Revision Checklist

WORTHWHILE CONTENT

The essay's main point is clear and sharply focused.
- ☐ Does the title attract attention and give a forecast? (52)
- ☐ Is the topic limited enough? (31)
- ☐ Do you get to your main point quickly? (53)
- ☐ Is the thesis definite, informative, and easy to find? (32)

The discussion delivers on the promise of the thesis.
- ☐ Will readers learn something new and useful (79)
- ☐ Do you support every assertion with enough details? (77)
- ☐ Does everything belong, or can anything be cut? (83)
- ☐ Have you used only your best material? (82)

SENSIBLE ORGANIZATION

The essay has a definite introduction, body, and conclusion.
- ☐ Will your introduction make readers want to read on? (53)
- ☐ Does each body paragraph develop *one* supporting point? (88)
- ☐ Does the order of body paragraphs reveal a clear line of thought and emphasize what is most important? (57)
- ☐ Does the conclusion give a real sense of an ending? (58)
- ☐ Is everything connected? (60)
- ☐ If you varied this organization, was it for good reason? (155)

Except for paragraphs of transition or special emphasis, each body (or support) paragraph usually is a mini-essay.
- ☐ Does the paragraph have a topic (or orienting) statement? (89)
- ☐ Does the topic statement come at the beginning or end, depending on your emphasis? (89)
- ☐ Does everything stick to the point (unity), and stick together (coherence)? (92)
- ☐ Is the paragraph developed enough to support the point? (89)

READABLE STYLE

Sentences are clear, concise, and fluent.
- ☐ Can each sentence be understood the first time it is read? (109)
- ☐ Is the information expressed in the fewest words? (118)
- ☐ Are sentences put together with enough variety? (125)

Each word does its job.
- ☐ Is a real person speaking, and is the voice likable? (139)
- ☐ Is everything in plain English? (139)
- ☐ Is your meaning precise, concrete, and specific? (134)
- ☐ Is your tone appropriate for this situation and audience? (138)

Numbers in parentheses refer to the first page of major discussion in the text.

SIXTH **EDITION**

THE WRITING PROCESS

A CONCISE RHETORIC

JOHN M. LANNON

**University of Massachusetts,
Dartmouth**

 LONGMAN

An imprint of Addison Wesley Longman, Inc.

New York ■ Reading, Massachusetts ■ Menlo Park, California ■ Harlow, England
Don Mills, Ontario ■ Sydney ■ Mexico City ■ Madrid ■ Amsterdam

Publishing Partner: Anne Elizabeth Smith
Developmental Editor: Tom Maeglin
Supplements Editor: Donna Campion
Project Coordination and Text Design: Ruttle, Shaw & Wetherill, Inc.
Cover Designer: Mary McDonnell
Electronic Production Manager: Christine Pearson
Manufacturing Manager: Willie Lane
Electronic Page Makeup: Ruttle, Shaw & Wetherill, Inc.
Printer and Binder: R. R. Donnelley & Sons Company
Cover Printer: Phoenix Color Corp.

For permission to use copyrighted material, grateful acknowledgment is made to the copyright holders on pp. 459–461, which are hereby made part of this copyright page.

Library of Congress Cataloging-in-Publication Data

Lannon, John M.
      The writing process : a concise rhetoric / John M. Lannon.—6th ed.
         p.   cm.
      Includes index.
      ISBN 0-321-01109-0
      1. English language—Rhetoric.   2. Report writing.   I. Title.
   PE1408.L3188   1997
808'.042—dc21   97-14278
                                                                   CIP

ISBN 0-321-01109-0

12345678910—DOC—00999897

DETAILED CONTENTS

SECTION THREE

ESSAYS FOR VARIOUS GOALS 151

SECTION FOUR

THE RESEARCH REPORT PROCESS: A RESEARCH GUIDE FOR THE INFORMATION AGE   297

INTRODUCTION   298

CHAPTER 19

ASKING QUESTIONS AND FINDING ANSWERS   307

CHAPTER 20

RECORDING, EVALUATING, AND INTERPRETING YOUR FINDINGS   330

CHAPTER 21

DOCUMENTING YOUR SOURCES   346

CHAPTER 22

COMPOSING THE RESEARCH REPORT   374

CHAPTER 23

CASE STUDY: A SAMPLE RESEARCH PROJECT   395

*T*his text promotes rhetorical awareness by treating the writing process as a set of deliberate and recursive decisions. It promotes rhetorical effectiveness by helping develop the problem-solving skills essential to reader-centered writing.

ORGANIZATION

Section One, **THE PROCESS,** covers reading, planning, drafting, and revising. Students learn to invent, select, organize, and express their material recursively. They see how decisions about purpose and audience influence decisions about what will be said and how it will be said. They see that reading and writing are linked, and that writing is essentially a "thinking" process. They learn to respond to their reading and to work collaboratively.

Section Two, **THE PRODUCT,** expands on composing and evaluation skills by focusing on content, organization, and style. Students learn to support their assertions; to organize for the reader; and to achieve prose maturity, precise diction, and appropriate tone.

Section Three, **ESSAYS FOR VARIOUS GOALS,** shows how the *strategies* (or modes) of discourse serve the particular *goals* of a discourse; that is, how description, narration, exposition, and argument are variously employed for expressive, referential, or persuasive ends. A balance of student and professional selections touch on current and lasting issues. Beyond studying these samples as models, students are asked to respond to the issues presented; that is, to write in response to a specific rhetorical situation.

Section Four, **THE RESEARCH REPORT PROCESS: A RESEARCH GUIDE FOR THE INFORMATION AGE,** approaches research as a process of deliberate inquiry. Students learn to formulate significant research questions; to explore a selective range of primary and secondary sources; to record, summarize, and document their findings; and, most importantly, to evaluate sources and evidence and interpret findings accurately.

Finally, for easy reference, Appendix A is a concise handbook, with exercises for the student. Appendix B, an additional, brief appendix offers advice on formatting a manuscript.

THE FOUNDATIONS OF *THE WRITING PROCESS*

- Writers with no rhetorical awareness overlook the decisions that are crucial for effective writing. Only by defining their rhetorical problem and asking the important questions can writers formulate an effective response to the problem.

- Although it follows no single, predictable sequence, the writing process is not a collection of random activities; rather it is a set of deliberate decisions in problem solving. Beyond emulating this or that model essay, students need to understand that effective writing requires critical thinking.

- Students write for audiences other than teachers and purposes other than completing an assignment. To view the act of writing as only a mere display of knowledge or fluency, an exercise in which writer and reader (i.e., "the teacher") have no higher stake or interest, is to ignore the unique challenges and constraints posed by each writing situation. In every forum beyond the classroom, we write to forge a specific connection with a specific audience.

- Students at any level of ability can develop audience awareness and learn to incorporate within their writing the essential rhetorical features: worthwhile content, sensible organization, and readable style.

- As well as being a fluent *communicator,* today's educated person needs to be a discriminating *consumer* of information, skilled in the methods of inquiry, retrieval, evaluation, and interpretation that constitute the research process.

- As an alternative to reiterating the textbook material, classroom workshops apply textbook principles by focusing on the students' writing. These workshops call for an accessible, readable, and engaging book to serve as a comprehensive resource. (Suggestions for workshop design are in the Instructor's Manual.)

- Finally, writing classes typically contain students with all types of strengths and weaknesses. *The Writing Process* offers explanations that are thorough, examples and models that are broadly intelligible, and goals that are rigorous yet realistic. The textbook is flexible enough to allow for various course plans and customized assignments.

The Writing Process proceeds from writer-centered to reader-centered discourse. Beginning with personal topics and a basic essay structure, the fo-

cus shifts to increasingly complex rhetorical tasks, culminating in argument. Within this cumulative structure each chapter is self-contained for flexible course planning. The sample essays represent a balance of student and professional authorship. Exercises (or Applications) in each chapter offer various levels of challenge. All material has been class-tested.

NEW TO THIS EDITION

- Case studies of student writers at work as they read, plan, draft, and revise. (See Chapters 1, 2, 3, 4, 5, and 23.)
- Guidelines and applications for collaborative work. (See Introduction and Chapter 3 as well as applications throughout.)
- Guidelines for reviewing and editing the work of others. (See Chapter 5.)
- Computer projects and guidelines. (See Chapter 4 and easily adaptable applications throughout.)
- Advice on avoiding excessive informality and offensive usage and on considering cultural differences in the observance of style guidelines. (See Chapters 3 and 9.)
- Discussions of how each rhetorical strategy might be used beyond the writing classroom. (See Section Three.)
- Readings and sample essays that have meaning for students today. Following each essay in Section Three are questions that promote critical analysis of the readings along with suggestions for discussion and response.
- E-mail communication guidelines. (See Chapter 20.)
- A fully revised Section Four, on research methods for the information age. Full coverage of MLA and APA styles as well as ACW (Alliance for Computers in Writing) style for documenting Internet sources (MOOs, FTPs, Telnet sites, and so on). Examples of other additions: achieving adequate depth in research, broadening and customizing electronic searches; understanding the essentials and limitations of interview and survey research; E-mail privacy and quality issues; guidelines for preparing summaries and abstracts; bias in printed and electronic sources; fallacies inherent in statistical data; a case study that follows one student through the research process. Two fully annotated research essays: one in APA style, one in MLA style.
- A broad range of challenging, class-tested ideas for essay topics.
- A revised and redesigned appendix on essentials of grammar, usage, and mechanics—including brief exercises.
- A separate instructor's manual written by the author.

- All chapters condensed and reorganized for greater clarity, conciseness, and emphasis.
- A user-friendly art program and page design for easy access and visual orientation:

  —In the margins, notes highlight key points and salient features of writing samples; icons announce material on collaborative and computer work; editing and correction symbols provide instant reference.

  —In the text, boxed "Questions," "Guidelines," and "Checklists" facilitate decisions and spell out criteria.

ACKNOWLEDGMENTS

Much of the improvement in this edition was inspired by helpful reviews from Dan Damerville, Tallahassee Community College; Suzanne Forster, University of Alaska—Anchorage; Lynn Goya, Leeward Community College; Paula Guetschow, University of Alaska—Anchorage; Judith Hinman, College of the Redwoods; Edward Klein, University of Notre Dame.

I am especially grateful to Virginia Anderson, a Ph.D. graduate of the University of Texas at Austin, who compressed and reorganized each chapter, wrote computer exercises, and offered invaluable insight and suggestions.

For examples, advice, and support, I thank colleagues and friends at the University of Massachusetts—Dartmouth, especially Tish Dace, Barbara Jacobskind, Louise Habicht, and Richard Larschan. As always, Raymond Dumont helped in countless ways.

A special thanks to my students who allowed me to reproduce versions of their work: Wendy Gianacoples for "Confessions of a Food Addict," Kim Fonteneau for "Suffering through Gym Class," Jeff Leonard for "Walk but Don't Run," Adam Szymkowicz for "Bonfire," Shirley Haley and Julia Conforti for their research essays and other excellent work, Chris Adey for selections on privacy in America, Mike Creeden on physical fitness, Pam Herbert on summer beaches, Liz Gonsalves on rap music, Joe Bolton on toys of violence, John Manning on the American Dream, and the many other student writers named in the text.

Once again, I enjoyed the excellent fortune of working with superb editors who are also my friends. Anne Smith inspired the shape and substance and most of what matters about this edition. Tom Maeglin and Patricia Rossi gave feedback, perspective, and support at every stage. Janet Nuciforo simply has no peer in project management.

For Chega, Daniel, Sarah, and Patrick—without whom not.

JOHN M. LANNON

THE PROCESS—DECISIONS IN PLANNING, DRAFTING, AND REVISING

INTRODUCTION

WRITING AS DECISION MAKING

Writing has no recipes

People who succeed usually are those who make the right decisions—about a career, an investment, a relationship, or anything else. Like any decision making, good writing requires hard work. If we had one recipe for all writing, our labors would be small. We could learn the recipe ("Do this; then do that"), and then apply it to every writing task—from love letters to lab reports. But we write about various subjects for various audiences for various purposes—at home, at school, on the job. For every writing task, we make our own decisions.

Most writers face problems like these

Still, most of us face identical problems: in deciding on who our audience is and how to connect with it; in deciding on what goal we want to achieve and on how to make the writing achieve that goal. This book introduces strategies that help us succeed as writers.

Writing is hard work for anyone

Most writing is a conscious, deliberate *process*—not the result of divine intervention, magic, miracles, or last-minute inspiration. Nothing ever leaps from the mind to the page in one neat and painless motion—not even for creative geniuses. Instead, we plan, draft, and revise. Sometimes we know right away what we want to express; sometimes we discover our purpose and meaning only as we write. But our finished product takes shape through our decisions at different stages in the writing process.

This book shows you how to plan, draft, and revise in a suggested sequence of activities. But just as no two people use an identical sequence of activities to drive, ski, or play tennis, no two people write in the same way. How you decide to use this book depends on your writing task and on what works for you.

HOW WRITING LOOKS

The neat and ordered writing samples throughout this book show the products of writing—not the process. Every finished writing task begins with messy scribbling, things crossed out, lists, arrows, and fragments of ideas, like the section from my first draft of this introduction shown in Figure I.1.

Writing appears in many shapes

Just as the writing process has no one recipe, the finished products have no one shape. In fact, very little writing published in books, magazines, and newspapers looks exactly like the basic college essay discussed in this book's early chapters (an introductory paragraph beginning or ending with a thesis statement; three or more support paragraphs, each beginning with a topic sentence; and a concluding paragraph). But all effective writers use identical skills: they know how to discover something worthwhile to write about, how to organize their material sensibly, and how to express their ideas clearly and gracefully.

Why college essays are important

College essays offer a good model for developing these skills because they provide you with a basic structure for shaping your thinking. They also

FIGURE I.1
Part of a typical
first draft

Messiness is a natural
and often essential part
of writing in its early
stages

*Wouldn't it be nice if there were a formula for writing:
*"this is the way you do it"? *Any kind of decision-
(USE) + (DEVELOP) making is hard

Introduction

In writing, as in the rest of life,
decisions are important

-buy a car
-a house
-getting married
-having children
(CHANGE THESE)

Later you will write all kinds of documents for all
kinds of purposes: -letters to the school board
all goals -job application letters
that need -love letters
a plan -requests for pay raises
All these -apologize for mistakes
are designed -memos or reports for clients and colleagues
to get the -poetry, fiction,?
reader to do -computer documentation
something, ? (Transitional writing)?
or at least
to like
you

Those who
succeed generally
are those who
make good
decisions

(NO)

Instead of
just letting
things happen

(?) So, what ~~does writing~~ do college essays have to do with
these varied tasks? "Why am I doing this?" is a
(MAYBE) question asked by ~~many~~ people who find themselves in
a composition class. ~~And this question deserves an answer.~~
(If there were I could write this section in a couple of hours,
There is no one way of "doing it right." instead of a week)
But all writers in all situations face certain ~~comm~~
(USE) common problems: they need to ~~figure out~~ decide what to say;
they need to ~~figure out~~ decide why they're saying it; they
need to organize to make their thinking clear; they
need to express themselves line of

supply an immediate, helpful audience—your instructor and classmates. Unlike many audiences who read only your final draft and from whom you could not reasonably expect helpful and sympathetic advice, your teacher and classmates can give you valuable feedback as you continue to shape and rework drafts of your writing.

What any reader expects

Like any audience, your classroom readers will expect you finally to give them something worthwhile—some useful information, a new insight on some topic, an unusual perspective or an entertaining story—in a form easy to follow and pleasing to read.

HOW WRITING MAKES A DIFFERENCE

Surface reasons for writing

All through school, we write too often for surface reasons: to show we can grind out a few hundred words on some topic, cook up a thesis, and organize paragraphs; to show we can punctuate, spell, and use grammar; or to pass the course. These surface reasons mask the deeper reasons we write: to explore something important to us, to connect with our readers, to make a difference—as students, as employees, as citizens, or as friends.

Deeper reasons for writing

Differences writing can make

What kind of difference can any writing make? It might move readers to act or reconsider their biases; it might increase their knowledge or win their support; it might broaden their understanding. Whether you're giving instructions for running an electric toothbrush or pouring out your feelings to a friend, effective writing brings writer and reader together.

As you read the essays in this book, you will see how student and professional writers in all kinds of situations manage to make a difference with their readers. These models, along with the advice and assignments, should help your writing make a difference of its own.

DECISIONS IN COLLABORATIVE WRITING

Many of the Applications in this book ask you to collaborate with peers. Especially with today's electronic communications, countless documents in the workplace are produced collaboratively; effective collaboration enables a group to synthesize the *best* from each member. Collaboration allows us to:

Benefits of collaboration

- Share in new perspectives.
- Test and sharpen ideas.
- Recognize our biases and assumptions.
- Get feedback from group members.
- Enjoy group support instead of working alone.

But like all writing, collaborative work demands decisions. Group members have to find ways of expressing their views persuasively, of accepting constructive criticism, of getting along and reaching agreement with others who hold different views. Collaborators may face these potential problems:

Things that go wrong
in collaborative work

- Differences in personality, working style, commitment, standards, or ability to take criticism.
- Disagreements about exactly what or how much the group should accomplish, who should do what, or who should make the final decisions.
- Feelings of intimidation or reluctance to speak out.

Guidelines in the following chapters will help make collaborative projects useful for you.

 ## DECISIONS ABOUT WRITING WITH COMPUTERS

Like collaborative writing, computers can provide tremendous advantages if you understand their limitations. Here are some of the decisions you will be making about computers as you progress through this book:

1. *Should I use computers to write my papers?* Working directly on the computer screen reduces the drudgery of writing and revising. You can brainstorm, develop different outlines, and design countless versions of a document without retyping the entire piece. You can also insert, delete, or move blocks of text; search the document to change a word or phrase; or have your document examined automatically for correct spelling, accurate word choice, and readable style. You then can file your finished document electronically, for easy retrieval.

2. *Should I use computers to enhance my research?* Instead of thumbing through newspapers, journals, reference books, or printed card catalogs, you can do much of your research at the computer terminal. See Chapter 19 for detailed descriptions of computerized research and reference tools (card catalogs, on-line databases, electronic encyclopedias, and so on).

3. *Should I use computers for collaborative projects?* Computers facilitate collaborative writing. For instance, group members might review, edit, or proofread your writing directly from a disk you have provided. The latest software even enables readers to comment on your writing without altering the text itself. Finally, when using *electronic mail,* you can transmit copies of your writing to classmates and they can respond.

But your decisions about these issues should take the following cautions into account:

Limitations of writing
with a computer

- Messages still need to be *written*. The task of sorting, organizing, and interpreting information still belongs to the writer.
- No computerized device can convert bad writing to good. Moreover, the ease of "fixing" our writing on a computer might encourage minimal revision. (Sometimes the very act of rewriting an entire page in longhand or type causes us to rethink that whole page or discover something new.)
- A computer is not a substitute brain. Shabby thinking produces shabby writing.

The following chapters will help you make thoughtful decisions about the part computers can play in your work.

APPLICATION A

Identify a situation in which your writing (or someone else's) has made a difference. Be prepared to describe the situation in class.

APPLICATION B

Locate a piece of nonfiction writing that you think "makes a difference." Bring a copy to class and be prepared to explain why this particular piece qualifies.

DECISIONS IN THE WRITING PROCESS

*D*uring the writing process you transform the material you discover—by inspiration, research, accident, or other means—into a message that makes a difference for readers. In short, writing is a process of making deliberate decisions.

For example, consider a Dear John or Jane letter, an essay exam, a job application, a letter to a newspaper, a note to a sick friend, or your written testimony as a witness to a crime. In each of these writing situations, you write because you feel strongly enough to have a definite *viewpoint* and to respond or speak out.

But merely expressing a viewpoint doesn't tell readers very much. To understand your ideas, readers need *explanations* that have been shaped so that readers can follow them. In any useful writing, whether in the form of a book, a news article, a memo, a report, or an essay, writers decide on a sensible line of thinking, often in a shape like this:

Much of your writing will have this basic shape.

INTRODUCTION
BODY
CONCLUSION

The shape of useful writing

- The **introduction** attracts attention, announces the viewpoint, and previews what will follow. All good introductions invite readers in.
- The **body** explains and supports the viewpoint, achieving *unity* by remaining focused on the viewpoint. It achieves *coherence* by carrying a line of thinking from sentence to sentence in logical order. Bodies come in all different sizes, depending on how much readers need and expect.
- The **conclusion** sums up the meaning of the piece, or points toward other meanings to be explored. Good conclusions give readers a clear perspective on what they have just read.

Writers also make decisions about whom they're writing to (their *audience*) and what they want to sound like: whether they want to sound formal, friendly, angry, or amused.

DECISION MAKING AND THE WRITING PROCESS

Composing words on paper or your computer screen is only one small part of the writing process. Your real challenge lies in making decisions like those in Figure 1.1:

FIGURE 1.1
Typical decisions during
the writing process

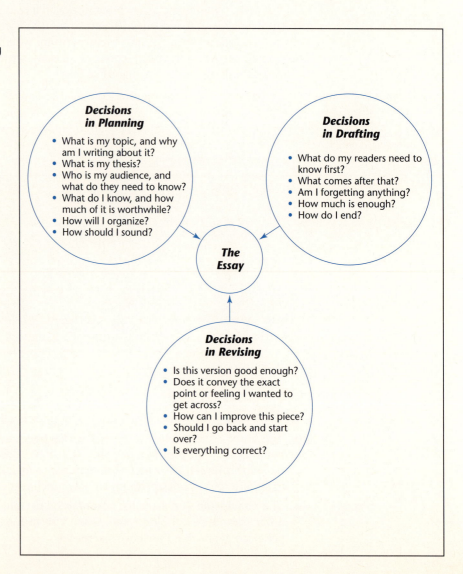

ONE WRITER'S DECISION MAKING PROCESS

To appreciate writing as a deliberate process, let's follow one student through two approaches to the same writing situation. We'll see how decisions about planning, drafting, and revising like those shown in Figure 1.1 distinguish this writer's quickest effort from her best effort.

Shirley Haley has been assigned an essay on this topic: How do you want your life to be different from (or similar to) that of your parents? Haley's twofold goal is to explore her feelings about this topic and to share that exploration with us. Her first response, a random piece of freewriting, took about 30 minutes:

Haley's freewriting

When my mother was my age, life was simple. Women really didn't have to study in college. They came primarily to find a husband, and they majored in liberal arts or teaching. They knew they were going to be wives and mothers. My mother says she got an education so she would have "something to fall back on" in case something ever happened to my father—which was a good thing, I suppose. Maybe it was her attitude about "family first, me second" that made our home life so stable.

I appreciate the fact that my parents have given me a stable home life, and I want parts of my life to turn out like theirs. But my parents are slaves to their house; they never go anywhere or do anything with their spare time. They just work on the house and yard. They never seem to do anything they want to do—only what other people expect of them.

I wish my parents would allow themselves to enjoy life, have more adventure. They go to the same place every year for their vacation. They've never even seen a country outside the United States.

I'll have a family some day, and I'll have responsibilities, but I never want to have a boring life. When I'm on my own, I want my life to soar. And even though I want to provide a stable home life for my children and husband some day, I hope I never forget my responsibility to myself as well.

Discussion of Haley's freewriting

Freewriting is a valuable invention tool—but only a first step. Haley's draft has potential, but she hints at lots of things in general and points at nothing in particular. Without a thesis to assert a controlling viewpoint, neither writer nor reader ever finds an orientation. Lacking a definite thesis, Haley never decided which material didn't belong, which was the most important, and which deserved careful development.

At first, the essay seems to be about a change in women's roles, but the end of the first paragraph and the beginning of the second suggest that Haley's topic has shifted to ways in which she wants her life to resemble her parents'. But the second, third, and fourth paragraphs discuss what Haley dislikes about her parents' lives. The final sentence adds confusion by looking back to a now-defunct topic in the first paragraph: stable family life.

The lack of an introduction and conclusion deprives us of a way of narrowing the possible meanings of the piece and of finding a clear perspective on what we have just read.

Also, the paragraphs either lack development or fail to focus on one specific point. And some sentences (like the last two in paragraph 1) lack logical connections.

Finally, we get almost no sense of a real person speaking to real people. Haley has written only for herself—as if writing a journal or diary.

A quick effort (as in a journal or diary) offers a good way to get started. But when writers go no further, they bypass the essential stages of *planning* and *revising*. In fact, putting *something* on the page or screen is relatively easy. Getting the piece to *succeed*, to make a difference for readers—here, the tougher decisions occur.

Now let's follow Haley's thinking as she struggles through her planning decisions.

Haley's planning decisions

What exactly is my topic, and why am I writing about it? *My intended topic was "How I Want My Life to Be Different from That of My Parents," but my first draft got off track. I need to focus on the specific differences!*

I'm writing this essay to discover my own feelings and to help readers understand these feelings by showing them specific parts of my parents' life-style that I hope will be different for me.

What is my thesis? *After countless tries, I think I've finally settled on my thesis: "As I look at my parents' life, I hope my own will be less ordinary, less duty-bound, and less predictable."*

Who is my audience, and what do they need to know? *My audience consists of my teacher and classmates (this essay will be discussed in class). Each reader already is familiar with this topic; everyone, after all, is someone's son or daughter! But I want my audience to understand specifically the differences I envision.*

What do I know about this topic? *A better question might be, "What don't I know?" I've spent my life with this topic, and so I certainly don't have to do any research.*

Of all the material I've discovered on this topic, how much of it is worthwhile (considering my purpose and audience)? *Because I could write volumes here, I'll have to resist getting carried away. I've already decided to focus on the feeling that my parents' lives are too ordinary, duty-bound, and predictable. One paragraph explaining each of these supporting points (and illustrating them with well-chosen examples) should do. How will I organize? I guess I've already made this decision by settling on my thesis: moving from "ordinary" to "duty-bound" to "predictable." Predictability is what I want to emphasize, and so I will save it for last.*

How do I want my writing to sound? I'm sharing something intimate with my classmates, so my tone should be relaxed and personal, as when people talk to people they trust.

In completing her essay, Haley went on to make similar decisions for drafting and revising. Here is her final draft.

Haley's final draft

Introductory paragraph (leads into the thesis)

LIFE IN FULL COLOR

I'm probably the only person I know who still has the same two parents she was born with. We have a traditional American family: we go to church and football games; we watch the Olympics on television and argue about politics; and we have Thanksgiving dinner at my grandmother Clancy's and Christmas dinner with my father's sister Jess, who used to let us kids put pitted olives on our fingertips when we were little. Most of my friends are struggling with the problems of broken homes; I'll always be grateful to my parents for giving me a loving and stable background. But sometimes I look at my parents' life and hope my life will be less ordinary, less duty-bound, and less predictable.

Thesis statement

Topic statement and first support paragraph

I want my life to be imaginative, not ordinary. Instead of honeymooning at Niagara Falls, I want to go to Paris. In my parents' neighborhood, all the houses were built alike about twenty years ago. Different owners have added on or shingled or painted, but the houses basically all look the same. The first thing we did when we moved into our house was plant trees; everyone did. Now the neighborhood is full of family homes on tree-lined streets, which is nice; but I'd prefer a condo in a renovated brick building in Boston. I'd have dozens of plants, and I'd buy great furniture one piece at a time at auctions and dusty shops and not by the roomful from the local furniture store. Instead of spending my time trying to be similar to everyone else, I'd like to explore ways of being different.

Topic statement and second support paragraph

My parents have so many obligations, they barely have time for themselves; I don't want to live like that. I'm never quite sure whether they own the house or the house owns them. They worry constantly about taxes, or the old furnace, or the new deck, or mowing the lawn, or weeding the garden. After spending every weekend slaving over their beautiful yard, they have no time left to enjoy it. And when they're not buried in household chores, other people are making endless demands on their time. My mother will stay up past midnight because she promised some telephone voice 3 cakes for the church bazaar, or 5 dozen cookies for the Girl Scout meeting, or 76 little sandwiches for the women's club Christmas party. My father coaches Little League, wears a clown suit for the Lions' flea markets, and both he and my mother are volunteer firefighters. In fact, both my parents get talked into volunteering for everything. I hate to sound selfish, but my first duty is to myself. I'd rather live in a tent than be owned by my house. And I don't want my life to end up being measured out in endless chores.

Topic statement and
third support paragraph

Although it's nice to take things such as regular meals and paychecks for granted, many other events in my parents' life are too predictable for me. Every Sunday at two o'clock we dine on overdone roast beef, mashed potatoes and gravy, a faded green vegetable, and sometimes that mushy orange squash that comes frozen in bricks. It's not that either of my parents is a bad cook, but Sunday dinner isn't food any more; it's a habit. Mom and Dad have become so predictable that they can order each other's food in restaurants. Just once I'd like to see them pack up and go away for a weekend, without telling anybody; they couldn't do it. They can't even go crazy and try a new place for their summer vacation. They've been spending the first two weeks in August on Cape Cod since I was 2 years old. I want variety in my life. I want to travel, see this country and see Europe, do things spontaneously. No one will ever be able to predict my order in a restaurant.

Concluding paragraph

Before long, Christmas will be here, and we'll be going to Aunt Jess's. Mom will bake a walnut pie, and Grandpa Frank will say, "Michelle, you sure know how to spoil an old man." It's nice to know that some things never change. In fact, some of the ordinary, obligatory, predictable things in life are the most comfortable. But too much of any routine can make life seem dull and gray. I hope my choices lead to a life in full color.

—*Shirley Haley*

Discussion of Haley's
final draft

Here are some of Haley's major improvements:

- The distinct shape (introduction, body, conclusion) enables us to organize our understanding and follow the writer's thinking.
- The essay no longer confuses us. We know where Haley stands because she tells us, with a definite thesis; and we know why because she shows us, with plenty of examples.
- She wastes nothing; everything seems to belong and everything fits together.
- Now each paragraph has its own design, a place for things that belong together. Each paragraph enhances the whole.
- We now see real variety in the ways in which sentences begin and words are put together. We hear a genuine voice.

All good writing has
these qualities

Because she made careful decisions, Haley produced a final draft that displays the qualities of all good writing: *content* that makes it worth reading; *organization* that reveals the line of thinking and emphasizes what is most important; and *style* that is economical and convincingly human.

Writers rarely struggle with these decisions about planning, drafting, and revising in a predictable sequence. Instead, writers choose sequences that work best for them. Figure 1.2 diagrams this looping ("recursive") structure of the writing process.

FIGURE 1.2
The looping structure of
the writing process

Decisions in the writing
process are recursive;
no one stage is
complete until all stages
are complete.

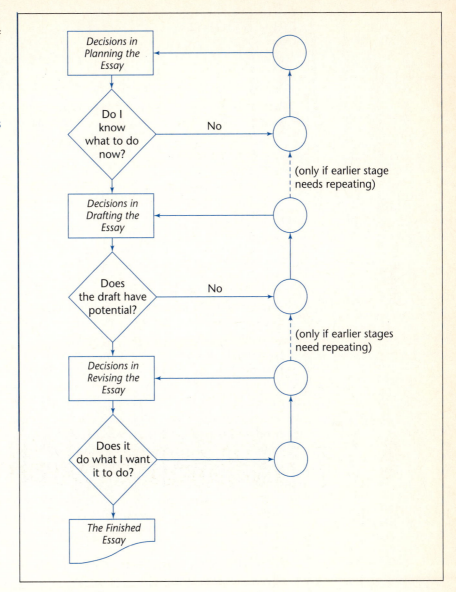

. . . .

APPLICATION 1-1

The essay that follows (a third draft) was written in response to this assignment:

> Identify a personal trait that is so strong you cannot control it (a quick temper, the need for acceptance, a fear of failure, shyness, a bad habit, a phobia, an obsession, or the like). In a serious or humorous essay, show how this trait affects your behavior. Provide enough details for readers to understand clearly this part of your personality.

Our writer, Wendy Gianacoples, decided to explore a personal obsession: food.

Read Wendy's essay once or twice. Then read it again, using the questions that follow the essay for your analysis.

Essay for analysis

CONFESSIONS OF A FOOD ADDICT

Like many compulsive eaters, I eat to fill a void—an emptiness within. I feed my feelings. Food can be my best friend, always there when I need it. This friend, however, actually is a tyrant that dominates my life through endless cycles of need, indulgence, and guilt.

Thanks to my food obsession, I seem to have two personalities: the respected, self-controlled Wendy who eats properly all day, and the fat Wendy who emerges after dark to gobble everything in sight. Lying in bed, I wait for the house to be silent. Feeling excited and giddy, I sneak to the kitchen and head straight for the freezer to begin my search. My initial prize is an unopened pint of Ben and Jerry's chocolate chip ice cream. I break the container's seal, dig in with my spoon, and shovel down massive gobs. (I have a love/hate relationship with food: I want all or nothing.) Next thing I know the container is empty.

Stashing the empty container deeply in the trash, I continue my rampage. From the cookie drawer, I snatch a nearly full package of Fig Newtons. As I tiptoe toward the milk, I ask myself what the folks at Weight Watchers would say if they could see me standing half-awake in my ice-cream splattered Lanz nightgown, popping down Fig Newtons and swigging milk from the carton. After pushing the few remaining cookies to the front of the package so it looks fuller, I rummage around for my next "fix."

Beneath a bag of frozen Bird's Eye vegetables, I find a frozen pizza—the ultimate midnight snack. The oven will take too long but the microwave is too noisy—all that beeping could get me busted. Feeling daring, I turn on the kitchen faucet to drown out the beeps, place the pizza in the microwave, set the timer, grab the last handful of Fig Newtons, and wait.

By the time I polish off the pizza, it's 1:00 a.m. and I crave Kraft Macaroni and Cheese. Standing on a chair I reach for a box from the overhead cabinet. Trying to be quiet, I dig out a spaghetti pot from a pile of pots and pans. Grabbing the handle, I hold my breath as I pull the pan from the clutter. While the water boils and the macaroni cooks, I fix a bowl of Rice Krispies. Just as I finish chowing down "Snap, Crackle, and Pop," the macaroni is ready. After eating the whole package, I bury the box in the trash.

After a binge, I panic: "What have I done?" Setting a hand on my bulging stomach, I think of the weight I'll gain this week. Climbing the stairs to my bed, I feel drained, like a person on drugs who is now "coming down." In my bedroom, I study myself in the full-length mirror, looking for visible signs of my sins. Lying in bed, I feel fat and uncomfortable. Although I usually sleep on my stomach, on "binge" nights, I assume the fetal position, cradling my full belly, feeling ashamed and alone, as if I were the only person who overeats and uses food as a crutch. When the sugar I've consumed keeps me awake, I plead with God to help me overcome this weakness.

The next morning I kick myself and feel guilty. I want to block out last night's memories, but my tight clothes offer a painful reminder. My stomach is sick all day and I have heartburn. During the following week, I'll eat next to nothing and exercise constantly, hoping to break even on the scale at Weight Watchers.

Most people don't consider compulsive eating an addiction. Substance abusers can be easy to spot, but food addicts are less obvious. Unlike drugs, one can't live without food. People would never encourage a drug addict or alcoholic to "have another hit" or "fall off the wagon." However, people constantly push food on overeaters: "Come on, one brownie won't hurt. I made them especially for you," says a friend. When I decline, she scowls and turns away. Little does she know, while she was in the bathroom, I had four.

—*Wendy Gianacoples*

Questions about the writing

Does the Content of the Essay Make It Worth Reading?

- Can you find a definite thesis that announces the writer's viewpoint?
- Do you have enough information to understand the viewpoint?
- Do you learn something new and useful?
- Does everything belong, or should any material be cut?

Does the Organization Reveal the Writer's Line of Thinking?

- Is there an introduction to set the scene, a middle to walk us through, and a conclusion to sum up the meaning?
- Does each support paragraph present a distinct unit of meaning?
- Does each paragraph stick to the point and stick together?

Is the Style Economical and Convincing?

- Can you understand each sentence the first time you read it?
- Should any words be cut?
- Are sentences varied in the way they're put together?
- Is the writer's meaning always clear?
- Can you hear a real person speaking?
- Do you like the person you hear?

Write out your answers to these questions and be prepared to discuss them in class.

APPLICATION 1-2

Collaborative Project: In class, write your "quickest effort" essay about a personal trait, or about this subject: "Important Differences or Similarities Between My Life and That of My Parents." Exchange papers with a classmate, and evaluate your classmate's paper, using the questions from Application 1-1. In one or two paragraphs, give your classmate advice for revising. Don't be afraid to mark up (with your own questions, comments, and suggestions) this paper you're evaluating. Discuss with your classmate your evaluation of his/her work. At home, read the evaluation of your paper carefully, and write your "best" version of your original essay. List the improvements you made in moving from your quickest effort to your best effort. Be prepared to discuss your improvements in class.

Also, in two or three paragraphs, trace your own writing process for this essay by describing the decisions you made. Be prepared to discuss your decisions in class.

Note: Don't expect miracles at this stage, but do expect some degree of frustration and confusion. Things will improve quickly, though.

APPLICATION 1-3

Collaborative Project: Out of class (drawing on your personal experience with group work if possible), write down one thing you look forward to in working with peers, and one potential problem you find especially important. In class, share your expectations and concerns with a small group. Do group members raise similar issues, or does everyone have different concerns? As a group, craft these issues and concerns into a list of group goals: benefits you hope to achieve and pitfalls you hope to avoid.

APPLICATION 1-4

Computer Project: Investigate your school's electronic facilities. Are computers available to students who don't have their own? If so, where? What kind are they: IBM or MacIntosh? Where can you buy disks and supplies? Do dorm rooms have Internet hookups? Does your school provide e-mail? If so, is there any charge? How do you open an account? Your instructor might divide this research among small groups, who will then report back to the class.

OPTIONS FOR ESSAY WRITING

The following topics offer ideas for essays to get you started. People write best about things they know, and so we begin with personal forms of writing. You might want to return to this list for topic ideas when essays are assigned throughout the early chapters of this book.

1. What major effects has television had on your life (your ambitions, hopes, fears, values, consumer habits, awareness of the world, beliefs, outlook, faith in people, and so on)? Overall, has television been a positive or negative influence? Have you learned anything from TV that you couldn't have learned elsewhere? Support your thesis with specific details.

2. How do advertising and commercials shape our values (notions about looking young, being athletic, being thin, smoking, beer drinking, and so on)? Does advertising present an unrealistic view of life? In what ways? What kinds of human weaknesses and aspirations do commercials exploit? Support your viewpoint with examples your readers will recognize.

3. If you could repeat your high school years, what three or four things would you do differently? Write for a younger brother or sister entering high school, and provide enough detail to get your viewpoint across.

4. Do some music videos communicate distorted and dangerous messages? If so, what should be done? Discuss specific examples and their effect on viewers.

5. Americans often are criticized for their emphasis on competing and succeeding (academically, financially, physically, socially, and so on). Is this criticism valid? Has emphasis on competition and success been mostly helpful or harmful for you? Why?

6. Our public schools have been accused of failing to educate America's students. Does your high school typify the so-called failure of American education? Why or why not? How well did your school prepare you for college—and for life?

7. College students commonly are stereotyped as party animals. Explain to a skeptical nonstudent audience that college life is harder than people imagine—but don't sermonize or complain. For instance, if you attend a public university, you might write for state legislators who want to cut the school budget.

DECISIONS ABOUT READING FOR WRITING

Much of this book asks you to read other people's writing in order to explore their decision making processes. Reading also provides raw material that will help you craft what you want to say. But to read effectively you need to decide what you want your reading to do.

DIFFERENT LEVELS OF READING

Reading to summarize

Different types of writing call for different levels of interacting with the text. Often, we read to retrieve information and understand facts. Then we write to demonstrate our knowledge or understanding. In this situation, we *summarize* the main ideas.

Reading to analyze

Other situations require us to go beyond merely retrieving information. In this situation, we *analyze* our reading by breaking it down and examining its parts systematically.

Summary and analysis are essential to the explanatory and persuasive writing covered in Section Three. But much of the energy for any writing comes from our unique response to what we have read.

Reading to respond

In reading to respond, we join a "conversation": reacting to something that was said, we respond with something of our own. We read to explore our own thinking or to make up our minds or to get in touch with buried feelings or ideas. Then we reinvent that material with a force and passion that will make a difference to readers of our own.

DIFFERENT LEVELS OF READING ANSWER DIFFERENT QUESTIONS

Reading to summarize:
- *What are the main ideas?*

Reading to analyze:
- *What are the basic principles?*
- *How does this all fit together?*

Reading to respond
- *What special meaning does this reading have for me?*
- *What grabs my attention?*
- *How do I want to reply?*

DIFFERENT READERS, DIFFERENT MEANINGS

The connection that writing creates is both public and private. On the one hand, a piece of writing makes a public connection with all its readers; on the other hand, the writing makes a private connection with each of its readers. Consider, for example, "Suffering Through Gym Class" (pages 59–60). Many of us who read this essay can feel the writer's anxiety, alienation, and sense of failure. Beyond our common reaction, however, each of us has a unique and personal reaction as well—special feelings or memories or thoughts.

QUESTIONS FOR RESPONDING TO READING

- *How do I feel about this reading? Angry, defensive, supportive, or what?*
- *Why do I feel this way?*
- *Does the piece present an accurate picture?*
- *With which statements do I agree or disagree?*

- *What is the most striking part of this essay?*
- *Do I like the way the writing sounds (the tone)?*
- *Has it reminded me of something, made me aware of something new, or changed my mind about anything?*

You as reader interpret and complete the "private" meaning of the text you read. And, like you, all other readers come away from this same text with a personal meaning of their own. This personal meaning serves as inspiration for your own writing.

CASE STUDY

RESPONDING TO READING

The following essay by Judy Brady (then Judy Syfers) was published in the very first issue of *Ms.* magazine, in Spring 1972. Even though Brady seems to write for married readers in particular, her essay addresses anyone familiar with married people in general. Please read the essay carefully.

Essay for analysis and response

WHY I WANT A WIFE

I belong to that classification of people known as wives. I am A Wife. And, not altogether incidentally, I am a mother.

Not too long ago a male friend of mine appeared on the scene fresh from a recent divorce. He had one child, who is, of course, with his ex-wife. He is looking for another wife. As I thought about him while I was ironing one evening, it suddenly occurred to me that I, too, would like to have a wife. Why do I want a wife?

I would like to go back to school so that I can become economically independent, support myself, and, if need be, support those dependent upon me. I want a wife who will work and send me to school. And while I am going to school I want a wife to take care of my children. I want a wife to keep track of the children's doctor and dentist appointments. And to keep track of mine, too. I want a wife to make sure my children eat properly and are kept clean. I want a wife who will wash the children's clothes and keep them mended. I want a wife who is a good nurturant attendant to my children, who arranges for their schooling, makes sure that they have an adequate social life with their peers, takes them to the park, the zoo, etc. I want a wife who takes care of the children when they are sick, a wife who arranges to be around when the children need special care, because, of course, I cannot miss classes at school. My wife must arrange to lose time at work and not lose the job. It may mean a small cut in my wife's income from time to time, but I guess I can tolerate that. Needless to say, my wife will arrange and pay for the care of the children while my wife is working.

I want a wife who will take care of my physical needs. I want a wife who will keep my house clean. A wife who will pick up after my children, a wife who will pick up after me. I want a wife who will keep my clothes clean, ironed, mended, replaced when need be, and who will see to it that my personal things are kept in their proper place so that I can find what I need the minute I need it. I want a wife who cooks the meals, a wife who is a good cook. I want a wife who will plan the menus, do the necessary grocery shopping, prepare the meals, serve them pleasantly, and then do the cleaning up while I do my studying. I want a wife who will care for me when I am sick and sympathize with my pain and loss of time from school. I want a wife to go along when our family takes a vacation so that someone can continue to care for me and my children when I need a rest and change of scene.

I want a wife who will not bother me with rambling complaints about a wife's duties. But I want a wife who will listen to me when I feel the need to explain a rather difficult point I have come across in my course of studies. And I want a wife who will type my papers for me when I have written them.

I want a wife who will take care of the details of my social life. When my wife and I are invited out by my friends, I want a wife who will take care of the babysitting arrangements. When I meet people at school that I like and want to entertain, I want a wife who will have the house clean, will prepare a special meal, serve it to me and my friends, and not interrupt when I talk about things that interest me and my friends. I want a wife who will have arranged that the children are fed and ready for bed before my guests arrive so that the children do not bother us. I want a wife who takes care of the needs of my guests so that they feel comfortable, who makes sure that they have an ashtray, that they are passed the hors d'oeuvres, that they are offered a second helping of the food, that their wine glasses are replenished when necessary, that their coffee is served to them as they like it. And I want a wife who knows that sometimes I need a night out by myself.

I want a wife who is sensitive to my sexual needs, a wife who makes love passionately and eagerly when I feel like it, a wife who makes sure that I am satisfied. And, of course, I want a wife who will not demand sexual attention when I am not in the mood for it. I want a wife who assumes the complete responsibility for birth control, because I do not want more children. I want a wife who will remain sexually faithful to me so that I do not have to clutter up my intellectual life with jealousies. And I want a wife who understands that my sexual needs may entail more than strict adherence to monogamy. I must, after all, be able to relate to people as fully as possible.

If, by chance, I find another person more suitable as a wife than the wife I already have, I want the liberty to replace my present wife with another one. Naturally, I will expect a fresh, new life; my wife will take the children and be solely responsible for them so that I am left free. When I am through with school and have a job, I want my wife to quit working and remain at home so that my wife can more fully and completely take care of a wife's duties.

My God, who *wouldn't* want a wife?

—*Judy Brady*

Discussion

Now let's examine our reactions to "Why I Want A Wife." We all presumably extract a common meaning from this piece: namely the viewpoint that women in the traditional "wifely" role are overworked and underappreciated. But, beyond its bleak portrait of the "housewife's" destiny, what particular meaning does this essay have for you?

Maybe Brady's essay makes you feel angry with (1) men, (2) the writer, (3) yourself, or (4) someone else. Or maybe you feel threatened or offended. Or maybe you feel amused or confused about your own attitudes toward gender roles. The questions on page 23 may help you explore your reactions to the reading. Keep a journal for recording your impressions.

Before you decide how you feel about Brady's essay, read how one student writer responded. Here are some of the notes that Jacqueline LeBlanc wrote in her journal after first reading Brady's essay:

One initial response to Brady's essay

This essay makes me angry because it reminds me too much of some women in my own generation who seem to want nothing more than a wifely role for themselves. For all we hear about "equal rights," women still feel the pressure to conform to old-fashioned notions. I can really take this essay personally.

After reading the essay and reviewing her journal entries, Jackie decided to write from the viewpoint that the stereotypical role condemned by Brady two decades ago continues to be disturbingly evident. Jackie expresses her viewpoint in this thesis statement: "Although today's 'equality-minded' generation presumably sees marriage as more than just an occupation, the wifely stereotype persists." Here, after several revisions, is the essay that explains Jackie's viewpoint:

One final response to
Brady's essay

A LONG WAY TO GO

Judy Brady's portrait of a servile wife might appear somewhat dated—until we examine some of today's views about marriage. Brady defines a wife by the work she does for her husband: she is a secretary, housemaid, babysitter, and sex object. She is, in a word, her husband's employee. Although today's "equality-minded" generation presumably sees marriage as more than an occupation, the wifely stereotype persists.

Among my women friends, I continue to encounter surprisingly traditional attitudes. Last week, for instance, I was discussing my career possibilities with my roommate, who added to the list of my choices by saying, "You can always get married." In her view, becoming a wife seems no different from becoming a teacher or journalist. She implied that marriage is merely another way of making a living. But where do I apply for the position of wife? The notion struck me as absurd. I thought to myself, "Surely, this person is an isolated case. We are, after all, in the nineties. Women no longer get married as a substitute for a job—do they?"

Of course many women do have both job and marriage, but as I look closely at others' attitudes, I find that my roommate's view is not so rare. Before the recent wedding of a female friend, my conversations with the future bride revolved around her meal plans and laundry schedule. To her vows "to love, honor, and cherish" she could have added, "to cook, serve, and clean up." She had been anticipating the first meal she would prepare for her husband. Granted, nothing is wrong with wanting to serve and provide for the one you love—but she spoke of this meal as if it were a pass-or-fail exam given by her employer on her first day on the job. Following the big day of judgment, she was elated to have passed with flying colors.

I couldn't help wondering what would have happened if her meal had been a flop. Would she have lost her marriage as an employee loses a job? As long as my friend retains such a narrow and materialistic view of wifely duties, her marriage is not likely to be anything more than a job.

Not all my friends are obsessed with wifely duties, but some do have a definite sense of husbandly duties. A potential husband must measure up to the qualifications of the position, foremost of which is wealth. One of the first questions about any male is "What does he do?" Engineering majors or premed students usually get highest ranking, and humanities or music majors end up at the bottom. College women are by no means opposed to marriage based on true love, but, as we grow older, the fantasy of a Prince Charming gives way to the reality of an affluent provider. Some women look for high-paying marriages just as they look for high-paying jobs.

Some of my peers may see marriage as one of many career choices, but my parents see it as the only choice. To my parents, my not finding a husband is a much more terrifying fate than my not finding a job. In their view, being a wife is no mere occupation, but a natural vocation for all women. But not just any man will do as a husband. My parents have a built-in screening procedure for each man I date. Appearance, money, and general background are the highest qualifications. They ignore domestic traits because they assume that his parents will be screening me for such qualifications.

I have always tried to avoid considering male friends simply as prospective husbands; likewise, I never think of myself as filling the stereotypical position of wife. But sometimes I fall into my parents' way of thinking. When I invite a friend to dinner at my house, I suddenly find myself fretting about his hair, his religion, or his job. Will he pass the screening test? Is he the right man for the role of husband? In some ways my attitudes seem no more liberated than those of my peers or parents.

Today's women have made a good deal of progress, but apparently not enough. Allowing the practical implications of marriage to overshadow its emotional implications, a surprising number of us seem to feel that we still have to fit the stereotype that Brady condemns.

—*Jacqueline LeBlanc*

Our second student respondent, David Galuski, discovered in Brady's essay the possibility for humor, summed up in this thesis:

Instead of a wife, I need an assistant.

Galuski's response pokes fun at his own inability to cope with an impossibly busy schedule. Also, he discovered that (like all of us, at times) he is merely looking for a little sympathy.

Another response to Brady's essay

I NEED AN ASSISTANT

I am much too busy. Being eighteen takes a lot out of a person—especially one who attends college full time, works two part-time jobs, plays sports, and tries to have a social life. I need someone to help me get through the day. Instead of a wife, I need an assistant.

For one thing, my assistant would help with school chores. Although I usually find time to do homework, it is never without a lot of pain. My assistant could ease the pain by doing some of my reading, which he could then summarize and explain to me. Maybe he could do some of my research and type my papers. Fluent in all subjects, my assistant would be able to transfer his knowledge to me.

Studying is easy—when I have enough time. But keeping up my grades while holding down two part-time jobs is another story. I spend twenty hours weekly at Max's, a gourmet restaurant, where I am expected to cater to my customers. But when I'm exhausted from studying, I'm likely to be forgetful and irritable. My assistant would stand by me at all times, to help with the work and cover for any lapses in my patience or attention.

My work as timekeeper for hockey games consumes five hours weekly. I need an assistant to cover games I miss because of the restaurant job or homework and to take over when I fall asleep during the late hours these games are scheduled.

> Even though I need these jobs to pay college expenses, my life isn't all work and study. I save at least one hour daily to run, cycle, or swim. No matter what my other commitments, without daily exercise, I feel useless. I need an assistant to encourage me to run that extra step or swim that extra lap. He would push me out the door to exercise in the cold and rain. He would compete alongside me in the six triathlons I do each year. He would be a good hockey player, who would attend practices in my place, leaving the team happy and giving me time to finish homework or earn money.
>
> I try—without much success—to maintain an active social life. I need an assistant to keep me informed about my friends and girlfriend. I never have time to call them and hardly ever see them. *My* assistant would make my phone calls and arrange my dates at times when I can squeeze them in.
>
> Dates are something I can't really make with my parents, but I try to see them as much as possible. I try to help out at home, but that could be a job for my assistant. He could do my household chores, wash the cars, and mow the lawn. My assistant would make my bed and wash my clothes while I hurry off to some pressing engagement.
>
> Finally, I need an assistant who will give me emotional support. I want an assistant to whisper in my ear, saying that everything will turn out all right—one who will sing me to sleep and hold me when I cry. Maybe all I'm looking for after all is a little pity.
>
> —*David Galuski*

These two student writers reached deep into their reading and into themselves to discover a real connection. Their writing, in turn, makes us part of that connection.

The possible responses to Brady's essay are almost infinite. What are some possibilities for your own response?

SUGGESTIONS FOR READING AND WRITING

Some of the readings in later chapters are professionally written, others student written. Besides triggering your own writing, each reading provides a model of worthwhile content, sensible organization, and readable style.

Here are suggestions for reading to respond to the selections assigned throughout the semester:

GUIDELINES FOR READING TO RESPOND

1. Read the essay at least three times: first, to get a sense of the geography; next, to explore your reactions; finally, to see what you find most striking or important or outrageous.
2. List (or underline) the statements that strike you or set you off.
3. Answer any questions on page 23 that are relevant here.
4. Once you've identified your reaction, decide what to say in reply.
5. Settle on the main thing you want to say—your viewpoint.
6. State your viewpoint in a thesis statement (see pages 32–35).

APPLICATION 2-1

Respond to any essay in this chapter with an essay of your own. Share with us a new way of seeing. Imagine that you are conversing with the writer: How would you reply if someone had just spoken what you have read? The questions on page 23 will help you reach deep into your reading experience. Record your responses in a reading journal.

APPLICATION 2-2

Collaborative Project: Share your essay from Application 2-1 with others in your class who have responded to the same essay. Can you pinpoint any places where your responses were very similar or where they were radically different? As a group, discuss the possible reasons for the differences. Have one group member record the reasons for discussion with the entire class.

APPLICATION 2-3

Computer Project: One of the most important uses of computers is word processing. You will need to become familiar with one or more of the standard word processing programs available at your school. Use a computer to record your answers to the page 23 questions as you work on Application 2-1. Practice entering, deleting, and changing text. Also learn how to save your work to a floppy disk after you have finished.

DECISIONS IN PLANNING

Writing is a battle with impatience, a fight against the natural urge to "be done with it." Effective writers win this battle by *planning:* analyzing their writing situation, exploring their assets, and finding a voice. Of course, planning continues throughout the writing process, but an initial plan gives you a place to start and a direction for your decisions.

DECIDING ON A TOPIC, PURPOSE, THESIS, AND AUDIENCE

Your earliest planning decisions will require that you analyze your writing situation:

QUESTIONS FOR ANALYZING A WRITING SITUATION

- *What, exactly, is my topic?*
- *Why am I writing about it?*
- *What is my viewpoint?*
- *Who is my audience?*

Of course, you won't always follow a single order in making these decisions; in Chapter 1, Shirley Haley discovers her thesis before brainstorming for material. The key is to make all the decisions—in whichever order works best for you.

As with any stage in the writing process, you might have to return again and again to your plan.

DECIDE ON YOUR TOPIC

In most out-of-school writing ("Why I deserve a promotion"; "Why you should marry me"; "How we repaired the computer"), topics are decided for you by the situation. But when you are asked to choose your own topic, remember one word: *focus*.

"What, exactly is my topic?"

Sometimes, afraid we'll have too little to say, we mistakenly choose the broadest topic. But a focused topic actually provides more to write about by allowing for the nitty-gritty details that show readers what we mean.

For instance, if you wanted to know the "personality" of a particular town, walking around and talking with the people would show a lot more than flying over the place at 10,000 feet. A *focused topic*, then, is something you know and really can talk about, something that has real meaning for you.

DECIDE ON YOUR PURPOSE

"Why am I writing?"

Finding a *purpose* means asking yourself, "Why am I writing this piece?" Each writing situation has a specific goal. Perhaps you want audience members to see what you saw, to feel what you felt, or to think differently. To achieve your goal, you will need a definite *strategy*.

Goal plus strategy equals purpose. Consider one writer's inadequate answers to the familiar question, "Why am I writing this paper?"

Inadequate statements of purpose	**(a)** I'm writing this essay to pass the course.
	(b) My goal is to write an essay about yoga.
	(c) My goal is to write an essay persuading classmates to try yoga.

Responses **a** and **b** above tell nothing about the specific goal. Response **c** defines the goal, but offers no strategy. Here, finally, is our writer's *purpose statement* (goal plus strategy):

A useful statement of purpose	My purpose is to write an essay persuading my classmates to try yoga by showing how it relaxes the body, clears the mind, and stimulates the imagination.

Sometimes you will be unable to define your purpose immediately. You might need to jot down as many purposes as possible until one pops up. Or you might need to write a rough draft first or make some type of outline.

DECIDE ON YOUR THESIS

"What is my viewpoint?"

Your *thesis statement* makes a definite commitment. It tells readers what to expect by making your viewpoint absolutely clear. Here are some different ways of announcing your viewpoint:

As an opinion	College is not for everyone.
As an observation	My high school education was a waste of time.
As a suggestion	Computer literacy should be required for all applicants.
As an attitude	I want my life to be better than that of my parents.
As a question	What is friendship?

Any of these thesis statements creates clear expectations. They don't keep readers guessing. They make their points fast.

Thesis as Framework.   Consciously or unconsciously, readers look for a thesis, usually in the essay's early paragraphs. Even a single paragraph is hard to understand if the main point is missing. Read this paragraph once, only—and then try answering the questions that follow.

A paragraph with its main point omitted	His [or her] job is not to punish, but to heal. Most students are bad writers, but the more serious the injuries, the more confusing the symptoms, the

> greater the need for effective diagnostic work. When an accident victim is carried into the hospital emergency ward, the doctor does not start treating the patient at the top and slowly work down without a sense of priority, spending a great deal of time on the black eye before [getting] to the punctured lung. Yet that is exactly what the English teacher too often does. The doctor looks for the most vital problem; he [or she] wants to keep the patient alive, and . . . goes to work on the critical injury.
>
> —*Donald Murray*

Can you identify the paragraph's main idea? Probably not. Without the topic sentence, you have no framework for understanding this information in its larger meaning.

Now, insert the following sentence at the beginning and reread the paragraph.

The missing main idea | The writing teacher must be not a judge, but a physician.

This orientation makes the message's exact meaning obvious.

In the basic essay framework, each body paragraph supports its own *topic statement,* which focuses on one aspect of the thesis. The thesis is the controlling idea; each topic statement treats one part of the controlling idea, as diagramed here:

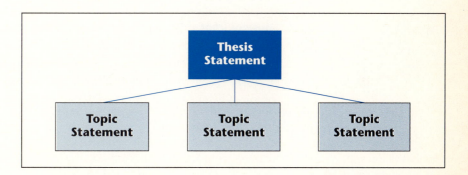

Some writers include in the thesis a preview of supporting points; some don't. For instance, an essay titled "Beef Cost and the Cattle Rancher" might have this thesis statement:

A thesis that includes a preview | Because of rising costs, unpredictable weather, and long hours, many cattle ranchers have trouble staying in business.

Including a preview in their thesis helps some writers stay on track as they develop each support paragraph. With or without the preview, be sure that supporting points appear as topic statements in subsequent paragraphs.

Your thesis statement often grows out of your purpose statement. While the purpose statement is part of the discovery process, the thesis is part of the finished essay. (See pages 59–60.)

Evaluating Your Thesis. Always check to see that your thesis provides a sharp focus and a definite and significant viewpoint.

A. *Is the Topic Sharply Focused?* In a short essay, avoid broad topics such as this one:

> **Too broad** Some experiences can be unforgettable

B. *Is a Definite and Informative Viewpoint Expressed?* Preview your exact meaning. These next thesis statements offer no such preview:

> **No clear viewpoint expressed** I will discuss a memory of high school gym class.
>
> In high school, I had a weekly gym class.
>
> High school experiences can be complex.

C. *Is the Viewpoint Significant?* Whether your thesis is expressed as an opinion, attitude, observation, suggestion, or question, it should trigger some fresh insight or have some value or importance for readers. A thesis that holds no surprise is worthless:

> **Insignificant viewpoints** The high school years can be traumatic. *[Everyone would agree, and so why discuss it?]*
>
> Everyone has some vivid memories of high school. *[No big surprise here!]*

Variations in Your Thesis. The thesis statement can appear in different forms and different locations:

How thesis form and location can vary

- The main supporting points are not always previewed.
- A thesis does not automatically call for only three supporting points. Three is a good minimum, but some topics call for more, others for less.
- The thesis usually is the final sentence in the introduction. In this position it "bridges" the introduction and the body. But for some purposes it can appear elsewhere in the introduction (as on page 53).
- The thesis need not be limited to one sentence.

How you phrase the thesis and where you place it depends on your purpose and audience.

When to Compose Your Thesis. In an ideal world, writers would be able to (1) settle on a topic, (2) compose a purpose statement, and (3) compose a thesis. But these steps rarely occur in such neat order. If you have trouble coming up with a thesis right away, go on to some other activity: list some ideas, work on an outline, do some freewriting, or take a walk. Writing, after all, is a way of discovering what you want to say.

Even if you do begin with a workable thesis, it might not be the one you end up with. As you work and discover new meanings, you might need to revise or start again.

DECIDE ON YOUR AUDIENCE

"Who is my audience and what do they expect?"

Except for a diary or a journal, everything you write is for readers who will react to your information. You might write to a prospective employer who wants to know why you quit a recent job; or to a committee who wants to know why you deserve a scholarship; or to a classmate who wants to know you better; or to a professor who wants to know whether you understand the material. For any audience, your task is to deliver a message that makes a difference with readers, that helps them see things your way.

Audiences you might encounter

What audiences expect

Out of school you will write for diverse audiences (customers, employers, politicians, and so on). But in school, you can envision a definite audience besides your instructor: your classmates. Like any audience, they expect your writing to be clear, informative, and persuasive. Whoever your readers are, they need enough material to understand your position and to react appropriately. Readers don't need repetition of material they already know. To put readers in your place, first put yourself in theirs. Anticipate their most probable questions.

Anticipating your readers' questions gives you a better chance of discovering and selecting material that really makes a difference—that offers readers what they need and expect.

CASE STUDY

ANALYZING YOUR WRITING SITUATION

Assume your instructor has requested an essay about a vivid memory. This time, part of your focusing job is done (memory ⟶ a vivid memory). But you need even more focus:

Focusing your topic

A vivid memory

↓

A memory from high school

↓

High school gym class

↓

Unpleasant memories of my gym class

The last subject seems focused enough for a short essay. But what in this subject do you wish to explore? What do you want readers to know and understand?

Your focused topic

| Why I hated high school gym class

You have now converted a broad subject to a suitable topic; you're on your way. You might get stuck later and have to discard the whole thing, but for now you can decide on your purpose.

Because the essay examines "Why," you organize a rough outline to follow the sequence of causes and effects in your painful experience:

Your rough outline

a.   What the class was like

b.   How I performed

c.   How my peers and teachers reacted to my performance

d.   How I ended up feeling

Now you can compose your statement of purpose:

Your purpose statement

My purpose is to explain to classmates why I hated high school gym class. I'll show what the class was like, how I performed, how everyone reacted, and how I ended up feeling.

This is your map for reaching your goal.

Based on the above purpose statement, assume you derive the following thesis:

Your thesis

| For three long years, gym class was my weekly exercise in failure.

As you consider your audience here (teacher and classmates), you anticipate the following questions:

Audience questions you can anticipate

■ *What was it?*

■ *What happened?*

■ *When, where, and why did it happen?*

■ *How did it make you feel?*

■ *Who was involved?*

■ *Who cares?*

As this case continues, after the following section, you will identify more specific audience questions you need to answer.

DISCOVERING, SELECTING, AND ORGANIZING YOUR MATERIAL

Once you have analyzed your writing situation, you set out to answer these questions:

QUESTIONS FOR EXPLORING YOUR ASSETS

- *What do I know about the topic?*
- *How much of my material is useful in this situation?*
- *How will readers want this organized?*

DISCOVER USEFUL MATERIAL

"What do I know about the topic?"

Discovering useful material is called *invention*. When you begin working with an idea or exloring a topic, you search for useful material, for content: insights, facts, statistics, opinions, examples, images, that might help answer this question: *How can I find something worthwhile to say—something that will advance my meaning?*

Some people use invention as an early writing step, a way of getting started. Others save the invention stage until they've made other decisions. Regardless of the sequence, all writers use invention throughout the writing process.

The goal of invention is to get as much material as possible on paper, through the use of strategies like the following.

Keeping a Journal.   A *journal* is an excellent way to build a personal inventory of ideas and topics. Here you can write for yourself only.

How to make a journal

To start, buy a hardcover notebook with a sewn binding (so that whatever you write becomes a permanent part of your journal). Record your reactions to something you've read or seen; ask questions or describe people, places, things, feelings; explore fantasies, daydreams, nightmares, fears, hopes; write conversations or letters that never will be heard or read; examine the things you hate or love. Write several times a day, once a week, or whenever you get the urge—or put aside some regular time to write. Every so often, go back and look over your entries—you might be surprised by the things you find.

Freewriting.   *Freewriting* is a version of the "quickest-effort" approach discussed in Chapter 1. Shirley Haley's first attempt (page 11) is the product of freewriting. As the term suggests, when freewriting you simply write whatever comes to mind, hoping that the very act of recording your thinking will generate some useful content.

How to freewrite

Try freewriting by exploring what makes you angry or happy or frightened or worried. Write about what surprises you or what you think is unfair or what you would like to see happen. Don't stop writing until you've filled a whole page or two, and don't worry about organization or correctness—just get it down. Although it will never produce a finished essay, freewriting can give you a good start by uncovering all kinds of buried ideas. It can be especially useful for curing "writer's block."

Using Journalists' Questions. To probe the many angles and dimensions of a topic, journalists ask these questions:

QUESTIONS JOURNALISTS ASK

- *Who was involved?*
- *What happened?*
- *When did it happen?*
- *Where did it happen?*
- *How did it happen?*
- *Why did it happen?*

Unlike freewriting, the journalists' questions offer a built-in organizing strategy—an array of different "perspectives" on your topic.

Asking Yourself Questions. If you can't seem to settle on a definite viewpoint, try answering any of these questions that apply to your topic.

DISCOVERY QUESTIONS YOU CAN ASK

- *What is my opinion of X?*
- *Am I for it or against it?*
- *Does it make me happy or sad?*
- *It is good or bad?*
- *Will it work or fail?*
- *Does it make sense?*
- *What have I observed about X?*
- *What have I seen happen?*
- *What is special or unique about it?*
- *What strikes me about it?*
- *What can I suggest about X?*
- *What would I like to see happen?*
- *What should or should not be done?*

From your answers, you can zero in on the viewpoint that will provide the organizing insight for your essay.

Brainstorming.   You can also try brainstorming—a sure bet for coming up with useful material. Here is how brainstorming works:

GUIDELINES FOR BRAINSTORMING

1. Find a quiet spot, and bring an alarm clock, a pencil, and plenty of paper.

2. Set the alarm to ring in 30 minutes.

3. Try to protect yourself from interruptions: phones, music, or the like. Sit with eyes closed for two minutes, thinking about absolutely nothing.

4. Now, concentrate on your writing situation. If you've already spelled out your purpose and your audience's questions, focus on these. Otherwise, repeat this question: *What can I say about my topic, at all?*

5. As ideas begin to flow, record every one. Don't stop to judge relevance or worth, and don't worry about complete sen-tences (or even correct spelling). Simply get everything on paper. Even the wildest idea might lead to some valuable insight.

6. Keep pushing and sweating until the alarm rings.

7. If the ideas are still flowing, reset the alarm and go on.

8. At the end of this session, you should have a chaotic mixture of junk, irrelevancies, and useful material.

9. Take a break.

10. Now confront your list. Strike out what is useless, and sort the remainder into categories. Include any other ideas that crop up. Your finished list should provide plenty of raw material.

Reading and Researching.   Some of our best ideas, insights, and questions often come from our reading (as discussed in Chapter 2). Or we might want to consider what others have said or discovered about our topic (as discussed in Chapter 19), before we reach our own conclusions. Reading and research are indispensable tools for any serious writer.

SELECT YOUR BEST MATERIAL

"How much of my material is useful in this situation?"

Invention invariably produces more material than a writer needs. Select only the material that best advances your meaning (see Chapter 6, Achieving Worthwhile Content).

If you do find yourself trying to include everything you've discovered, you probably need to refocus on your purpose and audience.

ORGANIZE FOR READERS

"How will readers want this organized?"

When material is left in its original, unstructured form, readers waste time trying to understand it. With an outline, you move from a random listing of items as they occurred to you to a deliberate map that will guide readers from point to point.

All readers expect a definite beginning, middle, and ending that provide orientation, discussion, and review. But specific readers want these sections tailored to their expectations. Identify your readers' expectations by (1) anticipating their probable questions about your thesis, and (2) visualizing the sequence in which readers would want these questions answered.

Some writers can organize merely by working from a good thesis statement. Others prefer to begin with some type of outline. And some writers like to write a draft and then an outline to check their line of thinking. You might outline early or later. But you need to move from a random collection of ideas to an organized list that helps readers to follow your material.

Note: No single form of outline should be followed slavishly by any writer. The organization of any writing ultimately is determined by its audience's needs and expectations.

CASE STUDY   **EXPLORING AND ARRANGING ASSETS**

For your gym class essay, assume you've developed the brainstorming list that follows.

Your brainstorming list

1. gym teacher expected too much
2. terror every Monday morning
3. like a walk to the guillotine
4. teachers should learn to control their biases
5. they should be trained to deal with students of all abilities
6. winning was everything
7. drums beating
8. losing teams punished
9. teachers teach students, not phys. ed. or other subjects
10. always one of the last players picked
11. always the loser
12. trying hard only made me feel incompetent
13. teacher liked only the athletes
14. fun—instead of victory—should be the goal in athletics
15. teammates groaned at my efforts
16. my gift grade was a C minus
17. I felt blacklisted

18. effort versus performance

19. nicknamed "the athlete"

20. I laughed, but it wasn't funny

21. missed the backboard

22. I had no talent

23. sure to fail

With your raw material collected, you can now move into the selection phase—leaving open the possibility that new material may surface.

As you review your brainstorming list, you decide to cut items 4, 5, 9, and 14.

Your selection of material to omit

■ *Item 4 sounds too much like a sermon and doesn't relate to the purpose (to describe a memory—not to argue for changes in teaching approaches).*

■ *Item 5 is a cliché, which again is too abstract to have real meaning—much less any relevance—to this essay.*

■ *Item 9, again, is not directly related to experiences in the gym. Also, the notion of such "subjects" is too abstract to have real meaning in this context.*

■ *Item 14 is overstated. Athletics could have value other than fun (exercise, relaxation, team spirit, and so on).*

Next you try to anticipate readers' questions about your essay, and you come up with this list of possibilities:

Reader questions you anticipate

■ *Can you set the scene for us, and re-create your feelings or mood?*

■ *What were the teacher and the class like?*

■ *What did you do that was so bad?*

■ *How did everyone react to what you did?*

■ *How did you react?*

Your readers' expectations give you a basis for organizing your brainstorming material into categories:

Your general outline

I. How I Dreaded Monday Morning Gym Class

II. How Our Teacher's Standards Were Too High

III. How I Failed to Meet These Standards

IV. How I Was Continually Reminded of My Failures

V. How the Experience Left Me Feeling Defeated

Within each category, you arrange your brainstorming items, along with any other worthwhile material that occurs to you. Your final outline might resemble this one:

Your final outline

I. I dreaded Monday morning gym class.

    A. I knew what was waiting for me.

    B. I could sense the dampness and the stale smell.

    C. My hands would tremble, and I would sweat.

    D. I had no athletic talent, and was so terrified.

    E. It felt like a walk to the guillotine, with drums in the background.

    F. **Thesis:** For three long years, my high school gym class was my weekly exercise in failure.

II. Our teacher's standards were too high.

    A. She was not unkind, but not realistic, either.

    B. Athletic prowess was expected of each student.

    C. Only the athletes were liked.

    D. Winning meant everything.

    E. All fun disappeared.

III. I never could measure up to the high standards.

    A. I always lost—even when my team won.

    B. I couldn't hit the backboard.

    C. I tripped over my own feet.

    D. Any sport meant failure.

    E. The more I tried, the more I felt inferior.

IV. I was continually reminded of my failures.

    A. My classmates grew to expect the worst from me.

    B. I was always one of the last picked for teams.

    C. People groaned when I came up to bat.

    D. My friends nicknamed me "the athlete."

    E. I laughed on the outside, but not inside.

    F. My C– "gift grade" killed my otherwise high average.

V. The whole experience left me feeling defeated.

    A. I should have been able to learn something about self-confidence.

    B. But I only felt "blacklisted."

    C. Intimidated, I developed a kind of mental paralysis.

    D. I accepted the certainty of failure.

    E. Never have my personal shortcomings received such public display.

This outline takes the form of short, kernel sentences that include key ideas for later expansion. Some writers might use a less formal outline—a simple list of phrases without numerals or letters. (Use the form that works best for you.)

During later drafts you will discover more material, and probably will delete some original material (as in the final draft, pages 59–60).

FINDING YOUR VOICE

Your planning inventory is nearly complete: you have a topic and a thesis, a clear sense of purpose and audience, a stock of material, and some sort of outline. In fact, if you were writing merely to get your message across, you could begin drafting the essay immediately. Except for diaries or some technical reports, however, we write not only to transmit information, but also to connect with readers.

Why voice matters

Whether your writing connects with readers depends on how it "sounds." The way your writing sounds depends on its *tone,* your personal mark—the voice readers hear between the lines. Readers who like the tone like the writer; they allow contact.

Consciously or unconsciously, readers ask three big questions about the writer:

Readers' questions in sizing up a writer

- *What type of person is this (somebody businesslike, serious, silly, sincere, phony, boring, bored, intense, stuck-up, meek, confident, friendly, hostile)?*
- *How is this person treating me (as a friend, acquaintance, stranger, enemy, nobody, superior, subordinate, bozo, somebody with a brain and feelings)?*
- *What does this person really think about the topic (really involved or merely "going through the motions")?*

How readers answer these questions will depend on your voice.

Why fancy words don't always work

Some inexperienced writers mistakenly think that fancy words make them sound more intelligent and important. And sometimes, of course, only the complex word will convey your exact meaning. Instead of saying "Sexist language contributes to the ongoing existence of stereotypes," you could say more accurately and concisely, "Sexist language perpetuates stereotypes." (One "fancy" word effectively replaces six "simpler" words.) But when you use fancy words only to impress, your writing sounds stuffy and pretentious.

FIND A VOICE THAT CONNECTS WITH READERS

Personal essays ordinarily employ a conversational tone: you write to your audience as if you were speaking to them. Look again at Shirley Haley's opening lines from page 13:

Conversational tone

> I'm probably the only person I know who still has the same two parents she was born with. We have a traditional American family: we go to church and football games; we watch the Olympics on television and argue about politics; and we have Thanksgiving dinner at my grandmother Clancy's and Christmas dinner with my father's sister Jess, who used to let us kids put pitted olives on our fingertips when we were little.

Haley's tone is friendly and relaxed—the voice of a writer who seems at home with herself, her subject, and her readers. We are treated to comfortable images of family things. But the long list of "traditional" family activities also hints at the writer's restlessness, lets us share her mixed feelings of attraction and repulsion.

Suppose Haley had decided to sound more "academic":

Academic tone

> Among my friends and acquaintances, I am apparently the only individual with the good fortune to have parents who remain married. Our family activities are grounded in American tradition: we attend church services and football games; we watch televised sporting events and engage in political debates; at Thinksgiving, we dine at Grandmother's, and at Christmas, with an aunt who has always been quite tolerant of children's behavior.

Which is better? To see for yourself which version is more inviting, test each against readers' three big questions on page 43.

AVOID AN OVERLY INFORMAL TONE

How tone can be too informal

We generally do not write in the same way we would speak to friends at the local burger joint or street corner. Achieving a conversational tone does not mean lapsing into substandard usage, slang, profanity, or excessive colloquialisms. *Substandard usage* ("He ain't got none"; "I seen it today"; "She brang the book") ignores standards of educated expression. *Slang* ("hurling," "belted," "bogus," "bummed") usually has specific meaning only for members of a particular in-group. *Profanity* ("Pissed off"; "This idea sucks"; "What the hell") not only displays contempt for the audience but often triggers contempt for the person using it. *Colloquialisms* ("O.K.," "a lot," "snooze," "in the bag,") are understood more widely than slang, but tend to appear more in speaking than in writing.

How tone can offend

Tone is considered offensive when it violates the reader's expectations: when it seems disrespectful or tasteless, or distant and aloof, or too "chummy," casual, or otherwise inappropriate for the topic, the reader, and the situation.

When to use an academic tone

A formal or academic tone, in fact, is perfectly appropriate in countless writing situations: a research paper, a job application, a report for the company president, and so on. In a history essay, for example, we would not refer to George Washington and Abraham Lincoln as "those dudes, George and Abe." Whenever we begin with freewriting or brainstorming, our tone might be overly informal and is likely to require some adjustment during subsequent drafts.

But while slang is usually inappropriate in school or workplace writing, some situations call for a measure of informality. The occasional colloquial expression helps soften the tone of any writing.

THE WRITER'S PLANNING GUIDE

Decisions and strategies covered in this chapter apply to almost any writing situation. You can make sure your own planning decisions are complete by following the Planning Guide whenever you write. Items in the Planning Guide are reminders of things to be done.

PLANNING GUIDE

Broad subject:

Limited topic:

Purpose statement:

Thesis statement:

Audience:

Probable audience questions:

Brainstorming list (with irrelevant items deleted):

Outline:

Appropriate tone for audience and purpose:

Your instructor might ask you to use the Planning Guide for early assignments and to submit your responses along with your essay. Remember that your decisions for completing the Planning Guide need not follow the strict order of the items listed—so long as you make all the necessary decisions.

This next Planning Guide has been completed to show a typical set of decisions for the gym class essay.

THE COMPLETED PLANNING GUIDE

Broad topic: A vivid memory

Limited topic: Why I hated high school gym class

Purpose statement (what you want to do): My purpose is to explain to my classmates why I have such a painful memory of high school gym class. I'll have to show what the class was like, how I performed, how everyone reacted, and how I ended up feeling.

Thesis statement (what you want to say): For three long years, gym class was my weekly exercise in failure.

Audience: Classmates

Probable audience questions:
> Can you set the scene for us, and re-create your feelings or mood?
> What were the teacher and the class like?
> What did you do that was so bad?
> How did everyone react to what you did?
> How did you react?
> Who cares?

Brainstorming list:
> 1. gym teacher expected too much
> 2. terror every Monday morning
> 3. like a walk to the guillotine . . . and so on

Outline:
> I. I dreaded Monday morning gym class.
>   A. I knew what was waiting for me.
>   B. I could sense the dampness and the stale smell.
>   C. My hands would tremble, and I would sweat.
>   D. Monday was physical education day . . . and so on.

Appropriate tone for audience and purpose: personal and serious

PLANNING FOR GROUP WORK

In the Introduction to Section One, you practiced thinking ahead to the kinds of decisions groups must make if they are to benefit from all members' contributions. The following guidelines will enable your group to prepare for collaborative work.

GUIDELINES FOR WRITING COLLABORATIVELY

1. *Appoint a group manager.* The manager assigns tasks, enforces deadlines, conducts meetings, consults with the instructor, and generally "runs the show."

2. *Compose a purpose statement (pages 31–32).* Spell out the project's goal and the group's plan for achieving the goal.

3. *Decide how the group will be organized.* Some possibilities:

   a. The group researches and plans together, but each person writes a different part of the document.

   b. Some members plan and research; one person writes a complete draft; others review, edit, revise, and produce the final version. Keep in mind that the final revision should display one consistent style throughout—as if written by one person only.

4. *Divide the task.* Who will be responsible for which parts of the essay or report or which phases of the project? Who is best at doing what (writing, editing, using a word processor)?

5. *Establish specific completion dates for each phase.* This will keep everyone focused on what is due and when.

6. *Decide on a meeting schedule and format.* How often will the group meet, and for how long? In or out of class? Who will take notes?

7. *Establish a procedure for responding to the work of other members.* Will reviewing and editing (pages 67–72) be done in writing, face-to-face, as a group, one-on-one, or even via computer? Will this process be supervised by the project manager?

8. *Establish procedures for dealing with group problems.* How will gripes and disagreements be aired and resolved? How will irrelevant discussion be curtailed? Can inevitable conflict be used positively?

9. *Decide how to evaluate each member's contribution.* Will members evaluate each other? Criteria for evaluation might include dependability, cooperation, effort, quality of work, and the ability to meet deadlines.

APPLICATION 3-1

Narrow two or three of the broad topics in this list to a topic suitable for a short essay. (Review page 31.)

EXAMPLE

social rituals

↓

high-school proms

↓

how the romantic image of prom night has become a myth

↓

how today's typical prom night is based on competition and appearances and polluted by drugs, alcohol, and sex

TOPICS TO BE NARROWED

entertainment	careers	war	family
life	sports	crime	sex
social rituals	automobiles	fashion	music
marriage	alcohol	studying	drugs

· ·

APPLICATION 3-2

Compose statements of purpose for essays on three or more of the topics in Application 3-1. (Review pages 31–32.)

EXAMPLE

Topic   The problems with prom night

Purpose statement   My purpose is to persuade past and present high school students that high school proms have become a waste of time. I will discuss four major problems with prom night: drugs and alcohol, sexual promiscuity, competition, and danger.

· ·

APPLICATION 3-3

Convert your statements of purpose from Application 3-2 into thesis statements. (Review pages 32–35.)

EXAMPLE

Purpose statement   My purpose is to persuade past and present high school students that proms have become a waste of time. I will discuss four major problems with prom night: drugs and alcohol, sexual promiscuity, competition, and danger.

Thesis statement   High school proms have lost their value as social events and have become expensive and exaggerated rituals that entrap students in situations they often despise.

······················

APPLICATION 3-4

For each thesis statement in Application 3-3, brainstorm and write three or four topic statements for individual supporting paragraphs. Arrange your topic statements in logical order. (Review pages 37–39.)

EXAMPLE

Thesis statement	High school proms have lost their value as social events and have become expensive and exaggerated rituals that entrap students in situations they often despise.
First topic statement	Parents, teachers, coaches, and other role models seem to merely accept the fact that students are going to drink or get high on prom night.
Second topic statement	It is almost an unspoken law that a couple (no matter how unacquainted) should have sex on prom night.
Third topic statement	Competition over who has the most expensive dress, the most unusual tux, the biggest limousine, or the cutest date also detracts from the evening.
Fourth topic statement	Not only do many feel obliged to attend the prom in order to fit in, but they also feel obliged to participate in often dangerous after-prom events.

······················

APPLICATION 3-5

From Application 3-4, select the most promising set of materials, and write your best essay. Use selected items from your brainstorming list to develop each support paragraph. Outline as necessary. Provide an engaging introduction and a definite conclusion. Use the questions on pages 17–18 as guidelines for revising your essay.

······················

APPLICATION 3-6

Collaborative Project: Organize into small groups. Choose a subject from the list at the end of this exercise. Then decide on a thesis statement and (not necessarily in this order) brainstorm. Identify a specific audience. Group similar items under the same major categories, and develop an outline. When each group completes this procedure, one representative can write the outline on the board for class suggestions about revision. (Review pages 39–40.)

a description of the ideal classroom

instructions for surviving the first semester of college

instructions for surviving a blind date

suggestions for improving one's college experience

causes of teenage suicide

arguments for or against a formal grading system

an argument for an improvement you think this college needs

the qualities of a good parent

what you expect the world to be like in ten years

young people's needs that parents often ignore

· ·

APPLICATION 3-7

 Computer Project: Many word processing programs offer an outline function. If the program you are using permits, use the computer to develop an outline for one of the applications in this chapter. Alternatively, brainstorm headings for a kernel outline, and then use the computer commands for moving text from one place to another to try out different arrangements of your headings, inserting new headings or deleting inappropriate ones as they occur.

· ·

DECISIONS IN DRAFTING

Once you have a definite plan, you are ready to draft your essay. Here is where you decide on answers to some tough questions:

DECISIONS IN DRAFTING YOUR ESSAY

- *How do I begin the essay?*
- *What does my reader need to know first?*
- *What comes after that?*

- *How much is enough?*
- *Am I forgetting anything?*
- *How do I end?*

As you work, remember that each writing sample in this book is the product of multiple drafts and revisions. None of these writers expected to get it right the first time—neither should you.

DRAFTING THE TITLE AND INTRODUCTION

Why titles are important

Titles—which are sometimes chosen after the essay is complete—should forecast an essay's subject and approach. Clear, attention-getting titles, such as "Let's Shorten the Baseball Season," or "Instead of Running, Try Walking," help readers plan how to interpret what they read.

Assume you are continuing your work from Chapter 3 where you planned your essay about your feelings of personal failure in gym class. You have chosen the title, "Suffering Through Gym Class."

THE INTRODUCTORY PARAGRAPH

Introductions differ in shape and size and may consist of more than one paragraph; however, basic introductory paragraphs often have a funnel shape:

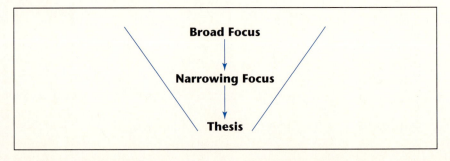

Broad Focus

Narrowing Focus

Thesis

Now that you have decided on a title—"Suffering Through Gym Class"— you can introduce your essay's final draft, using a funnel pattern:

SUFFERING THROUGH GYM CLASS

Broad focus (1)
Narrowing focus (2–4)

[1]In high school my Monday mornings were awful. [2]Even before the school's front door had slammed behind me, I could sense a nauseating dampness rising up from the locker room, a mist of stale sweat. [3]Monday for me was physical education day. [4]And because I was no athlete, each of my 8:00 a.m. trips downstairs to the gym seemed like a clammy and quivering walk to the guillotine, my heartbeat like a drumbeat, my ego about to suffer its ritual of public execution. [5]For three long years, gym class was my weekly exercise in failure.

Thesis (5)

Why introductions are important

Introductory paragraphs do more than just lead into the essay; they invite readers in and set a tone. The tone of this painful account is personal and urgent, created by the first-person *I*, *my*, and *our*, and by images such as "a clammy and quivering walk to the guillotine." If your only aim were to lead into the main discussion, you might have given this introduction instead:

I always did poorly in high school gym class.

But this version lacks the vivid images ("nauseating dampness," "a mist of stale sweat") that engage our attention, make us want to read on.

PLACING THE THESIS

In a standard essay, the thesis often appears at the end of the introductory paragraph, as a bridge to the discussion. Sometimes, though, you will want your readers to know where you stand immediately, especially when the topic is controversial.

A controversial thesis as opener

Corporal punishment doesn't belong in our public schools, because it creates a regimented atmosphere that stifles the desire to learn, generates hostility toward the teacher, and causes antisocial behavior. A school, after all, is not a prison. And among the different learning experiences school should provide is the opportunity to learn through mistakes.

Sometimes, even personal writing can open directly with the thesis, especially when the viewpoint is unexpected.

A surprising thesis as opener

I hate summer beaches. Ocean swimming is impossible; upon conquering a wave, I simply lose to the next, getting pushed back onto the hard-packed, abrasive sand. Booby-traps of bottles, soda cans, toys, and rocks make walking hazardous. Heavy with the stench of suntan lotion, greasy French fries, dead fish, and sweat, the thick, searing air hangs motionless about the scorching sand. Blasting radios and growling hot rods cut the slap-swoosh of the green-gray surf to a weak hiss. People devour a summer

> beach, gouging the sand with umbrella spikes and gripping it with oiled limbs, leaving only trampled debris at summer's end.

In some essays, the thesis appears later, even near the end (as on page 284). A delayed thesis is especially useful in a story leading to some larger meaning (*Here is what happened,* and then, *Here is what it means*).

SELECTING AN OPENING STRATEGY

"How do I begin?"

The specifics of your introduction are determined by what you know about your readers and your purpose.

DECISIONS IN ANALYZING YOUR AUDIENCE

- *Are my readers likely to be interested in this topic?*
- *How can I make them want to read on?*
- *Are they likely to react defensively?*
- *Is my purpose to describe something, to tell a story, to explain something, to change somebody's mind?*

The opening strategies that follow offer various possibilities for connecting with your audience.

Open with an Anecdote. An anecdote is a brief, personal story that makes a point.

> Last weekend, I gave a friend's younger brother a ride from the mall. As we drove, I asked him the same old questions about high school, grades, football, and girlfriends. He answered me in one-word sentences and then pulled out a cassette tape. "Wanna hear somethin' cool?" I shrugged and popped it into the tape player. What came pouring through my car speakers made me run a stop sign. The "rap" song spelled out, in elaborate detail, 101 ways to violate a woman's body. Needless to say, it was a long ride across town.
>
> I borrowed the tape and listened to every song, horrified by their recurrent theme of sexual violence and domination. But most horrifying is that a 15-year-old kid actually considers this music "cool."

Open with a Background Story. For example, in an essay that challenges a popular attitude, trace the development of that attitude.

> In 1945, a terrifying blast shook the New Mexico desert. Shortly afterward, the new, awesome force literally vaporized hundreds of thousands of lives, to end World War II. Thus began the atomic era. This horrid beginning, along with recent nuclear accidents and scandals, has caused increasing criticism. However, as we enter a new century the nuclear breeder reactor offers a promising energy alternative, but critics have drastically reduced its development and production. We need the breeder reactor, because it is one of our best long-range sources of energy.

This kind of opening is especially effective in persuasive writing, because it acknowledges opposing views, creating empathy (identification with the reader's attitude).

Open with a Question. An opening question can get readers thinking right away, especially when you write instructions, give advice, or argue for action.

> What do you do when you find yourself in the produce room cooler with your manager and he nonchalantly wraps his arm around your waist? Or how about when the guys you work with come out with a distasteful remark that makes you seem like a piece of meat? These are just a couple of problems you might face as the only female in a department. There are, however, ways of dealing with this kind of harassment.

Open with a Short Quotation. If a quotation can summarize your point, use it—and clarify its significance immediately.

> "The XL Roadster—anything else is just a car," unless the XL happens to be mine. In that case, it's just a piece of junk.

Open with a Direct Address. The second-person *you* can involve the readers and helps them pay attention—especially when you are giving instructions or advice or writing persuasively.

> Does the thought of artificially preserved, chemically treated food make you lose your appetite? Do limp, tasteless, frozen vegetables leave you cold? Then you should try your hand at organic gardening.

Use direct address in ads, popular articles, and brochures but not in academic reports or most business and technical documents.

Open with a Brief, Vivid Description. Instead of a thesis, some descriptive essays simply have an orienting sentence to set a scene or create a mood, to place readers at the center of things.

> The raft bobs gently as the four divers help each other with scuba gear. We joke and laugh casually as we struggle in the cramped space; but a restlessness is in the air because we want to be on our way. Finally, everyone is ready, and we split into pairs. I steal a last glance over the blue ocean. I hear the waves slap the boat, the mournful cry of a seagull, and a steady murmur from the crowded beach a mile away. With three splashes my friends jump in. I follow. There is a splash and then silence. The water presses in, and all I hear is the sound of my regulator as I take my first breath. All I see is blue water, yellow light, and endless space. While the world rushes on, we feel suspended in time. Then my buddy taps me on the shoulder, and we begin a tour of a hidden world.

Description can also be a powerful way to make a point.

> They appear each workday morning from 7:00 to 9:00, role models for millions of career-minded women. Their crisp, clear diction and articulate reporting are second only to their appearance. Slender and lovely, the female co-hosts of morning news shows radiate that businesslike "chic" that networks consider essential in their newswomen. Such perfection is precisely why the networks hire these women as anchors. Network television rarely tolerates women commentators who are other than young, stylish, and attractive.

Notice how the businesslike tone parallels the topic itself.

Open with Examples. Examples enable readers to visualize the issue or problem.

> Privacy in America is disappearing. New technologies enable users to unearth anyone's health, credit, e-mail, and legal records with a few keystrokes. Beyond these computerized records, our telephones, television sets, and even our trash can be monitored by government agencies, banks, businesses, political groups—or just plain nosy people. Current United States law does disturbingly little to protect our right to privacy.

Open with a Definition. Clarify abstract terms for both writer and reader. This next essay, on the limits of the American Dream, begins by defining that key term.

> The American Dream has taken on different meanings for different people, but its original meaning derived from a seemingly unlimited potential for growth: in the sense of the country's great westward expansion followed by the Industrial Revolution. From this combination of geographic and economic progress emerged the correlation between the American Dream and freedom. The seemingly endless supply of land and employment let people

feel there was nothing stopping them from "moving up in the world." We now recognize, however, that the Dream does have a limit.

As you draft your introduction, consider the following suggestions:

Hints for an engaging introduction

- The introduction can be the hardest part of an essay. Many writers complete it last. If you do write your introduction first, be sure to revise it later.
- In most college writing, avoid opening with personal qualifiers such as "it is my opinion that," "I believe that," and "in this paper I will."
- Let your introduction create suspense that is resolved by your thesis statement, usually at the end of the paragraph(s).
- If the opening is boring, vague, long-winded, or toneless, readers may give up. Don't waste their time.

DRAFTING THE BODY SECTION

"How much is enough, and how can I shape it?"

The body section delivers on the commitment made in your thesis. Readers don't want details that just get in the way, or a jigsaw puzzle they have to unscramble for themselves. To develop the body, therefore, answer these questions:

DECISIONS IN DEVELOPING THE BODY OF YOUR ESSAY

- *How much is enough?*
- *How much information or detail should I provide?*
- *How can I stay on track?*
- *What shape will reveal my line of thought?*

Decide about purpose and unity. Here you discard some material you thought you might keep, and maybe discover additional material. Look hard at everything you've discovered during freewriting, brainstorming, or questioning. Stand in the reader's place. Keep whatever belongs, and discard whatever doesn't.

Decide how many support paragraphs to include. College essays typically have three or more, but use as many as you need. Decide how to develop each support paragraph and how to order them. What paragraph order will make the most sense and provide the best emphasis?

Elements affecting the shape of your writing (unity, coherence, emphasis, and transition) are discussed fully in Chapter 7, "Shaping the Paragraphs." Principles of developing the individual paragraph are principles as well of creating the whole essay—or of writing at any length.

DRAFTING THE CONCLUSION

An essay's conclusion refocuses on the thesis and leaves a final—and lasting—impression on readers. Your conclusion might evaluate the meaning or significance of the body section, restate your position, predict an outcome, offer a solution, request an action, make a recommendation, or pave the way for more exploration. Avoid conclusions that repeat, apologize, or belabor the obvious:

Don't repeat   I have just discussed my reasons for disliking gym class. I never did well at any sport I played.

Don't apologize   Although some readers might be bored reading about my experiences in gym class, they mean a lot to me.

Don't belabor the obvious   Now that you've read my essay, you should have a clear picture of what my gym class was like.

SELECTING A CLOSING STRATEGY

Forgettable endings drain the life from any writing. This list of strategies samples ways of closing with meaning and emphasis.

Close with a Summary. A review of main points helps readers remember what is most important.

Close with a Question. A closing question provides readers something to think about.

> Overall, the advantages of the breeder reactor seem immeasurable. Because it can produce more fuel than it uses, it will theoretically be an infinite source of energy. And efficient use of the fuel it does burn makes it highly desirable in this energy-tight era. What other source promises so much for our long-range energy future?

Close with a Call to Action. Tell readers exactly what you want them to do.

> Just imagine yourself eating a salad of crisp green lettuce, juicy red tomato chunks, firm white slices of cucumber, and crunchy strips of green pepper—all picked fresh from your own garden. If this picture appeals to you, begin planning your summer garden now, and by July the picture of you eating that salad will become a reality. *Bon appetit!*

Close with a Quotation. This next writer quotes from journalist Ellen Goodman's essay, "Blame the Victim."

> I agree with Ellen Goodman's assertion that there is "something malignant about some of the extremists who make a public virtue of their health." The cancer is in the superior attitudes of the "health elite"—an attitude that actually discourages exercise and healthy habits by making average people feel too intimidated and inferior even to begin a fitness program.

Close with an Interpretation or Evaluation. Help readers understand the meaning of things.

> A growing array of so-called private information about American citizens is collected daily. And few laws protect our right to be left alone. In the interest of pursuing criminals, government too often sacrifices the privacy of innocent people, and new technology is making old laws obsolete. Huge collections of data are becoming available to your insurance company, to prospective employers, to companies doing mass mailings, and even to your neighbor. The invasion continues, and no one seems to know how to stop our world from fulfilling the prophecy in George Orwell's *1984*.

Whichever strategy or combination of strategies you select, be sure that your conclusion is in some way memorable and that it refocuses on your main point without repeating it.

CASE STUDY

DRAFTING THE ESSAY

As an illustration of how these drafting decisions produce a completed essay, consider "Suffering Through Gym Class," reproduced here. (Chapter 5 traces the steps in revision that created the final version shown here.)

Notice that the thesis and each topic sentence appear in boldface and italics.

The finished essay

Introduction

SUFFERING THROUGH GYM CLASS

In high school my Monday mornings were awful. Even before the school's front door had slammed behind me, I could sense a nauseating dampness rising up from the locker room, a mist of stale sweat. Monday for me was physical education day. And because I was no athlete, each of my 8:00 a.m. trips downstairs to the gym seemed like a clammy and quivering walk to the guillotine, my heartbeat like a drumbeat, my ego about to suffer its ritual of public execution. *For three long years, gym class was my weekly exercise in failure.*

First support paragraph

Although I respected my gym teacher's focus on excellence, the standards in this class were beyond my ability. Everybody was expected to be an athlete—and nothing less would do. Effort was ignored in favor of performance. Winning became all-important, and losing teams were punished with extra laps. The fun in any game quickly disappeared. To make matters worse, some gung ho classmates seemed to mirror our teacher's attitude; within a few weeks, a caste system had developed: jocks on top, the marginally acceptable in the middle, and klutzes like me—the untouchables—at the bottom.

Second support paragraph

Whatever sport we played, I could count on being the loser, even when my team won. In baseball, I was the sure strikeout, the right fielder whose glove had a hole in it. In basketball, I had a hard time hitting the backboard, much less scoring a basket. In soccer, I tripped over my own feet. Also, team sports were not the only disaster: Parallel bars, hurdles, broad jumps, or high jumps—all were occasions for my world-class embarrassment. The more pathetic attempts I made, the more I came to feel incompetent and inferior.

Third support paragraph

I was continually reminded of my failures. Whenever players were picked for teams, I was sure to be last—huddled among the few remaining rejects trying to look nonchalant. Bracing myself at home plate for the inevitable swing-and-miss, I could count on a few hisses and groans from teammates, and at least one reassuring "easy out!" from opponents. Even my friends affectionately nicknamed me "the athlete." More charitable than my peers, our teacher mostly ignored those of us who qualified as wimps. And, as if to certify my incompetence, my C-minus grade (a gift, I guess, for passing "showers") would destroy an otherwise impressive grade average. At all these indignities I laughed on the outside, but not on the inside.

Conclusion

The whole experience left me feeling defeated. Instead of having fun and gaining confidence, I felt like a jerk. Intimidated by a standard impossible for me to achieve, I never gave myself the chance to discover my personal best. Taking fewer and fewer risks, I grew to accept the certainty of failure in sports. Those painful years are now behind me, but I still have trouble playing even a sport as casual as volleyball without feeling self-conscious. Looking back, I can appreciate the value of challenge in any class, but I can't help resenting a system that forces personal shortcomings into public display.

—*Kim Fonteneau*

Discussion

This essay presents a focused picture, enabling readers to feel what the writer felt. And the picture is unified: nothing gets in the way; everything belongs.

But content alone cannot ensure contact. Thoughts need shaping to help us grasp the experience and appreciate its importance. Each paragraph helps detail the weekly sequence of anxiety, alienation, inadequacy, and then humiliation.

Finally, the conclusion explores the meaning of this experience. The first four concluding sentences tell us how repeated failures affected the writer's sense of self-worth. The fifth tells about the lasting effects of such an experience. The final sentence brings everything together by reemphasizing the writer's ambivalence and resentment about an experience that challenges all students but humiliates some.

Readers remember last things best, and this essay's conclusion leaves us with something worth remembering.

DRAFTING ON THE COMPUTER

Word processing is especially useful as a drafting tool, enabling you to delete, move, or design text instantly. The following guidelines will help you capitalize on all the benefits a computer can offer.

Guidelines for Writing with a Computer

1. *Explore your school's computer facilities.* Sign up for training sessions on your school's computers. If possible, attend a workshop on the Internet. If you own a computer, ask about a modem connection to the school's mainframe computer.

2. *Decide whether to draft on the computer or by hand for later transfer to the computer.* Experiment with each approach before deciding which works best for you.

3. *Beware of computer junk.* The ease of cranking out words on a computer can produce long, windy pieces that say nothing. Edit your final drafts to eliminate anything that fails to advance your meaning. (See pages 118–124 for ways to achieve conciseness.)

4. *Never confuse style with substance.* Laser printers and choices of typefaces, type sizes, and other highlighting options can make documents highly attractive. But not even the most attractive formatting can redeem a document whose content is worthless or inaccessible.

5. *Save and print your work often.* One wrong keystroke might wipe out pages of writing forever. Save each paragraph as you write it and print out each page as you complete it.

6. *Make backup disks.* A single electrical surge or other malfunction can destroy the contents of an entire file, or even an entire floppy disk or hard disk!

7. *Always revise from hard copy.* Nothing beats scribbling and scratching on the printed page with pen or pencil. The hard copy provides the whole text, right in front of you.

8. *Never depend only on automated "checkers."* Even the most sophisticated writing aids cannot substitute for careful proofreading. A synonym offered up in an electronic thesaurus may not accurately convey your meaning. The spellchecker cannot differentiate among correctly spelled words such as "their," "they're" or "there" or "it's" versus "its." Although spell and grammar checkers can be a big help, they cannot evaluate the subtle choices of phrasing that determine tone and emphasis. Page 149 summarizes the limitations of many computerized aids.

9. *Always print two final copies.* With all the paperwork that writing instructors (and their students) shuffle, papers sometimes get misplaced. Submit one copy and keep one for yourself—just in case!

APPLICATION 4-1

Plan and draft an essay about something special to you; it might be a place, a person, an experience, an activity, or anything else—but it has to be something you are sure is worth writing about. Decide on an audience: your classmates, a friend, readers of the campus paper, or someone close to you. Your purpose here is to share your way of seeing, and to help your audience understand why your subject is special. Let your reader or readers see what you experience and let them feel your responses to it. Have a thesis and deliver on it.

Also, find a voice that will appeal to your readers. Create unity so that your writing sticks to the point; create order and use transitions so that it stands together. Have a beginning, a middle, and an ending. Use the questions on pages 17–18 for guidance in improving your essay.

APPLICATION 4-2

Using the strategies in this chapter, return to an essay you wrote earlier (maybe your first, or one your instructor recommends), and write a better draft. List the improvements you make, and be prepared to discuss them.

APPLICATION 4-3

Collaborative Project: Locate a good introduction or a good conclusion to a short article in a popular magazine such as *Time, Newsweek,* or *Reader's Digest.* As a group, analyze the strategies that make the writing effective. (Review pages 52–57 and 58–59.)

APPLICATION 4-4

Computer Project: Type your draft using a word processing program. Type either directly onto the computer or from a longhand original. Learn the commands for moving blocks of text and practice them by trying different placements of your body paragraphs. Most word processing programs allow you to save several versions of a document under different names. Use this function to save both backup copies of your draft and at least two alternative versions of the draft. Learn how to print your documents; then print hard copies of all three versions.

DECISIONS IN REVISING

*B*esides being a battle with impatience, writing is a battle with inertia: once we've written a draft, we are often too easily satisfied with what we've done. Good writers win the battle by revising often. For the sake of clarity, earlier chapters have presented a single sequence of steps for composing an essay. To review:

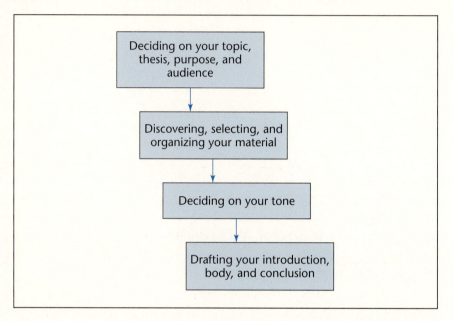

We have seen that writers rarely follow this exact sequence. But no matter what the sequence, any effective writer depends on revision—the one constant in the writing process. When you finish a first draft, you really have only begun.

THE MEANING OF REVISION

Why rhetorical elements are important

Revision involves more than proofreading for spelling, punctuation, or other mechanical details (all covered in Appendix A). Mechanical correctness is essential, but what matters most are the essay's *rhetorical elements: worthwhile content, sensible organization,* and *readable style.* The rhetorical elements determine whether your writing connects with readers—and makes a difference. Your instructor might write suggestions on your first draft or have you revise on your own. In any case, revision never means merely recopying; it always means *rethinking.*

Useful revision happens only when you can evaluate accurately what you already have written. Use the Revision Checklist to pinpoint possible improvements in content, organization, and style. (Numbers in parentheses refer to the first page of discussion.)

REVISION CHECKLIST

Worthwhile Content

The essay's main point is clear and sharply focused.

- ❑ Does the title attract attention and give a forecast? (52)
- ❑ Is the topic limited enough? (31)
- ❑ Do you get to your main point quickly? (53)
- ❑ Is the thesis definite, informative, and easy to find? (32)

The discussion delivers on the promise of your thesis.

- ❑ Will readers learn something new and useful? (79)
- ❑ Do you support every assertion with enough details? (77)
- ❑ Does everything belong, or can anything be cut? (83)
- ❑ Have you used only your best material? (82)

Sensible Organization

The essay has a definite introduction, body, and conclusion.

- ❑ Will your introduction make readers want to read on? (53)
- ❑ Does each body paragraph develop *one* supporting point? (88)
- ❑ Does the order of body paragraphs reveal a clear line of thought and emphasize what is most important? (57)
- ❑ Does the conclusion give a real sense of an ending? (58)

- ❑ Is everything connected? (60)
- ❑ If you varied this organization, was it for good reason? (155)

Except for paragraphs of transition or special emphasis, each body (or support) paragraph usually is a mini-essay.

- ❑ Does the paragraph have a topic (or orienting) statement? (89)
- ❑ Does the topic statement come at the beginning or end, depending on your emphasis? (89)
- ❑ Does everything stick to the point (unity), and stick together (coherence)? (92)
- ❑ Is the paragraph developed enough to support the point? (89)

Readable Style

Sentences are clear, concise, and fluent.

- ❑ Can each sentence be understood the first time it is read? (109)
- ❑ Are points made in the fewest words? (118)
- ❑ Are sentences put together with enough variety? (125)

Each word does its job.

- ❑ Is a real person speaking, and is the voice likable? (139)
- ❑ Is everything in plain English? (139)
- ❑ Is your meaning precise, concrete, and specific? (134)
- ❑ Is your tone appropriate for this situation and audience? (138)

USING THE CHECKLIST

As you use the Revision Checklist to rethink your essay, ask yourself questions such as these:

QUESTIONS FOR CRITICAL EVALUATION AND REVISION

- *Have I conveyed my exact point or feeling?*
- *Do vivid details from the event come to mind now that I've finished writing?*
- *What facts or figures or ideas do I now remember?*

- *Can I reorganize for greater emphasis or clarity?*
- *Can I find a better way of saying what I want to?*
- *Does this draft sound as I wanted it to sound, or is it too corny or detached or arrogant or humble?*

Eventually you will find that you can revise almost automatically, without following the checklist item by item.

CASE STUDY

REVISING THE DRAFT

Assume you've written this early draft of "Suffering Through Gym Class" (whose final version appears on pages 59–60):

A draft to be revised

Like any other student, I feel that many of my high school experiences were memorable. Few of them, however, were as memorable as my gym class. Every Monday morning, I would feel my anxiety rising as I thought about facing the most hateful part of my week.

In all fairness, I'm sure my gym teacher was kind. But athletic prowess was expected of every student, and nothing less would do. The fun in any game quickly disappeared. The students' efforts were ignored in favor of performance. The students seemed to take on the same attitude as the teacher; students with athletic skill were seen as superior to those who lacked athletic skill. The whole thing made me sick. Physical education teachers should learn to control their biases and accept students who lack athletic abilities. The whole system otherwise ends up doing more harm than good.

Whatever sport we played, I could count on being the loser, even when my team won. In both team sports and individual sports, all I seemed to be able to do in each gym class was to make some kind of pathetic attempt. Some people simply have little or no athletic ability, and I'm one of them. It seemed as if every effort I made resulted in embarrassment. All I could do on these occasions was feel incompetent.

I was always one of the last players picked for teams. As I waited at home plate to swing and miss, I could already hear the hisses and groans from other players on my team, and the "easy-out" chant from members of the opposing team. Even people who were my friends nicknamed me "the athlete." Although these friends were only joking, they nevertheless caused me to suffer emotionally. My teacher seemed to ignore all those students who failed to excel in the achievement of athletic goals. At semester's end, I always received a C– grade.

What really are the underlying elements of sports? I would say that the elements are these: rules, teamwork, and tolerance. Combining all these concepts into a grade makes more sense than counting the number of home runs in a semester. Faculty, students, and administrators should work together to improve the system.

Discussion

This draft needs a good deal of revision. First, the content leaves many reader questions unanswered:

- What, exactly, was the class like?
- What, exactly, did you do that was so bad?
- What was the meaning of this whole experience for you?

Next, the organization of this draft hints at an introduction, body, and conclusion, but some paragraphs lack topic sentences and clear connections between ideas. The style also needs work: sentence structure is too similar and sentences often sound stuffy or too much like a sermon.

The following pages show how the Revision Checklist can help you revise to achieve the finished essay on pages 59–60. For reference, the paragraphs from the essay are labeled A through E. Specific needed improvements are explained on the facing page. (This revision treats only the *rhetorical* features: content, organization, and style. See the rear endsheet for a checklist on grammar, punctuation, and mechanics.)

Revision has created an essay with worthwhile content, sensible organization, and readable style. (For detailed advice on achieving these qualities in a final draft, see Chapters 6 to 9.)

REVISING WITH PEERS

All writing can benefit from feedback. As part of the revision process, your writing course may include workshops that require peer reviewing and editing. *Reviewing* means evaluating how well the writing connects with its intended audience:

Suffering Through Gym Class

Rewrite introduction to invite readers in

A

~~Like every student, I feel that many of my high school experiences were memorable. Few of them, however, were as memorable as~~ my gym class. Every Tuesday morning, I would feel my anxiety rising as I thought about facing the most hateful part of my week. *Although I respected my gym teacher's commitment to excellence the standards in this class simply were impossible for me to reach.*

Give more of a forecast in the thesis.

~~In all fairness, I'm sure my gym teacher was kind.~~ *Everybody was expected to be an athlete*
~~But athletic prowess was expected of every student~~, and

Sentence variety

nothing less would do. The fun in the game quickly disappeared. ~~The students~~ Effort was ignored in favor of performance. The students seemed to take on the same attitude as the teacher; students with athletic skill were seen as superior to those who lacked athletic skill. The whole thing made me sick. ~~Physical education teachers should learn to control their biases and accept students who lack athletic abilities. The whole system otherwise ends up doing more harm than good.~~

B

More description here

C

Whatever sport we played, I could count on being the loser, even when my team won. In both team sports and individual sports, *(parallel bars, hurdles, etc.)* all I seemed to be able to do ~~in each gym class~~ was to make some kind of pathetic attempt. *In baseball, I was the sure strike-out, the right-fielder whose glove had a hole in it. In basketball, I had a hard time hitting the backboard, much less scoring a basket. In soccer, I tripped over my own feet.*

Give examples.

FIGURE 5.1
A draft edited for revision

Paragraph A: The essay lacks a title and the introduction doesn't give readers a clear sense of what to expect. The two opening sentences are so general and obvious as to be meaningless. The final sentence (the thesis?) suggests an attitude, but readers are not sure why gym class was such a hateful experience (because it was boring, too hard, too easy?). The thesis should be more definite and informative.

Paragraph B: The first support paragraph needs a topic statement to forecast the content of the paragraph. Sentences throughout need variety, especially to cut down on the many "the" sentence openers. The final two sentences sound too much like a sermon. And readers need some kind of transition to the next paragraph.

Paragraph C: This paragraph contains needless words and too few details. What were some of the "pathetic attempts"? Readers need to visualize what happened. The third sentence repeats earlier material; it can be cut.

~~Some people simply have little or no athletic ability,~~

~~and I'm one of them.~~ ~~It seemed as if~~ [E] every effort I
seemed to

made, resulted in embarrassment. All I could do ~~on~~

~~these occasions~~ was ~~to~~ feel incompetent. *and inferior*
I was continually reminded of my failures.

I was always one of the last players picked for
along with the other rejects.

teams. As I waited at home plate to swing and miss, I

could already hear the hisses and groans from other

players on my team, and the "easy out" chant from ~~mem-~~
opponents.

~~bers of the opposing team.~~ Even ~~people who were~~ my
affectionately

friends nicknamed me "the athlete." Although ~~these~~
hurt

~~friends were~~ only joking, they nevertheless ~~caused~~
my feelings

~~me to suffer emotionally~~. My teacher seemed to ignore
qualified as wimps

all those students who ~~failed to excel in the achieve-~~

~~ment of athletic goals.~~ At semester's end, I always

recieved a C-minus grade. [#] *(a gift for passing "showers" I guess)*
At all these indignities I laughed on the outside, but not on the inside.

~~What really are the underlying elements of sports?~~

~~I would say that the elements are these: rules, team~~

~~work, and tolerance. Combining all these concepts into~~

~~a grade makes more sense than counting the number of~~

~~home runs in a semester. Faculty, students, and admin-~~

~~istrators should work together to improve the system.~~

The whole experience left me feeling defeated.

Margin notes:

D

E

Loosen the tone.

Relate the ending directly to the painful memory.

Show the overall meaning of the experience.

Talk about this in detail.

FIGURE 5.1
A draft edited for revision (*Continued*)

Paragraph D: Although this paragraph provides informative details, it lacks a topic sentence to frame readers' understanding of these details. The tone often seems stuffy: "caused me to suffer emotionally" instead of "hurt my feelings." Lightening the tone also would help eliminate many needlessly big words. And some sort of transition to the concluding paragraph is needed.

Paragraph E: This conclusion strays from the essay's purpose: sharing with us this painful memory. It seems to belong to some other essay about how gym classes should be run. A good conclusion would sum up the meaning of this experience. Also, the preachy tone clashes with the tone of earlier paragraphs.

What reviewers look for

- accurate, appropriate, and useful content
- material organized for the readers' understanding
- clear, easy to read, and engaging style

In reviewing you explain to the writer how you respond as a reader; you point out what works or doesn't work. This feedback helps a writer envision ways of revising. Criteria for reviewing an essay appear on page 65; for an argument, pages 279–280; and for a Research Report, page 377.

Editing means actually "fixing" the piece:

Ways in which editors "fix" writing

- rephrasing or reorganizing sentences
- clarifying a thesis or topic sentence
- choosing a better word
- correcting spelling, usage, or punctuation, and so on.

Your task as editor is to help improve the writing—without altering the author's original meaning. Criteria for editing appear inside the rear cover.

GUIDELINES FOR PEER REVIEWING AND EDITING

1. *Read the entire piece at least twice before you comment.* Develop a clear sense of the assignment's purpose and its intended audience.

2. *Remember that mere correctness offers no guarantee of effectiveness.* Poor usage, punctuation, or mechanics do distract readers and harm the writer's credibility. However, a "correct" piece of writing still might contain faulty rhetorical elements (inferior content, confusing organization, or unsuitable style).

3. *Understand the acceptable limits of editing.* In the workplace, "editing" can range from fine-tuning to an in-depth rewrite. In school, however, rewriting a piece to the extent that it ceases to belong to the writer may constitute plagiarism.

4. *Be honest but diplomatic.* Many of us are sensitive to criticism—even the most

constructive! Begin with something positive before moving to critique. Support rather than judge.

5. *Always explain "why" something doesn't work.* Instead of "this paragraph is confusing," say "because this paragraph lacks a clear topic sentence, I had trouble discovering the main idea" (see pages 65, 279, 377).

6. *Make specific recommendations for improvements.* Write out your suggestions in enough detail to give the writer a clear sense of how to proceed.

7. *Be aware that not all feedback has equal value.* Even professional reviewers and editors sometimes disagree. If you receive conflicting opinions from different readers, seek the advice of your instructor.

APPLICATION 5-1

Using the Revision Checklist on page 65 as a guide, return to an essay you have written earlier, and revise it.

At this early stage, you are bound to feel a little confused about the finer points of content, organization, and style. But try your best.

In later chapters you will learn to improve your skill for diagnosing problems and prescribing cures.

Along with your revised essay, submit the original essay and an explanation of the improvements you've made.

APPLICATION 5-2

Collaborative Project: Take an essay you have written earlier, and exchange it for a classmate's. Assume your classmate's essay has been written specifically for you as the audience. Write a detailed evaluation of your classmate's essay, making specific suggestions for revision. Using the Revision Checklist on page 65, evaluate all three rhetorical features: content, organization, and style. Use Appendix A to recommend improvements in grammar, punctuation, and mechanics. Do plenty of scribbling on the essay, and sign your evaluation.

APPLICATION 5-3

Computer Project: Try out the "spellchecker" supplied by the word processing program you're using. First, learn how to add words you use often (your name, for example) to the computer's dictionary, so the machine won't question you each time it encounters these words. Second, make a list of the words the computer lists as misspelled and the suggested corrections. Compare the computer's suggestions with the entries in a good dictionary. Do they match? Keep a log of the words you misspell.

Then proof your paper carefully, watching for the kinds of errors computers can't catch: *homonyms,* or words that sound alike but are spelled differently and have different meanings (*their* and *there, heel* and *heal*); and *transpositions* (*form* for *from*). Also note that the spellchecker won't catch missing or extra words! How many of these corrections did you find?

TWO

THE PRODUCT—SUBSTANCE, SHAPE, STYLE

ACHIEVING WORTHWHILE CONTENT

*R*eaders hate to waste time. They expect an insightful thesis backed by solid content and support.

The first requirement of worthwhile content is *unity*: every word, every detail belongs. Three other qualities are also essential to worthwhile content: *credibility, informative value,* and *completeness.**

CREDIBILITY

Anyone can assert opinions; *supporting* your assertion is the real challenge. We all have opinions about political candidates, cars, or controversial subjects such as abortion or nuclear energy. But *many* of our *opinions are uninformed;* instead of resting on facts, they lean mostly on a chaotic collection of beliefs repeated around us, notions we've inherited from advertising, things we've read but never checked, and so on.

Uninformed Opinions

Christopher Columbus was a hero.

Christopher Columbus was an oppressor.

Grindo toothpaste is best for making teeth whiter.

In a democracy, religion deserves a voice in government.

Informed opinion, in contrast, rests on fact or good sense. Any fact (*My hair is brown; Professor Glum fails more than 50 percent of his students; Americans have more televisions than bathtubs*) can be verified by anyone, either by observation (*I saw Felix murder his friend*); by research (*Wood smoke contains the deadly chemical dioxin*); by experience (*I was mugged this morning*); or by measurement (*less than 60 percent of our first-year students eventually earn a degree*).

Informed Opinions

Felix is guilty of murder.

Homes with woodstoves need good ventilation.

This has been a bad day for me.

College clearly is not for everyone.

To *support an opinion,* you often must consider a variety of facts. You might be able to support with facts the claim that Grindo toothpaste makes

---

*Adapted from James L. Kinneavy's assertion that discourse should be factual, unpredictable, and comprehensive. See James L. Kinneavy, *A Theory of Discourse* (Englewood Cliffs, NJ: Prentice, 1971).

teeth whiter, but a related fact may be that Grindo contains tiny silicone particles—an abrasive that "whitens" by scraping enamel from teeth. The second fact could change your opinion about Grindo.

The Grindo example illustrates that no two facts about anything are likely to have equal relevance. Assume you've asserted this opinion:

This opinion needs supporting facts

| The Diablo Canyon nuclear plant is especially dangerous.

In deciding how to support this opinion, you compare the relevance of each of these facts:

Not all supporting facts are equal

1. The road system is inadequate for rapid evacuation of local residents.
2. Nuclear plants have found no suitable way to dispose of radioactive wastes.
3. The plant is only 100 miles from sizable population centers.
4. The plant is built near a major earthquake fault.

Although all these facts support the label "dangerous," the first three can apply to many nuclear plants. Only the fourth addresses the danger specific to the Diablo Canyon plant—and therefore has most relevance. Because readers can tolerate only so many details, you must decide which of your facts offer the best support.

Besides unifying your facts, arrange them for emphasis. Consider this opening passage:

Passage A—An Opinion Supported by Fact

Child abuse has become our national disgrace. In the past decade, reported incidence has increased an average of 20 percent yearly. This year alone, more than 500,000 children (fewer than 20 percent of cases) will be the reported victims of physical, sexual, or emotional violence by one or both parents. And among the reported offenders, only 3 percent are ever convicted. Even more tragic, the pattern of violence is cyclical, with many abused children later becoming abusive parents themselves.

We move from the disquieting numbers to the tragically cyclical process.

Moral or emotional issues (prayer in public schools, the existence of God, the distribution of wealth) cannot be supported by facts. Opinions on such issues rest mainly on common sense and insight. The following passage supports the opinion that Americans should do more to help the world's hungry.

Passage B—An Opinion Supported by Good Sense

If we as a nation allow people to starve while we could, through some sacrifice, make more food available to them, what hope can any person have for the future of international relations? If we cannot agree on this most basic of values—feed the hungry—what hopes for the future can we entertain? Technology is imitable and nuclear weaponry certain to proliferate. What appeals to trust and respect can be made if the most rudimentary of moral impulses—feed the hungry—is not strenuously incorporated into national policy?

—*James R. Kelly*

Athough the passage offers no statistics, research data, or observable facts (except that technology can be imitated), the support is credible because of its basis in our intuition about our shared humanity.

INFORMATIVE VALUE

Are you one of those writers who enter college as experts in the art of "stuffing"? The stuffing expert knows how to fill pages by cramming into the essay every thought that will pile up 500 words (or any required total) with minimal pain. But readers expect *something new and useful*. Writing has informative value when it does at least one of these things:

Elements of informative value

- Shares something new and significant
- Reminds us about something we know but ignore
- Offers fresh insight or perspective on something we already know

In short, informative writing gives readers exactly what they need.

Readers approach most topics with some prior knowledge (or old information). They might need reminding, but they don't need a rehash of old information; they can "fill in the blanks" for themselves. On the other hand, readers don't need every bit of new information you can think of, either.

As a reader of this book, for example, you expect to learn something worthwhile about writing, and my purpose is to help you do that. Which of these statements would you find useful?

a. Writing is hard and frustrating work.
b. Writing is a process of deliberate decisions.

Statement a offers no news to anyone who ever has picked up a pencil. But Statement b reminds you that producing good writing can be a lot more complex than we would like. Because Statement b offers new insight into a familiar process, then, we can say it has informative value.

We see that Passages A and B (pages 78–79) satisfy our criteria for informative value. Passage A offers surprising evidence about child abuse; Passage B gives fresh insight into the familiar issue of international relations.

Sometimes we write for a mixed group of readers with varied needs. How, then, can our writing have informative value for each reader?

Imagine you are an ex-jogger and a convert to walking for aerobic exercise. You decide to write an essay for classmates on the advantages of walking over running. You can assume a few classmates are runners; others swim, cycle, or do other exercise; some don't do much, but are thinking of starting; and some have no interest in any exercise. Your problem is to address all these readers in one essay that each reader finds worthwhile. Specifically, you want to:

- Persuade runners and other exercisers to consider walking as an alternative
- Encourage the interested nonexercisers to try walking
- Create at least a spark of interest among the diehard nonexercisers—and maybe even inspire them to rise up out of their easy chairs and hit the bricks

First, you will need to answer questions shared by all readers:

Audience questions you can anticipate

- *Why is walking better than running?*
- *How are they similar or different?*
- *What are the benefits in walking?*
- *Can you give examples?*
- *Why should I?*

But some readers will have special questions. Nonexercisers might ask, *What exactly is aerobic exercise, anyway?* And the true couch potatoes might ask, *Who cares?* Your essay will have to answer all these questions.

Assume that many hours of planning, drafting, and revising have enabled you to produce this final draft:

An Essay with Informative Value

WALK BUT DON'T RUN

Our bodies gain aerobic benefits when we exercise at a fast enough pace for muscles to demand oxygen-rich blood from the heart and lungs. During effective aerobic exercise, the heart rate increases roughly 80 percent above normal. Besides strengthening muscle groups—especially the heart—aerobic exercise makes blood vessels stronger and larger.

Running, or jogging, has become a most popular form of aerobic exercise. But millions of Americans who began running to get in shape are now limping to their doctors for treatment of running injuries. To keep yourself in one piece as you keep yourself in shape, try walking instead of running.

All the aerobic benefits of running can be yours if you merely take brisk walks. Consider this comparison. For enough aerobic training to increase cardiovascular (heart, lungs, and blood vessels) efficiency, you need to run three times weekly for roughly 30 minutes. (Like any efficient system, an efficient cardiovascular system produces maximum work with minimum effort.) You can gain cardiovascular benefits equivalent to running, however, by taking a brisk walk three times weekly for roughly 60 minutes. Granted, walking takes up more time than running, but it carries fewer risks.

Because of its more controlled and deliberate pace, walking is safer than running. A walker stands far less chance of tripping, stepping in potholes, or slipping and falling. And the slower pace causes less physical trauma. Anyone who has ever run at all knows that a runner's foot strikes the ground with sizable impact. But the shock of this impact travels beyond the foot—to the shins, knees, hips, internal organs, and spine. Walking, of course, creates an impact of its own, but the walker's foot strikes the ground with only half as much force as the runner's foot.

Beyond its apparent physical dangers, running can provoke subtle stress for the devoted exerciser. Because running is generally seen as more competitive than just walking, we too easily can be tempted to push our bodies too far, too fast. Even though we might not compete in races or marathons, we often tend to compete against ourselves—maybe just to keep up with a jock neighbor or to break a personal record. And by ignoring the signals of overexertion and physical stress, we can easily run ourselves into an injury—if not the grave. Slowing to a walk instead is a safe way of leaving the "competition" behind.

—*Jeff Leonard*

Will this essay have informative value for all readers? Probably so. It seems to answer all the readers' questions we anticipated on page 80. Will all readers become converts? Probably not. But each should have something to think about. A worthwhile message makes some kind of a difference for its readers—even if it triggers only the slightest insight.

Now let's assume that you had written the walking essay by using the old high school strategy of filling up the page. Your opening paragraph might look like this:

An Opening without Informative Value

WALK BUT DON'T RUN

Medical science has made tremendous breakthroughs in the past few decades. Research has shown that exercise is a good way of staying healthy, beneficial for our bodies and our minds. More people of all ages are exercising today than ever before. Because of its benefits, one popular form of exercise for Americans is aerobic exercise.

Your readers (in the situation described on page 80) already know all this.

Even new material lacks informative value when it is irrelevant:

Material Irrelevant to the Situation

> To avoid the perils of running, the Chinese attend sessions of T'ai-chi, a dancelike series of stretching routines designed to increase concentration and agility. Although T'ai-chi is less dangerous than running, it fails to provide a truly aerobic workout.

The above material might serve in an essay comparing certain aerobic and nonaerobic exercises, but not in this comparison between walking and running.

Nor would highly technical details have informative value here, as in this next example:

Material too Technical for the Situation

> Walking and jogging result in forward motion because you continually fall forward and catch yourself. With each stride, you lift your body, accelerate, and land. You go faster when running because you fall farther, but you also strike the ground harder, and for less time. Your increase in speed and distance fallen combine with the shorter contact period to cause an impact on your body that is more than double the impact from walking.

The above material would serve for students of biophysics, exercise physiology, or sports medicine, but seems too detailed for a mixed audience.

COMPLETENESS

All writers struggle with this question: *How much is enough?* (Or, *How long should it be?*) Again, anticipate readers' questions about your thesis.

Assume, for instance, that a friend now living in another state is thinking of taking a job similar to one you held last summer. Your friend has written to ask how you liked the job; your response will influence the friend's decision. Here is a passage from a first draft that tells but doesn't show:

Not Enough Detail

> My job last summer as a flagger for a road construction company was boring, tiresome, dirty, and painful. All I did was stand in the road and flag cars. Every day I just stood there, getting sore feet. I was always covered with dirt and breathing it in. To make matters worse, the sun, wind, and bugs ruined my skin. By the end of summer, I vowed never to do this kind of work again.

The above passage has only limited informative value because it fails to make the experience vivid for readers. The sketchy details fail to answer our obvious questions.

- *Can you show me what the job was like?*
- *What, exactly, made it boring, tiresome, dirty, and painful?*

This next passage, on the other hand, is revised to include graphic details that make readers feel a part of it all:

Enough Detail

> My job last summer as a flagger for a road construction company was boring, tiresome, dirty, and painful. All day I stood like a robot; waving a stupid red flag at oncoming traffic; my eardrums blasted by the racket of road machinery, each day dragging by more slowly than the last. My feet would swell, and my legs would ache from standing on the hard clay and gravel for up to fifteen hours a day. And the filth was disgusting. The fumes, oil, and grime from the road machinery and the exhaust from passing cars became like a second skin. Each breath sucked up more dust, clogging my sinuses, irritating my eyes. But worst of all was the weather. Blistering from sunburn, I was being sandblasted and rubbed raw by windstorms, pounded by hail, or chewed by mosquitoes and horseflies. By the end of summer, I was a freak: swollen feet and ankles, the skin of a water buffalo, and chronic sinusitis. I'd starve before taking that job again.

In the above situation, even more details (say, a day-by-day description of every event) probably would clutter the message. The reader here needed and *wanted* just enough information to make an informed decision.

Giving enough detail is not the same as merely adding more words. Whatever does nothing but fill the page is puffery:

Hot Air

> My job last summer as a flagger for a road construction company was boring, tiresome, dirty, and painful. ~~Day in and day out,~~ I stood ~~on that road~~ for endless hours getting ~~a severe case of~~ sore feet. My face and body were ~~always completely~~ covered with ~~the~~ dust blown up from the ~~passing cars and various other~~ vehicles, and I was forced to breathe in all ~~of~~ this ~~horrible~~ junk ~~day after day.~~ ~~To add to the problems of boredom, fatigue, and dirt,~~ the weather murdered my skin. ~~Let me tell you that~~ by the time ~~the~~ summer ended, I ~~had~~ made ~~myself~~ a solemn promise never to ~~victimize myself by~~ tak~~ing~~ this kind of awful job again.

Although the above passage is nearly twice as long as the original (page 82), it adds no meaning; hot air (shown crossed out) offers no real information.

Don't worry about not having enough to say. Once you have begun the writing process (searching for details, rephrasing, making connections), you probably will find it harder to stay within the limit than to reach it. Your purpose is to *make your point*—not to show how smart you are. Instead of including every word, fact, and idea that crosses your mind, learn to select. Sometimes one single detail is enough. To make the point about a "boring" job, the passage on page 83 describes the writer standing like a robot, waving a red flag.

The passages above show how you can measure the completeness of your own writing, *providing details that show,* by answering questions like the following:

Details answer these questions

- *Who, what, when, where, and why?*
- *What did you see, feel, hear, taste, smell?*
- *What would a camera record?*
- *What are the dates, numbers, percentages?*
- *Can you compare it to something more familiar?*

. . . .

APPLICATION 6-1

Each sentence below states either a fact or an opinion. Rewrite all statements of opinion as statements of fact. Remember that a fact can be verified. (Review pages 77–78.)

EXAMPLE

Opinion   My roommate isn't taking college work seriously.

Fact   My roommate never studies, sleeps through most classes, and has missed every exam.

1. Professor X grades unfairly.
2. My vacation was too short.
3. The salary for this position is $15,000 yearly.
4. This bicycle is reasonably priced.
5. We walked 5 miles last Saturday.
6. He drives recklessly.
7. My motorcycle gets great gas mileage.
8. This course has been very helpful.
9. German shepherds eat more than cocker spaniels do.
10. This apartment is much too small for our family.

APPLICATION 6-2

Return to Shirley Haley's essay on pages 13–14. Underline all statements of fact, and circle all statements of opinion. Are all the opinions supported by facts or by good sense? Now, perform the same evaluation on an essay you have written. (Review pages 77–78.)

APPLICATION 6-3

Assume you live in the Northeast, and citizens in your state are voting on a solar energy referendum that would channel millions of tax dollars toward solar technology. The next paragraphs are designed to help you, as a voter, make an educated decision. Do both these versions of the same message have informative value? Explain. (Review pages 79–82.)

> Solar power offers a realistic solution to the Northeast's energy problems. In recent years the cost of fossil fuels (oil, coal, and natural gas) has risen rapidly while the supply has continued to decline. High prices and short supply will continue to cause a worsening energy crisis. Because solar energy comes directly from the sun, it is an inexhaustible resource. By using this energy to heat and air-condition our buildings, as well as to provide electricity, we could decrease substantially our consumption of fossil fuels. In turn, we would be less dependent on the unstable Middle East for our oil supplies. Clearly, solar power is a good alternative to conventional energy sources.

> Solar power offers a realistic solution to the Northeast's energy problems. To begin with, solar power is efficient. Solar collectors installed on fewer than 30 percent of roofs in the Northeast would provide more than 70 percent of the area's heating and air-conditioning needs. Moreover, solar heat collectors are economical, operating for up to 20 years with little or no maintenance. These savings recoup the initial cost of installment within only ten years. Most important, solar power is safe. It can be transformed into electricity through photovoltaic cells (a type of storage battery) noiselessly and with no air pollution—unlike coal, oil, and wood combustion. In sharp contrast to its nuclear counterpart, solar power produces no toxic wastes and poses no catastrophic danger of meltdown. Thus, massive conversion to solar power would ensure abundant energy and a safe, clean environment for future generations.

APPLICATION 6-4

Collaborative Project: Review a classmate's essay and eliminate all statements that lack informative value (those that offer commonly known, irrelevant, or insignificant material). Be careful not to cut material the audience needs in order to understand the essay, such as

1. Details that help us see.
2. Details that help us feel.
3. Numerical details.
4. Vivid comparisons.
5. Details that a camera would record.
6. A detail that helps us hear.

Would some parts of your classmate's essay benefit from greater detail? Use the list above as a basis for making specific suggestions.

APPLICATION 6-5

Return to one of your earlier essays. Study it carefully, then brainstorm again to sharpen your details. Now write a revised version. (Review pages 37–39.)

APPLICATION 6-6

Computer Application: Working from the joint computer file for your group, complete Application 6-4.

APPLICATION 6-7

Computer Application: Select a paragraph you have written for an earlier assignment. Using the paragraph on page 83 as a guide, create and save at least two alternative versions of this paragraph by deleting different combination of words and phrases. Print out all three versions. Then, from among the alternatives, choose what you think is the most effective version of *each sentence.* Recombine these sentences into a fourth version of the paragraph—one that achieves completeness without clutter.

SHAPING THE PARAGRAPHS

An essay's basic design makes its content accessible for readers. But this larger design (introduction, body, conclusion) depends on the smaller design of each paragraph. A paragraph is a place for things that belong together.

SUPPORT PARAGRAPHS AS MINI-ESSAYS

Paragraphs in an essay have various shapes and purposes. Introductory paragraphs draw us into the writer's reality; concluding paragraphs ease us out; transitional paragraphs help hold things together. But here the subject is *support paragraphs*—those middle blocks of thought, each often a mini-shape of the whole essay. Just as the thesis is sustained by its supporting points, each major supporting point is sustained by its paragraph.

Although part of the essay's larger design, each support paragraph usually can stand alone in meaning and emphasis. Consider this paragraph by a noted psychiatrist:

A Typical Support Paragraph

Introduction (topic statement, 1)
Body (2–9)

¹*Crime is everybody's temptation.* ²It is easy to look with proud disdain upon "those people" who get caught—the stupid ones, the unlucky ones, the blatant ones. ³But who does not get nervous when a police car follows closely? ⁴We squirm over our income-tax statements and make some "adjustments." ⁵We tell the customs official that we have nothing to declare—well, practically nothing. ⁶Some of us who have never been convicted of any crime picked up over two billion dollars' worth of merchandise last year from the stores we patronize. ⁷Over a billion dollars was embezzled by employees last year. ⁸One hotel in New York lost over seventy-five thousand finger bowls, demitasse spoons, and other objects in its first ten months of operation. ⁹The Claims Bureau of the American Insurance Association estimates that 75 percent of all claims are dishonest in some respect and the amount

Conclusion (10–12)

of overpayment more than $350,000,000 a year. ¹⁰These facts disturb us or should. ¹¹They give us an uneasy feeling that we are all indicted. ¹²"Let him who is without sin cast the first stone."

—*Karl Menninger*

Menninger's paragraph is part of a much larger design: a chapter in his book *The Crime of Punishment*. But the paragraph's shape is familiar enough: the introduction asserts a definite viewpoint; the body walks us through the writer's reasoning: the conclusion offers perspective on what we've read.

PARAGRAPH FUNCTION

¶

Writers need definite paragraph divisions for control; readers need them for access.

Paragraphs increase your *writing control.* Each support paragraph is an idea unit, one distinct space for developing one supporting point. If Menninger begins his paragraph with the point that crime tempts everyone, he can tailor everything in the paragraph to advance his meaning. No matter how long your message, you can stay in control by looking for things that belong together—thinking in terms of paragraphs.

Paragraphs also *give readers orientation.* Readers need to know where they are and where they're going. By dividing a long piece of writing, paragraphs allow readers to focus on each point. The indention (five spaces) gives a breathing space, a signal that the geography is changing and that it's time to look ahead.

PARAGRAPH LENGTH

¶lgth

Paragraph length depends on *the writer's purpose* and the reader's capacity for understanding. Writing that carries highly technical information or complex instructions may use short paragraphs or perhaps a list. In a newspaper article, paragraphs of only one or two sentences keep the reader's attention. In writing that explains concepts, attitudes, or viewpoints (as in college essays), support paragraphs generally run from 100 to 300 words.

But word count really means very little. What matters is *how thoroughly the paragraph makes your point.* A flabby paragraph buries readers in needless words and details; but just skin-and-bones leaves readers looking for the meat. Each paragraph requires new decisions. Try to avoid too much of anything. A clump of short paragraphs can make some writing seem choppy and poorly organized, but a stretch of long ones is tiring. A well-placed short paragraph—sometimes just one sentence—can supply special emphasis:

> More than 30 percent of our state's groundwater contains toxic wastes.

For real impact, you can even use just one word:

> Exactly.

THE TOPIC STATEMENT

¶ts

A college essay needs a thesis that asserts the main point, and each support paragraph needs a *topic statement* that asserts a supporting point. Sometimes the topic statement comes at the end of the paragraph; sometimes in the middle; but usually it comes first. The paragraph's first sentence should focus and forecast.

THE TOPIC STATEMENT AS READERS' FRAMEWORK

Most paragraphs in college writing begin by *telling readers what to look for.* Don't write

No focus

| Some jobs are less stressful than others.

when you mean

Better

| Mortuary management is an ideal major for anyone craving a stress-free job.

The first topic statement above doesn't give a very clear forecast; the second helps us focus.
Don't write

No forecast

| Summers in Goonville are awful.

when you mean

Better

| I hate Goonville summers because of the chiggers, ticks, scorpions, and rattlesnakes.

THE TOPIC STATEMENT AS WRITER'S FRAMEWORK

Without a topic statement, writers struggle to make their paragraphs more than a collection of stuff. Always *take a definite stand; assert something significant.*

Imagine that you are a member of Congress, about to vote on abortion legislation. One of your constituents has responded to your request for citizens' viewpoints with a letter that begins like this:

No focus or forecast

Abortion is a very complex issue. There is a sharp division between those who are for it and those who are against it. Very few people take a neutral stand on this issue. The battle between supporters and opponents has raged for years. This is only one of the serious problems in our society. Every day, things seem to get worse.

Because this writer never identified his purpose, never discovered his own exact meaning, the above paragraph merely parrots a number of unrelated thoughts that are all common knowledge. If, instead, our writer had refined his meaning by asserting a definite viewpoint, he might have written a worthwhile paragraph. Depending on his purpose, he might have begun with, say:

Better

> *Abortion laws in our state discriminate against the poor.*

or

> *Abortion is wrong because of the irresponsibility it allows.*

Before you can explain yourself, you have to figure out exactly what you mean.

STRUCTURAL VARIATIONS IN SUPPORT PARAGRAPHS

Your main idea might have several distinct parts, which would result in an excessively long paragraph. You might then break up the paragraph, making your topic statement a brief introductory paragraph that forecasts various subparts, which are set off as independent paragraphs.

A Topic Statement that Serves Several Paragraphs

> *Common types of strip-mining procedures include open-pit mining, contour mining, and auger mining. The specific type employed will depend on the type of terrain covering the coal.*
>
> Open-pit mining is employed in the relatively flat lands in western Kentucky, Oklahoma, and Kansas. Here, draglines and scoops operate directly on the coal seams. This process produces long parallel rows of packed spoil banks, 10 to 30 feet high, with steep slopes. Between the spoil banks are large pits that soon fill with water to produce pollution and flood hazards.
>
> Contour mining is most widely practiced in the mountainous terrain of the Cumberland Plateau and eastern Kentucky. Here, bulldozers and explosives cut and blast the earth and rock covering a coal seam. Wide bands are removed from the mountain's circumference to reach the embedded coal beneath. The cutting and blasting result in a shelf along with a jagged cliff some 60 feet high at a right angle to the shelf. The blasted and churned earth is pushed over the shelf to form a massive and unstable spoil bank that creates a danger of mud slides.
>
> Auger mining is employed when the mountain has been cut so thin that it no longer can be stripped. It is also used in other difficult-access terrain. Here, large augers bore parallel rows of holes into the hidden coal seams to extract the embedded coal. Among the three strip-mining processes, auger mining causes least damage to the surrounding landscape.

As you can see, each paragraph begins with a clear statement of the subtopic discussed in it.

Remember that you won't always be able to think first of the right topic statement, and then of your support. Your actual framework might not appear until you've done some freewriting or brainstorming. The sequence is unimportant—as long as the finished paragraph offers a definite framework and solid support.

PARAGRAPH UNITY

¶un

Each paragraph in an essay requires *external unity* and *internal unity*. A paragraph has external unity when (as on pages 59–60) it belongs with all the other paragraphs in an essay. But each paragraph requires internal unity as well: everything in the paragraph should belong there.

Imagine that you're composing a paragraph beginning with this topic statement:

Chemical pesticides and herbicides are both ineffective and hazardous.

The words that signal the meaning here are **ineffective** and **hazardous;** everything in the paragraph should directly advance that meaning. Here is the unified paragraph:

A Unified Paragraph

Chemical pesticides and herbicides are both ineffective and hazardous. Because none of these chemicals has permanent effects, pest populations invariably recover and need to be resprayed. Repeated applications cause pests to develop immunity to the chemicals. Furthermore, most pesticides and herbicides attack species other than the intended pest, killing off its natural predators, thus actually increasing the pest population. Above all, chemical residues survive in the environment (and in living tissue) for years and often are carried hundreds of miles by wind and water. This toxic legacy includes such biological effects as birth deformities, reproductive failures, brain damage, and cancer. Although intended to control pest populations, these chemicals ironically threaten to make the human population their ultimate victims.

One way to destroy unity in the paragraph above would be to veer from the focus on **effective** and **hazardous** with material about the cost of the chemicals or their unpleasant odor or the number of people who oppose their use.

Every topic statement has a *signal term*, a key word or phrase that announces the viewpoint. In the paragraph below, the signal term is **intelligent,** causing readers to expect material about whale intelligence. But the shift to food problems fails to advance the meaning of intelligence, throwing the paragraph—and the reader—off track:

A Disunified Paragraph

Whales are among the most intelligent of all mammals. Scientists rank whale intelligence with that of higher primates because of whales' sophisticated group behavior. These impressive mammals have been seen teaching and disciplining their young, helping their wounded comrades, engaging in elaborate courtship rituals, and playing in definite gamelike patterns. Whales continually need to search for food in order to survive. Their search for krill and other sea organisms can cause them to migrate thousands of miles yearly.

PARAGRAPH COHERENCE

¶coh

In a coherent paragraph, everything not only belongs but sticks together: topic statement and support form *a connected line of thought*, like links in a chain.

This next paragraph (written by a track team veteran addressing new runners) is both unified and coherent: everything relates to the topic in a continuous line of thinking.

A Coherent Paragraph

[1]*To be among the first out of the starting blocks in any race, follow these instructions.* [2]First, when the starter says "Into your blocks," make sure you are the last runner down. [3]Take your sweet time; make all the others wait for you. [4]You take your time for three good reasons: one, you get a little more stretching than your competitors do; two, they are down in the blocks getting cold and nervous while you're still warm and relaxed from stretching; and three, your deliberate manner tends to weaken other runners' confidence. [5]The second step is to lean forward over your shoulders, in the "set" position. [6]This way, you will come out of the blocks forward and low, meeting less wind resistance. [7]The third and final step is to pump your arms as fast as you can when you come off the blocks. [8]The faster your arms pump, the faster your legs will move. [9]By concentrating on each of these steps, you can expect your quickest possible start.

The material in this paragraph seems easy enough to follow:

1. The topic statement sets a clear direction.
2. The first step is introduced.

3–4. The importance of "taking your time" is emphasized and explained.

5–6. The second step is introduced and its importance explained.

7–8. The third step is introduced and its importance explained.

9. The conclusion sums up.

Because the material follows a logical order (in this case, chronological), readers know exactly where they are at any place in the paragraph. Let's now examine specific ways of achieving coherence.

ORDERING IDEAS FOR COHERENCE

The mind works in structured ways to arrange and make sense of its many perceptions. If you decide you like a class (a general observation), you then identify your particular reasons (friendly atmosphere, interesting subject, dynamic teacher, and so on); your thinking has followed a *general-to-specific order*. Or, if you tell a friend about your terrific weekend, you follow the order of events, how things happened over the weekend; your thinking has followed a *chronological order*. These are just two of several ordering patterns the mind uses to create a sensible sequence of information. Here are the most common ordering patterns:

Common ways of arranging information

- general-to-specific order
- specific-to-general order
- emphatic order
- spatial order
- chronological order

These ordering patterns can help you answer these questions:

- *What comes first?*
- *What comes next?*
- *Does the subject have any features that suggest an order?*

Answers will be based on your subject and purpose. In a letter describing your new car (subject) to a friend, you might decide to move from outside to inside in a spatial order, as one would first see the car. Or, if you decided to concentrate on the car's computerized dashboard (subject), you might move from left to right (as one would see it from the driver's seat). If, instead, you were trying to persuade someone to stay in school or to quit smoking, you probably would present your reasons in an emphatic order, from least to most important or vice versa.

As we will see, some kinds of order call for your topic statement to come last instead of first. Even then, your opening sentence should tell readers what to expect. Before considering those variations, however, let's begin with the standard ordering pattern: general to specific.

General-to-Specific Order.   The most usual way of arranging a paragraph is from general to specific: a *general topic statement supported by specific details*. Most sample paragraphs we've seen so far follow a general-to-specific order, as this next one does:

Starting with the Big Picture

General assertion (topic statement, 1)
Specific support (2–8)

[1]Americans everywhere are obsessed with speed. [2]The airlines think it's so important that they've developed jets that can cross the ocean in a few hours. [3]Despite energy shortages, Detroit often makes the speed of a car and the power of its engine a focal point of its advertising campaign. [4]Ads for oil companies boast of ten-minute oil changes at their gas stations. [5]Even pedestrians aren't spared: some shoemakers will put soles and heels on shoes "while you wait." [6]Fast-food restaurants prosper as increasing millions gobble increasing billions of "all-beef" hamburgers and guzzle their Cokes in seconds flat. [7]And the Day of Rest, too, has given way to the stopwatch as more and more churches offer brief evening services or customize their offerings to suit "people on the go." [8]Some churches even offer drive-in ceremonies—pay your money, spit out your prayer, and hit the road, streaking toward salvation with Ronald McDonald. [9]These days, even the road to eternity has a fast lane.

Conclusion (9)

Paragraphs of general-to-specific order are the workhorses of virtually all nonfiction writing.

Specific-to-General Order. For some purposes, instead of narrowing and restricting your meaning, you will generalize and extend it. Thus, your *support will come first, and your topic statement last.* A specific-to-general order is especially useful for showing how pieces of evidence add up to a convincing conclusion, as in this next paragraph.

Starting with the Supporting Details

Orienting statements (1–2)

[1]For thousands of years, the single species Homo sapiens, to which you and I have the dubious honor of belonging, has been increasing in numbers. [2]In the past couple of centuries, the rate of increase has itself increased explosively.

Specific details (3–4)

[3]At the time of Julius Caesar, when Earth's human population is estimated to have been 150 million, that population was increasing at a rate such that it would double in 1,000 years if that rate remained steady. [4]Today, with Earth's population estimated at about 4,000 million (26 times what it was in Caesar's time), it is increasing at a rate which, if steady, will cause it to double in 35 years.

General conclusion (topic statement, 5)

[5]*The present rate of increase of Earth's swarming human population qualifies* Homo sapiens *as an ecological cancer, which will destroy the ecology just as sure as any ordinary cancer would destroy an organism.*

—Isaac Asimov

But even though the topic statement appears last, the opening statements forecast the paragraph. Whenever you decide to delay your topic sentence, be sure the paragraph's opening sentence gives readers enough orientation for them to know what's going on.

A specific-to-general order works well for supporting a position that some readers might disagree with, as in this next example:

Saving the Big Picture for Last

Specific observation in orienting statement (1)

Specific arguments (2–7)

General conclusion (topic statement, 8)

[1]Strange that so few ever come to the woods to see how the pine lives and grows and spires, lifting its evergreen arms to the light—to see its perfect success; but most are content to behold it in the shape of many broad boards brought to market, and deem *that* its true success! [2]But the pine is no more lumber than [the person] is, and to be made into boards and houses is no more its true and highest use than the truest use of a [person] is to be cut down and made into manure. [3]There is a higher law affecting our relations to pine as well as to [people]. [4]A pine cut down, a dead pine, is no more a pine than a dead human carcass is a [person]. [5]Can [one] who has discovered only some of the values of whalebone and whale oil be said to have discovered the true use of the whale? [6]Can [one] who slays the elephant for [its] ivory be said to have "seen the elephant"? [7]These are petty and accidental uses; just as if a stronger race were to kill us in order to make buttons and flutes of our bones; for everything may serve a lower as well as a higher use.[8] *Every creature is better alive than dead, [people] and moose and pine trees, and [one] who understands it correctly will rather preserve its life than destroy it.*

—Henry David Thoreau

Some readers (especially those in the paper and lumber industry, as well as hunters) would find Thoreau's main point harder to accept if it were placed at the beginning. By moving from the specific to the general, Thoreau presents his evidence before drawing his conclusion. Also, things that come last (last word in a sentence, last sentence in a paragraph, last paragraph in an essay) are the things readers remember best.

Emphatic Order.   In earlier chapters, we've seen how emphasis can make important things stand out, become easier to remember. Writers *achieve emphasis within paragraphs by positioning material* in two common ways: (1) *from least to most important* or serious or dramatic, and (2) *vice versa.* The next paragraph is from an essay analyzing television advertisements for toys of violence. Joe Bolton offers dramatic support for his opening assertion by saving his strongest example for last.

Helping Readers Focus

Topic statement (1–2)

Examples in increasing order of importance (3–5)

[1]*Too many toys advertised during television programs for children are of what I call the "death and destruction" variety: toys that simulate the killing of humans by humans.* [2]Such toys make children's "war games" seem far too real. [3]During the pre-Christmas season, children are bombarded with ads promoting all the new weapons: guns, tanks, boats, subs, helicopters, lasers, and more. [4]One new warplane is described as "the wickedest weapon yet,"

and a new mobile weapon resembles an old "Nike" missile, designed to be moved around on railroad tracks to avoid an enemy strike.[5] One of the enemy dolls is even dubbed a "paranoid schizophrenic killer" and advertised as such on the side of the box.

Spatial Order. Sometimes, you create a word picture by treating the parts of your subject in the same order that readers would follow if they actually were looking at it. In this next paragraph, the writer describes a missing friend to the police.

Helping Readers Visualize

Topic statement

My missing friend should be easy to recognize. When I last saw Roger, he was wearing dark blue jeans, a pair of dark brown hunting boots with red laces, and a light blue cableknit sweater with a turtleneck; he was carrying a red daypack with black trim filled with books. He stands about 6 feet 4 inches, has broad, slouching shoulders, and carries roughly 190 pounds on a medium frame. He walks in excessively long strides, like a cowboy. His hair is sunstreaked, sandy blond, cut just below his ears and feathered back on the sides. He has deep purple eyes framed by dark brown eyelashes and brows set into a clear, tanned complexion. The bridge of his nose carries a half-inch scar in the shape of an inverted crescent. His right front tooth has a small chip in the left corner.

A gradually narrowing focus

The above sequence follows the order of features readers would recognize in approaching Roger: first, from a distance, by his clothing, size, posture, and stride; next, from a closer view—the hair, eye color, and so on; and, finally, from right up close—the scar on his nose and the chip on his tooth. The earlier details, visible from a distance, would alert readers, and the later ones would confirm their impression as they moved nearer. The writer decided to take the angle of a movie camera gradually closing in.

Chronological Order. A chronological order follows the *actual sequence of events.* Writers use chronological order to give instructions (how to be first out of the starting blocks), to explain how something works (how the heart pumps blood), or to show how something happened. This paragraph from George Orwell's "Shooting an Elephant" shows how something brutal happened. As with many paragraphs that tell a story, this one has no topic statement. Instead, the opening sentence places us in the middle of the action.

Helping Readers Experience

Orienting statement (1–2)

[1]When I pulled the trigger I did not hear the bang or feel the kick—one never does when a shot goes home—but I heard the devilish roar of glee that went up from the crowd. [2]In that instant, in too short a time, one would have thought, even for the bullet to get there, a mysterious, terrible change had come over the elephant. [3]He neither stirred nor fell, but every line on his

body had altered. [4]He looked suddenly stricken, shrunken, immensely old, as though the frightful impact of the bullet had paralyzed him without knocking him down. [5]At last, after what seemed like a long time—it might have been five seconds, I dare say—he sagged flabbily to his knees. [6]His mouth slobbered. [7]An enormous senility seemed to have settled upon him. [8]One could have imagined him thousands of years old. [9]I fired again into the same spot. [10]At the second shot he did not collapse but climbed with desperate slowness to his feet and stood weakly upright, with legs sagging and head drooping. [11]I fired a third time. [12]That was the shot that did it for him. [13]You could see the agony of it jolt his whole body and knock the last remnant of strength from his legs. [14]But in falling he seemed for a moment to rise, for as his hind legs collapsed beneath him he seemed to tower upwards like a huge rock toppling, his trunk reaching skywards like a tree. [15]He trumpeted, for the first and only time. [16]And then down he came, his belly towards me, with a crash that seemed to shake the ground even where I lay.

—George Orwell

The actual chronology in Orwell's paragraph is simple:

a. With the first shot, the elephant falls to its knees.
b. With the second shot, instead of collapsing, the elephant drags itself up.
c. With the third shot, the elephant falls, rises, and then falls for good.

But note that if narrating these events in order were the writer's only purpose, the paragraph might look like this:

Tracing the Event

When I pulled the trigger, a change came over the elephant. He neither stirred nor fell, but every line on his body had altered as if the impact of the bullet had paralyzed him without knocking him down. At last, he sagged to his knees. His mouth slobbered. I fired again into the same spot. At the second shot, he did not collapse but climbed slowly to his feet and stood with legs sagging and head drooping. I fired a third time. That was the shot that did it for him. But in falling he seemed for a moment to rise. And then, down he came, with his belly towards me, with a crash that shook the ground.

The above paragraph presents the kinds of details a camera might record.

Compare the first and second version of Orwell's paragraph. Which has the greatest impact? Why?

Notice that this chapter asks you to practice specific strategies, but remember: when you write on your own, you won't begin by saying, "I've decided to write a spatial paragraph, and so now I need to find a subject that will fit that order." Instead, you will say, "I want to discuss X; therefore, I need to select the ordering pattern that best reveals my thinking. Much of your writing will, in fact, call for a combination of these ordering patterns.

PARALLELISM

Several other devices enhance coherence. The first is *parallelism*—similar grammatical structures and word order for similar items, or for items of equal importance. Note how parallelism is employed in this next paragraph:

Expressing Equal Items Equally

[1]*What is the shape of my life?* [2]The *shape* of my life today starts with a family. [3]I *have* a husband, five children, and a home just beyond the suburbs of New York. [4]I *have* also a craft, writing, and therefore work I want to pursue. [5]The *shape* of my life is, of course, determined by many other things: *my background and* childhood, *my mind and* its education, *my conscience and* its pressures, *my heart and* its desires. [6]I want *to give and take* from my children and husband, *to share* with friends and community, *to carry* out my obligations *to* [humanity] and *to the world, as a woman, as an artist, as a citizen.* [emphasis added]

—*Anne Morrow Lindbergh*

The above paragraph displays parallelism between as well as within sentences. Sentences 2 and 5 open with identical structures ("The shape of my life . . .") to signal that both sentences treat the same subject. Sentence 5 has four parallel phrases ("my background and . . . , my mind and . . . , my conscience and . . . , my heart and . . ."). These similar structures emphasize similarity between ideas, thereby tying the paragraph together. See pages 112–113 for further discussion of parallelism.

Can you identify additional examples of parallelism in Morrow-Lindbergh's paragraph?

REPETITION, RESTATEMENT, AND VARIATION

To help link ideas, repeat key words or phrases or rephrase them in different ways as in this next paragraph (emphasis added):

Forwarding the Main Idea

[1]The ultimate threat posed by *nuclear weapons* is not only *death* but *meaninglessness:* an unknown *death* by an unimaginable weapon. [2]War with *such weapons* is no longer heroic; *death* from *such weapons* is without valor. [3]*Meaninglessness* has become almost a stereotyped characterization of twentieth-century *life,* a central theme in modern art, theater, and politics. [4]The roots of this *meaninglessness* are many. [5]But crucial, we believe, is the anxiety deriving from the sense that all forms of human associations are perhaps

pointless because subject to sudden *irrational ends.* ⁶Cultural *life* thus becomes still more *formless.* ⁷No one form, no single *meaning* or style, appears to have any ultimate claim. ⁸The psychological implications of this *formlessness* are not fully clear; while there seem to be more *life* choices available, fewer are inwardly compelling.

—*Robert J. Lifton and Eric Olson*

The signal word **meaninglessness** in the topic statement reappears in sentences 3, 4, and 7 (its variant: *meaning*). **Formless** (or its variants), here treated as a symptom of meaninglessness, appears in sentences 5, 6, 7, and 8. Repetition of these two key words helps tie the paragraphs together. In sentence 5, **pointless** and **irrational** offer synonyms (different words with similar meaning) for the central theme of meaninglessness. And, throughout, the antonyms (words with opposite senses) **life** and **death** seem to clash, each uncertain of ultimate victory. Also, repetition of **weapon** from sentence 1 further enhances the connection.

Needless repetition, of course, makes writing seem tedious, juvenile, and annoying to read. For a clear distinction between effective and ineffective repetition, see page 120.

Does the Lifton/Olson paragraph contain parallel structures as well? If so, how does the parallelism reinforce the meaning?

PRONOUNS FOR COHERENCE

Instead of repeating certain nouns, it is sometimes more natural to use pronouns that refer to an earlier key noun. Pronouns improve coherence by relating sentences, clauses, and phrases to each other. This next paragraph uses pronouns to avoid repeating **the bull fighters** (emphasis added):

Using Pronouns as Connectors

The *bull fighters* march in across the sand to the president's box. *They* march with easy professional stride, swinging along, not in the least theatrical except for *their* clothes. *They* all have the easy grace and slight slouch of the professional athlete. From *their* faces *they* might be major league ball players. *They* salute the president's box then spread out along the barrera, exchanging *their* heavy brocaded capes for the fighting capes that have been laid along the red fence by the attendants.

—*Ernest Hemingway*

Be sure each pronoun refers clearly to the appropriate noun. The pronouns in Hemingway's paragraph, for example, clearly refer to the **bull fighters**. See page 111 for a full discussion of pronoun-antecedent agreement.

CONSISTENCY FOR COHERENCE

Coherence always relies on consistent tense, point of view, and number. In general, do not shift from past to present tense, from third- to first-person point of view, or from singular to plural nouns or pronouns. See Appendix A for a discussion of shifts that destroy coherence.

trans

TRANSITIONS

The above devices for achieving coherence (order, parallelism, repetition and restatement, pronouns) *suggest* specific relations between ideas. Transitional expressions, on the other hand, *announce* those relations. Words or phrases such as **for example, meanwhile, however,** and **moreover** work like bridges between thoughts. Each has a definite meaning—even without a specific context—as shown below.

Transition	*Relation*
X; meanwhile, Y	X and Y are occurring at the same time.
X; however, Y	Y is in contrast or exception to X.
X; moreover, Y	Y is in addition to X.
X; thus, Y	Y is a result of X.

Here is a paragraph in which these transitions are used to clarify the writer's line of thinking (emphasis added):

Using Transitions to Bridge Ideas

Psychological and social problems of aging too often are aggravated by the final humiliation: poverty. One of every three older Americans lives near or below the poverty level. *Meanwhile,* only one of every nine younger adults lives in poverty. The American public assumes that Social Security and Medicare provide adequate support for the aged. These benefits alone, *however,* rarely are enough to raise an older person's living standards above the poverty level. *Moreover,* older people are the only group living in poverty whose population recently has increased rather than decreased. More and more of our aging citizens *thus* confront the prospect of living with less and less.

Note: Transitional expressions should be a limited option for achieving coherence. Use them sparingly, and only when a relationship is not already made clear by the devices discussed earlier.

Note, too, that whole sentences can serve as transitions between paragraphs and a whole paragraph can serve as a transition between sections of writing. Assume, for instance, that you work as a marketing intern for a stereo manufacturer. You have just completed a section of a memo on the

COMMON TRANSITIONS AND THE RELATIONS THEY INDICATE

An addition: *moreover, in addition, and, also*

> I am majoring in naval architecture; *also,* I spent three years crewing on a racing yawl.

Results: *thus, hence, therefore, accordingly, thereupon, as a result, and so, as a consequence*

> Mary enjoyed all her courses; *therefore,* she worked especially hard last semester.

An example or illustration: *for instance, to illustrate, namely, specifically*

> Competition for part-time jobs is fierce; *for example,* 80 students applied for the clerk's job at Sears.

An explanation: *in other words, simply stated, in fact*

> Louise had a terrible semester; *in fact,* she flunked three courses.

A summary or conclusion: *in closing, to conclude, to summarize, in brief, in summary, to sum up, all in all, on the whole, in retrospect, in conclusion*

> Our credit is destroyed, our bank account is overdrawn, and our debts are piling up; *in short,* we are bankrupt.

Time: *first, next, second, then, meanwhile, at length, later, now, the next day, in the meantime, in turn, subsequently*

> Mow the ball field this morning; *afterwards,* clean the dugouts.

A comparison: *likewise, in the same way, in comparison*

> Our reservoir is drying up because of the drought; *similarly,* water supplies in neighboring towns are dangerously low.

A contrast or alternative: *however, nevertheless, yet, still, in contrast, otherwise, but, on the other hand, to the contrary, notwithstanding, conversely*

> Felix worked hard; *however,* his grades remained poor.

advantages of the new AKS amplifier and are now moving to a section on selling the idea to consumers. This next paragraph might link the two sections:

A Transitional Paragraph

> Because the AKS amplifier increases bass range by 15 percent, it should be installed as a standard item in all our stereo speakers. Tooling and installation adjustments, however, will add roughly $50 to the list price of each model. We must, therefore, explain the cartridge's long-range advantages to consumers. Let's consider ways of explaining these advantages.

Notice that this transitional paragraph *contains* transitional expressions as well.

APPLICATION 7-1

This next essay is shown without appropriate paragraph divisions. Mark the spot where each new paragraph should begin. *Hint:* Here is a rough (six-paragraph) outline: (1) introduction, (2) description of the plant, (3) a typical night shift, (4) the writer's specific job, (5) overview, (6) concluding story. Material that belongs together—and not length—should dictate specific paragraph divisions. (Review pages 88–89.)

SWING SHIFT

Have you ever worked in a factory? Have you ever worked swing shift? Can you stand to function like a machine in 95-degree heat or more? Let alone stand it—can you work in it for eight hours of endless repetition and mindless labor? I did, for more than eight years. The Acme Tire and Rubber Company, about 5 miles east of our campus, resembles a prison. (Look for a massive and forbidding three-story building occupying two city blocks on Orchard Street.) The plant was built 50 years ago, and its windows, coated by the soot and grit of a half-century, admit no light, no hope of seeing in or out. Add to this dismal picture the drab red bricks and the stench of burned rubber. This is what I faced five nights a week at 10:00 P.M. when I reported for work. A worker's life inside the plant is arranged so as not to tax the mind. At exactly 10:00 P.M. a loud bell rings. Get to work. The bell has to be loud in order to be heard over the roar of machinery and hissing steam escaping from the high-pressure lines. In time you don't even notice the noise. It took me about two weeks. At midnight the bell rings again: a ten-minute break. At 2:00 A.M. it rings again: lunch, 20 minutes. Two hours later, it rings for the last break of the night. At 6:00 A.M. the final bell anounces that the long night is over; it's time to go home. My dreary job was stocking tires. (I say "was" because I quit the job last year.) I had to load push trucks, the kind you see in railroad depots. I picked the tires up from the curing presses. A curing press is an 8-foot-high by 6-foot-wide by 6-foot-deep pressure cooker. There are 18 curing presses all in a row, and the temperature around them is over 100 degrees. Clouds of steam hang just below the 20-foot ceiling. By the time I had worked for ten minutes, my clothes were drenched with sweat and reeked with the acrid stench of steamed rubber. Once the truck was full, I'd push it to the shipping department on the other side of the plant. It's quiet there; they ship only during the day. And it's cooler. I'd feel chilled even though the temperature was around 75 degrees. Here I would leave the full truck, look for an empty one, push it back, and start again. It was the same routine every night: endless truckloads of tires, five nights a week—every week. Nothing ever changed except the workers; they got older and worn out. I wasn't surprised to hear that a worker had hanged himself there a few weeks ago. He was a friend of mine. Another friend told me that the work went on anyway. The police said to leave the body hanging until the medical examiner could clear it—like so much meat hanging on a hook. Someone put a blanket around the hanging body. They had to move around it. The work went on.

—*Glenn Silverberg*

APPLICATION 7-2

Most paragraphs employ a combination of devices for achieving coherence; not every paragraph employs them all. The next paragraph contains a variety of such devices. How many can you identify?

[1]*In a society based on self-reliance and free will, the institutionalization of life scares me.* [2]Today, America has government-funded programs to treat all society's ills. [3]We have day-care centers for the young, nursing homes for the old, psychologists in schools who use mental health as an instrument of disciplines, and mental hospitals for those whose behavior does not conform to the norm. [4]We have drug-abuse programs, methadone-maintenance programs, alcohol programs, vocational programs, rehabilitation programs, learning-how-to-cope-with-death-for-the-terminally-ill programs, make-friends-with-your-neighborhood-policeman programs, helping-emotionally-disturbed-children programs, and how-to-accept-divorce programs. [5]Unemployment benefits and welfare are programs designed to institutionalize a growing body of citizens whose purpose in life is the avoidance of work. [6]They are dependent on the state for their livelihood. [7]We can't even let people die in peace. [8]We put them in hospitals for the dying, so that they can be programmed into dying correctly. [9]They don't need to be hospital-

ized; they would be better off with their families, dying with dignity instead of in these macabre halfway houses. [10]All this is a displacement of confidence from the individual to the program. [11]We can't rely on people to take care of themselves anymore so we have to funnel them into programs. [12]This is a self-perpetuating thing, for the more programs we make available, the more people will become accustomed to seeking help from the government. [emphasis added]

—Ted Morgan

APPLICATION 7-3

Identify the subject and the signal term in each of these sentences. (Review pages 92–93.)

EXAMPLE

The pressures of the sexual revolution are everywhere.   *—Joyce Maynard*

Subject   pressures of the sexual revolution
Signal term   everywhere

1. High voltage from utility transmission lines can cause bizarre human and animal behavior.
2. Nuclear power plants need stricter supervision.
3. Producers of television commercials have created a loathsome gallery of men and women patterned, presumably, on Mr. and Mrs. America.
   —Marya Mannes
4. From the very beginning of school, we make books and reading a constant source of possible failure and possible humiliation.   *—John Holt*
5. High interest rates cripple the auto and housing industries.

APPLICATION 7-4

Collaborative Project and Computer Project: The paragraph below is unified but not coherent, because the sentences are not in logical order. On computer disks, each member of your group should individually rearrange the sentences so that the line of thinking is clear, and then print a hard copy. As a group, compare your different versions, with each member explaining the order he or she chose. Then agree on a final version, which one group member will create by rearranging the sentences on his or her disk. Print this final version for the entire class, justifying your group's decisions.

> [1]The Supreme Court's ruling against sex discrimination has touched all parts of American life—even the doll industry. [2]For example, Mattel, a large manufacturer of dolls, decided to change its ways—and make a little profit as well. [3]Now, little girl mommies might not have realized the significance of this arrival had it not been for the television announcement that "No family is complete without a tender Baby Brother." [4]Where would they find that little boy before Christmas? [5]In short, the doll was one small step for Mattel, but one giant leap for man. [6]Thus sexism died, and a new doll was born: Mattel's Baby Brother Tender Love, a soft, lovable doll complete with boy parts. [7]Not only did it give children a dose of sex education, but it also made men grin with satisfaction upon having invaded the doll industry. [8]As a consequence, parents quivered with anxiety that they would be unable to meet the demand of little mothers. [9]Yes, Baby Brother Tender Love was Mattel's gift to society that year.

APPLICATION 7-5

Select one of these assignments and write a paragraph organized from the general to the specific.

- Picture the ideal summer job. Explain to an employer why you would like the job.
- Assume that it's time for end-of-semester student evaluations of courses. Write a one-paragraph evaluation of your favorite course to be read by the professor's department chairperson.
- Explain your views on video games. Write for your classmates.
- Describe the job outlook in your chosen field. Write for a high school senior interested in your major.

APPLICATION 7-6

Identify a problem in a group to which you belong (such as family, club, sorority). Or select a topic from the list or make up one of your own. After reviewing pages 96–97, write two emphatic paragraphs, one featuring the emphatic material at the beginning and the other positioning it at the end. Be prepared to explain which versions work best for you and why.

- Advice to an entering freshman about surviving in college
- Your life goal, to your academic advisor, who is recommending you for a scholarship
- Your reasons for wanting to live off campus, to the dean of students

APPLICATION 7-7

Select the best paragraph or essay you have written thus far (or one that your instructor suggests). Using the strategies in this chapter, revise the paragraph or essay for improved coherence. After revising, list the specific strategies you employed (logical order, parallelism, repetition of key terms, restatement, pronouns, transitions).

WRITING READABLE SENTENCES

*N*o matter how vital your content and how sensible your organization, your writing will mean little unless it is easy to understand—in a word, readable. A readable sentence requires no more than a single reading.

One requirement for readable sentences, of course, is correct grammar, punctuation, and mechanics. But "correctness" alone is no guarantee of readability. Readers also are distracted when writing is hard to interpret, slow to make the point, or choppy. Sentences that are clear, concise, and fluent emphasize relationships, make every word count, and flow smoothly.

Before working with this section, you may wish to review some basic grammatical elements in Appendix A.

MAKING SENTENCES CLEAR

These guidelines will help you write clear sentences that convey your meaning on the first reading.

AVOID FAULTY MODIFIERS

mod

Modifiers explain, define, or add detail to other words or ideas. Prepositional phrases usually define or limit adjacent words. Defining or limiting modifiers can be:

Prepositional phrases:

> the foundation **with the cracked wall**
> the journey **to the moon**

Phrases with "-ing" verbs:

> the student **painting the portrait**
> **Opening the door,** we entered quietly.

Phrases with "to + verb" forms:

> **To succeed,** one must work hard.

Clauses:

> the person **who came to dinner**
> the job **that I recently accepted**

If a modifier is too far from the words it modifies, the message can be ambiguous.

Misplaced modifier   At our campsite, **devouring the bacon,** I saw a huge bear.

Was it *I* who was devouring the bacon? Moving the modifier next to bear clarifies the sentence:

Revised   At our campsite, I saw a huge bear **devouring the bacon.**

The order of adjectives and adverbs also affects the meaning of sentences:

I often remind myself to balance my checkbook.

I remind myself to balance my checkbook **often.**

Position modifiers to reflect your meaning:

Misplaced modifier   Jeanette read a report on using nonchemical pesticides **in our conference room.** [*Are the pesticides to be used in the conference room?*]

Revised   In our conference room, Jeanette read a report on using nonchemical pesticides.

Misplaced modifier   **Only** press the red button in an emergency. [*Does "only" modify "press" or "emergency"?*]

Revised   Press **only** the red button in an emergency.

or

Press the red button in an emergency **only.**

Misplaced modifier   Nonsmokers are harmed by tobacco smoke **as well as smokers.** [*Do smokers harm nonsmokers?*]

Revised   Nonsmokers **as well as smokers** are harmed by tobacco smoke.

Another problem with ambiguity occurs when a modifying phrase has no word to modify.

Dangling modifier   **Answering the telephone,** the cat ran out the door.

The cat obviously did not answer the telephone. But because the modifier **Answering the telephone** has no word to modify, the noun beginning the main clause (**cat**) seems to name the one who answered the phone. Without any word to connect to, the *modifier dangles.* Inserting a subject repairs this absurd message.

Revised   **As Mary answered the telephone,** the cat ran out the door.

A dangling modifier also can obscure your meaning.

<table>
<tr><td>**Dangling modifier**</td><td>**After completing the student financial aid applica-tion form,** the Financial Aid Office will forward it to the appropriate state agency.</td></tr>
</table>

Who completes the form—the student or the financial aid office?
Here are some other dangling modifiers:

<table>
<tr><td>**Dangling modifier**</td><td>**By planting different varieties of crops,** the pests were unable to adapt.</td></tr>
<tr><td>**Revised**</td><td>By planting different varieties of crops, **farmers** prevented the pests from adapting.</td></tr>
<tr><td>**Dangling modifier**</td><td>**As an expert in this field,** I'm sure your advice will help.</td></tr>
<tr><td>**Revised**</td><td>**Because of your expertise in this field,** I'm sure your advice will help.</td></tr>
</table>

KEEP YOUR PRONOUN REFERENCES CLEAR

ref

Pronouns (**she, it, his, their,** and so on) must refer to one clearly identified noun that they replace. If the pronoun's referent (or antecedent) is vague or ambiguous, readers will be confused.

<table>
<tr><td>**Vague referent**</td><td>Our patients enjoy the warm days while **they** last. [*Are the patients or the warm days on the way out?*]</td></tr>
<tr><td>**Clear referent**</td><td>While these warm days last, our patients enjoy them.</td></tr>
<tr><td></td><td>*or*</td></tr>
<tr><td></td><td>Our terminal patients enjoy these warm days.</td></tr>
<tr><td>**Ambiguous**</td><td>Sally told Sarah that **she** was obsessed with **her** job.</td></tr>
<tr><td>**Revised**</td><td>Sally told Sarah, "I'm obsessed with my job."
Sally told Sarah, "I'm obsessed with your job."</td></tr>
</table>

What other interpretations are possible for the ambiguous sentence above?
Avoid using **this, that,** or **it**—especially to begin a sentence—unless the pronoun refers to a specific antecedent (referent).

<table>
<tr><td>**Vague**</td><td>As Pierre drove away from his menial job, boring lifestyle, and damp apartment, he was happy to be leaving **it** behind.</td></tr>
</table>

Revised	As Pierre drove away, he was happy to be leaving his menial job, boring lifestyle, and damp apartment behind.
Vague	The problem with our defective machinery is only compounded by the new operator's incompetence. **This** annoys me!
Revised	I am annoyed by the problem with our defective machinery as well as by the new operator's incompetence.

AVOID CRAMMING

A sentence that crams in too many ideas forces the reader to struggle over its meaning.

Crammed	A smoke-filled room causes not only teary eyes and runny noses but also can alter people's hearing and vision, as well as creating dangerous levels of carbon monoxide, especially for people with heart and lung ailments, whose health is particularly threatened by "second-hand" smoke.

Clear things up by sorting out the relationships:

Revised	Besides causing teary eyes and runny noses, a smoke-filled room can alter people's hearing and vision. One of "second-hand" smoke's biggest dangers, however, is high levels of carbon monoxide, a particular health threat for people with heart and lung ailments.

KEEP EQUAL ITEMS PARALLEL

To reflect relationships among items of equal importance, express them in identical grammatical form (see also page 99).

For example, if you begin the series with a noun, use nouns throughout the series; likewise for adjectives, adverbs, and specific types of clauses and phrases.

Faulty	The new tutor is **enthusiastic, skilled,** and **you can depend on her.**
Revised	The new tutor is **enthusiastic, skilled,** and **dependable.** [*all subjective complements*]
Faulty	In his new job Ramon felt **lonely** and **without a friend.**
Revised	In his new job Ramon felt **lonely** and **friendless.** [*both adjectives*]

Faulty	Lulu plans **to study** all this month and **on scoring** well in her licensing examination.
Revised	Lulu plans **to study** all this month and **to score** well in her licensing examination. [*both infinitive phrases*]

wo

ARRANGE WORD ORDER FOR COHERENCE AND EMPHASIS

In coherent writing, everything sticks together; each sentence builds on the preceding sentence and looks ahead to the following sentence. Sentences generally work best when the beginning looks back at familiar information and the end provides the new (or unfamiliar) information.

Familiar		*Unfamiliar*
My dog	has	fleas.
Our boss	just won	the lottery.
This company	is planning	a merger.

Besides helping a message stick together, the familiar-to-unfamiliar structure emphasizes the new information. Just as every paragraph has a key sentence, every sentence has a key word or phrase that sums up the new information. That key word or phrase usually is emphasized best at the end of the sentence.

Faulty emphasis	We expect a **refund** because of your error in our shipment.
Correct	Because of your error in our shipment, we expect a **refund.**
Faulty emphasis	After your awful behavior, an apology is something I expect. But I'll probably get an excuse.
Correct	After your awful behavior, I expect an **apology.** But I'll probably get an excuse.

One exception to placing key words last occurs with a statement in the imperative mood (a command, an order, an instruction) with the subject [*you*] understood. For instance, each step in a list of instructions should contain an action verb (**insert, open, close, turn, remove, press**). To give readers a forecast, place the verb in that instruction at the beginning.

Correct	**Insert** the diskette before activating the system.
	Remove the protective seal.

With the key word at the beginning of the instruction, readers know immediately the action they need to take.

USE PROPER COORDINATION

Give equal emphasis to ideas of equal importance by joining them, within simple or compound sentences, with coordinating conjunctions: **and, but, or, nor, for, so,** and **yet.**

Correct	This course is difficult, **but** it is worthwhile.
	My horse is old **and** gray.
	We must decide to support **or** reject the dean's plan.

But too much coordination can confound your meaning. Below, notice how the meaning becomes clear when the less important ideas (**nearly floating, arms and legs still moving, my mind no longer having**) are shown as dependent on, rather than equal to, the most important idea (**jogging almost by reflex**).

Excessive coordination	The climax in jogging comes after a few miles **and** I can no longer feel stride after stride **and** it seems as if I am floating **and** jogging becomes almost a reflex **and** my arms and legs continue to move **and** my mind no longer has to control their actions.
Revised	The climax in jogging comes after a few miles, when I can no longer feel stride after stride. By then I am jogging almost by reflex, nearly floating, my arms and legs still moving, my mind no longer having to control their actions.

Avoid coordinating ideas that cannot be sensibly connected:

Faulty	I was late for work **and** wrecked my car.
Revised	Late for work, I backed out of the driveway too quickly, hit a truck, and wrecked my car.

USE PROPER SUBORDINATION

Proper subordination shows that a less important idea is dependent on a more important idea. A dependent (or subordinate) clause in a complex sentence is signaled by a subordinating conjunction: **because, so that, if, unless, after, until, since, while, as,** and **although.** Consider these complete ideas:

| Joe studies hard. He has severe math anxiety.

Because these ideas are expressed as simple sentences, they appear coordinate (equal in importance). But if you wanted to indicate your opinion of Joe's chances of succeeding, you would need a third sentence: **His handicap prob-**

ably will prevent him from succeeding or **His willpower will help him succeed** or some such. To communicate the intended meaning concisely, combine the two ideas. Subordinate the one that deserves less emphasis and place
the idea you want emphasized in the independent (main) clause.

> Despite his severe math anxiety [*subordinate idea*], Joe studies hard [*indepen-
> dent idea*].

Below, the subordination suggests the opposite meaning:

> Despite his diligent study [*subordinate idea*], Joe is unlikely to overcome his
> learning disability [*independent idea*].

Do not coordinate when you should subordinate:

> **Faulty**   Television viewers can relate to a person they idolize, and
> they feel obliged to buy the product endorsed by their hero.

Of the two ideas in the sentence above, one is the cause, the other the effect.
Emphasize this relationship through subordination.

> **Revised**   Because television viewers can relate to a person they idolize,
> they feel obliged to buy the product endorsed by their hero.

USE ACTIVE VOICE OFTEN

av

A verb's voice signals whether a sentence's subject acts or is acted upon. The
active voice (**I did it**) is more direct, concise, and persuasive than the passive
voice (**It was done by me**). In the active voice, the agent performing the action serves as subject:

	AGENT	ACTION	RECIPIENT
Active	Leslie	lost	your report.
	SUBJECT	VERB	OBJECT

The passive voice reverses the pattern, making the recipient of an action serve
as subject:

	RECIPIENT	ACTION	AGENT
Passive	Your report	was lost	by Leslie.
	SUBJECT	VERB	PREPOSITIONAL PHRASE

Sometimes the passive eliminates the agent altogether:

> **Passive**   Your report was lost. [*Who lost it?*]

Some writers mistakenly rely on the passive voice because they think it sounds more objective and important. But the passive voice often makes writing seem merely wordy or evasive:

Concise and direct (active)	**I underestimated** expenses for this semester. [*7 words*]
Wordy and indirect (passive)	Expenses for this semester **were underestimated by me.** [*9 words*]
Evasive (passive)	Expenses for this semester **were underestimated.**

Do not evade responsibility by hiding behind the passive voice:

Passive "irresponsibles"	A mistake was made in your shipment. [*By whom?*]
	It was decided not to hire you. [*Who decided?*]

Use the active voice when you want action. Otherwise, your statement will have no power:

Weak passive	If my claim is not settled by May 15, the Better Business Bureau will be contacted, and their advice on legal action will be taken.
Strong active	If you do not settle my claim by May 15, I will contact the Better Business Bureau for advice on legal action.

Ordinarily, use the active voice for giving instructions:

Faulty passive	The door to the cobra's cage should be locked.
	Care should be taken with the dynamite.
Correct active	Lock the door to the cobra's cage.
	Be careful with the dynamite.

USE PASSIVE VOICE SELECTIVELY

pv

Passive voice is appropriate in lab reports and other documents in which the agent's identity is immaterial to the message.

Use the passive voice if the person behind the action needs to be protected.

Correct passive	The criminal **was identified.**
	The victim **was asked** to testify.

Similarly, use the passive when the agent is unknown, unapparent, or unimportant:

Correct passive   Mr. Jones **was brought** to the emergency room.

The bank failure **was publicized** statewide.

Mary's article **was published** last week.

Prefer the passive when you want to be indirect or inoffensive:

Active but offensive   **You have not paid** your bill.

You need to overhaul our filing system.

Inoffensive passive   This bill **has not been paid**.

Our filing system **needs overhauling**.

APPLICATION 8-1

These sentences are unclear because of faulty modification, unclear pronoun reference, overstuffing, faulty parallelism, or key words buried in midsentence. Revise them so that their meaning is clear. For sentences suggesting two meanings, write separate versions—one for each meaning intended. (Review pages 109–113.)

1. Bill told Fred that he was mistaken.
2. In all writing, revision is required.
3. Only use this elevator in a fire.
4. Making the shelves look neater was another of my tasks at X-Mart that is very important to a store's business because if the merchandise is not always neatly arranged, customers will not have a good impression, whereas if it is neat they probably will return.
5. Wearing high boots, the snake could not hurt me.
6. When my ninth-grade teacher caught daydreamers, she would jab them in the shoulder with gritted teeth and a fierce eye.
7. While they eat dead fish, our students enjoy watching the alligators.
8. Education enables us to recognize excellence and to achieve it.
9. Student nurses are required to identify diseases and how to treat them.
10. My car needs an oil change, a grease job, and the carburetor should be adjusted.

APPLICATION 8-2

Use coordination or subordination to clarify relationships in these sentences. (Review pages 114–115.)

1. Martha loves John. She also loves Bruno.
2. You will succeed. Work hard.
3. I worked hard in calculus and flunked the course.
4. Now I have no privacy. My cousin moved into my room.
5. The instructor entered the classroom. Some students were asleep.

APPLICATION 8-3

Convert these passive voice sentences to concise, forceful, and direct expressions in the active voice. (Review pages 115–116.)

1. The evaluation was performed by us.
2. The essay was written by me.
3. Unless you pay me within three days, my lawyer will be contacted.
4. Hard hats should be worn at all times.
5. It was decided to decline your invitation.

APPLICATION 8-4

The sentences below lack appropriate emphasis because of improper use of the active voice. Convert each to passive voice. (Review pages 116–117.)

1. Joe's company fired him.
2. You are paying inadequate attention to student safety.
3. A power surge destroyed more than 2000 lines of our new computer program.
4. You did a poor job editing this report.
5. The selection committee awarded Mary a Fulbright Scholarship.

MAKING SENTENCES CONCISE

Concise writing conveys the most meaning in the fewest words. But it does not omit the details necessary for clarity. Use fewer words whenever fewer will do.

Cluttered   At this point in time I must say that I need a vacation.

Concise   I need a vacation now.

First drafts rarely are concise. Trim the fat:

Avoid Wordy Phrases

w

Each needless phrase here can be reduced to one word.

at this point in time	=	now
has the ability to	=	can
aware of the fact that	=	know
due to the fact that	=	because
dislike very much	=	hate
athletic person	=	athlete
the majority of	=	most
being in good health	=	healthy
on a daily basis	=	daily
in close proximity	=	near

Eliminate Redundancy

red

A redundant expression says the same thing twice in different words, as in **fellow classmates.**

a [dead] corpse	enter [into]
the reason [why]	[totally] monopolize
the [final] conclusion	[totally] oblivious
[utmost] perfection	[very] vital
[mental] awareness	[past] experience
[the month of] August	correct [amount of] change
[mutual] cooperation	[future] prospects
mix [together]	[valuable] asset
[viable] alternative	[free] gift

Avoid Needless Repetition

rep

Unnecessary repetition clutters writing and dilutes meaning.

Repetitious   In trauma victims, breathing is restored by **artificial respiration.** Techniques of **artificial respiration** include mouth-to-mouth **respiration** and mouth-to-nose **respiration.**

Repetition in the above passage disappears when sentences are combined.

Concise   In trauma victims, breathing is restored by artificial respiration, either mouth-to-mouth or mouth-to-nose.

But don't hesitate to repeat, or at least rephrase, if you feel that readers need reminders.

AVOID *THERE* AND *IT* SENTENCE OPENERS

Th

Many **there is, there are,** and **it** sentence openers can be eliminated.

Faulty   There are several good reasons why Boris dropped out of school.

Concise   Boris dropped out of school for several good reasons.

Of course, in some contexts, proper emphasis would call for a *there* opener.

Correct   People often have wondered about the rationale behind Boris's sudden decision. Actually, there are several good reasons for his dropping out of school.

Most often, however, *there* openers are best dropped.

Faulty   There is a serious fire danger created by your smoking in bed.

Concise   Your smoking in bed creates danger of fire.

Wordy   [It was] his negative attitude [that] caused him to fail.

Wordy   It gives me great pleasure to introduce our speaker.

Concise   I am pleased to introduce our speaker.

AVOID NEEDLESS PHRASES

np

To be, as well as **that** and **which** phrases, can often be cut.

Wordy   She seems [to be] upset.

Wordy   I find some of my classmates [to be] brilliant.

Wordy   The Batmobile is a car [that is] worth buying.

Wordy   This [is a] math problem [that] is impossible to solve.

Wordy   The book [,which is] about Hemingway[,] is fascinating.

AVOID WEAK VERBS

wv

Prefer verbs that express a definite action: **open, close, move, continue, begin.** Avoid verbs that express no specific action: **is, was, are, has, give, make,**

come, take. All forms of the verb **to be** are weak. This sentence can be revised for conciseness by substituting a strong verb:

Weak and wordy	Please **take into consideration** my application.
Concise	Please **consider** my application.

Here are some weak verbs converted to strong:

give a summary of	=	summarize
make an assumption	=	assume
come to the conclusion	=	conclude
take action	=	act
make a decision	=	decide
come to the realization	=	realize

AVOID EXCESSIVE PREPOSITIONS

prep

Wordy	Some **of** the members **of** the committee made these recommendations.
Concise	Some committee members made these recommendations.
Wordy	I gave the money **to** Sarah.
Concise	I gave Sarah the money.

AVOID NOMINALIZATIONS

nom

Nouns manufactured from verbs (nominalizations) often accompany weak verbs and needless prepositions.

Weak and wordy	We ask for the **cooperation** of all students.
Strong and concise	We ask that all students **cooperate**.
Weak and wordy	Give **consideration** to the possibility of a career change.
Strong and concise	**Consider** a career change.

Besides causing wordiness, nominalizations can be vague—by hiding the agent of an action.

Wordy and vague	A need for immediate action exists. [*Who should take the action? We can't tell.*]
Precise	We must act immediately.

Nominalizations drain the life from your style. In cheering for your favorite team, you wouldn't say:

| Blocking of that kick is a necessity!

instead of

| Block that kick!

Here are nominalizations restored to their verb forms:

conduct an investigation of	=	investigate
provide a description of	=	describe
conduct a test of	=	test
engage in the preparation of	=	prepare
make a discovery of	=	discover

MAKE NEGATIVES POSITIVE

A positive expression is easier to understand than a negative one.

Indirect and wordy	I did **not** gain anything from this course.
Direct and concise	I gained nothing from this course.
Confusing and wordy	Do **not** distribute this memo to employees who have **not** received security clearance.
Clear and concise	Distribute this memo only to employees who have received security clearance.

Besides the directly negative words (**no, not, never**), some indirectly negative words (**except, forget, mistake, lose, uncooperative**) also force readers to translate.

Confusing and wordy	**Do not neglect** to activate the alarm system.
	My conclusion was **not inaccurate**.
Clear and concise	Be sure to activate the alarm system.
	My conclusion was **accurate**.

Some negative expressions, of course, are perfectly correct, as in expressing disagreement.

Correct negatives	This is **not** the best plan.
	Your offer is **unacceptable**.
	This project **never** will succeed.

Here are other negative expressions translated into positive versions:

did not succeed	=	failed
does not have	=	lacks
did not prevent	=	allowed
not unless	=	only if
not until	=	only when
not absent	=	present

CLEAR OUT CLUTTER WORDS

cl

Clutter words stretch a message without adding meaning. Here are some of the commonest: **very, definitely, quite, extremely, rather, somewhat, really, actually, situation, aspect, factor.**

Cluttered	**Actually**, one **aspect** of a relationship **situation** that could **definitely** make me **very** happy would be to have a **somewhat** adventurous partner who **really** shared my **extreme** love of traveling.
Concise	I'd like to meet an adventurous person who loves traveling.

DELETE NEEDLESS PREFACES

pref

Don't keep readers waiting for the new information in your sentence. Get right to the point.

Wordy	[I am writing this letter because] I wish to apply for the position of dorm counselor.
Wordy	[The conclusion we can draw is that] writing is hard work.

DELETE NEEDLESS QUALIFIERS

qual

Qualifiers such as **I feel, it would seem, I believe, in my opinion,** and **I think** express uncertainty or soften the tone and impact of a statement.

Appropriate qualifiers	Despite Frank's poor academic performance last semester, he will, **I think**, do well in college.
	Your product **seems to be** what I need.

But when you are certain, eliminate the qualifier so as not to seem tentative or evasive.

Needless qualifiers
[It seems that] I've wrecked the family car.

[It would appear that] I've lost your credit card.

[In my opinion,] you've done a good job.

In communicating across cultures, keep in mind that a direct, forceful style might be considered offensive (page 146).

....

APPLICATION 8-5

Make these sentences more concise by eliminating redundancies and needless repetition. (Review pages 119–120.)

1. She is a woman who works hard.
2. I am aware of the fact that Sam is a trustworthy person.
3. Clarence completed his assignment in a short period of time.
4. Bruno has a stocky build.
5. Sally is a close friend of mine.
6. I've been able to rely on my parents in the past.

....

APPLICATION 8-6

Make these sentences more concise by eliminating **There is** and **There are** sentence openers, and the needless use of **it, to be, is, of, that,** and **which.** (Review page 120.)

1. I consider Martha to be a good friend.
2. Our summer house, which is located on Cape Cod, is for sale.
3. The static electricity that is generated by the human body is measurable.
4. Writing must be practiced in order for it to become effective.
5. Another reason the job is attractive is because the salary is excellent.
6. There are many activities and sports that I enjoy very much, but the one that stands out in my mind is the sport of jogging.
7. Friendship is something that people should be honest about.

8. Smoking of cigarettes is considered by many people to be the worst habit of all habits of human beings.

9. There are many students who are immature.

10. It is necessary for me to leave immediately.

···

APPLICATION 8-7

Make these sentences more concise by replacing weak verbs with strong ones and nouns with verbs, by changing negatives to positives, and by clearing out clutter words, needless prefatory expressions, and needless qualifiers. (Review pages 121–124.)

1. I have a preference for Ferraris.

2. Your conclusion is in agreement with mine.

3. We request the formation of a committee of students for the review of grading discrepancies.

4. I am not unappreciative of your help.

5. Actually, I am very definitively in love with you.

6. I find Susan to be an industrious and competent employee.

7. It seems that I've made a mistake in your order.

8. Igor does not have any friends at this school.

9. In my opinion, winter is an awful season.

10. As this academic year comes upon us, I realize that I will have trouble commuting to school this semester.

11. There is an undergraduate student attrition causes study needed at our school.

12. A need for your caution exists.

13. Never fail to attend classes.

14. Our acceptance of the offer is a necessity.

···

MAKING SENTENCES FLUENT

Fluent sentences are easy to read because of clear connections, variety, and emphasis. Their varied length and word order eliminate choppiness and monotony. Fluent sentences enhance *clarity,* allowing readers to see ideas that are most important. Fluent sentences enhance *conciseness,* often replacing several short, repetitious sentences with one longer, more economical sentence. To write fluently, use the following strategies:

comb

COMBINE RELATED IDEAS

Disconnected	Jogging can be healthful. You need the right equipment. Most necessary are well-fitting shoes. Without this equipment you take the chance of injuring your legs. Your knees are especially prone to injury. [*5 sentences*]
Clear, concise, and fluent	Jogging can be healthful if you have the right equipment. Shoes that fit well are most necessary because they prevent injury to your legs, especially your knees. [*2 sentences*]

Most sets of information can be combined in different relationships depending on what you want to emphasize. Imagine that this set of facts describes an applicant for a ski instructor's position:

- Sarah James has been skiing since age 3.
- She has no experience teaching skiing.
- She has won several slalom competitions.

Assume that you are Snow Mountain Ski Area's head instructor, writing to the manager to convey your impression of this candidate. To convey a negative impression, you might combine the facts in this way:

Strongly negative emphasis	Although Sarah James has been skiing since age 3 and has won several slalom competitions, **she has no experience teaching skiing.**

The *independent idea* (in boldface) receives the emphasis (also see page 114 on subordination). But if you are undecided, yet leaning in a negative direction, you might write:

Slightly negative emphasis	Sarah James has been skiing since age 3 and has won several slalom competitions, **but** she has no experience teaching skiing.

In the sentence above, the ideas before and after **but** are both independent. These independent ideas are joined by the coordinating word **but**, which suggests that both sides of the issue are equally important (or "coordinate"). Placing the negative idea last, however, gives it slight emphasis.

Finally, to emphasize stong support for the candidate, you could say:

Positive emphasis	Although Sarah James has no experience teaching skiing, **she has been skiing since age 3 and has won several slalom competitions.**

In the version above, the earlier idea is subordinated by **although,** leaving the two final ideas independent.

Caution: Combine sentences only to ease the reader's task. Remember that overstuffed sentences with too much information and two many connections can be hard for readers to sort out. Notice how many times you have to read the following overstuffed instruction in order to understand what to do:

> **Overcombined**   In developing less than a tankful of film, be sure to put in enough empty reels to fill all the space in the tank so that the film-loaded reels won't slide around when the tank is agitated.

VARY SENTENCE CONSTRUCTION AND LENGTH

var

We have just seen how related ideas often need to be linked in one sentence so that readers can grasp the connections.

> **Disconnected**   The nuclear core reached critical temperature. The loss-of-coolant alarm was triggered. The operator shut down the reactor.
>
> **Connected**   As the nuclear core reached critical temperature, triggering the loss-of-coolant alarm, the operator shut down the reactor.

But an idea that should stand alone for emphasis needs a whole sentence of its own:

> **Correct**   Core meltdown seemed inevitable.

However, an unbroken string of long or short sentences can bore and confuse readers, as can a series with identical openings:

> **Dreary**   There are some drawbacks about diesel engines. They are difficult to start in cold weather. They cause vibration. They also give off an unpleasant odor. They cause sulfur dioxide pollution.
>
> **Varied**   Diesel engines have some drawbacks. Most obvious are their noisiness, cold-weather starting difficulties, vibration, odor, and sulfur dioxide emission.

Similarly, when you write in the first person, overusing **I** makes you appear self-centered. Do not, however, avoid personal pronouns if they make the writing more readable (say, by eliminating passive constructions).

USE SHORT SENTENCES FOR SPECIAL EMPHASIS

All this talk about combining ideas might suggest that short sentences have no place in good writing. Wrong. Short sentences (even one-word sentences) provide vivid emphasis and stick in the reader's mind. Consider a student pilot's description of taking off:

> Our airspeed increases. The plane vibrates. We reach the point where the battle begins.

Instead, the student might have written:

> As our airspeed increases, the plane vibrates, and we reach the point where the battle begins.

However, she wanted to emphasize three discrete phases here: (1) the acceleration, (2) the vibration, and (3) the critical point of lifting off the ground.

. . . .

APPLICATION 8-8

The sentence sets below lack fluency because they are disconnected, have no variety, or have no emphasis. Combine each set into one or two fluent sentences.

Choppy   The world's forests are now disappearing. The rate of disappearance is 18 to 20 million hectares a year (an area half the size of California). Most of this loss occurs in humid tropical forests. These forests are in Asia, Africa, and South America.

Revised   The world's forests are now disappearing at the rate of 18 to 20 million hectares a year (an area half the size of California). Most of this loss is occurring in the humid tropical forests of Africa, Asia, and South America.*

1. The world's population will grow.

   It will grow from 4 billion in 1975.

   It will reach 6.5 billion in 2000.

   This will be an increase of more than 50 percent.

---

*Sample sentences are adapted from *Global Year 2000 Report to the President: Entering the* 21st *Century* (Washington, DC: Government Printing Office, 1980).

2. In sheer numbers, population will be growing.
   It will be growing faster in 2000 than it is today.
   It will add 100 million people each year.
   This figure compares with 75 million in 1975.

3. Energy prices are expected to increase.
   Many less-developed countries will have increasing difficulty.
   Their difficulty will be in meeting energy needs.

4. One-quarter of humanity depends primarily on wood.
   They depend on wood for fuel.
   For them, the outlook is bleak.

5. The world has finite fuel resources.
   These include coal, oil, gas, oil shale, and uranium.
   These resources, theoretically, are sufficient for centuries.
   These resources are not evenly distributed.

. . . .

APPLICATION 8-9

Combine each set of sentences below into one or two fluent sentences that provide the requested emphasis.

Sentence set	John is a loyal employee.
	John is a motivated employee.
	John is short-tempered with his colleagues.
Combined for positive emphasis	Even though John is short-tempered with his colleagues, he is a loyal and motivated employee.
Sentence set	This word processor has many excellent features.
	It includes a spelling checker.
	It includes a thesaurus.
	It includes a grammar checker.
Combined to emphasize the thesaurus	Among its many excellent features, such as spelling and grammar checkers, this word processor includes a thesaurus.

1. The job offers an attractive salary.
   It demands long work hours.

Promotions are rapid.

(Combine for negative emphasis.)

2. The job offers an attractive salary.

   It demands long work hours.

   Promotions are rapid.

   (Combine for positive emphasis.)

3. Company X gave us the lowest bid.

   Company Y has an excellent reputation.

   (Combine to emphasize Company Y.)

4. Superinsulated homes are energy efficient.

   Superinsulated homes can promote indoor air pollution.

   The toxins include radon gas and urea formaldehyde.

   (Combine for negative emphasis.)

5. Computers cannot think for the writer.

   Computers eliminate many mechanical writing tasks.

   They speed the flow of information.

   (Combine to emphasize the first assertion.)

. . . .

APPLICATION 8-10

Collaborative Project and Computer Application: Have each group member revise this next passage to improve fluency by combining related ideas; by varying sentence structure, openings, and length; and by using short sentences for special emphasis. (*Note:* When rephrasing to achieve conciseness, be sure to preserve the meaning of the original.) Then compare your versions and collaborate on an effective revision to present to the class.

Each summer, semitropical fish appear in New England salt ponds. They are carried northward by the Gulf Stream. The Gulf Stream is a warm ocean current. It flows like a river through the cold Atlantic. It originates in the Caribbean. It winds through the Florida straits. It meanders northward along the eastern coast of the United States. Off the shore of Cape Hatteras, North Carolina, the Gulf Stream's northerly course veers. It veers slightly eastward. This veering moves the stream and its warming influence farther from the coast. Semitropical fish are swept into the Gulf Stream from their breeding ground. The breeding ground is south of Cape Hatteras. The fish are carried northward. The strong current carries them. The current is often 20 degrees warmer than adjacent waters. Some of these fish are trapped in eddies. Eddies are pools of warm water that split from the Gulf Stream. These pools drift shoreward. By midsummer the ocean water off the New England coast is warm. It is warm enough to attract some fish out of the eddies and nearer to shore. In turn, even warmer water flows from the salt ponds. It flows to the ocean. It attracts these warm-water fish. They are attracted into the ponds. Here they spend the rest of the summer. They die off in the fall. The ponds cool in the fall.

APPLICATION 8-11

Computer Application: Try the grammar function of your word processing program. First, look for problems with clarity, conciseness, and fluency yourself. Then compare your changes with those the computer suggests. If the computer contradicts your own judgment, ask a classmate or your peer group for feedback. If the computer suggests changes that seem ungrammatical or incorrect, consult a good handbook for confirmation. Try to assess when and how the grammar function can be useful and when you can revise best on your own.

CHOOSING THE RIGHT WORDS

Any sentence is only as effective as the words it contains. The following suggestions will help you choose words that are convincing, precise, informative, and engaging.

MAKING YOUR MESSAGE CONVINCING

Readers will consider worthless any message that is trite, slang-ridden, overstated, or insincere:

AVOID TRITENESS

Writers who rely on tired old phrases (clichés) like the following come across as too lazy or too careless to find exact ways to say what they mean:

first and foremost	tough as nails
in the final analysis	holding the bag
needless to say	up the creek
work like a dog	over the hill
last but not least	bite the bullet
dry as a bone	fly off the handle
victim of circumstance	get on the stick

If it sounds like a "catchy phrase" you've heard before, don't use it.

AVOID OVERSTATEMENT

When they exaggerate to make a point, writers lose credibility. Be cautious when using words such as **best, biggest, brightest, most,** and **worst.** Recognize the differences among **always, usually, often, sometimes,** and **rarely** or among **all, most, many, some,** and **few.**

> **Overstated**   You never listen to my ideas.
>
> Everything you say is obnoxious.
>
> This is the worst essay I've ever read.

How would you rephrase the above examples to make them more reasonable?

AVOID MISLEADING EUPHEMISMS

A form of understatement, euphemisms are expressions aimed at politeness or at making unpleasant subjects seem less offensive. Thus, we **powder our**

noses or **use the boy's room** instead of **using the bathroom**; we **pass away** or **meet our Maker** instead of **dying.**

When euphemisms avoid offending or embarrassing our audience, they are perfectly legitimate. But they are unethical if they understate the truth when only the truth will serve:

- Instead of being **laid off** or **fired,** employees are **surplused** or **deselected,** or the company is **downsized.**
- Instead of **lying** to the public, the government engages in a **policy of disinformation.**
- Instead of **wars** and **civilian casualties,** we have **conflicts** and **collateral damage.**

APPLICATION 9-1

Revise these sentences to eliminate triteness, overstatements, and euphemisms.

1. This course gives me a pain in the neck.
2. There is never a dull moment in my dorm.
3. Television is rotting everyone's brain.
4. I was less than candid.
5. This student is poorly motivated.
6. You are the world's most beautiful person.
7. Marriage in America is a dying institution.
8. I love you more than life itself.
9. We have decided to terminate your employment.
10. People of our generation are all selfish.

MAKING YOUR LANGUAGE PRECISE

Even words listed as synonyms can carry different shades of meaning. Do you mean to say "I'm slender; you're slim; he's lean; and she's scrawny"? The wrong choice could be disastrous. A single, wrong word can be offensive, as in this statement by a college applicant:

| Another attractive feature of the college is its adequate track program.

While **adequate** might convey honestly the writer's intended meaning, the word seems inappropriate in this context (an applicant expressing a judgment about a program). Although the program may not have been ranked highly, the writer could have used any of several alternatives (**solid, promising, growing**—or no modifier at all).

Be especially aware of similar words with dissimilar meanings, as in these examples:

affect/effect	fewer/less
all ready/already	healthy/healthful
among/between	imply/infer
continual/continuous	uninterested/disinterested
eager/anxious	worse/worst
farther/further	

Does your professor expect **fewer** or **less** technical details in your essay? Do not write **Skiing is healthy** when you mean that skiing promotes good health (is healthful). **Healthy** means to be in a state of health. **Healthful** things help keep us healthy.

Be on the lookout for imprecisely phrased (and therefore illogical) comparisons:

Faulty	Your bank's interest rate is higher than BusyBank. [*Can a rate be higher than a bank?*]
Revised	Your bank's interest rate is higher than BusyBank's.

Imprecision can create ambiguity. For instance, is **send us more personal information** a request for more information that is personal or for information that is more personal?

Precision ultimately enhances conciseness, when one exact word replaces multiple inexact words.

Wordy and less exact	I have **put together** all the financial information.
	Keep doing this exercise for ten seconds.
Concise and more exact	I have **assembled** all the financial information.
	Continue this exercise for ten seconds.

· ·
APPLICATION 9-2

Revise these sentences to make them precise.

1. Our outlet does more business than San Francisco.
2. Low-fat foods are healthy.

3. Marie's license is for driving an automatic car only.

4. This is the worse course I've taken.

5. Unlike many other children, her home life was good.

6. State law requires that restaurant personnel serve food with a sanitation certificate.

MAKING YOUR WRITING SPECIFIC AND CONCRETE

General words name broad classes of things, such as **job, car,** or **person.** Such terms usually need to be clarified by more *specific* ones:

job = senior accountant for Rockford Press

car = red, four-door, Ford Escort station wagon

person = male Caucasian, with red hair, blue eyes (and so on)

The more specific your words, the sharper your meaning:

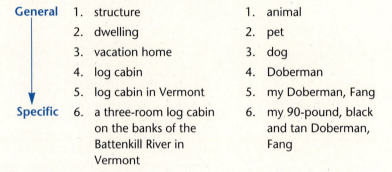

General		
1. structure	1. animal
2. dwelling	2. pet
3. vacation home	3. dog
4. log cabin	4. Doberman
5. log cabin in Vermont	5. my Doberman, Fang
Specific 6. a three-room log cabin on the banks of the Battenkill River in Vermont	6. my 90-pound, black and tan Doberman, Fang

Notice how the picture becomes more vivid as we move to lower levels of generality. To understand your way of seeing and your exact meaning, readers need specifics.

Abstract words name qualities, concepts, or feelings (**beauty, luxury, depression**) whose exact meaning has to be nailed down by *concrete* words—words that name things we can know through our five senses:

a beautiful view = snowcapped mountains, a wilderness lake, pink granite ledge, and 90-foot blue spruce trees

a luxury condominium = redwood hot tub, hand-painted Mexican tile counters, floor-to-ceiling glass walls, oriental rugs

a depressed person = suicidal urge, feeling of worthlessness, no hope for improvement, insomnia

Your discussion must be concrete and specific enough to provide clear and convincing support. Let's say that your topic statement is this one:

> Pedestrians crossing the street in front of my house place their lives in danger.

In supporting your main point you need to **show** with concrete and specific examples.

Abstract	For example, a person was injured there by a vehicle recently.
Concrete	My Uncle Albert was hit by a speeding garbage truck last Tuesday and had his leg broken.

Similarly, don't write **thing** when you mean **problem, pencil,** or **gift.** Instead of evaluating a coworker as **nice, great,** or **terrific,** use terms that are more concrete and verifiable, such as **reliable, skillful,** and **competent** or **dishonest, irritable,** and **awkward**—further clarified by examples (**never late for work**).

In some instances, of course, you may wish to generalize. Instead of writing **Bill, Mary, and Sam have been tying up the office phones with personal calls,** you might prefer **Some employees have been tying up** .... The second version gets your message across without pointing the finger.

Most good writing offers both general and specific information. The more general material is in the topic statement and sometimes in the conclusion because these parts, respectively, set the paragraph's direction and summarize its content. Informative writing invariably has a balance of *telling* and *showing*. Abstract and general expressions tell, and concrete and specific expressions show.

Meaningless abstraction	Professor Able's office is a sight to behold. [*What does "a sight to behold" mean?*]
Informative abstraction	Professor Able's office looks like a dump.

Now, the telling needs clarification through concrete and specific showing:

Concrete showing	The office has a floor strewn with books, a desk buried beneath a mountain of uncorrected papers, and ashtrays overflowing with ripe cigar butts.

....

APPLICATION 9-3

In each set of terms, identify the most abstract or general and the most concrete or specific. Give reasons for your choices.

1. a presidential candidate, a U.S. senator, Edward Kennedy, a politician

2. a favorite spot, a beautiful place, an island in the Bahamas, a hideaway

3. woman, surgeon, person, professional individual

4. an awful person, a cruel and dishonest person, a nasty person

5. a competitor, a downhill racer, an athlete, a skier, a talented amateur

6. violence, assassination, terrorism, political action

MAKING THE TONE APPROPRIATE

Your tone is your personal stamp—the personality that takes shape between the lines. The tone you create depends on (1) the distance you impose between yourself and the reader, and (2) the attitude you show toward the subject.

Assume that a friend is going to take over a job you've held. You're writing your friend instructions for parts of the job. Here is your first sentence:

Informal

> Now that you've arrived in the glamorous world of office work, put on your track shoes; this is no ordinary clerical job.

First, we notice that the sentence imposes little distance between the writer and the reader (it uses the direct address, **you,** and the humorous suggestion to **put on your track shoes**). And the ironic use of **glamorous** suggests that the writer means just the opposite, that the job holds little glamour.

For a different reader (say, the recipient of a company training manual) the writer would have chosen some other opening:

Semiformal

> As an office assistant with Acme Explosives Corporation, you will spend little of your day seated at your desk.

The tone now is serious, no longer intimate, and the writer expresses no distinct attitude toward the job. For yet another audience (say, those who will read an annual report for clients or investors), the writer again might have altered the tone:

Formal

> Office assistants at Acme Explosives are responsible for duties that extend far beyond desk work.

Here, the businesslike shift from second- to third-person address makes the tone too impersonal for any writing addressed to the assistants themselves.

Similarly, letters to your professor, your grandmother, and your friend, each about a disputed grade, would have different tones:

Formal

> Dear Professor Snapjaws:
>   I am convinced that my failing grade in calculus did not reflect a fair evaluation of my work over the semester.

Semiformal | Dear Granny,
> Thanks for your letter. I'm doing well in school, except for my unfair grade in calculus.

Informal | Dear Carol,
> Have I been shafted or what? That old turkey, Snapjaws, gave me an F in calculus.

ESTABLISH AN APPROPRIATE DISTANCE

We already know how tone works in speaking. When you meet someone new, you respond in a tone that defines your relationship.

Tone announces interpersonal distance | Honored to make your acquaintance. [*formal tone—greatest distance*]

How do you do? [*formal*]

Nice to meet you. [*semiformal—medium distance*]

Hi. [*informal—least distance*]

What's happening? [*informal*]

Each of these responses is appropriate in specific situations, inappropriate in others.

To decide on an appropriate distance for addressing a particular audience, follow these guidelines:

GUIDELINES FOR DECIDING ABOUT TONE

1. Use a formal or semiformal tone in writing for superiors, professionals, or academics (depending on what you think the reader expects).
2. Use a semiformal or informal tone in essays and letters (depending on how close you feel to your reader).
3. Use an informal tone when you want your writing to be conversational, or when you want it to sound like a person talking.
4. Above all, find out what tone your particular readers prefer.

Whichever tone you decide on, be consistent throughout your message:

Inconsistent tone | My dorm room isn't fit for a pig: it is ungraciously inattractive.

Revised | My dilapidated dorm room is unfit to live in.

In general, lean toward an informal tone without falling into slang. Make your writing conversational by following these suggestions:

GUIDELINES FOR ACHIEVING A CONVERSATIONAL TONE

1. Use simple and familiar words.
2. Use an occasional contraction.
3. Address readers directly when appropriate.
4. Use **I** and **We** when appropriate.
5. Prefer active to passive voice.

Use Simple and Familiar Wording. Say it in plain English. Try not to use a three-syllable word when one syllable will do. Don't write like the author of a report from the Federal Aviation Administration who suggested that manufacturers of the DC-10 be directed to **reevaluate the design of the entire pylon assembly to minimize design factors which are resulting in sensitive and/or critical maintenance and inspection procedures** (*25 words, 50 syllables*). Here is a plain-English translation: **Redesign the pylons so they are easier to maintain and inspect** (*11 words, 18 syllables*). Here are other instances of inflated language:

Inflated   Upgrade your present employment situation. [*5 words, 12 syllables*]

Revised   Get a better job. [*4 words, 5 syllables*]

Inflated   I am thoroughly convinced that Sam is a trustworthy individual.

Revised   I trust Sam.

Whenever possible, trade for less and more familiar:

utilize	=	use
to be cognizant	=	to know
to endeavor	=	to try
endeavor	=	effort
to secure employment	=	to find a job
concur	=	agree
effectuate	=	do
terminate	=	end
deem	=	think

Of course, now and then the complex or more elaborate word is best—if it expresses your exact meaning or if it replaces a handful of simpler words.

Weak	Six loops around **the outside edges** of the dome tent **are needed for** the pegs **to fit into.**
Informative and precise	Six loops around the dome tent's **perimeter accommodate** the pegs.
Weak	We need a **one-to-one exchange of ideas and opinions.**
Informative and precise	We need a **dialogue.**

Use an Occasional Contraction. Unless you have reason to be formal, use (but do not overuse) contractions. Balance an **I am** with an **I'm**, a **you are** with a **you're**, an **it is** with an **it's**. Generally, use contractions only with pronouns—not with nouns or proper nouns (names).

Awkward contractions	Barbara'll be here soon.
	Health's important.
	Love'll make you happy.
Ambiguous contractions	The dog's barking.
	The baby's crying.

These ambiguous contractions could be confused with possessive constructions.

Address Readers Directly. Use the personal pronouns **you** and **your** to connect with readers.

Impersonal tone	Students at our college will find the faculty always willing to help.
Personal tone	As a student at our college, **you** will find the faculty always willing to help.

Research shows that readers relate better to something addressed to them directly.

Caution: Use **you** and **your** only to correspond *directly* with the reader, as in a letter, instructions, or some form of advice, encouragement, or persuasion. By using **you** and **your** in a situation that calls for first or third person, you might write something like this:

Wordy and awkward	When **you** are in northern Ontario, **you** can see wilderness lakes everywhere around **you.**
Appropriate	Wilderness lakes are everywhere in northern Ontario.

Use I and we When Appropriate.   Instead of disappearing behind your writing, use **I** or **we** when referring to yourself or your group.

Distant	This writer would like a refund.
Revised	I would like a refund.
Distant	The fear was awful until the police arrived.
Revised	We were terrified until the police arrived.

Prefer the Active Voice.   Because the active voice is more direct and economical than the passive voice, it generally creates a less formal tone. Review pages 115–117 for use of active and passive voice.

EXPRESS A CLEAR AND APPROPRIATE ATTITUDE

In addition to setting the distance between writer and reader, your tone implies your attitude toward the subject and the reader:

Tone announces attitude

> We dine at seven.
>
> Dinner is at seven.
>
> We eat at seven.
>
> We chow down at seven.
>
> We strap on the feedbag at seven.
>
> We pig out at seven.

The words we choose tell readers a great deal about where we stand.

One problem with tone occurs when your attitude is unclear. Don't force readers to translate. Say **I enjoyed the course** instead of **My attitude toward the course was one of high approval.** Try to convey an attitude that reflects your relationship with the reader. For instance, in an upcoming conference about a late paper, does the professor expect to **discuss the situation, talk it over, have a chat,** or **chew the fat?** Decide how casual or serious your attitude should be.

Don't be afraid to inject personal commentary when it's called for. Consider how the message below increases in force and effectiveness with the boldfaced commentary:

> In 1972, 56,000 people died on America's highways; 200,000 were injured, 15,000 children were orphaned. In that year, if you were a member of a family of five, chances are that someone related to you, by blood or law, was killed or injured by **one of the most violent forms of self-elimination ever devised by humanity**—an auto accident.

If, however, your job is to report objectively, try to suppress any bias you might have; do not volunteer your attitude.

bias

AVOID BIAS

Even controversial subjects deserve unbiased treatment. Imagine, for instance, that you are a campus newspaper reporter, investigating a confrontation between part-time faculty and the administration. Your initial report, written for tomorrow's edition, is intended simply to describe what happened. Here is how an unbiased description might read:

A factual account

> At 10:00 a.m. on Wednesday, October 24, 80 adjunct faculty members set up picket lines around the college's administration building, bringing business to a halt. The group issued a formal protest, claiming that their salary scale was unfair, and their fringe benefits [health insurance, and so on] inadequate, and their job security nonexistent. The group insisted that the college's wage scales and employment policies be revised. The demonstration ended when Glenn Tarullo, vice-president in charge of personnel, promised to appoint a committee to investigate the group's claims and to correct any inequities.

Notice the absence of implied judgments. A less impartial version of the event, from a protester's point of view, might read like this:

A biased version

> Last Wednesday, adjunct faculty struck another blow against exploitation when 80 members paralyzed the college's repressive administration for more than six hours. The timely and articulate protest was aimed against unfair salary scales, inadequate fringe benefits and lack of job security. Stunned administrators watched helplessly as the group organized their picket lines, determined to continue their protest until their demands for fair treatment were met. An embarrassed vice-president quickly agreed to study the group's demands and to revise the college's discriminatory policies. The success of this long-overdue confrontation serves as an inspiration to oppressed adjunct faculty everywhere.

But writing teacher Marshall Kremers reminds us that being unbiased, of course, doesn't mean remaining "neutral" about something you know to be wrong or dangerous.* If, for instance, you conclude that the college protest was clearly justified, say so.

AVOID SEXIST LANGUAGE

The way we as a culture use language reflects the way we think about ourselves. Usage that gives people in general a male identity allows no room for females. In fact, females become virtually invisible in a world of **policemen, congressmen, firemen, foremen, selectmen,** and **aldermen.**

---

*See *IEEE Transactions on Professional Communication* 32.2 (1989):58–61.

Sexist usage refers to doctors, lawyers, and other professionals as **he** or **him** while referring to nurses, secretaries, and homemakers as **she** or **her.** In this traditional stereotype, males do the jobs that really matter and that pay higher wages, whereas females serve only as support and decoration. And when females do invade traditional "male" roles, we might express our surprise at their boldness by calling them **female executives, female sportscasters, female surgeons,** or **female hockey players.** Likewise, to demean males who have taken "female" roles, we refer to **male secretaries, male nurses, male flight attendants,** or **male models.**

In the biased reality of sexist usage, the title **Mr.** protects the privacy of a male who might be married or unmarried, whereas **Mrs.** and **Miss** announce a female's marital status to the world. Moreover, an unmarried male is fondly referred to as a **bachelor,** although his female counterpart is stigmatized as an **old maid** or a **spinster.**

GUIDELINES FOR NONSEXIST USAGE

1. Use neutral expressions:

chair, or chairperson	rather than	chairman
supervisor	rather than	foreman
police officer	rather than	policeman
letter carrier	rather than	postman
homemaker	rather than	housewife
humanity	rather than	mankind
actor	rather than	actor vs. actress

2. Rephrase to eliminate the pronoun, if you can do so without altering your original meaning.

Sexist   A writer will succeed if he revises.

Revised   A writer who revises succeeds.

3. Use plural forms.

Sexist   A writer will succeed if **he** revises.

Revised   Writers will succeed if **they** revise. (But *not A writer will succeed if **they** revise.*)

When using a plural form, don't create an error in pronoun-referent agreement by having the plural pronoun **they** or **their** refer to a singular referent:

Each writer should do **their** best.

4. When possible (as in direct address) use you:

Direct address   You will succeed if you revise.

But use this form only when addressing someone directly. (See page 141.)

AVOID OFFENSIVE USAGE OF ALL TYPES

Enlightened communication respects all people in reference to their specific cultural, racial, ethnic, and national background; sexual and religious orientation; age or physical condition. References to individuals and groups should be as neutral as possible; no matter how inadvertent, any expression that seems condescending or judgmental or that violates the reader's sense of appropriateness is offensive. Detailed guidelines for reducing biased usage appear in these two works:

Schwartz, Marilyn et al. *Guidelines for Bias-Free Writing.* Bloomington: Indiana UP, 1995.

Publication Manual of the American Psychological Association, 4th ed. Washington: American Psychological Association, 1994.

5. Use occasional pairings (**him or her, she or he, his or hers, he/she**):

| **Effective pairing** | A writer will succeed if **she or he** revises. |

But note that overuse of such pairings can be awkward:

| **Awkward pairing** | A writer should do **his or her** best to make sure that **he or she** connects with **his or her** readers. |

6. Use feminine and masculine pronouns alternately:

| **Alternating pronouns** | An effective writer always focuses on **her** audience. The writer strives to connect with all **his** readers. |

7. Drop condescending diminutive endings such as -**ess** and -**ette** used to denote females (**poetess, drum majorette, actress,** etc.).

8. Use **Ms.** instead of **Mrs.** or **Miss,** unless you know that the person prefers one of the traditional titles. Or omit titles completely: **Jane Kelly** and **Roger Smith; Kelly and Smith.**

9. In quoting sources that have ignored present standards for nonsexist usage, consider these options:

- Insert [**sic**] (for **thus** or **so**) following the first instance of sexist terminology in a particular passage.
- Use ellipses to omit sexist phrasing.
- Paraphrase instead of quoting directly.

Below is a sampling of suggestions adapted from the previous works.

GUIDELINES FOR INOFFENSIVE USAGE

1. When referring to members of a particular culture, be as specific as possible about that culture's identity: Instead of **Latin American** or **Asian** or **Hispanic**, for instance, prefer **Cuban American** or **Korean** or **Nicaraguan.** Instead of **American students,** specify **U.S. students** when referring to the United States.

   Avoid judgmental expressions: Instead of **third-world** or **undeveloped nations** or the **Far East,** prefer **developing** or **newly industrialized nations** or **East Asia.** Instead of **nonwhites,** refer to **people of color.**

2. When referring to someone who has a disability, avoid terms that could be considered pitying or overly euphemistic, such as **victims, unfortunates, special** or **challenged** or **differently abled.** Focus on the individual instead of the disability: instead of **blind person** or **amputee** refer to a **person who is blind** or a **person who has lost an arm.**

   In general usage, avoid expressions that demean those who have medical conditions: **retard, mental midget, insane idea, lame excuse, the blind leading the blind, able-bodied workers,** and so on.

3. When referring to members of a particular age group, prefer **girl** or **boy** for people of age 14 or under; **young person, young adult, young man** or **young woman** for those of high-school age; and **woman** or **man** for those of college age. (**Teenager** or **juvenile** carries certain negative connotations.) Instead of **the elderly,** prefer **older persons.**

Keep in mind that standards and conventions for bias-free communication continue to evolve. In addition to consulting the two works listed on page 145, keep up-to-date on new developments and always rely on careful and conscientious audience analysis for addressing a specific readers' expectations.

CONSIDERING THE CULTURAL CONTEXT

Cultures differ in their style preferences

The style guidelines throughout Chapters 8 and 9 apply specifically to standard English in North America. But practices and preferences can differ widely in different cultural contexts.

Certain cultures might prefer complicated sentences and elaborate language, to convey an idea's full complexity. Other cultures value expressions of politeness, praise, and gratitude more than mere clarity or directness (Hein 125–26; Mackin 349–50).

Writing in non-English languages tends to be more formal than in English, and some relies heavily on the passive voice (Weymouth 144). French readers, for example, may prefer an elaborate style that reflects sophisticated and complex modes of thinking. In contrast, our "plain English," conversational style might connote simple-mindedness, disrespect, or incompetence (Thrush 277).

In translation or in a different cultural context, certain words carry offensive or unfavorable connotations. A few notable disasters (Gesteland 20; Victor 44):

- The Chevrolet *Nova*—meaning "don't go" in Spanish
- The Finnish beer *Koff*—for an English-speaking market
- Colgate's *Cue* toothpaste—an obscenity in French
- A bicycle brand named *Flying Pigeon*—imported for a U.S. market

Idioms ("strike out," "over the top,") hold no logical meaning for other cultures. Slang ("bogus," "fat city") and colloquialisms ("You bet," "Gotcha") can strike readers as being too informal and crude.

Offensive writing can alienate audiences—toward you *and* your culture (Sturges 32).

....

APPLICATION 9-4

Rewrite these statements in plain and precise English, with special attention to tone.

1. This writer desires to be considered for a position with your company.
2. My attitude toward your behavior is one of disapproval.
3. A good writer is cognizant of how to utilize grammar in correct fashion.
4. Replacement of the weak battery should be effectuated.
5. Sexist language contributes to the ongoing prevalence of gender stereotypes.
6. Make an improvement in your studying situation.
7. We should inject some rejuvenation into our lifeless and dull relationship.

....

APPLICATION 9-5

Find examples of overly euphemistic language (such as "chronologically challenged") or of insensitive language. Discuss your examples in class.

APPLICATION 9-6

Collaborative Project and Computer Application: A version of this next letter was published in a local newspaper. Working on the computer, each group member should rewrite the letter in plain English and then print a hard copy for comparison. Agree on a final version that one group member will compose. Print this final version for the whole class, justifying your group's revision.

> In the absence of definitive studies regarding the optimum length of the school day, I can only state my personal opinion based upon observations made by me and upon teacher observations that have been conveyed to me. Considering the length of the present school day, it is my opinion that the school day is excessive lengthwise for most elementary pupils, certainly for almost all of the primary chidren.
>
> To find the answer to the problem requires consideration of two ways in which the problem may be viewed. One way focuses upon the needs of the children, while the other focuses upon logistics, scheduling, transportation, and other limits imposed by the educational system. If it is necessary to prioritize these two ideas, it would seem most reasonable to give the first consideration to the primary and fundamental reason for the very existence of the system itself, i.e., to meet the educational needs of the children the system is trying to serve.

APPLICATION 9-7

Rewrite these statements to eliminate sexist and other offensive expressions—without altering the meaning.

1. An employee in our organization can be sure he will be treated fairly.
2. Almost every child dreams of being a fireman.
3. The average man is a good citizen.
4. The future of mankind is uncertain.
5. Being a stewardess is not as glamorous as it may seem.
6. Everyone has the right to his opinion.
7. Every married surgeon depends on his spouse for emotional support.
8. Dr. Marcia White is not only a female professor, but also chairman of the English department.
9. The accident left me blind as a bat for nearly an hour.
10. What a dumb idea!

AVOIDING RELIANCE ON AUTOMATED TOOLS

Many of the strategies in Chapters 8 and 9 could be executed rapidly with word-processing software. By using the global *Search-and-replace function* in some programs, you can command the computer to search for ambiguous pronoun references, overuse of passive voice, **to be** verbs, **There** and **It** sentence openers, negative constructions, clutter words, needless prefatory expressions and qualifiers, sexist language, and so on. With an on-line dictionary or thesaurus, you can check definitions or see a list of synonyms for a word you have used in your writing.

But these editing aids can be extremely imprecise. They can't eliminate the writer's burden of choice. None of the "rules" offered in Chapters 8 and 9 applies universally. Ultimately the informed writer's sensitivity to meaning, emphasis, and tone—the human contact—determines the effectiveness of any message.

....

APPLICATION 9-8

Computer Application: Explore the thesaurus function on your word-processing program. Remember that a thesaurus never can provide an exact synonym. Check the computer's suggestions against the dictionary definitions of the words. Compare the computer's suggestions with a good traditional thesaurus. How would you assess the advantages and disadvantages of the two?

....

WORKS CITED

Gesteland, Richard R. "Cross-Cultural Compromises." *Sky* May 1993:20+.

Hein, Robert G. "Culture and Communication." *Technical Communication* 38.1 (1991): 125–26.

Mackin, John. "Surmounting the Barrier between Japanese and English Technical Documents." *Technical Communication* 36.4 (1989): 346–51.

Sturges, David L. "Internationalizing the Business Communication Curriculum." *Bulletin of the Association for Business Communication* 55.1 (1992): 30–39.

Thrush, Emily A. "Bridging the Gap: Technical Communication in an Intercultural and Multicultural Society." *Technical Communication Quarterly* 2.3 (1993): 271–83.

Victor, David A. *International Business Communication.* New York: Harper, 1992.

Weymouth, L. C. "Establishing Quality Standards and Trade Regulations for Technical Writing in World Trade." *Technical Communication* 37.2 (1990): 143–47.

ESSAYS FOR VARIOUS GOALS

INTRODUCTION

*E*arlier chapters have stressed the importance of deciding on a goal and of refining the goal into a purpose (goal plus plan). This section shows you how to focus on your purpose in order to achieve a variety of writing goals.

THREE MAJOR GOALS OF WRITING

Most writing can be categorized according to three major goals: expressive, referential, and persuasive.

Expressive writing is mostly about you, the writer (your feelings, experiences, impressions, personality). This personal form of writing helps readers understand something about you or your way of seeing.

Expressive writing situations

- You write to cheer up a sick friend with a tale about your latest blind date.
- You write a Dear John (or Jane) letter.
- You write to your parents, explaining why you've been feeling down-in-the-dumps.

Examples of expressive writing appear in the sample essays in Section One on pages 13, 16, and 59. Many students find expressive writing easiest because it is a kind of storytelling.

Instead of focusing on the writer, *referential (or explanatory) writing* involves analysis of some outside subject. Your goal might be (a) to inform readers about something they need to know or (b) to explain something they need to understand. Referential writing doesn't focus on your feelings and experiences but on the subject at hand.

Referential writing situations

- You write to describe the exterior of your new dorm so that your parents can find it next weekend.
- You define *condominium* for your business law class.
- You report on the effects of budget cuts at your college for the campus newspaper.
- You write to advise a younger sibling about how to prepare for college-level work.

An example of referential writing appears on page 179.

Persuasive writing is mostly about your audience. Beyond merely imparting information or making something understandable, your goal is to win readers' support, to influence their thinking, or motivate them in some way. Persuasive writing appeals both to the audience's reason and emotions.

- You write an editorial for the campus newspaper, calling for a stricter alcohol policy in the dorms.

- You write a diplomatic note to your obnoxious neighbor, asking him to keep his dogs quiet.

- You write to ask a professor on sabbatical to reconsider the low grade you received in history.

- You write to persuade citizens in your county to vote against a proposal for a toxic-waste dump.

These three goals (expressive, referential or explanatory, and persuasive) often overlap. For example, persuading the dean to beef up campus security might mean discussing your personal fears (expressive goal) and explaining how some students have been attacked (referential goal). But most writing situations have one primary goal. Keeping that goal in focus can help you choose the best strategies for getting the job done.

Traditionally, the strategies for writing are considered to be *description, narration, exposition* (or explanation), and *argument.* But description, narration, and exposition can be used for expressive, referential, or persuasive goals. While Section One focuses on expressive writing, Section Three is mostly about communication between readers and writers on subjects of interest to both. Therefore, it focuses primarily on referential and persuasive uses of these strategies—that is, writing to inform, explain, or make a point. Persuasive writing, however, raises special concerns that we will cover in Chapters 17 and 18.

MAJOR DEVELOPMENT STRATEGIES

A *development strategy* is simply a plan for coming up with the details, events, examples, explanations, and reasons that convey your exact meaning—a way of answering readers' questions. *Description* paints a word picture, while *narration* tells a story or depicts a series of related events, usually in chronological order. Narration relies on descriptive details to make the events vivid. *Exposition,* meanwhile, relies on description and narration, but it does more than paint a picture or tell a story: this strategy explains the writer's viewpoint. Strategies of exposition include *illustration, classification, process analysis, cause-effect analysis, comparison-contrast,* and *definition,* all of which are explored in the following chapters. Essays often employ some combination of these strategies but usually have one primary strategy.

Finally, *argument* strives to win readers to our point of view. Whereas the main point in exposition can usually be shown to be true or valid, the main point in an argument is debatable—capable of being argued by reasonable people on either side. The stronger argument, then, would be the one that makes the more convincing case.

USING THIS SECTION

The chapters that follow begin with an introduction to a particular strategy, then demonstrate how the strategy can support referential and persuasive writing. Next, the chapters provide guidelines for using the strategy yourself. Finally, they offer exercises to sharpen your skills, including a "practice" essay for analysis. When you read these practice essays, refer to the following list of questions as well as to the more specific questions provided in each chapter.

QUESTIONS FOR ESSAY PRACTICE

QUESTIONS ABOUT CONTENT

- Is the title effective? Explain.
- Is the essay primarily referential or persuasive? How would you characterize the writer's goal?
- What is the thesis? Is it stated, or is it implicit? Where does it appear? Does this placement contribute to the reader's understanding?
- Is the essay convincing? What kinds of support does the writer offer for the main points?

QUESTIONS ABOUT ORGANIZATION

- How is the introduction structured? Are the writer's decisions effective? Explain.
- Does the essay vary the standard introduction-body-conclusion format (see the discussion below)? If so, how? Do the writer's decisions help promote the goal?
- How is the conclusion structured? Is it effective? Why?

QUESTIONS ABOUT STYLE

- What is the outstanding style feature of this essay? Give examples.
- Characterize the tone. Give examples of word choice and sentence structure that contribute to the tone.

A WORD ABOUT STRUCTURAL VARIATIONS

Most sample essays in earlier chapters have a basic introduction-body-conclusion structure: a one-paragraph introduction that leads into the thesis; several support paragraphs, each developed around a topic statement that treats one part of the thesis; and a one-paragraph conclusion that relates to the main point. But a quick glance at published writing shows much variation from this formula: Some topics call for several introductory paragraphs; some supporting points require that one topic statement serve two or more body paragraphs; some paragraphs may be interrupted by digressions like personal remarks or flashbacks that are linked to the main point; some conclusions take up more than one paragraph. Single-sentence paragraphs will open, support, or close an essay.

Instead of the final sentence in the introduction, the thesis might be the first sentence of the essay, or it may be saved for the conclusion or not stated at all—although a definite thesis almost always is unmistakably implied.

Still other essays have neither introductory nor concluding paragraphs. Instead, the opening or closing is incorporated into the main discussion. Such *structural variations are a part of a writer's deliberate decisions*—decisions that determine the ultimate quality of an essay. Many of the essays in the following chapters embody one or more of these variations. Use them as inspiration for your own writing, but remember that *effective writing always reveals a distinct beginning, middle, and ending*—and a clear line of thought.

HELPING OTHERS SEE AND SHARE AN EXPERIENCE

Description creates a word picture; it tells about things as they appear in space. Because it helps readers *visualize,* description is a common denominator in all writing.

<table>
<tr><td>What readers expect to learn from a description</td><td>

■ *What is it?*

■ *What does it look like?*

■ *How could I recognize it?*

■ *What is it made of?*

■ *What does it do?*

■ *How does it work?*

■ *What is your impression of it?*

■ *How does it make you feel?*

</td></tr>
</table>

Narration also creates a word picture, telling how events occur in time. It relies on the showing power of descriptive details to make the story vivid, but its main goal is to help readers follow events.

<table>
<tr><td>What readers expect to learn from a narrative</td><td>

■ *What happened?*

■ *Who was involved?*

■ *When did it happen?*

■ *Where did it happen?*

■ *Why did it happen?*

</td></tr>
</table>

Because any topic or event can be viewed in countless ways, your decisions about descriptive and narrative details depend on your purpose and the reader's needs. Both strategies can serve either *objective (referential) goals*— that is, they can merely report—or they can be selected and used differently by different writers. They then fill *subjective (and often persuasive) goals*— they make a point.

USING OBJECTIVE DESCRIPTION TO INFORM

Objective description filters out—as much as appropriate—personal impressions, focusing on observable details.* It provides factual information about something for someone who will use it, buy it, or assemble it, or who needs

---

*Pure objectivity is, of course, humanly impossible. Each writer has a unique perspective on the facts and their meaning, and chooses what to put in and what to leave out.

to know more about it for some good reason. Objective description records exactly what is seen from the writer's vantage point. If your CD player has been stolen, the police need a description that includes the brand name, serial number, model, color, size, shape, and identifying marks or scratches. For this audience, a subjective description (that the item was a handsome addition to your car; that its sound quality was superb; that it made driving a pleasure) would be useless.

An Objective Description

Orienting sentence (1)

View from water (2–5)

View from shoreline (6–7)

[1]The 2-acre site (lot 7) for my proposed log cabin is on the northern shore of Moosehead Lake, roughly 1000 feet east of the Seboomook Point camping area. [2]It is marked by a granite ledge, 30 feet long and 15 feet high. [3]The ledge faces due south and slopes gradually east. [4]A rock shoal along the westerly frontage extends about 30 feet from the shoreline. [5]On the easterly end of the frontage is a landing area on a small gravel beach immediately to the right of the ledge. [6]Lot boundaries are marked by yellow stakes a few feet from the shoreline. [7]Lot numbers are carved on yellow-marked trees adjacent to the yellow stakes.

The above paragraph, written to help a soil engineer locate the property by boat, follows a spatial order, moving from whole to parts—the same order in which we would actually view the property. Instead of a standard topic statement, the paragraph begins with a simple description, which nonetheless gives us a definite sense of what to expect.

Because the goal above is referential, only factual information appears: a brief but specific catalog of the lot's major features. Other situations might call for more specifics. For instance, the soil engineer's evaluation of the Moosehead site, written for officials who approve building permits, might look like this:

Hand-dug test holes revealed a well-draining, granular material, with a depth of at least 48 inches to bedrock.

The quantity of detail in a description is keyed to the writer's purpose and the audience's needs.

USING SUBJECTIVE DESCRIPTION TO MAKE A POINT

No useful description can be strictly subjective; to get the picture, readers need some observable details. Subjective description colors objective details with personal impressions and metaphors. It usually strives to draw readers into the writer's view of the world, often by creating a mood or sharing a feeling, as shown in the italicized expressions on page 160.

....

USING DESCRIPTION BEYOND THE WRITING CLASSROOM

■ **In other courses:** Whether you are describing a lab experiment, a field trip or a fire hazard in the dorm, you would focus on the observable details, not on your feelings. What specific types of objective description have you written in other courses?

■ **In the workplace:** Your descriptions might inform customers about a new product or service. Banks require applicants for loans to describe the property or venture. Architects and engineers would describe their proposed building on paper before construction begins. Medical professionals write detailed records of a patient's condition and treatment. Whenever readers need to visualize the item itself, objective description is essential. What specific types of objective description do you expect to write in your career?

■ **In the community:** You might describe the problems with discipline or drugs or violence or overcrowding at the local junior high in an attempt to increase community awareness.

Can you think of other situations in which objective description could make a difference?

A Subjective Description

[1]One of my own favorite approaches to a rocky seacoast is by a rough path through an evergreen forest that has its own peculiar enchantment. [2]It is usually an early morning tide that takes me along the forest path, so that the light is still pale and the fog drifts in from the sea beyond. [3]It is almost a *ghost forest,* for among the living spruce and balsam are many dead trees—some still erect, some sagging earthward, some lying on the floor of the forest. [4]All the trees, the living and the dead, are *clothed* with green and silver crusts of lichens. Tufts of the bearded lichen or old man's beard hang from the branches *like bits of sea mist* tangled there. [5]Green woodland mosses and a *yielding carpet* of reindeer moss cover the ground. [6]In the quiet of that place even the *voice* of the surf is reduced to a *whispered echo* and the sounds of the forest are but the *ghosts of sound*—the *faint sighing* of evergreen needles in the moving air; the creaks and heavier groans of half-fallen trees *resting against their neighbors* and rubbing bark against bark; the *light rattling* fall of a dead branch broken under the feet of a squirrel and sent bouncing and ricocheting earthward. [emphasis added]

—*Rachel L. Carson*

Carson's paragraph blends objective and subjective description to help us visualize a forest with "its own peculiar enchantment." Concrete and specific details—the "early morning . . . light is still pale and the fog drifts in . . ."; "all the trees are clothed with green and silver crusts of lichens"—are those any reader could visualize. But these details alone would not persuade readers to share the dominant impression of "peculiar enchantment." To create that special mood, the writer filtered the facts through her own feelings.

Beyond creating a mood or sharing a feeling, description can serve practical purposes. For example, Rachel Carson used her vivid writing to enlist readers against the use of deadly pesticides. The following selection also conveys personal impressions to make a persuasive point.

Subjective Description in Persuasive Writing

Close your eyes for a moment, and picture a professional baseball game. You probably see something like this: a hot summer afternoon, complete with sizzling bats, fans clad in the reds and yellows and pastels of summer, and short-sleeved vendors yelling "ICE CREAM HEEERE!" If you recall some recent World Series, though, you might envision a scene more like this: a c-c-cold starlit night highlighted by players in Thinsulate gloves and turtlenecks, fans in ski hats instead of baseball caps, and vendors hurriedly hawking coffee. This "football-like" image suggests that baseball season is just plain too long!

—Mike Cabral

GUIDELINES FOR DESCRIPTION

1. *Always begin with some type of orienting statement.*   Objective descriptions rarely call for a standard topic or thesis statement, because their goal merely is to catalog the details that readers can visualize. Any description, however, should begin by telling readers what to look for.

2. *Choose descriptive details to suit your purpose and the reader's needs.*   Brainstorming yields more details than a writer can use. Select only those details that advance your meaning. Use objective details to provide a clear and exact picture and subjective details to convey your point.

3. *Select details that are concrete and specific enough to convey an unmistakable picture.*

Most often description works best at the lowest levels of abstraction and generality.

Vague	Exact
at high speed	80 miles an hour
a tiny office	an 8-by-12-foot office
some workers	the accounting staff
a high salary	$80,000 per year

4. *Order details in a clear sequence.*   Descriptions generally follow a spatial or general-to-specific order—whichever parallels the angle of vision readers would have if viewing the item. Or the details are arranged according to the dominant impression desired.

Similarly, a colorful description of your messy dorm or apartment might encourage roommates to clean up their act. Or a nauseating catalog of greasy food served in the college dining hall might prompt school officials to improve the menu. Subjective writing can move readers to see things your way.

USING OBJECTIVE NARRATION TO EXPLAIN

To see how narration, like description, can serve both referential and persuasive purposes, let's look first at narration that informs, reports, or explains. These narratives simply give a picture of what happened, without stating—or even implying—any particular viewpoint. Newspaper stories or courtroom testimonies often provide only the bare facts. This next paragraph simply describes events without inserting personal impressions.

A Narrative that Merely Reports

The climactic scene (1)

A related detail (2)

Background (3–9)

Conclusion (10–11)

[1]Two [suspects] hobbled into Federal Court in Brooklyn on crutches yesterday, each with a leg missing and each charged with smuggling cocaine and marijuana stored in the hollowed-out parts of their confiscated artificial limbs. [2]A third suspect, a . . . woman, was also accused of taking part in the smuggling of $1 million worth of cocaine from Bogota to Kennedy International Airport. [3]Acting on confidential information, customs agents took the three into custody Monday night. [4]The agents took one of the suspects . . . to St. Vincent's Hospital in Manhattan, where physicians removed his plastic leg. [5]Inside, they said, they found one kilo (2.2 pounds) of cocaine wrapped in plastic bags. [6]The suspect told them he had lost his leg during a guerrilla uprising in Colombia two years ago. [7]Agents said they found six ounces of marijuana in the artificial right limb worn by . . . another suspect. [8]The woman . . . was allegedly found to be wearing three girdles, each concealing quantities of plastic-wrapped cocaine totaling one kilo. [9]Agents reported that each suspect had more than $400 and return tickets to Bogota. [10]United States Magistrate Vincent A. Catoggio held each in $100,000 bail. [11]Expressing concern over the missing artificial limbs, which had been described as damaged, he directed that customs agents return them in good condition. . . .

—*The New York Times*

This paragraph implies no main point. The writer simply reports the details of the bizarre smuggling strategy.

Note, however, that the writer juggles the sequence of events to attract our interest. The first two sentences place us at the story's climax. Then the background details follow strict chronological order so that we can keep track of events leading to the courtroom scene. Consistent use of past tense and third-person point of view helps us follow the story.

Using Narrative Reports Beyond the Writing Classroom

- **In other courses:** You might report on experiments or investigations in chemistry, biology, or psychology. Or you might retrace the events leading up to the Russian Revolution or the 1929 stock market crash. What specific types of narrative reports have you written in other courses?

- **On the job:** You might report on the events that led up to an accident on the assembly line or provide daily accounts of your crew's progress on a construction project. Whenever readers need to understand *what happened,* narrative reporting is essential. What specific types of narrative reports might you write in your career?

- **In the community:** As a witness to an accident, a crime, or some other incident, you might report what took place.

In what other situations might a narrative report make a difference?

USING SUBJECTIVE NARRATION TO MAKE A POINT

Narration can be an excellent strategy for advancing some definite viewpoint or thesis. When you recount last night's date, your purpose usually is to suggest a particular viewpoint: say, that some people can be fickle, or that first dates can be disastrous. This next story of a scene witnessed from a commuter train makes the point that urban dwellers can become desensitized to tragedy.

A Narrative that Makes a Point

Orienting sentence

[1]One afternoon in late August, as the summer's sun streamed into the car and made little jumping shadows on the windows, I sat gazing out at the tenement-dwellers, who were themselves looking out of their windows from the gray crumbling buildings along the tracks of upper Manhattan. [2]As we crossed into the Bronx, the train unexpectedly slowed down for a few miles. [3]Suddenly from out of my window I saw a large crowd near the tracks, held back by two policemen. [4]Then, on the other side, from my window, I saw a sight I would never be able to forget: a little boy almost severed in halves, lying at an incredible angle near the track. [5]The ground was covered with blood, and the boy's eyes were opened wide, strained and disbelieving in his

> sudden oblivion. [6]A policeman stood next to him, his arms folded, staring straight at the windows of our train. [7]In the orange glow of late afternoon, the policeman, the crowd, the corpse of the boy were for a brief moment immobile, motionless, a small tableau to violence and death in the city. [8]Behind me, in the next row of seats, was a game of bridge. [9]I heard one of the four men say as he looked out at the sight, "God, that's horrible." [10]Another said in a whisper, "Terrible, terrible." [11]There was a momentary silence, punctuated only by the clicking of the wheels on the track. [12]Then, after a pause, I heard the first man say: "Two hearts."
>
> —Willie Morris

Although the awful details of this story are filtered only slightly through the author's own impressions (sentences 4, 5, and 7), the point implied is all too clear. Sometimes, narration can be the best form of showing.

Past tense and first-person point of view give Morris's paragraph a consistent sense of direction (the writer tells of his own experience). An alternative point of view for narration is the third person (telling of someone else's experience).

Like description, narratives also can move readers to change their attitudes or take action. For instance, you might tell about a boating accident to elicit voter support for tougher boating laws. You might recount the details of a conflict among employees to persuade your boss to institute a stress-management program. By telling the story, you can help readers see things your way.

Subjective Narration in Persuasive Writing

> I entered community college at 17 and began taking classes with some 25- and 30-year-old students. Such an age difference made me feel much luckier than these older people. What were they doing in a freshman class, anyway? Compared to them, I had unlimited time to succeed—or so I thought. Soon after my eighteenth birthday, the horrid piece of lung tissue I coughed into the sink gave a whole new meaning to my notion of "youth." Five years of inhaling hot smoke, carbon monoxide, nicotine, and tobacco pesticides finally had produced enough coughing and sickness to terrify me. "Oh, my god, I'm going to die young; I'm going to die before all those 30-year-olds." For years, I had heard my mother tell me that I was committing suicide on the installment plan. Now I seemed to be running out of installments.
>
> —Chris Adey

By letting the story make the point, Chris's narrative seems more persuasive than the usual sermons: "Smoking is bad for you," and so on.

The main point in a narrative might be expressed as a topic or thesis statement at the beginning or end of the story. Or, as in the two narratives above, the main point might not be stated at all, but only implied by the story. But even when its point is saved for last or just implied, the story often opens with some statement that orients readers to the events.

The most powerful narratives often are those that combine objective and subjective details to reveal their point. In the following essay, an African American explores how a black man can induce paranoia among people who react to a racial stereotype. As you read, think about how the writer's analysis compels the audience to examine their biases.

BLACK MEN AND PUBLIC SPACE

My first victim was a woman—white, well dressed, probably in her early twenties. I came upon her late one evening on a deserted street in Hyde Park, a relatively affluent neighborhood in an otherwise mean, impoverished section of Chicago. As I swung onto the avenue behind her, there seemed to be a discreet, uninflammatory distance between us. Not so. She cast back a worried glance. To her, the youngish black man—a broad six feet two inches with a beard and billowing hair, both hands shoved into the pockets of a bulky military jacket—seemed menacingly close. After a few more quick glimpses, she picked up her pace and was soon running in earnest. Within seconds she disappeared into a cross street.

That was more than a decade ago. I was twenty-two years old, a graduate student newly arrived at the University of Chicago. It was in the echo of that terrified woman's footfalls that I first began to know the unwieldy inheritance I'd come into—the ability to alter public space in ugly ways. It was clear that she thought herself the quarry of a mugger, a rapist, or worse. Suffering from a bout of insomnia, however, I was stalking sleep, not defenseless wayfarers. As a softy who is scarcely able to take a knife to a raw chicken—let alone hold one to a person's throat—I was surprised, embarrassed, and dismayed all at once. Her flight made me feel like an accomplice in tyranny. It also made it clear that I was indistinguishable from the muggers who occasionally seeped into the area from the surrounding ghetto. That first encounter, and those that followed, signified that a vast, unnerving gulf lay between nighttime pedestrians—particularly women—and me. And I soon gathered that being perceived as dangerous is a hazard in itself. I only needed to turn a corner into a dicey situation, or crowd some frightened, armed person in a foyer somewhere, or make an errant move after being pulled over by a policeman. Where fear and weapons meet—and they often do in urban America—there is always the possibility of death.

In that first year, my first away from my hometown, I was to become thoroughly familiar with the language of fear. At dark, shadowy intersections, I could cross in front of a car stopped at a traffic light and elicit the thunk, thunk, thunk, thunk of the driver—black, white, male, or female—hammering down the door locks. On less traveled streets after dark, I grew accustomed to but never comfortable with people crossing to the other side of the street rather than pass me. Then there were the standard unpleasantries with policemen, doormen, bouncers, cabdrivers, and others whose business it is to screen out troublesome individuals before there is any nastiness.

I moved to New York nearly two years ago and I have remained an avid night walker. In central Manhattan, the near-constant crowd cover minimizes tense one-on-one street encounters. Elsewhere—in SoHo, for example, where sidewalks are narrow and tightly spaced buildings shut out the sky—things can get very taut indeed.

After dark, on the warrenlike streets of Brooklyn where I live, I often see women who fear the worst from me. They seem to have set their faces on neutral, and with their purse straps strung across their chests bandolier-style, they forge ahead as though bracing themselves against being tackled. I understand, of course, that the danger they perceive is not a hallucination. Women are particularly vulnerable to street violence, and young black males are drastically overrepresented among the perpetrators of that violence. Yet these truths are no solace against the kind of alienation that comes of being ever the suspect, a fearsome entity with whom pedestrians avoid making eye contact.

It is not altogether clear to me how I reached the ripe old age of twenty-two without being conscious of the lethality nighttime pedestrians attributed to me. Perhaps it was because in Chester, Pennsylvania, the small, angry industrial town where I came of age in the 1960s, I was scarcely noticeable against a backdrop of gang warfare, street knifings, and murders. I grew up one of the good boys, had perhaps a half-dozen fistfights. In retrospect, my shyness of combat has clear sources.

As a boy, I saw countless tough guys locked away; I have since buried several, too. They were babies, really—a teenage cousin, a brother of twenty-two, a childhood friend in his mid-twenties—all gone down in episodes of bravado played out in the streets. I came to doubt the virtues of intimidation early on. I chose, perhaps unconsciously, to remain a shadow—timid, but a survivor.

The fearsomeness mistakenly attributed to me in public places often has a perilous flavor. The most frightening of these confusions occurred in the late 1970s and early 1980s, when I worked as a journalist in Chicago. One day, rushing into the office of a magazine I was writing for with a deadline story in hand, I was mistaken for a burglar. The office manager called security and, with an ad hoc posse, pursued me through the labyrinthine halls, nearly to my editor's door. I had no way of proving who I was. I could only move briskly toward the company of someone who knew me.

Another time I was on assignment for a local paper and killing time before an interview. I entered a jewelry store on the city's affluent Near North Side. The proprietor excused herself and returned with an enormous red Doberman pinscher straining at the end of a leash. She stood, the dog extended toward me, silent to my questions, her eyes bulging nearly out of her head. I took a cursory look around, nodded, and bade her good night.

GUIDELINES FOR NARRATION

1. *Convey your viewpoint, whether stated or implied, through the narrative details.*   A narrative that simply reports, of course, has no main point. But when the main point is stated, the topic or thesis statement often appears at the end. The narrative always begins with a clear orienting statement that places readers at the center of the action.

2. *Choose details to serve specifically your purpose and the reader's needs.*   Again, select only those details that directly advance your meaning. Focus on the important details, but don't leave out lesser details that hold the story together. Decide whether to filter the events through your own impressions.

3. *Choose details that are concrete and specific enough to show clearly what happened.*   Narration is most effective at the lowest levels of abstraction and generality. Whenever you can, show people talking.

4. *Order details in a clear sequence.*   Chronological ordering often works best in a narrative, because it enables readers to follow events as they occurred. But for special emphasis, the sequence sometimes can be revised (as in the paragraph by Willie Morris, pages 163–164).

5. *Use consistent tense and point of view, as well as transitions as time and sequence markers, to provide coherence.*   Instead of past tense, you might use present tense to create a greater sense of immediacy, making readers feel like actual participants. Also, decide whether you are writing from the point of view of a spectator, a participant, or both (as in "Back at the Ranch," pages 169–171), and stick to that one point of view. Review pages 101–103 for use of transitions.

Relatively speaking, however, I never fared as badly as another black male journalist. He went to nearby Waukegan, Illinois a couple of summers ago to work on a story about a murderer who was born there. Mistaking the reporter for the killer, police officers hauled him from his car at gunpoint and but for his press credentials would probably have tried to book him. Such episodes are not uncommon. Black men trade tales like this all the time.

Over the years, I learned to smother the rage I felt at so often being taken for a criminal. Not to do so would surely have led to madness. I now take precautions to make myself less threatening. I move about with care, particularly late in the evening. I give a wide berth to nervous people on subway platforms during the wee hours, particularly when I have exchanged business clothes for jeans. If I happen to be entering a building behind some people who appear skittish, I may walk by, letting them clear the lobby before I return, so as not to seem to be following them. I have been calm and extremely congenial on those rare occasions when I've been pulled over by the police.

> And on late-evening constitutionals I employ what has proved to be an excellent tension-reducing measure: I whistle melodies from Beethoven and Vivaldi and the more popular classical composers. Even steely New Yorkers bunching toward nighttime destinations seem to relax, and occasionally they even join in the tune. Virtually everybody seems to sense that a mugger wouldn't be warbling bright, sunny selections from Vivaldi's Four Seasons. It is my equivalent of the cowbell that hikers wear when they know they are in bear country.
>
> —*Brent Staples*

Staples analyzes the links between events to argue that a racial stereotype has a double effect: in narrowing the perceptions of those who impose the stereotype, and in narrowing the choices of those who endure the stereotype.

Can you identify five memorable objective details in Staples' narrative? Five subjective ones?

APPLICATION 10-1

Paragraph Warm-Up: Description that Informs

Assume that a close friend has been missing for two days. The police have been called in. Because you know this person well, the police have asked you for a written description. Write an objective description that would help the police identify this person. To create a clear picture, stick to details any observer could recognize. If possible, include one or more unique identifying features (scar, mannerisms, and so on). Leave out personal comments, and give only objective details. Refer to Guidelines for Description, page 161. Use the paragraph on page 97 as a model.

APPLICATION 10-2

Paragraph Warm-Up: Description that Makes a Point

Assume that your college newspaper runs a weekly column titled "Memorable Characters." You have been asked to submit a brief sketch of a person you find striking in some way. Create a word portrait of this person in one paragraph. Your description should focus on a dominant impression, blending objective details and subjective commentary. Be sure to focus on personal characteristics that support your dominant impression. Develop your description according to the Guidelines for Description on page 161.

APPLICATION 10-3

Paragraph Warm-Up: Narration that Informs

Assume that you have recently witnessed an event or accident in which someone has been accused of an offense. Because you are an objective witness, the authorities have asked you to write a short report, telling them exactly what you saw. Your report will be used as evidence. Tell what happened without injecting personal impressions or interpretations. Refer to the Guidelines for Narration on page 167.

APPLICATION 10-4

Paragraph Warm-Up: Narration that Makes a Point

Tell about a recent experience or incident you witnessed that left a strong impression on you. Write for your classmates, and be sure to include the facts of the incident as well as your emotional reaction to it. In other words, give your audience enough details so that they will understand and ideally share your reaction. Use Willie Morris's or Chris Adey's paragraph as a model, letting the details of the story imply your main point. Refer to the Guidelines for Narration on page 167.

APPLICATION 10-5

Essay Practice

The following narrative, "Back at the Ranch," recalls how a dreadful moment during the writer's adolescence changed his own perception of "manhood."

ESSAY FOR ANALYSIS AND RESPONSE

BACK AT THE RANCH

A young boy molts. Tender skin falls off, or gets scraped off, and is replaced by a tougher, more permanent crust. The transition happens in moments, in events. All of a sudden, something is gone and something else is in its place. I made a change like that standing in the back of a pickup truck when I was 15.

It was 1967 and I had a summer job at a camp in Wyoming. It was beautiful there, high-pasture country with a postcard view of the Tetons. As an apprentice counselor I straddled the worlds of boys and men, breathing the high air, watching over kids, hanging out with cowboys. The cowboys wrangled the horses for the camp and were mostly an itinerant group, living in summer cabins below the barn, and they tolerated my loitering down there. I hitched up my jeans just like them, braided my lasso like them, smoked and cursed and slouched like them.

On the day it happened, I was standing with a group of cowboys by the ranch office. We heard the sound of a big engine coming in the long driveway, and after a while a red Corvette Sting Ray convertible, of all things, motored up in front of us. Conversation stopped. In the driver's seat was a hippie. His hair fell straight down his back and a bandanna was tied around his head. His style may have been standard for somewhere, but not for Jackson, Wyo.

The guy was decked out with beads and earrings and dressed in fantastic colors, and next to him his girlfriend, just as exotic, with perfect blond hair, looked up at us over little square glasses with a distracted, angelic expression. All in a red Corvette.

I was fascinated, mesmerized. I looked around me with a big grin and realized that I was alone in this feeling. The cowboys all had hard stares, cold eyes. I adjusted, a traitor to myself, and blanked out my expression in kind.

The hippie opened up a big smile, and said: "I went to camp here when I was a kid . . . came by to say hi. Is Weenie around?"

In that moment, Weenie, the owner of the place, having heard the throb of the engine, appeared in the ranch office door and walked toward us with a bowlegged stride, his big belt buckle coming first. He walked right up to the driver and looked down on him.

"Get out." Weenie didn't say hi. "Get out of here now."

"What? Wait a minute. I came to say hi. I went to camp here. I just came to say hi."

"Get the hell off this ranch. Now." And staring at the hippie, Weenie kicked some dust up on the side of the Corvette.

"What's wrong with you, man?"

"You're what's wrong with me, son."

I noticed the cowboys were nodding. I nodded. Weenie's right. The guy should leave. He doesn't belong here.

"But you sent me a Christmas card!" By this time, the hippie had choked up a little. "I don't believe it. You sent me a goddam Christmas card!"

The group of us closed in a little around the car. We-don't-like-that-kind-of-talk-from-a-hippie was the feeling I was getting. Thumbs came out of belt-loops. Jaws began to work.

"Looks like the little girlie's cryin'," said one of the cowboys, a tough one named Hondu. He spoke with his lips turned down on one side as if he was mouthing a cigarette. "Maybe so," said another, with mock consideration.

The notion rested in the air peacefully for a moment, then, in a sudden whipping motion, Hondu's jackknife was out, open and raised. With his other hand, he reached down and grabbed a fat bunch of the hippie's hair and pulled it toward him. Smiling grimly, he hacked it off and held it up for us to see.

During this, I looked down at the hippie's face, which was lifted up and sideways in such a way that he was looking right at me. Involuntarily, my head tilted just like his and we froze like that for a second.

"There now, that's better, ain't it?" asked Hondu.

The hippie, stunned, turned to his girlfriend, whose eyes and mouth had been wide open as long as he had been sitting there. Then he turned back to us, his face contorted, helpless. And then he went wild. He threw open his door and tried to jump up from the seat, but forgot that his seat belt was fastened and it held him in place. He struggled against it, scream-ing, swinging his arms like a bar fighter trying to shrug off his buddies re-straining him. It was funny. Like a cartoon.

I looked around. We were all laughing. Our group closed up a little more, and came toward the car. The air bristled. He was the one who started the trouble. Well, he would get what he was looking for, all right.

The hippie stopped struggling, threw the Vette into gear, and fishtailed in the dust. We all jumped out of the way, but the open door of the car bumped into Weenie's favorite dog, a Rhodesian Ridgeback, an inside-out-looking animal that gave a wild yelp and ran straight into a willow thicket. We could hear his yips over the sound of the big engine as the hippie gunned it and took off.

That settled it. The hippie hit the dog.

Without hesitation, we jumped into one of the trucks. Rifles were drawn from the rack in the cab. Other weapons were thrown up into the bed of the pickup. I was standing there and caught one.

We took off, and because the rough road slowed down the Corvette, we were gaining. I was filled with a terrible, frightening righteousness. I was holding a rifle, chasing a man and a woman with a rifle in my hand. I looked around at my partners in the truck, and the air came out of me. We meant harm. We didn't care. I wondered who I was exactly. I needed to know. And in that moment, it happened: I switched sides and never said a word about it.

We hit the asphalt road and floored it, but we couldn't catch the Corvette. No way. The smoke from its exhaust settled around us like fog in the valley.

Still, 23 years later, I can see the two of us clearly, chosen by the same moment. Memory cuts back and forth between our faces. The wind pulls tears from the hippie's eyes; his long hair waves behind him in his fiery con-vertible rocketing down Route 191 under the Tetons. I with my short hair stand in the back of a pickup truck watching after him, chasing after him, following, facing the same wind.

—Jay Allison

QUESTIONS ABOUT THE READING

Refer to the general questions on page 155 as well as these specific questions:

CONTENT

- Does this essay merely inform or does it make a point, and if so, what is the point?
- In your view what does Allison want the audience to be thinking or feeling after reading this piece?
- Does the essay succeed in making a difference with readers? If so, how?
- Can you identify any new insights or unusual perspectives?

ORGANIZATION

- What major devices lend coherence to this narrative? Give examples of each.

STYLE

- What about the short sentences and paragraphs? Are they effective? Explain.
- What is the writer's attitude toward his subject, toward his audience? How do we know? What are the signals?
- Which images here most help us visualize?

RESPONDING TO YOUR READING

"Back at the Ranch" proves that an essay about "What I Did Last Summer" can be much more than a tired list of worn-out images and travel clichés—that telling your own story can make a difference. Explore your reactions to this essay by using the questions on page 23. Then respond with your own narrative about an event that has made a difference in your life. Work to recapture for the reader the force of the event and its impact on you. Write in detail about what happened, but be sure to let him or her know what meaning the event ultimately had for you.

APPLICATION 10-6

Computer Application: Working from your group computer or E-mail network, exchange your reactions to "Back at the Ranch" with a classmate. Respond to each other's reactions, noting where you agree and disagree.

OPTIONS FOR ESSAY WRITING

1. Explore your reactions to "Black Men and Public Space" by using the questions on page 23 and those below.

   - For whom does Staples seem to be writing?
   - What assumptions does he make about his audience's knowledge and attitudes? Are these assumptions accurate? Why or why not?
   - What are the main issues here? How has this essay affected your thinking about these issues?
   - What point is Staples making about stereotypes?
   - What is this writer's attitude toward his subject? Toward his audience? How do we know? What are the signals?
   - How would you characterize the tone of this essay? Is it appropriate for this writer's audience and purpose?

   Most of us want to be liked, accepted, and respected. As you reread the essay, try to recall a situation in which you or a close person were the object of someone's hostility or rejection—say, because of resentment or fear or anger or scorn. (Or perhaps someone else was the object of yours!) Perhaps the reaction was based on a stereotype or misunderstanding or personal bias. Perhaps, after realizing rejection, you modified your behavior to fit in; you invented a self that seemed more acceptable. Identify your audience, and decide what you want these readers to be doing or thinking or feeling after reading your essay.

   Describe the events and your reactions in enough detail for readers to visualize what happened and what resulted. Without preaching or moralizing, try to explain your view of this experience's *larger meaning*.

2. Do you have a hero or villain? Describe this person in an essay for your classmates. Provide enough descriptive details for your audience to understand why you admire or despise this person. Supply at least three characteristics to support your dominant impression.

3. Assume that you are applying for your first professional job after college. Respond to the following request from the job application:

   Each of us has been confronted by an "impossible situation"—a job that appeared too big to complete, a situation that seemed too awkward to handle, or a problem that felt too complex to deal with. Describe such a situation and how you dealt with it. Your narrative should make a point about the situation, problem solving, or yourself.

4. Tell about the event that has caused you the greatest guilt and how you have dealt with that guilt.

ILLUSTRATING FOR READERS

*T*he backbone of explanation, *examples* are concrete and specific instances of a writer's main point.

What readers expect to learn from examples

- *What makes you think so?*
- *Can you show me?*

Examples provide the evidence that enables readers to understand your meaning and accept your viewpoint. The best way to illustrate what you mean by an "inspiring teacher" is to use one of your professors as an example. You might illustrate this professor's qualities by describing several of her teaching strategies. Or you might give an extended example (say, how she helped you develop confidence). Either way, you have made the abstract notion "inspiring teacher" concrete and thus understandable. (Notice how this paragraph's main point is clarified by the professor example.)

USING ILLUSTRATION BEYOND THE WRITING CLASSROOM

- **In other courses:** For a psychology course, you might give examples of paranoid behavior among world leaders; for an ecology course, an example of tree species threatened by acid rain.
- **On the job:** You might give examples of how the software developed by your company can be used in medical diagnosis, or examples of how certain investments have performed in the recent decade.
- **In the community:** You might give examples of how your town can provide a favorable economic climate for new industry, or examples of how other towns have coped with cutbacks in school funding.

What other specific uses of examples can you envision in any of the above three areas?

USING EXAMPLES TO EXPLAIN

In referential writing, *examples help readers grasp an abstract term or a complex principle.* You could explain what grunge music is by pointing out examples of well-known bands that have incorporated its influence. Or suppose you wanted to explain how the *liberal arts* have practical value in one's career; for this purpose, the paragraph below would not be very understandable:

A Passage Needing Examples

The irony of the emphasis being placed on careers is that nothing is more valuable for anyone who has had a professional or vocational education than to be able to deal with abstractions or complexities, or to feel comfortable with subtleties of thought or language, or to think sequentially. People who have such skills will have a major advantage in just about any career. In all these respects, the liberal arts have much to offer. Just in terms of career preparation, therefore, a student is shortchanging himself or herself by shortcutting the humanities.

Because this paragraph tells, but doesn't show, it fails to make a convincing case for a liberal arts education. Any reader will have unanswered questions:

- *What do you mean by "abstractions or complexities," "subtleties of thought or language," or "to think sequentially"?*
- *How, exactly, do students "shortchange" themselves by shortcutting the humanities?*
- *Can you show me how a liberal arts education is useful in one's career?*

Now consider the revised version of the same paragraph:

A Revision that Includes Examples

Main point (1)

¹The irony of the emphasis being placed on careers is that nothing is more valuable for anyone who has had a professional or vocational education than to be able to deal with abstractions or complexities, or to feel comfortable with subtleties of thought or language, or to think sequentially. ²*The doctor* who knows only disease is at a disadvantage alongside the doctor who knows at least as much about people as [he or she] does about pathological organisms. ³*The lawyer* who argues in court from a narrow legal base is no match for the lawyer who can connect legal precedents to historical experience and who employs wide-ranging intellectual resources. ⁴*The business executive* whose competence in general management is bolstered by an artistic ability to deal with people is of prime value to [her] company. ⁵For *the technologist,* the engineering of consent can be just as important as the engineering of moving parts. ⁶In all these respects, the liberal arts have much to offer. ⁷Just in terms of career preparation, therefore, a student is short-changing himself by shortcutting the humanities. [*emphasis added*]

Examples (2–5)

Summary (6)
Conclusion (7)

—*Norman Cousins*

The examples (in italics) help convince us that the author has a valid point.

USING EXAMPLES TO MAKE A POINT

Because examples so often provide the evidence to back up assertions, they have great persuasive power. For one thing, they can make writing more convincing simply by making it more interesting. This next writing sample employs vivid examples to express outrage over a proposal to "improve" national parks through commercial development.

Examples that Make a Point
LABOR DAY

Now here comes another clown with a scheme for the utopian national park: Central Park National Park, Disneyland National Park. Look here, he says, what's the matter with you fellows?—let's get cracking with this dump. Your road is bad; pave it. Better yet, build a paved road to every corner of the park; better yet, pave the whole damned place so any damn fool can drive anything anywhere—is this a democracy or ain't it? Next, charge a good stiff admission fee, you can't let people in free; that leads to socialism and regimentation. Next, get rid of all these homely rangers in their Smokey the Bear suits. Hire a crew of pretty girls, call them rangerettes, let them sell the tickets and give the campfire talks. And advertise, for godsake, advertise! How do you expect to get people in here if you don't advertise? Next, these here Arches—light them up. Floodlight them, turn on colored, revolving lights—jazz it up, man, it's dead. Light up the whole place, all night long, get on a 24-hour shift, keep them coming, keep them moving, you got two hundred million people out there waiting to see your product—is this a free country or what the hell is it? Next your campgrounds, you gotta do something about your campgrounds, they're a mess. People can't tell where to park their cars or which spot is whose—you gotta paint lines, numbers, mark out the campsites nice and neat. And they're still building fires on the ground, with wood! Very messy, filthy, wasteful. Set up little grills on stilts, sell charcoal briquettes, better yet hook up with the gas line, install jets and burners. Better yet do away with the campgrounds altogether, they only cause delay and congestion and administrative problems—these people want to see America, they're not going to see it sitting around a goddamned campfire; take their money, give them the show, send them on their way—that's the way to run a business. . . .

I exaggerate. Slightly. Was he real or only a bad dream? Am I awake or sleeping? Will Tuesday never come? No wonder they call it Labor Day.

—*Edward Abbey*

In what order (chronological, general-to-specific, and so on) are the above examples presented? Is this order effective? Explain.

In contrast to the previous writing sample, with its series of brief examples, this next persuasive paragraph relies on two extended examples:

Extended Examples

Main point (1)
Extended example of
the problem (2–6)

Extended example of
the solution (8–11)

Conclusion (12)

¹This seems to be an era of gratuitous inventions and negative improvements. ²Consider the beer can. ³It was beautiful—as beautiful as the clothespin, as inevitable as the wine bottle, as dignified and reassuring as the fire hydrant. ⁴A tranquil cylinder of delightfully resonant metal, it could be opened in an instant, requiring only the application of a hand gadget freely dispensed by any grocer. ⁵Who can forget the small, symmetrical thrill of these two triangular punctures, the dainty pfff, the little crest of suds that foamed eagerly in the exultation of release? ⁶Now we are given, instead, a top beetling with an ugly, shmoo-shaped "tab," which, after fiercely resisting the tugging, bleeding fingers of the thirsty [person], threatens [the] lips with a dangerous and hideous hole. ⁷However, we have discovered a way to thwart Progress, usually so unthwartable. ⁸Turn the beer can upside down and open the bottom. ⁹The bottom is still the way the top used to be. ¹⁰True, this operation gives the beer an unsettling jolt, and the sight of a consistently inverted beer can might make people edgy, not to say queasy. ¹¹But the latter difficulty could be eliminated if manufacturers would design cans that looked the same whichever end was up, like playing cards. ¹²What we need is Progress with an escape hatch.

—*John Updike*

To support his notion that "gratuitous inventions and negative improvements" masquerade as Progress, Updike selects the familiar example of the beer can. His purpose, however, is not only to point out the problem but also to offer a solution. Thus the two extended examples follow a logical order: from problem to solution.

GUIDELINES FOR ILLUSTRATING WITH EXAMPLES

1. *Fit the examples to your purpose and the readers' needs.*   An effective example fits the point it is designed to illustrate. Also, the example is familiar and forceful enough for readers to recognize and remember.

2. *Make the example more specific and concrete than the point it illustrates.*   Vivid examples usually occupy the lowest level of generality and abstraction.

3. *Arrange examples in a series in an accessible order.*   If your illustration is a narrative or some historical catalog, order your examples chronologically. Otherwise, try a "least-to-most" (least-to-most-dramatic or important or useful) order. Placing the most striking example last ensures greatest effect.

4. *Know "how much is enough."*   Overexplaining insults a reader's intelligence.

··

APPLICATION 11-1

Paragraph Warm-Up: Using Examples to Explain

Pierre, a French student who plans to attend an American university, has asked what the typical American college student is like. He has inquired about interests, activities, attitudes, and tastes. Selecting one or more characteristics *you* think typify American college students, write a response to Pierre.

··

APPLICATION 11-2

Paragraph Warm-Up: Using Examples to Make a Point

Assume your campus newspaper is inviting contributions for a new section called "Insights," a weekly collection of one-paragraph essays by students. Student contributors should focus on examples gained by close observation of campus life and American values or habits to offer some fresh insight on a problem facing our culture. Using the paragraph by Cousins or Updike as a model, write such a paragraph for the newspaper. Choose examples to convince your audience that the problem you discuss really exists.

··

APPLICATION 11-3

Essay Practice

The following essay appeared in *Newsweek* magazine. Read this essay, and answer the questions that follow it, as well as those on page 155 of the Introduction. Then select one of the essay assignments.

ESSAY FOR ANALYSIS AND RESPONSE

A CASE OF "SEVERE BIAS"

[1]This is who I am not. I am not a crack addict. I am not a welfare mother. I am not illiterate. I am not a prostitute. I have never been in jail. My children are not in gangs. My husband doesn't beat me. My home is not a tenement. None of these things defines who I am, nor do they describe the other black people I've known and worked with and loved and befriended over these 40 years of my life.

[2]Nor does it describe most of black America, period.

[3]Yet in the eyes of the American news media, this is what black America is: poor, criminal, addicted and dysfunctional. Indeed, media coverage of black America is so one-sided, so imbalanced that the most victimized and hurting segment of the black community—a small segment, at best—is presented not as the exception but as the norm. It is an insidious practice, all the uglier for its blatancy.

[4]In recent months, oftentimes in this very magazine, I have observed a steady offering of media reports on crack babies, gang warfare, violent youth, poverty and homelessness—and in most cases, the people featured in the photos and stories were black. At the same time, articles that discuss other aspects of American life—from home buying to medicine to technology to nutrition—rarely, if ever, show blacks playing a positive role, or for that matter, any role at all.

[5]Day after day, week after week, this message—that black America is dysfunctional and unwhole—gets transmitted across the American landscape. Sadly, as a result, America never learns the truth about what is actually a wonderful, vibrant, creative community of people.

[6]Most black Americans are not poor. Most black teenagers are not crack addicts. Most black mothers are not on welfare. Indeed, in sheer numbers, more white Americans are poor and on welfare than are black. Yet one never would deduce that by watching television or reading American newspapers and magazines.

[7]Why does the American media insist on playing this myopic, inaccurate picture game? In this game, white America is always whole and lovely and healthy while black America is usually sick and pathetic and deficient. Rarely, indeed, is black America ever depicted in the media as functional and self-sufficient. The free press, indeed, as the main interpreter of American culture and American experience, holds the mirror on American reality—so much so that what the media says is, even if it's not that way at all. The media is guilty of a severe bias and the problem screams out for correction. It is worse than simply lazy journalism, which is bad enough; it is inaccurate journalism.

[8]For black Americans like myself, this isn't just an issue of vanity—of wanting to be seen in a good light. Nor is it a matter of closing one's eyes to the very real problems of the urban underclass—which undeniably is disproportionately black. To be sure, problems besetting the black underclass deserve the utmost attention of the media, as well as the understanding and concern of the rest of American society.

[9]But if their problems consistently are presented as the only reality for blacks, any other experience known to the black community ceases to have validity, or to be real. In this scenario, millions of blacks are relegated to a sort of twilight zone, where who we are and what we are isn't based on fact but on image and perception. That's what it feels like to be a black American whose lifestyle is outside of the aberrant behavior that the media presents as the norm.

[10]For many of us, life is a curious series of encounters with white people who want to know why we are "different" from other blacks—when, in fact, most of us are only "different" from the now common negative images of black life. So pervasive are these images that they aren't just perceived as the norm; they're accepted as the norm.

[11]I am reminded, for example, of the controversial Spike Lee film, "Do the Right Thing," and the criticism by some movie reviewers that the film's ghetto neighborhood isn't populated by addicts and drug pushers—and thus is not a true depiction.

[12]In fact, millions of black Americans live in neighborhoods where the most common sights are children playing and couples walking their dogs. In my own inner-city neighborhood in Denver—an area that the local press consistently describes as "gang territory"—I have yet to see a recognizable "gang" member or any "gang" activity (drug dealing or drive-by shootings), nor have I been the victim of "gang violence."

[13]Yet to students of American culture—in the case of Spike Lee's film, the movie reviewers—a black, inner-city neighborhood can only be one thing to be real: drug-infested and dysfunctioning. Is this my ego talking? In part, yes. For the millions of black people like myself—ordinary, hard-working, law-abiding, tax-paying Americans—the media's blindness to the fact that we even exist, let alone to our contributions to American society, is a bitter cup to drink. And as self-reliant as most black Americans are—because we've had to be self-reliant—even the strongest among us still crave affirmation.

[14]I want that. I want it for my children. I want it for all the beautiful, healthy, funny, smart black Americans I have known and loved over the years.

[15]And I want it for the rest of America, too.

[16]I want America to know us—all of us—for who we really are. To see us in all our complexity, our subtleness, our artfulness, our enterprise, our specialness, our loveliness, our American-ness. That is the real portrait of black America—that we're strong people, surviving people, capable people. That may be the best-kept secret in America. If so, it's time to let the truth be known.

—Patricia Raybon

QUESTIONS ABOUT THE READING

Refer to the general questions on page 155 as well as these specific questions.

CONTENT

- What are Raybon's assumptions about her audience's knowledge and attitudes? Are these assumptions accurate? Why or why not?

- Identify one paragraph developed through an extended example and one through a series of brief examples.
- Should the examples be more specific? Why, or why not?

ORGANIZATION

- Is there a purpose behind the ordering of the examples? Explain.
- Are the two single-sentence paragraphs (numbers 2 and 15) appropriate? Explain.

STYLE

- What is the writer's attitude toward her subject? Toward her audience? How do we know? Where are the signals?
- Is the tone appropriate for this writer's audience and purpose? Explain.

RESPONDING TO YOUR READING

Explore your reactions to "A Case of Severe Bias" by using the questions on page 23. Then respond with an essay of your own, using powerful examples to make your point.

Perhaps someone has misjudged or stereotyped you or a group to which you belong. If so, set the record straight in a forceful essay to a specified audience. Or perhaps you can think of other types of media messages that seem to present a distorted or inaccurate view (say, certain commercials or sports reporting or war movies, and so on). For instance, do certain movies or TV programs give the wrong message? Give your readers examples they can recognize and remember.

APPLICATION 11-4

Collaborative Project and Computer Application: If possible, have your teacher set up a "listserv" for your class: a computer address to which you can all send messages that will then be distributed to everyone on the list. Or, set up your own list with some of your classmates by listing their addresses and assigning the list a "nickname": a single, short name that, when typed into the address line on a message, will direct the message to all the addresses you have designated. Use your *listserv* to brainstorm collectively for examples to support one or more claims your group has generated in response to one of the Readings or essay options in this chapter.

OPTIONS FOR ESSAY WRITING

1. Write a human interest essay for your campus newspaper in which you illustrate some feature of our society that you find humorous, depressing, contemptible, or admirable. Possible subjects: our eating, consumer, or dress habits; our idea of a vacation or a good time; the cars we drive, and so on. Provide at least three well-developed examples to make your point. Edward Abbey's passage, page 177, offers one example of how you might approach this assignment.

2. What pleases, disappoints, or surprises you most about college life? Illustrate this topic for your parents (or some other specific audience) with at least three examples.

3. Assume you've been assigned a faculty adviser who likes to know as much as possible about each advisee. The adviser asks each student to write an essay on this topic:

Is your hometown (city, neighborhood) a good or a bad place for a child to grow up?

Notice that you are not asked to write about yourself directly (as in a personal narrative). Support your response with specific examples that will convince the reader of your sound judgment.

CHAPTER 12

EXPLAINING PARTS AND CATEGORIES: DIVISION AND CLASSIFICATION

*D*ivision and classification are both strategies for sorting things out, but each serves a distinct purpose. *Division* deals with *one thing only*. It separates that thing into parts, pieces, sections, or categories—for closer examination (say, an essay divided into introduction, body, and conclusion).

What readers expect to learn from a division

- *What are its parts?*
- *What is it made of?*

Classification deals with *an assortment of things* that share certain similarities. It groups these things systematically (say, a record collection into categories—jazz, rock, country and western, classical, and pop).

What readers expect to learn from a classification

- *What relates to what?*
- *In what categories do X, Y, and Z belong?*

We use division and classification in many aspects of our lives. Say you are shopping for a refrigerator. If you are mechanically inclined, you could begin by thinking about the major parts that make up a refrigerator: storage compartment, cooling element, motor, insulation, and exterior casing. You can now ask questions about these individual parts to determine the efficiency or quality of each part in different kinds of refrigerators. You have *divided* the refrigerator into its components.

After shopping, you come home with a list of 20 refrigerators that seem to be built from high-quality parts. You make sense of your list by grouping items according to selected characteristics. First, you divide your list into three *classes* according to size in cubic feet of capacity: small, middle-sized, and large refrigerators. But you want economy, too, so you group the refrigerators according to cost. Or you might *classify* them according to color, weight, or energy efficiency. Here is how division and classification are related:

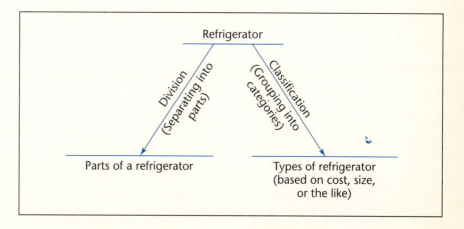

Whether you choose to apply division or classification depends on your purpose. An architect designing a library will think almost entirely of *division*. Once she has defined the large enclosed area that is needed, she must identify the parts into which that space must be divided: the reference area, reading areas, storage areas, checkout facilities, and office space. She might consider providing space for special groups of users (such as reading areas for children). In very large libraries she might need to divide further into specialized kinds of space (such as highly secure areas for rare manuscripts or special collections, or areas with special acoustic provisions for listening to recorded materials). But however simple or complex her problem, she is thinking now only about the appropriate division of space. She is not worrying about how the library will classify its books and other material.

But *classification* is one of the library staff's main problems. The purpose of a library is not only to store books and other forms of information, but above all to make the information retrievable. In order for us to find a book or item, the thousands or millions of books stored in the library must be arranged in logical categories. That arrangement becomes possible only if the books are carefully classified.

USING DIVISION TO EXPLAIN

We encounter referential uses of division every day. Division is used in manuals to help us understand how a computer or a car engine, for example, works. Division allows readers to tackle one aspect of a complex task at a time, as in the following instructions for campers.

A Division that Explains

Before pitching your tent, take the time to prepare the area that will be under the tent. Not only does this step prevent damage to the tent floor, but it also helps you get a good night's sleep. Begin by removing all stones, branches and other debris. Use your camping shovel for anything too large or deep to remove by hand. Next, fill in any holes with dirt or leaves. Finally, make a few light sweeps with the shovel or a leafy branch to smooth the area.

To increase readability, the steps or substeps in a complex task often appear in list form.

USING DIVISION TO MAKE A POINT

In the following paragraph, Watts uses division to explain his view of the ideal education. If we accept his divisions, we are more likely to agree that his opinion makes sense.

Division that Makes a Point

Lead-in to main point
(1–3)

¹It is perhaps idle to wonder what, from my present point of view, would have been an ideal education. ²If I could provide such a curriculum for my children they, in their turn, might find it all a bore. ³But the fantasy of what I would have liked to learn as a child may be revealing, since I feel un-equipped by education for problems that lie outside the cloistered, literary domain in which I am competent and at home.

Main point (4)

⁴Looking back, then, I would have arranged for myself to be taught survival techniques for both natural and urban wildernesses.

Parts of the "ideal education" (5)

⁵I would want to have been instructed in self-hypnosis, in aikido (the esoteric and purely self-defensive style of judo), in elementary medicine, in sexual hygiene, in vegetable gardening, in astronomy, navigation, and sailing; in cookery and clothesmaking, in metalwork and carpentry, in drawing and painting, in printing and typography, in botany and biology, in optics and acoustics, in semantics and psychology, in mysticism and yoga, in electronics and mathematical fantasy, in drama and dancing, in singing and in playing an instrument by ear; in wandering, in advanced daydreaming, in prestidigitation, in techniques of escape from bondage, in disguise, in conversation with birds and beasts, in ventriloquism, in French and German conversation, in planetary history, in morphology,* and in Classical Chinese.

Most important part (6)

⁶Actually, the main thing left out of my education was a proper love for my own body, because one feared to cherish anything so obviously mortal and prone to sickness.

—*Alan Watts*

The topic statement *tells*; the rest *shows* by dividing the ideal education into specific kinds of instruction. This writer knew the guidelines on page 188.

USING CLASSIFICATION TO EXPLAIN

Like division, classifying as a referential or informative strategy is a part of our lives. Your biology textbook shows you how scientists have classified life-forms into plants, animals, bacteria, and other categories; scientists examining fossils write up their discoveries by assigning them to one of these classes. A city planner might write a report classifying plans for conserving water on the basis of cost, efficiency, or some other basis. The following classification explains major career specialties in computer science on the basis of their central tasks.

Classification that Explains

Specialties in computer science can be grouped into three major categories. First, systems programmers write programs that run the computer

---

*The structure of organisms.

GUIDELINES FOR DIVISION

1. *Apply the division to a singular item.* Only one item at a time can be divided (ideal education; not ideal education and ideal career).

2. *Make the division consistent with your purpose.* Watts could have divided education into primary, secondary, and higher education; into social sciences, humanities, sciences, and mathematics—and so on. But his purpose was to explain a view that goes beyond traditional categories. We are given "parts" of an education that we may not yet have considered.

3. *Make your division complete.* Only 100 percent of something can be divided, and the parts, in turn, should add up to 100 percent. If a part is omitted, the writer should say so ("some of the parts of an ideal education").

4. *Subdivide the subject as needed to make the point.* Watts's first division is into survival techniques for (a) natural and (b) urban wildernesses. He then subdivides each of these into the specific parts listed in sentences 5 and 6. If he had stopped after the first division, he would not have made his point.

5. *Follow a logical order.* In sentence 5 the parts of an ideal education range from practical to recreational to intellectual skills. In sentence 6 the most important part appears last—for emphasis.

equipment itself. Next, applications programmers develop programs that put the computer to work on specific jobs (such as keeping track of bank accounts). Finally, systems analysts troubleshoot, debug, and update both systems and applications programs and they develop specifications for new computer systems. All three specialties involve analyzing a problem and then reducing it to a sequence of small, deliberate steps that a computer can carry out.

USING CLASSIFICATION TO MAKE A POINT

Like division, classification also can be persuasive. This next paragraph uses classification to analyze the motives behind attending the high school prom.

Classification that Makes a Point

Why must everyone who counts be at the prom? The answer is simple: peer pressure. Prom-goers often feel compelled to attend, as the prom represents in many ways their last chance, their last hurrah. For the popular, it is their final opportunity to saunter into a room filled with people who admire them not so much for who they are or what they've achieved, but instead for the shallow ideal they represent—the football star, the homecoming queen, the rich kid. For the borderline types, the prom is their final chance

> to mimic the popular, to rub elbows with those who really matter. For the losers—the nerds, geeks, dweebs, wallflowers, and other loners—prom night is their last, desperate chance to try fitting in, to matter at all.
>
> —*Julia Conforti*

In developing her message, Conforti observed the following guidelines.

GUIDELINES FOR CLASSIFICATION

1. *Apply the classification to a plural subject.* In Conforti's paragraph, the subject is types who attend the prom.

2. *Make the basis of the classification consistent with your purpose.* To make her point about needs, Conforti classifies the three groups on the basis of their respective popularity. For a different purpose, she might have classified students on prom night according to their behavior, style of dress, and so on.

3. *Make the classification complete.* All three broad stereotypes of high school culture are represented.

4. *Arrange the categories in logical order.* The categories Conforti uses move from "winners" to "losers."

5. *Don't let categories overlap.* If she had added the category *truly needy* to the three stereotypes she identifies, Conforti's classification would overlap, because all three categories represent some type of need.

   Or suppose a supermarket classified its meats as *pork, beef, ham,* and *lamb.* This classification would overlap because ham is a product of pork meat rather than an exclusive category.

APPLICATION 12-1

Paragraph Warm-Up: Dividing to Explain

Addressing a prospective new member, use division to explain either the organization or the function of committees in a social or service group you belong to.

APPLICATION 12-2

Paragraph Warm-Up: Dividing to Make a Point

Using the paragraph on page 187 as a model, write a paragraph for the college curriculum committee, explaining your idea of an ideal education.

APPLICATION 12-3

Paragraph Warm-Up: Classifying to Explain

You are helping prepare the orientation for next year's incoming students. Your supervisor asks you to write a paragraph outlining the jobs available to graduates in your major by organizing the jobs into major categories. Your piece will be published in a career pamphlet for new students. (You may need to do some library research, say in *The Occupational Outlook Handbook*.)

APPLICATION 12-4

Paragraph Warm-Up: Classifying to Make a Point

Identify a group you find in some way interesting. Sort the members of that group into at least three categories. Your basis for sorting (say, driving habits, attitudes toward marriage, hairstyles) will depend on the particular point you want to make about the group.

APPLICATION 12-5

Essay Practice

Read the Lutz essay, and answer the questions that follow it as well as those on page 155. Then select one of the essay assignments.

ESSAY FOR ANALYSIS AND RESPONSE

DOUBTS ABOUT DOUBLESPEAK

¹During the past year, we learned that we can shop at a "unique retail biosphere" instead of a farmers' market, where we can buy items made of "synthetic glass" instead of plastic, or purchase a "high velocity, multipurpose air circulator," or electric fan. A "waste-water conveyance facility" may "exceed the odor threshold" from time to time due to the presence of "regulated human nutrients," but that is not to be confused with a sewage plant that stinks up the neighborhood with sewage sludge. Nor should we confuse a "resource development park" with a dump. Thus does doublespeak continue to spread.

²Doublespeak is language which pretends to communicate but doesn't. It is language which makes the bad seem good, the negative seem positive, the unpleasant seem attractive, or at least tolerable. It is language which

avoids, shifts or denies responsibility; language which is at variance with its real or purported meaning. It is language which conceals or prevents thought.

[3]Doublespeak is all around us. We are asked to check our packages at the desk "for our convenience" when it's not for our convenience at all but for someone else's convenience. We see advertisements for "preowned," "experienced" or "previously distinguished" cars, not used cars and for "genuine imitation leather," "virgin vinyl" or "real counterfeit diamonds." Television offers not reruns but "encore telecasts." There are no slums or ghettos just the "inner city" or "substandard housing" where the "disadvantaged" or "economically nonaffluent" live and where there might be a problem with "substance abuse." Nonprofit organizations don't make a profit, they have "negative deficits" or experience "revenue excesses." With doublespeak it's not dying but "terminal living" or "negative patient care outcome."

[4]There are four kinds of doublespeak. The first kind is the euphemism, a word or phrase designed to avoid a harsh or distasteful reality. Used to mislead or deceive, the euphemism becomes doublespeak. In 1984 the U.S. State Department's annual reports on the status of human rights around the world ceased using the word "killing." Instead the State Department used the phrase "unlawful or arbitrary deprivation of life," thus avoiding the embarrassing situation of government-sanctioned killing in countries supported by the United States.

[5]A second kind of doublespeak is jargon, the specialized language of a trade, profession or similar group, such as doctors, lawyers, plumbers or car mechanics. Legitimately used, jargon allows members of a group to communicate with each other clearly, efficiently and quickly. Lawyers and tax accountants speak to each other of an "involuntary conversion" of property, a legal term that means the loss or destruction of property through theft, accident or condemnation. But when lawyers or tax accountants use unfamiliar terms to speak to others, then the jargon becomes doublespeak.

[6]In 1978 a commercial 727 crashed on takeoff, killing three passengers, injuring 21 others and destroying the airplane. The insured value of the airplane was greater than its book value, so the airline made a profit of $1.7 million, creating two problems: the airline didn't want to talk about one of its airplanes crashing, yet it had to account for that $1.7 million profit in its annual report to its stockholders. The airline solved both problems by inserting a footnote in its annual report which explained that the $1.7 million was due to "the involuntary conversion of a 727."

[7]A third kind of doublespeak is gobbledygook or bureaucratese. Such doublespeak is simply a matter of overwhelming the audience with words—the more the better. Alan Greenspan, a polished practitioner of bureaucratese, once testified before a Senate committee that "it is a tricky problem to find the particular calibration in timing that would be appropriate to stem

the acceleration in risk premiums created by falling incomes without prematurely aborting the decline in the inflation-generated risk premiums."

[8]The fourth kind of doublespeak is inflated language, which is designed to make the ordinary seem extraordinary, to make everyday things seem impressive, to give an air of importance to people or situations, to make the simple seem complex. Thus do car mechanics become "automotive internists," elevator operators become "members of the vertical transportation corps," grocery store checkout clerks become "career associate scanning professionals," and smelling something becomes "organoleptic analysis."

[9]Doublespeak is not the product of careless language or sloppy thinking. Quite the opposite. Doublespeak is language carefully designed and constructed to appear to communicate when in fact it doesn't. It is a language designed not to lead but mislead. Thus, it's not a tax increase but "revenue enhancement" or "tax-base broadening." So how can you complain about higher taxes? Those aren't useless, billion dollar pork barrel projects; they're really "congressional projects of national significance," so don't complain about wasteful government spending. That isn't the Mafia in Atlantic City; those are just "members of a career-offender cartel," so don't worry about the influence of organized crime in the city.

—William Lutz

QUESTIONS ABOUT THE READING

Refer to the general questions on page 155 as well as these specific questions.

CONTENT

■ What basis can you identify in Lutz's classification? Is this basis consistent with the writer's purpose? Explain.

■ Is the classification offered there complete? Explain.

ORGANIZATION

■ Does the arrangement of supporting paragraphs help make the classification convincing? Explain.

■ What major devices lend coherence to this essay? Give samples of each.

STYLE

■ What is the writer's attitude toward his subject? Toward his audience? How do we know? Where are the signals?

■ Is the tone appropriate for this writer's audience and purpose? Explain.

RESPONDING TO YOUR READING

Explore your reactions to the Lutz essay by using the questions on page 23. Then respond with an essay of your own that supports some particular point about deceptive uses of language. You might describe an experience in which you have been misled by doublespeak. Or you might discuss situations in which doublespeak can be beneficial. Whether your approach is humorous or serious, be sure your essay makes a definite point.

APPLICATION 12-6

Computer Application: A World Wide Web home page is an excellent example of classification and division at work. If your institution has its own Home page, obtain the electronic address from the campus computer center and access the page by using a web "browser" such as *Yahoo, Mosaic,* or *Netscape.* Explore the arrangement of the page, deciding to what extent the divisions and classifications follow the guidelines in this chapter.

- Do all the arrangements make sense?
- How do the divisions and classifications made by the creators of the page affect the way visitors to the page see the school?
- Could the page have been arranged differently for different effects? Your instructor may ask that your analysis/critique be submitted in writing.

OPTIONS FOR ESSAY WRITING

1. Television seems to invade every part of our lives. It can influence our buying habits, political views, attitudes about sex, marriage, family, and violence. Identify a group of commercials, sitcoms, talk shows, sports shows, or the like that have a bad (or good) influence on viewers. Sort the group according to a clear basis, using at least three categories, and be sure your essay supports a definite viewpoint.

2. Reread the passage by Alan Watts (page 187) and respond with an essay that lays out as specifically as possible the types of knowledge that you hope to acquire in college or the types you think everyone should acquire in higher education.

CHAPTER 13

EXPLAINING STEPS AND STAGES IN PROCEDURES AND PROCESSES

A process is a sequence of actions or changes leading to a product or result (say, in producing maple syrup). A *procedure* is a way of carrying out a process (say, in swinging a golf club). A *process analysis* explains these various steps and stages to instruct or inform readers.

USING PROCESS ANALYSIS BEYOND THE WRITING CLASSROOM

■ **In other courses:** You might instruct a classmate in dissecting a frog or in using the school's E-mail network. You might answer an essay question about how economic inflation occurs or how hikers and campers can succumb to hypothermia.

■ **On the job:** You might instruct a colleague or customer in accessing a database or shipping radioactive waste. You might explain to coworkers how the budget for various departments is determined or how the voice-mail system works.

■ **In the community:** You might instruct a friend in casting for largemouth bass or preparing for a job interview. You might explain to parents the selection process for new teachers followed by your PTA.

What additional audiences and uses for process analysis can you think of?

USING PROCESS ANALYSIS TO EXPLAIN

The most common referential uses of process analysis are to give instructions and to explain how something happens.

EXPLAINING HOW TO DO SOMETHING

As the examples show, almost anyone might need to write instructions. And everyone reads some sort of instructions. The new employee needs instructions for operating the office machines; the employee going on vacation writes instructions for the person filling in. A car owner reads the manual for service and operating instructions.

What readers want to know about a procedure

■ *How do I do it?*

■ *Why do I do it?*

■ *What materials or equipment will I need?*

- *Where do I begin?*
- *What do I do next?*
- *Are there any precautions?*

Instructions emphasize the reader's role, explaining each step in enough detail for the reader to complete the task safely and efficiently. This next passage is aimed at inexperienced joggers:

Explaining How to Do Something

Main point (1)
First step (2)

Supporting detail (3)
Second step (4)
Supporting detail (5)
Transitional sentence (6)
Third step (7–8)

Precaution (9–10)
Supporting details (11–15)

¹Instead of breaking into a jog too quickly and risking injury, take a relaxed and deliberate approach. ²Before taking a step, spend at least ten minutes stretching and warming up, using any exercises you find comfortable. ³(After your first week, consult a jogging book for specialized exercises.) ⁴When you've completed your warm-up, set a brisk pace walking. ⁵Exaggerate the distance between steps, taking long strides and swinging your arms briskly and loosely. ⁶After roughly 100 yards at this brisk pace, you should feel ready to jog. ⁷Immediately break into a very slow trot: lean your torso forward and let one foot fall in front of the other (one foot barely leaving the ground while the other is on the pavement). ⁸Maintain the slowest pace possible, just above a walk. ⁹Do not bolt like a sprinter! ¹⁰The biggest mistake is to start fast and injure yourself. ¹¹While jogging, relax your body. ¹²Keep your shoulders straight and your head up, and enjoy the scenery—after all, it is one of the joys of jogging. ¹³Keep your arms low and slightly bent at your sides. ¹⁴Move your legs freely from the hips in an action that is easy, not forced. ¹⁵Make your feet perform a heel-to-toe action: land on the heel; rock forward; take off from the toe.

Note that these instructions do not explain terms such as *long stride*, *torso*, and *sprinter* because these should be clear to the general reader. But a *slow trot* is explained in detail; different readers might have differing interpretations of this term.

EXPLAINING HOW SOMETHING HAPPENS

Besides showing how to do something, you often have to explain how things occur: how sunlight helps plants make chlorophyll; how a digital computer works; how your town decided on its zoning laws. *Process explanation* emphasizes the process itself—instead of the reader's or writer's role.

What readers want to know about a process

- *How does it happen? Or, how is it made?*
- *When and where does it happen?*
- *What happens first, next, and so on?*
- *What is the result?*

GUIDELINES FOR GIVING INSTRUCTIONS

1. *Know the process.* Unless you have performed the task, do not try to write instructions for it.

2. *Make instructions complete but not excessive.* Don't assume that people know more than they really do, especially when you can perform the task almost automatically. Think about when someone taught you to drive a car—or perhaps you have tried to teach someone else. As in the jogging instructions, include enough detail for your reader to understand and perform the task successfully, but omit general information that readers probably know. Excessive details get in the way.

3. *Organize instructions logically.* Instructions almost always are arranged in chronological order, with warnings and precautions inserted for specific steps.

4. *Make instructions immediately readable.* Instructions must be understood at the first reading, because readers usually take immediate action. Because they emphasize the reader's role, write instructions in the second person, as direct address.

   Begin all steps with action verbs by using the *active voice* (*move your legs* instead of *your legs should be moved*) and the *imperative mood* (*rock forward* instead of *you should rock forward*), giving an immediate signal about the specific action to be taken.

   Use shorter sentences than usual: use one sentence for one step, so readers can perform one step at a time.

   Finally, use transitional expressions (*while, after, next*) to improve readability by marking time and sequence.

USING PROCESS ANALYSIS TO MAKE A POINT

Although many process explanations are referential, others are closely related to cause and effect (see Chapter 14). In these cases, providing complete explanations and clear connections between steps helps convince readers that the process you're describing really does happen as you say. These kinds of causal chains often support larger arguments. In the next example, Julia Conforti uses a process analysis to lay the groundwork for her claim that credit cards and college students create a dangerous combination.

Process Analysis that Makes a Point

Orienting statement (1)
Details of the process and its results (2–8)

[1]It's almost too tempting to refuse. [2]Credit card companies marketing on campus offer free cards and sign-up gifts "with no obligation." [3]The "gifts" might include candy, coffee mugs, T-shirts, sports squeeze bottles, hip bags, and other paraphernalia. [4]The process seems harmless enough: Just fill in your social security number and other personal information, take your pick from the array of gifts, and cancel the card when it arrives. [5]But these companies know exactly what they're doing. [6]They know that misus-

Main point (9)

ing the card is often easier than cancelling it. [7]They know that many of us work part time and are paid little. [8]They know that most of us will be unable to pay more than the minimum balance each month—meaning big-time interest for years. [9]Don't be seduced by instant credit.

—Julia Conforti

APPLICATION 13-1

Paragraph Warm-Up: Giving Instructions

Choose some activity you perform well. Think of a situation requiring you to write instructions for that activity. Single out a major step within the process (such as pitching a baseball or adjusting ski bindings for safe release). Provide enough details so that the reader can perform that step safely and efficiently.

APPLICATION 13-2

Paragraph Warm-Up: Explaining How Something Happens

Select some process in your university—admissions, registration, changing majors, finding a parking place. Write a process analysis that could anchor an argument for changes in the procedure.

APPLICATION 13-3

Essay Practice: Giving Instructions

Read Frank White's essay, and answer the questions following it. Then select one of the essay assignments.

The writer of these instructions is a counselor at the North American Survival School, which offers courses ranging from mountaineering to desert survival. Besides being a certified Emergency Medical Technician, White has extensive experience hiking and camping in snake-infested terrain. The school is preparing a survival manual for distribution to all its students. This writer's contribution is a set of instructions on dealing with snakebites. Many of the readers will have no experience with snakes (or first aid), and so White decides to be brief and simple, for quick, easy reading as needed.

ESSAY FOR ANALYSIS AND RESPONSE

HOW TO DEAL WITH SNAKEBITES

[1]Every year, thousands of Americans are injured—sometimes fatally—by poisonous snakebites. Fewer than one percent of poisonous snakebites are fatal. But many of the injuries and most fatalities can be avoided as long as you are alert and cautious and follow a few instructions.

[2]Although most snakes bite, in the United States only rattlesnakes, copperheads, coral snakes, and water moccasins are poisonous. All these are most dangerous in early spring, when venom sacs are full from winter hibernation. Rattlers are found in most of the United States, while copperheads are only in the East. Coral snakes range throughout the South, while water moccasins live in Southern lowlands and swampy areas.

[3]Some simple precautions can help you avoid snakebites. Since most bites occur around the ankles, wear long, thick pants and high boots of heavy rubber or leather. Also, watch where you walk, swim, or sleep. As you walk, watch where you put your feet, especially in climbing over fallen trees or stone walls. In moccasin country, swim only where the water is moving and the shoreline is free of heavy vegetation. If you cannot sleep in a closed tent with a snakeproof floor, place your sleeping bag on a high, dry, open spot, and keep it zipped. When you do encounter a snake, freeze! Then move backwards *very* slowly, making no moves that will frighten the snake. In case these precautions fail, always carry a snakebite kit.

[4]A poisonous snakebite is easy enough to recognize. Within minutes the wound will swell and turn bright red. You will feel a throbbing pain that radiates from the bite. The swelling, redness, and pain will spread gradually and steadily. (Bites from nonvenomous snakes, in contrast, resemble mere pinpricks.) You may experience nausea and/or hot flashes. In any case, if you are not certain whether the bite is poisonous, treat it as poisonous.

[5]If you have been bitten, *do nothing to hasten the spread of the poison.* Above all, don't panic. Resist the temptation to walk, run, or move quickly. And stay away from stimulants such as coffee, tea, cola, alcohol, or aspirin. In fact, don't ingest anything. Instead, take a minute to think calmly about what you *should* do.

[6]Take the following steps immediately. Remain calm and move as little as possible. Keep the wound lower than the rest of your body so the poison remains localized. Have companions get you to a hospital as quickly as possible, without causing you needless exertion. If the hospital is more than an hour away, apply an icepack to retard the spread of the poison, or a tourniquet (snugly enough to stop venous flow but not so tight as to stop arterial flow—and loosened briefly every five minutes). If you lack a snakebite kit, you might cut a small X about $1/4$-inch deep at the point of greatest swelling on the wound to suck out and spit out some poison. Perform this last procedure *only* if you have no oral cuts or injuries and there is no chance of getting medical treatment for several hours.

> [7]By taking precautions and remaining alert, you should not have to fear snakebites. But if you are bitten, your best bet is to remain calm.
>
> —*Frank White*

QUESTIONS ABOUT THE READING

CONTENT

- What opening strategy is used to create interest?
- Is the information adequate and appropriate for the stated audience and purpose? Explain.
- What specific readers' questions are answered here?

ORGANIZATION

- What is the order of the body paragraphs? Is this the most effective order? Explain.
- Is the conclusion adequate and appropriate? Explain.

STYLE

- Are these instructions immediately readable? Explain.
- Is the tone of these instructions too "bossy"? Explain.

RESPONDING TO YOUR READING

Assume a specific situation and audience (like those for snakebite procedures), and write instructions for a specialized procedure, or for anything that you can do well (no recipes, please). Be sure you know the process down to the smallest detail. Narrow your subject (perhaps to one complex activity within a longer procedure) so you can cover it fully. Avoid day-to-day procedures that college readers would already know (brushing teeth, washing hair, and other such elementary activities).

....

APPLICATION 13-4

Computer Application: Most Web browsers allow you to do keyword searches (see pages 319–320 in Chapter 19) by using one of several "search engines" like *Yahoo*, *Lycos*, *Alta Vista*, or *Infoseek*. Each search engine, however, has its own guidelines and peculiarities; these usually are explained in a "help" file or user guide. Learn to use at least one search engine; for your classmates, write instructions for designing and conducting a Web search.

······························

APPLICATION 13-5

Essay Practice: Explaining How Something Happens

The next essay was written by Bill Kelly, a biology major, for a pamphlet on environmental pollution. It is aimed at an uninformed audience.

ESSAY FOR ANALYSIS AND RESPONSE

HOW ACID RAIN DEVELOPS, SPREADS, AND DESTROYS

[1]Acid rain is environmentally damaging rainfall that occurs after fossil fuels burn, releasing nitrogen and sulfur oxides into the atmosphere. Acid rain, simply stated, increases the acidity level of waterways, because these nitrogen and sulfur oxides combine with the air's normal moisture. The resulting rainfall is far more acidic than normal rainfall. Acid rain is a silent threat because its effects, although slow, are cumulative. This analysis explains the cause, the distribution cycle, and the effects of acid rain.

[2]Most research shows that power plants burning oil or coal are the primary cause of acid rain. Fossil fuels contain a number of elements that are released during combustion. Two of these, sulfur oxide and nitrogen oxide, combine with normal moisture to produce sulfuric acid and nitric acid. The released gases undergo a chemical change as they combine with atmospheric ozone and water vapor. The resulting rain or snowfall is more acid than normal precipitation.

[3]Acid level is measured by pH readings. The pH scale runs from 0 through 14; a pH of 7 is considered neutral. (Distilled water has a pH of 7.) Numbers above 7 indicate increasing degrees of akalinity. (Household ammonia has a pH of 11.) Numbers below 7 indicate increasing acidity. Movement in either direction on the pH scale, however, means multiplying by 10. Lemon juice, which has a pH value of 2, is 10 times more acidic than apples, which have a pH of 3, and 1000 times more acidic than carrots, which have a pH of 5.

[4]Because of carbon dioxide (an acid substance) normally present in air, unaffected rainfall has a pH of 5.6. At this time, the pH of precipitation in the northeastern United States and Canada is between 4.5 and 4. In Massachusetts, rain and snowfall have an average pH reading of 4.1. A pH reading below 5 is considered to be abnormally acidic, and therefore a threat to aquatic populations.

[5]Although it might seem that areas containing power plants would be most severely affected, acid rain can in fact travel thousands of miles from its source. Stack gases escape and drift with the wind currents. The sulfur and nitrogen oxides thus are able to travel great distances before they return to earth as acid rain.

[6]For an average of two to five days after emission, the gases follow the prevailing winds far from the point of origin. Estimates show that about 50 percent of the acid rain that affects Canada originates in the United States; at the same time, 15 to 25 percent of the U.S. acid rain problem originates in Canada.

[7]The tendency of stack gases to drift makes acid rain a widespread menace. More than 200 lakes in the Adirondacks, hundreds of miles from any industrial center, are unable to support life because their water has become so acidic.

[8]Acid rain causes damage wherever it falls. It erodes various types of building rock, such as limestone, marble, and mortar, which are gradually eaten away by the constant bathing in acid. Damage to buildings, houses, monuments, statues, and cars is widespread. Some priceless monuments and carvings already have been destroyed, and even trees of some varieties are dying in large numbers.

[9]More important, however, is acid rain damage to waterways in the affected areas. Because of its high acidity, acid rain dramatically lowers the pH in lakes and streams. Although its effect is not immediate, acid rain eventually can make a waterway so acidic it dies. In areas with natural acid-buffering elements such as limestone, the dilute acid has less effect. The northeastern United States and Canada, however, lack this natural protection, and so are continually vulnerable.

[10]The pH level in an affected waterway drops so low that some species cease to reproduce. In fact, a pH level of 5.1 to 5.4 means that fisheries are threatened; once a waterway reaches a pH level of 4.5, no fish reproduction occurs. Because each creature is part of the overall food chain, loss of one element in the chain disrupts the whole cycle.

[11]In the northeastern United States and Canada, the acidity problem is compounded by the runoff from acid snow. During the cold winter months, acid snow sits with little melting, so that by spring thaw, the acid released is greatly concentrated. Aluminum and other heavy metals normally present in soil also are released by acid rain and runoff. These toxic substances leach into waterways in heavy concentrations, affecting fish in all stages of development.

—*Bill Kelly*

QUESTIONS ABOUT THE READING

CONTENT

- Is the information appropriate for the intended audience (uninformed readers)? Explain.
- What specific readers' questions are answered in the body?

ORGANIZATION

- Are the body paragraphs arranged in the best order for readers to follow the process? Explain.
- Why does this essay have no specific conclusion?

STYLE

- Is the discussion easy to follow? If so, what style features help? If not, what might be changed?
- Give one example of each of the following sentence constructions, and explain briefly how each reinforces the writer's meaning: passive construction, subordination, short sentence.

RESPONDING TO YOUR READING

Select a specialized process that you understand well (from your major or an area of interest) and explain that process to uninformed readers. Choose a process that has several distinct steps, and write so that your composition classmates gain detailed understanding. Do not merely generalize. Get down to specifics.

. . . .

APPLICATION 13-6

Essay Practice: Using Process Analysis to Make a Point

Processes occur in our personal experiences as well—for example, our stages of maturation, of emotional growth and development, of intellectual awareness. The following essay traces a personal process some readers might consider horrifying: the stages of learning to live by scavenging through garbage. As you read, think about how the factual and "objective" style paints a gruesome portrait of survival at the margin of American affluence.

ESSAY FOR ANALYSIS AND RESPONSE

DUMPSTER DIVING

[1]I began Dumpster diving about a year before I became homeless.

[2]I prefer the term scavenging. I have heard people, evidently meaning to be polite, use the word foraging, but I prefer to reserve that word for gathering nuts and berries and such, which I also do, according to the season and opportunity.

[3]I like the frankness of the word scavenging. I live from the refuse of others. I am a scavenger. I think it a sound and honorable niche, although if I could I would naturally prefer to live the comfortable consumer life, per-

haps—and only perhaps—as a slightly less wasteful consumer owing to what I have learned as a scavenger.

[4]Except for jeans, all my clothes come from Dumpsters. Boom boxes, candles, bedding, toilet paper, medicine, books, a typewriter, a virgin male love doll, coins sometimes amounting to many dollars: all came from Dumpsters. And, yes, I eat from Dumpsters, too.

[5]There is a predictable series of stages that a person goes through in learning to scavenge. At first the new scavenger is filled with disgust and self-loathing. He [or she] is ashamed of being seen.

[6]This stage passes with experience. The scavenger finds a pair of running shoes that fit and look and smell brand-new. He finds a pocket calculator in perfect working order. He finds pristine ice cream, still frozen, more than he can eat or keep. He begins to understand: people do throw away perfectly good stuff, a lot of perfectly good stuff.

[7]At this stage he may become lost and never recover. All the Dumpster divers I have known come to the point of trying to acquire everything they touch. Why not take it, they reason, it is all free. This is, of course, hopeless, and most divers come to realize that they must restrict themselves to items of relatively immediate utility.

[8]The finding of objects is becoming something of an urban art. Even respectable, employed people will sometimes find something tempting sticking out of a Dumpster or standing beside one. Quite a number of people, not all of them of the bohemian type, are willing to brag that they found this or that piece in the trash.

[9]But eating from Dumpsters is the thing that separates the dilettanti from the professionals. Eating safely involves three principles: using the senses and common sense to evaluate the condition of the found materials; knowing the Dumpsters of a given area and checking them regularly; and seeking always to answer the question "Why was this discarded?"

[10]Yet perfectly good food can be found in Dumpsters. Canned goods, for example, turn up fairly often in the Dumpsters I frequent. I also have few qualms about dry foods such as crackers, cookies, cereal, chips, and pasta if they are free of visible contaminants and still dry and crisp. Raw fruits and vegetables with intact skins seem perfectly safe to me, excluding, of course, the obviously rotten. Many are discarded for minor imperfections that can be pared away.

[11]A typical discard is a half jar of peanut butter—though nonorganic peanut butter does not require refrigeration and is unlikely to spoil in any reasonable time. One of my favorite finds is yogurt—often discarded, still sealed, when the expiration has passed—because it will keep for several days, even in warm weather.

[12]No matter how careful I am I still get dysentery at least once a month, oftener in warm weather. I do not want to paint too romantic a picture. Dumpster diving has serious drawbacks as a way of life.

[13]I find from the experience of scavenging two rather deep lessons. The first is to take what I can use and let the rest go. I have come to think that there is no value in the abstract. A thing I cannot use or make useful, perhaps by trading, has no value, however fine or rare it may be. The second lesson is the transience of material being. I do not suppose that ideas are immortal, but certainly they are longer-lived than material objects.

[14]The things I find in Dumpsters, the love letters and rag dolls of so many lives, remind me of this lesson. Now I hardly pick up a thing without envisioning the time I will cast it away. This, I think, is a healthy state of mind. Almost everything I have now has already been cast out at least once, proving that what I own is valueless to someone.

[15]I find that my desire to grab for the gaudy bauble has been largely sated. I think this is an attitude I share with the very wealthy—we both know there is plenty more wherever we have come from. Between us are the rat-race millions who have confounded their selves with the objects they grasp and who nightly scavenge the cable channels for they know not what.

[16]I am sorry for them.

—*Lars Eighner*

QUESTIONS ABOUT THE READING

CONTENT

- What are Eighner's assumptions about his audiences' knowledge and attitudes? Are these assumptions accurate? Why or why not?

- Point out some of the referential details Eighner selects to make his point. How selective do you think he has been? Explain.

ORGANIZATION

- How does Eighner "frame" his process analysis through his introduction and conclusion? Do these framing elements make the depiction of the process itself more or less convincing? Explain.

STYLE

- What is the writer's attitude toward his subject? Toward his audience? How do we know? Where are the signals?

- Is the tone appropriate for this writer's audience and purpose? Explain.

RESPONDING TO YOUR READING

Explore your reactions to "Dumpster Diving" (pages 203–205) by using the questions on page 23. What is Eighner's point about values? What are the main issues here? How has this essay affected your thinking about these issues? As you reread the essay, try to recall some process that has played a role for you personally or for someone close to you. Perhaps you want to focus on the process of achievement (say, preparing for academic or athletic or career competition). Perhaps you have experienced or witnessed the process of giving in to human frailty (say, addiction to drugs, tobacco, alcohol, or food). Perhaps you know something about the process of enduring and recovering from personal loss or misfortune or disappointment. Identify your audience, and decide what you want these readers to do, think, or feel after reading your essay. Should they appreciate this process, try it themselves, avoid it, or what?

Whatever you write about—college or high school or family life or city streets—make a definite point about the larger meaning beyond the details of the process, about the values involved.

CHAPTER 14

EXPLAINING WHY IT HAPPENED OR WHAT WILL HAPPEN: CAUSE-AND-EFFECT ANALYSIS

*A*nalysis of reasons (causes) or consequences (effects) explains why something happened or what happens as a result of something.

What readers of causal analysis want to know

- ■ *Why did it happen?*
- ■ *What caused it?*
- ■ *What are its effects?*
- ■ *What will happen if it is done?*

For example, if you awoke this morning with a sore shoulder (effect), you might recall exerting yourself yesterday at the college Frisbee olympics (cause). You take aspirin, hoping for relief (effect). If the aspirin works, it will have *caused* you to feel better. But some causes and effects are harder to identify:

[CAUSE]   [EFFECT]
1. I tripped over a chair and broke my nose.

[EFFECT]   [CAUSE]
2. I never studied because I slept too much.

Other causes or effects could be identified for each of the above statements.

[EFFECT]   [CAUSE]
I tripped over the chair because my apartment lights were out.

[EFFECT]   [CAUSE]
The lights were out because the power had been shut off.

[EFFECT]   [CAUSE]
The power was off because my roommate forgot to pay the electric bill.

or

[CAUSE]   [EFFECT]
Because I slept too much, my grades were awful.

[EFFECT]   [CAUSE]
Because my grades were awful, I hated college.

[EFFECT]   [CAUSE]
Because I hated college, I dropped out.

[CAUSE]   [EFFECT]
Because I dropped out of college, I lost my scholarship.

In the examples above, the causes or effects become more distant. The *immediate* cause of example 1, however—the one most closely related to the effect—is that the writer tripped over the chair. Likewise, the *immediate* effect of example 2 is that the writer did no studying. Thus, the challenge is often to distinguish between immediate causes or effects and distant ones. Otherwise, we might generate illogical statements like these:

[CAUSE]   [EFFECT]
Because my roommate forgot to pay the electric bill, I broke my nose.

[EFFECT]   [CAUSE]
I lost my scholarship because I slept too much.

USING CAUSAL ANALYSIS TO EXPLAIN: DEFINITE CAUSES

As in process analysis (Chapter 13), writing that connects definite causes to their effects clarifies the relations among events in a causal chain. A *definite cause is apparent* ("The engine's overheating is caused by a faulty radiator cap"). You write about definite causes when you explain why the combustion in a car engine causes the wheels to move, or why the moon's orbit makes the tides rise and fall.

USING CAUSAL ANALYSIS BEYOND THE WRITING CLASSROOM

- **In other courses:** A research paper might explore the causes of the Israeli-Palestinian conflict or the effects of stress on college students. A report for the Dean of Students might explain students' disinterest in campus activities or the effect of a ban on smoking in public buildings.

- **On the job:** In workplace problem solving, you might analyze the high absenteeism among company employees or the malfunction of equipment.

- **In the community:** Perhaps local citizens need to know how air quality will be affected if your power plant changes from coal to oil or how increasing enrollment has affected education quality at your local high school.

In what other situations might causal analysis make a difference?

Explaining a Definite Cause

Topic sentence (1)
Causal chain (2–3)

Effects (4)
Conclusion (5)

[1]Some of the most serious accidents involving gas water heaters occur when a flammable liquid is used in the vicinity. [2]The heavier-than-air vapors of a flammable liquid such as gasoline can flow along the floor—even the length of a basement—and be explosively ignited by the flame of the water heater's pilot light or burner. [3]Because the victim's clothing often ignites, the resulting burn injuries are commonly serious and extremely painful. [4]They may require long hospitalization, and can result in disfigurement or death. [5]Never, under any circumstances, use a flammable liquid near a gas heater or burner.

—*Consumer Product Safety Commission*

USING CAUSAL ANALYSIS TO MAKE A POINT: POSSIBLE OR PROBABLE CAUSES

Causal writing often explores *possible or probable causes—causes that are not apparent.* In these cases, much searching, thought, and effort usually are needed to argue for a specific cause.

Suppose you ask: "Why are there no children's day-care facilities on our college campus?" Brainstorming yields these possible causes:

lack of need among students

lack of interest among students, faculty, and staff

high cost of liability insurance

lack of space and facilities on campus

lack of trained personnel

prohibition by state law

lack of legislative funding for such a project

Say you proceed with interviews, questionnaires, and research into state laws, insurance rates, and availability of personnel. You begin to rule out some items, and others appear as probable causes. Specifically, you find a need among students, high campus interest, an abundance of qualified people for staffing, and no state laws prohibiting such a project. Three probable causes remain: lack of funding, high insurance rates, and lack of space. Further inquiry shows that lack of funding and high insurance rates are issues. You think, however, that these causes could be eliminated through new sources of revenue: charging a fee for each child, soliciting donations, or diverting funds from other campus organizations. Finally, after examining available campus space and speaking with school officials, you conclude that the one definite cause is lack of space and facilities.

The persuasiveness of your causal argument will depend on the quality of research and evidence you bring to bear, as well as your ability to explain the links in the chain clearly. You must also convince audiences that you haven't overlooked important alternative causes.

Any complex effect is likely to have more than one cause; you have to make the case that the one you have isolated is the real issue.* You must also demonstrate sound reasoning. For example, the fact that one event occurs just before another is no proof that the first caused the second. You might have walked under a ladder in the hallway an hour before flunking your chemistry exam—but you would be hard-pressed to argue convincingly that the one event had caused the other.

REASONING FROM EFFECT TO CAUSE

In reasoning from effect to cause we examine a particular result, consequence, or outcome and we try to determine the circumstances that may produce such a result.

An Effect-to-Cause Analysis

Effect (main point) (1)
Distant cause and
examples (2)
Examples (3–4)

Evidence (5)

Immediate cause (6–7)

[1]In the right situation, a perfectly sane person can hallucinate. [2]It is most likely to happen when [he or she] is in a place that provides little stimulation to [the] senses, such as a barren, unbroken landscape or a quiet, dimly lit room. [3]Hallucinations are an occupational hazard of truck drivers, radar scanners, and pilots. [4]These occupations have in common long periods of monotony: lengthy stretches of straight highway, the regular rhythms of radar patterns, the droning hum of engines. [5]A. L. Mosely of the Harvard School of Public Health found that every one of 33 long-distance truck drivers he surveyed could recall having at least one hallucination. [6]Monotony means that the brain gets fewer sensory messages from the outside. [7]As external stimulation drops off, the brain responds more to messages from inside itself.

—Daniel Goleman

REASONING FROM CAUSE TO EFFECT

In reasoning from cause to effect, we examine a given set of circumstances and we try to ascertain the outcome of these circumstances.

---

*For example, one could argue that the lack of space and facilities somehow is related to funding. And the college's inability to find funds or space may be related to student need, which is not sufficiently acute or interest sufficiently high to exert real pressure.

GUIDELINES FOR EFFECT-TO-CAUSE ANALYSIS

1. *Be sure the cause fits the effect.* To clarify his point, Goleman shows examples of "right" situations and of "sane" persons. Research from Harvard provides convincing support.

2. *Make the links between effect and cause clear.* Goleman's reasoning goes like this:

   [DISTANT CAUSE]   [IMMEDIATE CAUSE]   [EFFECT]
   nonstimulating places ———▶ monotony ———▶ hallucination

   The distant cause is discussed first so that the immediate cause will make sense.

A Cause-to-Effect Analysis

¹What has the telephone done to us, or for us, in the hundred years of its existence? ²A few effects suggest themselves at once. ³It has saved lives by getting rapid word of illness, injury, or famine from remote places. ⁴By joining with the elevator to make possible the multistory residence or office building, it has made possible—for better or worse—the modern city. ⁵By bringing about a quantum leap in the speed and ease with which information moves from place to place, it has greatly accelerated the rate of scientific and technological change and growth in industry. ⁶Beyond doubt it has crippled if not killed the ancient art of letter writing. ⁷It has made living alone possible for persons with normal social impulses; by so doing, it has played a role in one of the greatest social changes of this century, the breakup of the multigenerational household. ⁸It has made the waging of war chillingly more efficient than formerly. ⁹Perhaps (though not probably) it has prevented wars that might have arisen out of international misunderstanding caused by written communications. ¹⁰Or perhaps—again not probably—by magnifying and extending irrational personal conflicts based on voice contact, it has caused wars. ¹¹Certainly it has extended the scope of human conflicts, since it impartially disseminates the useful knowledge of scientists and the babble of bores, the affection of the affectionate and the malice of the malicious.

—*John Brooks*

APPLICATION 14-1

Paragraph Warm-Up: Using Causal Analysis to Explain

Ordinary life in the 1990s depends on technology, but technology often frustrates us by letting us down when we most need it. Think of the last time you found

---

GUIDELINES FOR CAUSE-TO-EFFECT ANALYSIS

1. *Show that the effects fit the cause.* To clarify and support his point, Brooks shows the telephone's effects on familiar aspects of modern life. Because his purpose is to discuss effects in general (not only positive effects), he balances his development with both positive and negative effects.

2. *Make links between cause and effects clear.* The reasoning goes like this:

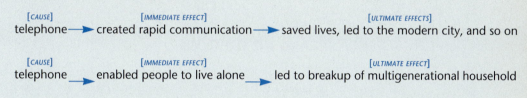

[CAUSE]   [IMMEDIATE EFFECT]   [ULTIMATE EFFECTS]
telephone ⟶ created rapid communication ⟶ saved lives, led to the modern city, and so on

[CAUSE]   [IMMEDIATE EFFECT]   [ULTIMATE EFFECT]
telephone   enabled people to live alone   led to breakup of multigenerational household

Without the link provided by the immediate effects, the ultimate effects would make no sense:

The telephone has saved lives. [*Why?*]

It has made possible the modern city. [*Why?*]

It perhaps has caused wars. [*Why?*]

For further linking, the paragraph groups definite effects (3–8), and then possible effects (9–10), with a conclusion that ties the discussion together.

---

yourself screaming at a machine. Using library research if necessary, explain the immediate and distant causes of the problem you experienced, limiting your discussion to definite causes as much as possible. Think of your paragraph as the heart of a letter to a friend explaining how to avoid the problem in the future.

· ·

APPLICATION 14-2

Paragraph Warm-Up: Using Causal Analysis to Make a Point

Identify a problem that affects you, your community, family, school, dorm, or other group ("The library is an awful place to study because____"). In a paragraph, analyze the causes of this problem as a prelude to an argument for change. Choose a subject you know about or one you can research to get the facts. Identify clearly the situation, the audience, and your purpose.

....

APPLICATION 14-3

Essay Practice: Analyzing Causes

In the following essay from *Newsweek* magazine, an irate mother examines causes of "premature sexual awakening" in today's children. As you read, think about how this writer's choice of phrasing and examples brings her analysis to life. Also think about how you would respond.

ESSAY FOR ANALYSIS AND RESPONSE

SEX, KIDS, AND THE SLUT LOOK

[1]The other day my 10-year-old daughter and I breached the prurient wilds of the Junior Fashion Department. Nothing in what she sneeringly calls the "little kid" department seems to fit anymore. She's tall for her age and at that awkward fashion stage between Little Red Riding Hood and Amy Fisher. She patrolled the racks, hunting the preteen imperative—a pair of leg-strangling white tights culminating in several inches of white lace. Everywhere were see-through dresses made out of little-flower-print fabric, lacy leggings, transparent tops and miniature bustiers for females unlikely to own busts. Many were garments that Cher would have rejected as far too obvious.

[2]Lace leggings? When I went to grade school, you were sent home if you wore even normal pants. The closest we got to leggings were our Pillsbury Doughboy snow pants, mummy-padding we pulled on under our dresses and clumped around in as we braved the frigid blasts of winter. Today's high-school girls have long dressed like street-corner pros; but since when did elementary school become a Frederick's of Hollywood showroom?

[3]Grousing that her dumb clothes compromised her popularity, the offspring had herded me to fashion's outer limits. She appeared to be the only 10-year-old in the area; the rest were 14 or so, unaccompanied by their mothers. She pranced up, holding out a hanger on which dangled a crocheted skirt the size of a personals ad and a top whose deep V-neck yawned like the jaws of hell.

[4]"Isn't this great! I want this!" she yodeled, sunshine beaming from her sweet face once more. "You're 10 years old," I said. "Shhh," she hissed, whipping her head around in frantic oh-God-did-anybody-hear mode. Then she accused me of not wanting her to grow up. She's 10 years old and the kid talks like a radio shrink.

[5]It's not really that I want her to be a little girl forever. It's just that it would be nice if she were a child during her childhood. Instead, she's been bathed in the fantasy of bodies and beauty that marinates our entire culture. The result is an insidious form of premature sexual awakening that is stealing our kids' youth.

[6]Meredith was 8 and we were in the car, singing along to some heart-broken musical lament on the radio, when she said, "Mom, why is everything in the world about sex?" I laughed and asked where she got that idea. But then, listening as she knowledgeably recited examples from music, movies, MTV and advertising, it hit me that she was right. The message of our popular culture for any observant 8-year-old is: *sex rules.* Otherwise, why would it deserve all this air time, all this agony and ecstasy, all this breathless attention?

[7]Kids pick up on the sexual laser focus of our society, then mimic what they see as the ruling adult craze, adding their own bizarre kid twist. Recently, I read that the authors of "The Janus Report on Sexual Behavior" were shocked to find how many had sex at 10, 11 and 12. Too young to know how to handle it, kids mix sex with the brutal competitiveness they learn in the two worlds they know best: sports and the streets. Sex is grafted onto their *real* consuming passion—to be the most radical dude or dudette in their crowd. Peer pressure—what I'm seeing now in my 10-year-old's wardrobe angst—takes over. The result is competitive sex: California gangs vying for the record in number of girls bedded; teenage boys raping girls my daughter's age in a heartless sexual all-star game where all that counts is the points you rack up. In Colorado Springs, not far from where I live, gangs are demanding that kids as young as 10 have sex as a form of initiation. It's the old "chicken" game in "Rebel Without a Cause," played with young bodies instead of cars.

[8]The adult reaction to all of this is outrage. But why should we be shocked? Children learn by example. Sex is omnipresent. What do we expect when we allow fashion designers to dress us, grown women, in garments so sheer that any passing stranger can see us nearly naked for the price of a casual glance?

[9]Or look at Madonna on the cover of Vanity Fair wearing only a pink inner tube and hair done up in cutesy '50s pigtails. Here's a 34-year-old heroine to little girls—the core of her fandom is about 14—posing as innocent jailbait. Inside, she romps on a playground in baby-doll nighties, toying with big, stuffed duckies and polar bears. This is a blatant child molester's fantasy-in-the-flesh. Does kiddie porn encourage sex crimes against chidren? Who cares!

[10]Rudimentary good sense must tell us that sexualizing children not only sullies their early years, but also exposes them to real danger from human predators. What our culture needs is a little reality check: in an era when sexual violence against children is heartbreakingly common—a recent study estimates that about one quarter of women have been victims of childhood sexual abuse—anything that eroticizes our children is irresponsible, at best.

[11]It's up to adults to explode the kids-are-sexy equation. Our kids need us to give them their childhood back. But this summer, the eroticization of our girl children proceeds apace. The crop tops! The tight little spandex

shorts! (Our moms wore them under their clothes and called them girdles.) My daughter's right, everybody struts her stuff. I've seen 5-year-old Pretty Babies.

[12]As for me, I don't care anymore if my kid has a hissy fit in the junior department. She's not wearing the Slut Look. Let her rant that I'm a hope-lessly pathological mom who wants to keep her in pacifiers and pinafores forever. Let her do amateur psychoanalysis on me in public until my ears fry—I've shaken the guilt heebie-jeebies and drawn the line. So you can put those white lace spandex leggings back on the rack, young lady.

—Joy Overbeck

QUESTIONS ABOUT THE READING

Refer to the general questions on page 155 as well as these specific questions.

CONTENT

- Are the causes presented here definite, probable, or possible? Explain.
- Are the causal links in this essay convincing? Do they seem complete? Has the author explored distant or alternative causes adequately? Explain.
- What assumptions does the author make about her audience's attitudes and awareness? Are these assumptions accurate? Explain.
- What are the main issues here? How has this essay affected your thinking about these issues?

ORGANIZATION

- What combination of opening strategies is used in the introduction?
- Is the introduction too long? Explain.
- Are the body paragraphs arranged in an order (such as general-to-specific) that emphasizes the thesis? If so, what is that order?

STYLE

- What is the author's attitude toward her subject? Toward her audience? How do we know? What are the signals?
- Is the tone appropriate for the intended audience and purpose? Explain.

RESPONDING TO YOUR READING

Explore your reactions to "Sex, Kids and the Slut Look" by using the questions on page 23. Think about how this essay has made a difference for you and then re-spond with an essay of your own that supports or refutes Overbeck's point that "an insidious form of premature sexual awakening . . . is stealing our kids' youth."

As an alternative writing project explore the causes of some other troubling reality, such as the dramatic increase in rates of teenage suicide.

Or you might want to analyze the appeal of some activity or behavior (harmful or beneficial, pleasurable or painful) that takes up much of your (and other people's) time. Feel free to inject humor. Here are activities or behaviors whose causes you could analyze:

- Why do I (or we) spend so much time watching football games (or some other sport)?
- Why am I so obsessed with exercise, fashion, or diet?
- Why am I a soap opera fan?
- Why are we such party animals?

Be sure your analysis supports some definite thesis.

APPLICATION 14-4

Essay Practice: Analyzing Effects

In this next selection, a psychologist points out the dangers of inflated self-esteem. As you read, think about how the essay challenges certain popular assumptions about the role of schools in student development.

ESSAY FOR ANALYSIS AND RESPONSE

SHOULD SCHOOLS TRY TO BOOST SELF-ESTEEM?— BEWARE THE DARK SIDE

[1]"We must raise children's self-esteem!" How often has this sentiment been expressed in recent years in schools, homes, and meeting rooms around the United States? The sentiment reflects the widespread, well-intentioned, earnest, and yet rather pathetic hope that if we can only persuade our kids to love themselves more, they will stop dropping out, getting pregnant, carrying weapons, taking drugs, and getting into trouble, and instead will start achieving great things in school and out.

[2]Unfortunately, the large mass of knowledge that research psychologists have built up around self-esteem does not justify that hope. At best, high self-esteem is a mixed blessing whose total effects are likely to be small and minor. At worst, the pursuit of high self-esteem is a foolish, wasteful, and self-destructive enterprise that may end up doing more harm than good.

[3]Writers on controversial topics should acknowledge their biases, and so let me confess mine: I have a strong bias in favor of self-esteem. I have been excited about self-esteem ever since my student days at Princeton, when I first heard that it was a topic of study. Over the past two decades I have probably published more studies on self-esteem than anybody else in the United States (or elsewhere). It would be great for my career if self-esteem could do everything its boosters hope: I'd be dining frequently at the White House and advising policymakers on how to fix the country's problems.

[4]It is therefore with considerable personal disappointment that I must report that the enthusiastic claims of the self-esteem movement mostly range from fantasy to hogwash. The effects of self-esteem are small, limited, and not all good. Yes, a few people here and there end up worse off because their self-esteem was too low. Then again, other people end up worse off because their self-esteem was too high. And most of the time self-esteem makes surprisingly little difference.

[5]Self-esteem is, literally, how favorably a person regards himself or herself. It is perception (and evaluation), not reality. For example, I think the world would be a better place if we could all manage to be a little nicer to each other. But that's hard: We'd all have to discipline ourselves to change. The self-esteem approach, in contrast, is to skip over the hard work of changing our actions and instead just let us all *think* we're nicer. That won't make the world any better. People with high self-esteem are not in fact any nicer than people with low self-esteem—in fact, the opposite is closer to the truth.

[6]High self-esteem means thinking well of oneself, regardless of whether that perception is based on substantive achievement or mere wishful thinking and self-deception. High self-esteem can mean *confident* and *secure*—but it can also mean *conceited, arrogant, narcissistic,* and *egotistical.*

[7]A recent, widely publicized study dramatized the fact that self-esteem consists of perception and is not necessarily based on reality. In an international scholastic competition, American students achieved the lowest average scores among all participating nationalities. But the American kids rated themselves and their performance the highest. This is precisely what comes of focusing on self-esteem: poor performance accompanied by plenty of empty self-congratulation. Put another way, we get high self-esteem as inflated perceptions covering over a rather dismal reality.

[8]Looking ahead, it is alarming to think what will happen when this generation of schoolchildren grows up into adults who may continue thinking they are smarter than the rest of the world—while actually being dumber. America will be a land of conceited fools.

[9]All of this might fairly be discounted if America were really suffering from an epidemic of low self-esteem, such as if most American schoolchildren generally had such negative views of themselves that they were unable

to tackle their homework. But that's not the case. On the contrary, as I'll explain shortly, self-esteem is already inflated throughout the United States. The average American already regards himself or herself as above average. At this point, any further boosting of self-esteem is likely to approach the level of grandiose, egotistical delusions.

Boosting Self-Esteem: The Problem of Inflation

[10]Most (though not all) of the problems linked to high self-esteem involve inflated self-esteem, in the sense of overestimating oneself. Based on the research findings produced in laboratories all over North America, I have no objection to people forming a sober, accurate recognition of their actual talents and accomplishments. The violence, the self-defeating behaviors, and the other problems tend to be most acute under conditions of threatened egotism, and inflated self-esteem increases that risk. After all, if you really are smart, your experiences will tend to confirm that fact, and so there's not much danger in high self-esteem that is based on accurate recognition of your intelligence. On the other hand, if you overestimate your abilities, reality will be constantly showing you up and bursting your bubble, and so your (inflated) self-opinion will be bumping up against threats—and those encounters lead to destructive responses.

[11]Unfortunately, a school system that seeks to boost self-esteem in general is likely to produce the more dangerous (inflated) form of self-esteem. It would be fine, for example, to give a hard test and then announce the top few scores for general applause. Such a system recognizes the successful ones, and it shows the rest what the important criteria are (and how much they may need to improve). What is dangerous and worrisome is any procedure that would allow the other students to think that they are just as accomplished as the top scorers even though they did not perform as well. Unfortunately, the self-esteem movement often works in precisely this wrong-headed fashion.

[12]Some students will inevitably be smarter, work harder, learn more, and perform better than others. There is no harm (and in fact probably some positive value) in helping these individuals recognize their superior accomplishments and talents. Such self-esteem is linked to reality and hence less prone to causing dangers and problems.

[13]On the other hand, there is considerable danger and harm in falsely boosting the self-esteem of the other students. It is fine to encourage them to work harder and try to gain an accurate appraisal of their strengths and weaknesses, and it is also fine to recognize their talents and accomplishments in other (including nonacademic) spheres, but don't give them positive feedback that they have not earned. (Also, don't downplay the importance of academic achievement as the central goal of school, such as by suggesting that success at sports or crafts is just as good.) To encourage the

lower-performing students to regard their performance just as favorably as the top learners—a strategy all too popular with the self-esteem movement—is a tragic mistake. If successful, it results only in inflated self-esteem, which is the recipe for a host of problems and destructive patterns.

[14]The logical implications of this argument show exactly when self-esteem should be boosted. When people seriously underestimate their abilities and accomplishments, they need boosting. For example, a student who falsely believes she can't succeed at math may end up short-changing herself and failing to fulfill her potential unless she can be helped to realize that yes, she does have the ability to master math.

[15]In contrast, self-esteem should not be boosted when it is already in the accurate range (or higher). A student who correctly believes that math is not his strong point should not be given exaggerated notions of what he can accomplish. Otherwise, the eventual result will be failure and heartbreak. Along the way he's likely to be angry, troublesome, and prone to blame everybody else when something goes wrong.

[16]In my years as an educator I have seen both patterns. But which is more common? Whether boosting self-esteem in general will be helpful or harmful depends on the answer. And the answer is overwhelmingly clear. Far, far more Americans of all ages have accurate or inflated views of themselves than underestimate themselves. They don't need boosting.

[17]Dozens of studies have documented how inflated self-esteem is. Research interest was sparked some years ago by a survey in which 90 percent of adults rated themselves as "above average" in driving ability. After all, only half can really be above average. Similar patterns are found with almost all good qualities. A survey about leadership ability found that only 2 percent of high school students rated themselves as below average. Meanwhile, a whopping 25 percent claimed to be in the top 1 percent! Similarly, when asked about ability to get along with others, no students at all said they were below average.

[18]Responses to scales designed to measure self-esteem show the same pattern. There are always plenty of scores at the high end and plenty in the middle, but only a few struggle down toward the low end. This seems to be true no matter which of the many self-esteem scales is used. Moreover, the few individuals who do show the truly low self-esteem scores probably suffer from multiple problems that need professional therapy. Self-esteem boosting from schools would not cure them.

[19]Obviously there's precious little evidence of low self-esteem in such numbers. By definition, plenty of people are in reality below average, but most of them refuse to acknowledge it. Meanwhile large numbers of people clearly overestimate themselves. The top 1 percent can really only contain 1 percent, not the 25 percent who claim to belong there. Meanwhile, the problem that would justify programs aimed at boosting self-esteem—people who significantly underestimate themselves—is extremely rare.

—*Roy F. Baumeister*

QUESTIONS ABOUT THE READING

Refer to the general questions on page 155 as well as these specific questions.

CONTENT

- What assumptions does the author seem to make about his audience's attitudes and awareness? Are these assumptions accurate? Explain.
- What are the main issues here? How has this essay affected your thinking about these issues? Explain.
- Is Baumeister's essay credible? Are you convinced this writer knows what he is talking about? Explain.
- Is the writer arguing for definite, probable, or possible effects? Support your answer with specific examples.
- Does the essay have informative value? Explain.

ORGANIZATION

- Trace the line of reasoning from paragraph to paragraph. Is this arrangement effective in supporting Baumeister's causal claims? Explain.
- Identify four devices that increase coherence in this essay, and give examples of each.

STYLE

- What attitude does Baumeister display toward his subject? Toward his audience? How do we know? What are the signals?
- Is the tone appropriate for the audience and purpose? Explain.

RESPONDING TO YOUR READING

Explore your reactions to "Should Schools Try to Boost Self-Esteem?" by using the questions on page 23. Then respond with an essay about your own views on the self-esteem issue.

As an alternative project, analyze the effects of a place, an event, or a relationship. You might trace the effects in your life from having a specific friend or belonging to a specific family or group. Or you might explain the effects on your family, school, or community of a tragic event (such as a suicide) or a fortunate one (say, a financial windfall). Or you might want to show how the socioeconomic atmosphere of your hometown or neighborhood or family has affected the person you have become. Or you might explain how the weather, landscape, or geography of your area affects people's values, behavior, and lifestyle. Or you might speculate about the effects that today's racial or gender or socioeconomic divisions will have on the next generation.

Whatever the topic, be sure your discussion supports a definite viewpoint about the effects of something.

APPLICATION 14-5

Computer Application and Collaborative Project: Application 14-1 suggested investigating the causes of common technological glitches. Using your *listserv* or E-mail, interview the group members to discover the problems they most commonly encounter when they use computers. Choose a glitch that seems to cause widespread frustration. With the help of your on-campus computer services, investigate the usual or probable causes of the glitch and write a report for one group member to present to the class. Note whether you are discovering definite, probable, or possible causes. How might the type of cause you find affect the way your readers should deal with the problem in the future?

CHAPTER 15

EXPLAINING SIMILARITIES OR DIFFERENCES: COMPARISON AND CONTRAST

Comparison examines similarities; contrast examines differences. Comparison and contrast (sometimes just called comparison) help us evaluate things or shed light on their relationship; they help us to visualize the Big Picture.

What readers of comparison and contrast want to know

- *In what significant ways are X and Y similar or alike?*
- *In what significant ways are X and Y different?*
- *Can something about X help us understand Y?*
- *In what significant ways is one preferable to the other?*

DEVELOPING A COMPARISON

Comparison offers perspective on one thing by pointing out its similarities with something else. The two items compared are of the same class: two cars, two countries, two professors. The next paragraph compares drug habits among people of all times and places to those among people of modern times:

A Comparison

Main point (1)

Historical similarity to modern habits (2–3)

Religious similarity to modern habits (4–5)

Modern continuation of habit (6–7)

Concluding point (8)

[1]All the natural narcotics, stimulants, relaxants, and hallucinants known to the modern botanist and pharmacologist were discovered by primitive [people] and have been in use from time immemorial. [2]One of the first things that *Homo sapiens* did with his newly developed rationality and self-consciousness was to set them to work finding out ways to bypass analytical thinking and to transcend or, in extreme cases, temporarily obliterate the isolating awareness of the self. [3]Trying all things that grew in the field or forest, they held fast to that which, in this context, seemed good—everything, that is to say, that would change the quality of consciousness, would make it different, no matter how, from everyday feeling, perceiving, and thinking. [4]Among the Hindus, rhythmic breathing and mental concentration have, to some extent, taken the place of mind-transforming drugs used elsewhere. [5]But even in the land of yoga, even among the religious and even for specifically religious purposes, *Cannabis indica* (marijuana) has been freely used to supplement the effects of spiritual exercises. [6]The habit of taking vacations from the more-or-less purgatorial world, which we have created for ourselves, is universal. [7]Moralists may denounce it; but, in the teeth of disapproving talk and repressive legislation, the habit persists, and mind-transforming drugs are everywhere available. [8]The Marxian formula, "Religion is the opium of the people," is reversible, and one can say, with even more truth, that "Opium is the religion of the people."

—*Aldous Huxley*

DEVELOPING A CONTRAST

A contrast is designed to point out differences between one thing and another. This next paragraph contrasts the beliefs of Satanism with those of Christianity:

A Contrast

Main point (1)
First difference (2–3)

Second difference (4)

Third difference (5–8)

Final—and major—
difference (9–10)

[1]The Satanic belief system, not surprisingly, is the antithesis of Christianity. [2]Their theory of the universe, their cosmology, is based upon the notion that the desired end state is a return to a pagan awareness of their humanity. [3]This is in sharp contrast to the transcendental goals of traditional Christianity. [4]The power associated with the pantheon of gods is also reversed: Satan's power is waxing (increasing); God's, if he still lives, waning. [5]The myths of the Santanic church purport to tell the true story of the rise of Christianity and the fall of paganism, and there is a reversal here too. [6]Christ is depicted as an early "con man" who tricked an anxious and powerless group of individuals into believing a lie. [7]He is typified as "pallid incompetence hanging on a tree." [8]Satanic novices are taught that early church fathers deliberately picked on those aspects of human desire that were most natural and made them sins, in order to use the inevitable transgressions as a means of controlling the populace, promising them salvation in return for obedience. [9]And finally, their substantive belief, the very delimitation of what is sacred and what is profane, is the antithesis of Christian belief. [10]The Satanist is taught to "be natural; to revel in pleasure and in self-gratification; to emphasize indulgence and power in this life."

—*Edward J. Moody*

DEVELOPING A COMBINED COMPARISON AND CONTRAST

A combined comparison and contrast examines similarities and differences displayed by two or more things. This next paragraph first contrasts education with training and, second, compares how each serves important needs of society:

A Combined Comparison/Contrast

Main point (1)

Difference of purpose (2)
How "trained" people serve society (3–5)

[1]To understand the nature of the liberal arts college and its function in our society, it is important to understand the difference between education and training. [2]Training is intended primarily for the service of society; education is primarily for the individual. [3]Society needs doctors, lawyers, engineers, teachers to perform specific tasks necessary to its operation, just as it needs carpenters and plumbers and stenographers. [4]Training supplies the immediate and specific needs of society so that the work of the world may

Similarity of effects (6)

How "educated"
people serve society
(7–11)

Conclusion (12)

continue. [5]And these needs, our training centers—the professional and trade schools—fill. [6]But although education is for the improvement of the individual, it also serves society by providing a leavening of men and women of understanding, of perception and wisdom. [7]They are our intellectual leaders, the critics of our culture, the defenders of our free traditions, the instigators of our progress. [8]They serve society by examining its function, appraising its needs, and criticizing its direction. [9]They may be earning their livings by practicing one of the professions, or in pursuing a trade, or by engaging in business enterprise. [10]They may be rich or poor. [11]They may occupy positions of power and prestige, or they may be engaged in some humble employment. [12]Without them, however, society either disintegrates or else becomes an anthill.

—Harry Kemelman

USING COMPARISON/CONTRAST BEYOND THE WRITING CLASSROOM

- **In other courses:** In sociology, you might assess the economic progress made by minority groups by comparing income figures from earlier decades with today's figures.

- **On the job:** You might compare the qualifications of various job applicants or the performance of various stock and bond portfolios.

- **In the community:** You might compare the voting records of two politicians or the SAT scores of local students compared to the national average.

In what other situations might comparison and contrast make a difference?

USING COMPARISON AND CONTRAST TO EXPLAIN

Referential comparison usually helps readers understand one thing in terms of another. For example, we could explain the effects of high-fat diets on heart disease and cancer by comparing disease rates in Japan (with its low-fat diet) with those in North America. To explain how new knowledge of earthquakes has affected the way engineers design buildings, we can contrast modern buildings with buildings constructed years ago.

Referential comparison also often permits us to explain a complex or abstract idea in terms of another. For example, it's easier to understand how earlier civilizations understood a term like "honor" if we contrast their concept with our own today.

USING COMPARISON AND CONTRAST TO MAKE A POINT

Like other development strategies, comparison and contrast can also support persuasion. For example, it is often used in evaluation, in which we judge the merits of something by measuring it in relationship to something else.

We might compare two (or more) cars, computers, political candidates, college courses, or careers to argue that one is better. In Chapter 1 (pages 13–14), Shirley Haley contrasts her parents' lifestyle with the one she prefers for herself.

Comparisons can support other kinds of arguments as well. Huxley's comparison of past and present drug habits, for example (page 224), supports the thesis that any habit so long entrenched will be hard to eliminate. Kemelman's analysis of the differences and similarities between training and education (page 225) supports his claim that the liberal arts college has an important function in our society.

Do you think that Moody's contrast of Christians and Satanists also supports an implied argument, or is it mainly referential? Explain.

As always, the evidence with which you support your content, your organizational skills, and your command of style are what make your argumentative comparisons persuasive.

A SPECIAL KIND OF COMPARISON: ANALOGY

Ordinary comparison shows similarities between two things of the same class (two teachers, two styles of dress, two political philosophies). *Analogy,* on the other hand, shows similarities between two things of *different classes* (writing and skiing, freshman registration and a merry-go-round, a dorm room and a junkyard). Analogy answers the reader's question:

Can you explain X by comparing it to something I already know?

Analogies are useful in explaining something abstract, complex, or unfamiliar, as long as the easier subject is broadly familiar to readers. This next analogy helps clarify an unfamiliar technical concept (dangerous levels of a toxic chemical) by comparing it to something more familiar (a human hair).

Analogy

A dioxin concentration of 500 parts per trillion is lethal to guinea pigs. One part per trillion is roughly equal to the thickness of a human hair compared to the distance across the United States.

—*Congressional Research Report*

GUIDELINES FOR COMPARISON AND CONTRAST

1. *Compare or contrast items in the same class.* Compare dogs and cats, but not dogs and trees; men and women, but not women and bicycles. Otherwise you have no logical basis for comparison.

2. *Rest the comparison on a clear and definite basis: costs, uses, benefits, appearance, results.* Huxley compares people of all times for their drug habits; Moody compares Satanism·and Christianity for their primary beliefs; Kemelman compares education and training by their function in our society.

3. *Give both items equal treatment.* Both Moody and Kemelman give roughly equal space to each item. In Huxley's paragraph, the other item in the comparison, modern drug use habits, is only briefly mentioned, but readers can intuit its place in the discussion from their own general knowledge. Huxley, then, offers an implied comparison. Points discussed for one item also are discussed (or implied) for the other, generally in the same order.

4. *Support and clarify the comparison or contrast through credible examples.* Use research, if necessary, for examples that readers can visualize.

5. *Follow either a block pattern or a point-by-point pattern.* In the block pattern, first one item is discussed fully, then the next, as in Kemelman: "trained" people in the first block; "educated" people in the second. Choose a block pattern when the overall picture is more important than the individual points.

In the point-by-point pattern, one point about both items is discussed, then the next point, and so on, as in Moody: the first difference between Satanism and Christianity is in their respective cosmologies; the second is in their view of God's power; the third, in their myths about the rise of Christianity, and so on. Choose a point-by-point pattern when specific points might be hard to remember unless placed side by side.

Block pattern	Point-by-point pattern
Item *A*	
first point	First point of *A*/first
second point	point of *B,* etc.
third point, etc.	
Item *B*	
first point	Second point of
second point	*A*/second point of *B,*
third point, etc.	etc.

APPLICATION 15-1

Paragraph Warm-Up: Comparison/Contrast

Using comparison or contrast (or both), write a paragraph discussing the likenesses or differences between two people, animals, attitudes, activities, places, or things. Identify clearly the situation, the audience, and your purpose. Then classify your paragraph: does it primarily inform, or does it make a point?

Here are some possible subjects:

two places I know well

two memorable teaching styles (good or bad)

two similar consumer items

two pets I've had

the benefits of two kinds of exercise

....

APPLICATION 15-2

Paragraph Warm-Up: Analogy

Develop a paragraph explaining something abstract, complex, or unfamiliar by comparing it to something concrete, simpler, or familiar. ("Writing is like . . . "; "Love is like . . . "; "Osmosis works like . . . "). Identify a specific purpose or audience. Do you have an informative or a persuasive goal?

....

APPLICATION 15-3

Essay Practice

In this next selection, a journalist summarizes findings from surveys and interviews that examine the attitudes of people below age 30. As you read, think about the types of comparisons presented and how you might respond with comparisons of your own.

ESSAY FOR ANALYSIS AND RESPONSE

PROFILES OF TODAY'S YOUTH: THEY COULDN'T CARE LESS

[1]John Karras, 28 years old, was in a card shop the other day as the radio, which provides the soundtrack for his generation, offered a report on the dead and missing in the floods that had just flashed through southeastern Ohio.

[2]The cashier, a man a bit younger than Mr. Karras, looked up at the radio and said: "I wish they'd stop talking about it. I'm sick of hearing about it."

[3]Mr. Karras, a doctoral student in education at Ohio State, recalled this incident to illustrate what he sees as a "pervasive" attitude among the members of his generation toward the larger world: the typical young person doesn't want to hear about it "unless it's knocking on my door."

[4]The findings of two national studies concur. The studies, one released today and the other late last year, paint a portrait of a generation of young adults, from 18 to 29 years of age, who are indifferent toward public affairs. It is a generation that, as the Times Mirror Center for the People and the Press put it in a report released today, "knows less, cares less, votes less, and is less critical of its leaders and institutions than young people in the past."

[5]Caught in the backwash of the baby boom, whose culture and attitudes still dominate American discourse, members of the "baby bust" seem almost to be rebelling against rebellion. Anyone who was hoping that the energy of this new generation would snap the nation out of its political lethargy, as young people helped awaken the nation from the quiescent 1950's, will probably be disappointed.

[6]"My teacher told me: 'Always question authority,'" said Paul Grugin, 22, one of two dozen young people interviewed this week by *The New York Times* in this mid-size city in the middle of the country. "You can question authority, but you can burden authority. Let them authoritate."

[7]The indifference of this generation—to politics, to government, even to news about the outside world—is beginning to affect American politics and society, the reports suggest, helping to explain such seemingly disparate trends as the decline in voting, the rise of tabloid television and the effectiveness of negative advertising.

[8]While apathy and alienation have become a national plague, the disengagement seems to run deeper among young Americans, those 18 to 29, setting them clearly apart from earlier generations.

[9]No one has yet offered a full explanation for why this should be so. The lack of mobilizing issues is part of the answer, as are the decline of the family and the rise of television.

[10]Young people themselves mention the weakness of their civics education, and they talk incessantly of stress—their preoccupation with getting jobs or grades and their concern about personal threats like AIDS and drugs. "There are a lot more pressures on them than there were on us," said 48-year-old Ron Zeller, who talked about the differences along with his 22-year-old daughter, Susan, and his 18-year-old son, John.

[11]The study by Times Mirror, a public opinion research center supported by Times Mirror Co., looked at 50 years of public opinion data and concluded, "Over most of the past five decades, younger members of the public have been at least as well informed as older people. In 1990 that is no longer the case."

[12]This concern was echoed in a second report, prepared last year by People for the American Way, a liberal lobby and research organization, which concluded that there is "a citizenship crisis" in which "America's youth are alarmingly ill-prepared to keep democracy alive in the 1990's and beyond."

[13]Susan Zeller, 22, who is about to enter Case Western law school, agreed. "I don't think many people my age group are very concerned," she

said. "They're only concerned about issues that affect them. When the drinking age went up, quite a few people were upset."

[14]The decline in voting is one illustration of how what seems to be a general problem is, in fact, most heavily concentrated among the young. Surveys by the census bureau show that since 1972 almost all of the decline in voting has been among those under 45, and that the sharpest drop is among those between 18 and 25. Among the elderly, voting has risen, according to the census bureau surveys.

[15]Older people, more settled than the young, have always participated more in elections. But the gap has widened substantially. In 1972, half of those between 18 and 24 said they voted, as did 71 percent of those 45 to 64, a gap of 21 percentage points. In 1988, 36 percent of the 18- to 24-year-olds and 68 percent of the 45- to 64-year-olds said they voted, a gap of 32 percentage points.

[16]Shonda Wolfe, 24, who has waited tables since dropping out of college, said she had voted only once, when she was 18 and still living at home. "I guess my mom was there to push me," she said.

[17]Now, she said, she does not pay much attention to politics or to the news. "I try to avoid it—all the controversy," she said. "It just doesn't interest me at this point in my life. I'd rather be outside doing something, taking a walk."

[18]Young people have always had to worry about getting started in life, beginning a career and a family. But this young generation, for whom Vietnam is a history lesson and Watergate a blurry childhood memory, seems to have adopted the cynicism of parents and older siblings without going through the activism and disappointments that produced that cynicism.

[19]Not one of the young people interviewed in Columbus, at the Street Scene Restaurant and the Short North Tavern, had a good word to say about politics or politicians. But unlike older people, who often express anger about news about sloth or corruption in government, these young people seem simply to be reporting it as a well-known fact. "Most politicians are liars," said Deborah Roberts, a 29-year-old secretary.

[20]People for the American Way, in its report, noted that young people seemed to have a half-formed understanding of citizenship, stressing rights but ignoring responsibilities.

[21]When asked to define citizenship, Shonda Wolfe said it meant the right not to be harassed by the police. She cited as an intrusion on her rights the security guards' insistence at a concert that she and her boyfriend stop turning on their cigarette lighters.

[22]Nancy Radcliffe-Spurgeon, 24, a student at Ohio State, said she thought that many of the attitudes of her generation were based on feeling safe. "It's easy to isolate yourself when you think things are going pretty well for you, so you don't rock the boat."

[23]Occasionally, someone in the interview would mention voting. None of the young people when asked about citizenship included in their defini-

tion of good citizenship running for office, attending a community board meeting, studying an issue, signing a a petition, writing a letter to the governor, or going to a rally.

[24]These young people are aware that some of their attitudes are a product of different times. Young people protesting the war in Vietnam were also engaged by an issue that affected them, but one that the rest of the country also accepted as being of central importance. "When people your age were our age, there was a lot more strife," Jeff Brodeur, a 22-year-old senior at Ohio State, told a 36-year-old visitor.

[25]Certain issues do get their attention, almost always involving government interference in personal freedoms. They generally favor access to abortion, and a few of the young people were upset by efforts to cut off Federal funds for art work deemed obscene.

[26]Their concern about the arts was not surprising because in the interviews the young people showed that their main contact with the larger world was through culture. Mr. Brodeur, for example, said he first became aware of apartheid in South Africa through the song "Biko," written by Peter Gabriel about Steve Biko, a prominent anti-apartheid leader in South Africa of the 1970's.

[27]But Mr. Brodeur's research seems more the exception than the rule. Andrew Kohut, director of surveys for Times Mirror, said there was a new generation gap, in which those under 30 were separated by their lack of knowledge and interest from those over 30.

[28]People in their 30's and 40's are disenchanted with the world, but remain aware, said Mr. Kohut. But those under 30, he said, "are not so much disillusioned as disinterested."

[29]The Times Mirror analysis was based on its own public opinion polling as well as comparisons with polling conducted by other organizations over the past 50 years.

[30]Deborah Roberts, the secretary, says she still reads a newspaper, sort of. "There's more bad news on the front page," she said, explaining why she skips over it. "I like to go to the local news; it's the fun news."

[31]"Attitudes like this are having a considerable effect on the news media," Mr. Kohut said. The number of people who read newspapers is declining, in general, but that number has plunged among the young. And not simply because they have turned to television, according to surveys. Viewing of traditional television news by the young is also shown to be down, although they do watch the new types of shows that concentrate on scandal and celebrity.

[32]"The generation gap in news and information is playing out in politics in very significant ways," Mr. Kohut added.

[33]"The 30-second commercial spot is a particularly appropriate medium for the MTV generation," he continued.

[34]"At the conclusion of the 1988 campaign, Times Mirror's research showed that young voters, who began the campaign knowing less than

older voters, were every bit as likely to recall advertised political themes such as pollution in Boston Harbor, Willie Horton and the flag.

[35]"Sound bites and symbolism, the principal fuel of modern political campaigns, are well suited to young voters who know less and have limited interest in politics and public policy. Their limited appetites and aptitudes are shaping the practice of politics and the nature of our democracy."

—*Michael Oreskes*

QUESTIONS ABOUT THE READING

CONTENT

- In your own words, restate the point of the comparison in a complete sentence.
- Would additional support for the comparison make it more convincing? Explain.

ORGANIZATION

- Does this comparison follow the block pattern or the point-by-point pattern? Comment on the effectiveness of the pattern.
- One subject of the comparison (today's youth) is discussed more extensively than the other (yesterday's youth). Is this imbalance justified? Explain.

STYLE

- Is this piece an example of relatively "objective reporting" or does the author insert his own attitude toward the material? Explain and give examples.
- Is the tone appropriate for the audience and purpose? Explain.

RESPONDING TO YOUR READING

Explore your reactions to "Profiles of Today's Youth," by using the questions on page 23. Do you agree with the negative comparisons offered? If you disagree, you might respond by offering *positive* comparisons (For example: In what ways is this generation superior to earlier counterparts?). If you agree with the comparisons, you might explore possible or probable causes (Why are we like this?). If you choose to explore causes, refer to Chapter 14 and try to be relatively objective in your analysis—instead of coming across as an indignant victim. Be sure your response supports a clear and definite thesis.

· ·

APPLICATION 15-4

Computer Application: Many schools now have World Wide Web sites, and some have made portions of their campus writing services available on-line. Services you can access may include exercises or tip sheets that you can download, or they may actually consist of opportunities for collaboration and consultation via electronic "chat rooms." In these chat rooms, participants from all over the world can exchange messages almost instantly (in "real-time"), as if they were having a face-to-face conversation. Using a Web browser, search for other colleges and universities and investigate their online writing services. (You might start with Purdue and the University of Texas at Austin, both of which provide access to their writing centers as well as links to other sources.) Choose two writing center sites and write a comparison/contrast paper assessing the quality of the services and the information provided.

APPLICATION 15-5

Collaborative Project—Gender Differences: Recent research on ways men and women communicate in meetings indicates a definite gender gap. Communication specialist Kathleen Kelley-Reardon offers this assessment of gender differences in group communication:

> Women and men operate according to communication rules for their gender, what experts call 'gender codes.' They learn, for example, to show gratitude, ask for help, take control, and express emotion, deference, and commitment in different ways. (88–89)

Professor Kelley-Reardon describes specific elements of a female gender code: Women are more likely than men to take as much time as needed to explore an issue, build consensus and relationship among members, use tact in expressing views, use care in choosing their words, consider the listener's feelings, speak softly, allow interruptions, make requests instead of giving commands ("Could I have the report by Friday?" versus "Have this ready by Friday."), and preface assertions in ways that avoid offending ("I don't want to seem disagreeable here, but . . . ").

Divide into small groups of mixed genders and complete the following tasks to test the hypothesis that women and men communicate differently.

Each group member prepares the following brief messages—without consulting with other members:

- A thank-you note to a friend who has done you a favor.

- A note asking a friend for help with a problem or project.

- A note asking a collaborative peer to be more cooperative or stop interrupting or complaining.

- A note expressing impatience, frustration, confusion, or satisfaction to members of your group.

- A note offering support to a good friend who is depressed.

- A note to a new student, welcoming this person to the dorm.
- A request for a higher grade, based on your hard work.
- The collaborative meeting is out of hand, so you decide to take control. Write out what you would say.
- Some members of your group are dragging their feet on a project. Write out what you would say.

As a group, compare messages, draw conclusions, and appoint one member to present the findings to the class.

OPTIONS FOR ESSAY WRITING

1. If you had your high school years to relive, what would you do differently?
2. During your years in school you've had much experience with both good teaching and bad. Based on your experiences, what special qualities are necessary for good teaching? Use a series of contrasts to make your point.

WORK CITED

Kelley-Reardon, Kathleen. *They Don't Get It, Do They?: Communication in the Workplace—Closing the Gap Between Women and Men.* Boston: Little, 1995.

EXPLAINING THE EXACT MEANING: DEFINITION

All successful writing shares one feature—clarity. Clear writing begins with clear thinking; clear thinking begins with an understanding of what all the terms mean. Therefore, clear writing depends on definitions that both reader and writer understand.

What readers of
definition want to know

- *What is it?*
- *What is its dictionary meaning?*
- *What personal meaning(s) does it suggest?*

Words can signify two kinds of meaning: *denotative* and *connotative*. Denotations—the meanings in a dictionary—usually appear in referential writing. A word's denotation means the same thing to everyone. *Apple* denotes the firm, rounded, edible fruit of the apple tree.

But words have *connotations* as well, overtones or suggestions beyond their dictionary meanings. A word can have different connotations for different people. Thus, *apple* might connote Adam and Eve, apple pie, Johnny Appleseed, apple polisher, or good health. These meanings play an important part in persuasive writing, because a writer uses the possible meanings his or her audience finds in words to elicit the emotions of the audience or to share a viewpoint.

USING DENOTATIVE DEFINITIONS TO EXPLAIN

Denotative definitions either explain a term that is specialized or unfamiliar to your readers or convey your exact definition of a word that has more than one meaning.

Most fields have specialized terms. Engineers talk about *prestressed concrete, tolerances,* or *trusses;* psychologists refer to *sociopathic behavior* or *paranoia;* attorneys discuss *liens, easements,* and *escrow accounts.* For readers outside the field, these terms must be defined.

Sometimes a term will be unfamiliar to some readers because it is new or no longer in use *(future shock, meltdown, uptalk)* or a slang word *(bad, diss, freak).*

Some readers, though, are unaware that some familiar terms such as *guarantee, disability, lease,* or *consent* take on very specialized meanings in some contexts. What *consent* means in one situation is not necessarily what it means in another. Denotative definition then becomes crucial if all parties are to understand.

CHOOSING THE LEVEL OF DETAIL

How much detail will readers need to understand a term or a concept? Can you use a synonym (a term with a similar meaning)? Will you need a sentence, a paragraph—or an essay?

Synonyms.   Often, you can clarify the meaning of an unfamiliar word by using a more familiar synonym:

> To **waffle** means to be evasive and misleading.
>
> The **leaching field** (sievelike drainage area) requires 15 inches of crushed stone.

Note: Be sure that the synonym clarifies your meaning instead of obscuring it. Don't say:

> A tumor is a neoplasm.

Do say:

> A tumor is a growth of cells that occurs independently of surrounding tissue and serves no useful function.

Sentence Definitions.   More complex terms may require a *sentence definition* (which may be stated in more than one sentence). These definitions follow a fixed pattern: (1) the name of the item to be defined, (2) the class to which the item belongs, and (3) the features that differentiate the item from all others in its class.

Term	Class	Distinguishing features
carburetor	a mixing device	in gasoline engines that blends air and fuel into a vapor for combustion within the cylinders
diabetes	a metabolic disease	caused by a disorder of the pituitary or pancreas and characterized by excessive urination, persistent thirst, and inability to metabolize sugar
brief	a legal document	containing all the facts and points of law pertinent to a case and filed by an attorney before the case is argued in court
stress	an applied force	that strains or deforms a body

These elements are combined into one or more complete sentences:

> Diabetes is a metabolic disease caused by a disorder of the pituitary or pancreas and characterized by excessive urination, persistent thirst, and inability to metabolize sugar.

Sentence definition is especially useful if you need to stipulate your precise definition for a term that has several possible meanings. For example, *qualified buyer* can have different meanings for readers in the construction industry, banking, or real estate business.

GUIDELINES FOR SENTENCE DEFINITIONS

1. *Classify the term precisely.* The narrower your class, the clearer your meaning. *Stress* is classified as an applied force; to say that stress "is what . . . " or "takes place when . . . " fails to reflect a specific classification. Diabetes is precisely classified as a *metabolic disease,* not as a *medical term.*

2. *Differentiate the term accurately.* If the distinguishing features are too broad, they will apply to more than this one item. A definition of *brief* as a "legal document used in court" fails to differentiate brief from all other legal documents (*wills, affidavits,* and the like).

3. *Avoid circular definitions.* Do not repeat, as part of the distinguishing feature, the word you are defining. "Stress is an applied force that places stress on a body" is a circular definition.

Expanded Definition. The sentence definition of carburetor on page 238 is adequate for a general reader who simply needs to know what a carburetor is. An instruction manual for mechanics, however, would define carburetor in much greater detail; these readers need to know how a carburetor works, how it is made, and what conditions cause it to operate correctly. Your choice of synonym definition, sentence definition, or expanded definition depends on the amount of information your readers need. Consider the two examples that follow.

A Sentence Definition

It [paranoia] refers to a psychosis based on a delusionary premise of self-referred persecution or grandeur (e.g., "The Knights of Columbus control the world and are out to get me" . . .), and supported by a complex, rigorously logical system that interprets all or nearly all sense impressions as evidence for that premise.

This definition is part of an article published in *Harper's,* a magazine whose general readership will require a more detailed definition of this specialized term. The expanded version below uses several explanatory strategies.

Expanded Definition of a Specialized Term

Main point (1)
Sentence definition (2)

[1]Paranoia is a word on everyone's lips, but only among mental-health professionals has it acquired a tolerably specific meaning. [2]It refers to a psychosis based on a delusionary premise of self-referred persecution or grandeur (e.g., "The Knights of Columbus control the world and are out to

Effect-cause analysis (3)
Process analysis (4)

Cause-effect analysis
(5–7)

Contrast (8)

get me" . . .), and supported by a complex, rigorously logical system that interprets all or nearly all sense impressions as evidence for that premise. [3]The traditional psychiatric view is that paranoia is an extreme measure for the defense of the integrity of the personality against annihilating guilt. [4]The paranoid (so goes the theory) thrusts his guilt outside himself by denying his hostile or erotic impulses and projecting them onto other people or onto the whole universe. [5]Disintegration is avoided, but at high cost; the paranoid view of reality can make everyday life terrifying and social intercourse problematical. [6]And paranoia is tiring. [7]It requires exhausting mental effort to construct trains of thought demonstrating that random events or details "prove" a wholly unconnected premise. [8]Some paranoids hallucinate, but hallucination is by no means obligatory; paranoia is an interpretive, not a perceptual, dysfunction.

—*Hendrik Hertzberg and David C. K. McClelland*

General readers are much more likely to understand this expanded definition than the sentence definition alone.

As we have seen in earlier chapters, synonyms and sentence definitions are part of most writing. But notice in turn how various development strategies from earlier chapters are employed in an expanded definition.

This following expanded definition, from an auto insurance policy, defines damages for *bodily injury to others,* a phrase that could have many possible meanings.

Expanded Definition of a Familiar Term with a Special Meaning

Main point (1)
Sentence definition (2)

Cause-effect (3–6)

Negation (7)

[1]Under this coverage, we will pay damages to people injured or killed by your auto in Massachusetts accidents. [2]Damages are the amount an injured person is legally entitled to collect through a court judgment or settlement. [3]We will pay only if you or someone else using your auto with your consent is legally responsible for the accident. [4]The most we will pay for injuries to any one person as a result of any one accident is $5,000. [5]The most we will pay for injuries to two or more people as a result of any one accident is a total of $10,000. [6]This is the most we will pay as the result of a single accident no matter how many autos or premiums are shown on the Coverage Selections page. [7]We will not pay: for injuries to guest occupants of your auto; for accidents outside of Massachusetts or in places in Massachusetts where the public has no right of access; for injuries to any employees of the legally responsible person if they are entitled to Massachusetts workers' compensation benefits.

This definition is designed to answer two basic questions:

- *Under what conditions will the insurer pay damages?*
- *Under what conditions will the insurer not pay?*

Thus the development patterns of cause-effect and negation (showing what something isn't) most logically serve the purpose of this definition.

USING CONNOTATIVE DEFINITIONS TO MAKE A POINT

A denotative definition cannot communicate the personal or special meaning a writer may intend. But connotative definitions explain terms that hold personal meanings for the writer. Because they are designed to draw readers into the writer's complex, private associations, connotative definitions almost always call for expanded treatment.

In the next paragraph, the denotative definition of house (a structure serving as a dwelling) is replaced by a more personal, artistic, and spiritual definition:

A Connotative Definition

Main point (1)
Analogies (2–4)

[1]What is a house? [2]A house is a human circumstance in Nature, like a tree or the rocks of the hills; a good house is a technical performance where form and function are made one; a house is integral to its site, a grace, not a disgrace, to its environment, suited to elevate the life of its individual inhabitants; a house is therefore integral with the nature of the methods and materials used to build it. [3]A house to be a good home has throughout what is most needed in American life today—integrity. [4]Integrity, once there, enables those who live in that house to take spiritual root and grow.

—*Frank Lloyd Wright*

Connotative definition is especially useful when we want people to accept a particular definition of a term that carries multiple, conflicting meanings (*freedom, love, patriotism,* or the like), and especially when the meaning we advocate is unconventional or controversial.

Unless you are sure that readers know the exact or special meaning you intend, always define a term the first time you use it.

APPLICATION 16-1

Sentence definitions require precise classification and detailed differentiation. Is each of these definitions adequate for a general reader? Rewrite those that seem inadequate. If necessary, consult dictionaries and specialized encyclopedias.

1. A bicycle is a vehicle with two wheels.
2. A transistor is a device used in transistorized electronic equipment.
3. Surfing is when one rides a wave to shore while standing on a board specifically designed for buoyancy and balance.

4. Mace is a chemical aerosol spray used by the police.

5. A Geiger counter measures radioactivity.

6. A cactus is a succulent.

7. In law, an indictment is a criminal charge against a defendant.

8. Friction is a force between two bodies.

9. Hypoglycemia is a medical term.

10. A computer is a machine that handles information with amazing speed.

APPLICATION 16-2

Paragraph Warm-Up: Denotative Definition that Explains

Using denotative definition, write a paragraph explaining the meaning of a term that is specialized, new, or otherwise unfamiliar to your reader. List in the margin the strategies for expansion you've used. Begin with a formal sentence definition (term-class-differentiation). Select a term from one of the lists below, from your major (defined for a nonmajor), or from your daily conversation with peers (defined for an elderly person). Identify clearly the situation, the audience, and your purpose.

Specialized terms	Slang terms
summons	jock
generator	Yuppie
dewpoint	nerd
capitalism	turkey
economic recession	fox
microprocessor	to break
T-square	awesome

APPLICATION 16-3

Paragraph Warm-Up: Connotative Definition that Makes a Point

Using connotative definition, write a paragraph explaining the special meaning or associations that a term holds for you. Select a term from the list below, or provide your own. List in the margin the expansion strategies you've used. Identify clearly the situation, the audience, and your purpose.

patriotism	education	freedom
trust	marriage	courage
friendship	God	peace
progress	guilt	morality
beauty	the perfect date	happiness
adult	sex appeal	fear

. . . .

APPLICATION 16-4

Essay Practice

In this next selection from *The New York Times*, a journalism professor defines a term that may seem unfamiliar—until we begin reading. As you read, identify the various development strategies used to expand this definition.

ESSAY FOR ANALYSIS AND RESPONSE

LIKE, UPTALK?

[1]I used to speak in a regular voice. I was able to assert, demand, question. Then I started teaching. At a university? And my students had this rising into-nation thing? It was particularly noticeable on telephone messages. "Hello? Professor Gorman? This is Albert? From feature writing?"

[2]I had no idea that a change in the "intonation contour" of a sentence, as linguists put it, could be as contagious as the common cold. But before long I noticed a Jekyll-and-Hyde transformation in my own speech. I first heard it when I myself was leaving a message. "This is Jim Gorman? I'm doing an article on Klingon? The language? From 'Star Trek'?" I realized then that I was unwittingly, unwillingly speaking uptalk.

[3]I was, like, appalled?

[4]Rising intonations at the end of a sentence or phrase are not new. In many languages, a "phrase final rise" indicates a question. Some Irish, English and Southern American dialects use rises all the time. Their use at the end of a declarative statement may date back in America to the 17th century.

[5]Nonetheless, we are seeing, well, hearing, something different. Uptalk, under various names, has been noted on this newspaper's Op-Ed page and on National Public Radio. Cynthia McLemore, a University of Pennsylvania linguist who knows as much about uptalk as anyone, says the frequency and repetition of rises mark a new phenomenon. And although uptalk has been most common among teen-agers, in particular young women, it seems to be spreading. Says McLemore, "What's going on now in America looks like a

dialect shift." In other words, what is happening may be a basic change in the way Americans talk.

[6]Nobody knows exactly where uptalk came from. It might have come from California, from Valley Girl talk. It may be an upper-middle-class thing, probably starting with adolescents. But everybody has an idea about what uptalk means. Some twentysomethings say uptalk is part of their attitude: cool, ironic, uncommitted.

[7]I myself was convinced that uptalk was tentative, testing, oversensitive: not feminine so much as wimpy, detumescent. Imagine how it would sound in certain cocksure, authoritative occupations, like police work:

You're under arrest? You have some rights?

Or surgery:

So, first I'll open up your chest?

[8]I also thought how some of the great dead white males of the much maligned canon might sound, reintoned:

It was really dark? Like, on the deep? The face of the deep?

Or:

Hi, I'm Ishmael? I'll be your narrator?

Or:

A horse? A horse? My kingdom for a horse?

[9]My speculations have some support; there are linguists who see uptalk as being about uncertainty and deference to the listener. But McLemore scoffs at these ideas. People tend to hear what they want to hear, she says. One can, for instance, take a speech pattern common among women and link it to a stereotype of women. (Uncertain? Deferential?)

[10]Deborah Tannen—a linguist at Georgetown, who, with her book "You Just Don't Understand: Women and Men in Conversation," may have overtaken Noam Chomsky and become the best-known linguist in America—contends that broad theorizing about uptalk is downright foolish. Speech patterns are contagious, she says, and they spread the way fads do. "There's a fundamental human impulse to imitate what we hear," she says. "Teen-agers talk this way because other teen-agers talk this way and they want to sound like their peers."

[11]That doesn't mean rises have no function. They can be used as a signal that "more is coming," says Mark Aronoff of the State University of New York at Stony Brook. An adolescent might be signaling "I have more to say; don't interrupt me." McLemore says an early study of telephone conversation suggested that rises may be used as a probe of sorts, to see if the hearer is getting what you are saying.

[12]A friend of mine (of no formal linguistic expertise) likes this latter in-

terpretation. He insists that the spread of uptalk indicates the lack of shared knowledge in our society. Our society, he contends, has become so fragmented that no one knows anymore whether another person will have a clue as to what he's saying. We need to test the hearer's level of understanding.

[13]*Like, suppose I want to talk about Sabicas? Or Charles Barkley? Or nitric oxide? The molecule of the year? For 1992?*

[14]By using the questioning tone, I'm trying to see if my conversational partner knows anything at all about flamenco guitar, professional basketball or neurochemistry.

[15]McLemore studied intonation in one very particular context. She observed uses of intonation in a Texas sorority, where uptalk was not at all about uncertainty or deference. It was used most commonly by the leaders, the senior officers. Uptalk was a kind of accent, or tag, to highlight new information for listeners: "We're having a bake sale? On the west mall? On Sunday?" When saying something like "Everyone should know that your dues should be in," they used a falling intonation at the end of the sentence.

[16]The sorority members' own interpretation of uptalk was that it was a way of being inclusive. McLemore's conclusions are somewhat similar. She says the rises are used to connect phrases, and to connect the speaker to the listener, as a means of "getting the other person involved."

[17]Since McLemore did her study, people are constantly calling to her attention other uses of uptalk. It seems to be a common speech pattern in Toronto, where, she says, a radio show called "Ask the Pastors" displays uptalk in spades. She also found that on another radio show the Mayor of Austin, Tex., used rises to mark items in a list. Asked to explain why he should maintain bike paths, he said things like: Austin has a good climate? It's good for bike riding? McLemore also observed a second-grade teacher who used rises freely for commands and statements. "Jason? Back to your chair? Thank you?"

[18]I confess to ambivalence about uptalk. When I use it, I judge it to mark a character flaw. On the other hand, there are some ritual utterances that could clearly benefit from a change in pitch contour.

[19]*Mea culpa? Mea culpa? Mea maxima culpa?*

[20]Or, to reflect the true state of matrimony in our society:

[21]*I do?*

[22]I do not, however, want the speech pattern to spread to airplane pilots. I don't want to hear: *This is Captain McCormick? Your pilot? We'll be flying to Denver? Our cruising altitude will be, like, 30,000 feet?*

[23]McLemore, however, says it seems possible that we will be hearing such an intonation among pilots in the future. After all, it looks as if pilots are getting younger every year. Once commercial airline pilots start using uptalk, McLemore notes, it will mean that a full-blown dialect shift has occurred. Uptalk won't be uptalk anymore. It will be, like, American English?

—*James Gorman*

QUESTIONS ABOUT THE READING

Refer to the general questions on page 155 and the specific ones here.

CONTENT

- Is Gorman's definition of *uptalk* primarily denotative or connotative? Explain and give examples.
- What is the primary expansion strategy in this definition? Explain.

ORGANIZATION

- Trace the line of thought in this essay. Is this the most effective order? Explain.
- Does the organization make the expansion strategies easier to follow? Explain.

STYLE

- Identify the major devices that increase coherence.
- What attitude does the author express toward his subject? How do we know? Where are the signals?

RESPONDING TO YOUR READING

Explore your reactions to "Like, Uptalk?" by using the questions on page 23. Then respond with your own essay. For instance, you might define some other term of recent vintage, such as *rap, grunge, skater,* or *homeboy.* Be sure your definition is connotative as well as denotative.

Or you might examine the origins of certain dialects (say, "New England" or "Southern") and explain how these speech patterns affect our perceptions of the speakers.

Your essay should make a clear and definite point about the larger meaning behind the examples you provide.

· ·

APPLICATION 16-5

Computer Application: Consult either a computer manual, a computer publication, or a newsgroup for computer enthusiasts. Find at least five technical terms that you—and probably most of your classmates—aren't familiar with or don't fully understand. Research these terms and then, for your classmates, write both sentence and expanded definitions for two of them. Some possibilities: *newsgroup, zip drive, FTP, MOO, MUD, IRC, baud, HTML, bookmark, URL, Netiquette.*

APPLICATION 16-6

Collaborative Project: Date rape has become a highly publicized issue. The following excerpts, "Antioch College Sexual Offense Policy" and the "Consensual Sex Contract," represent two attempts to address this contentious issue.

THE ANTIOCH COLLEGE SEXUAL OFFENSE POLICY [AN EXCERPT]

These rules, written by Antioch students and established by the college in 1992, require verbal "consent" for any level of sexual contact whatsoever.

1. For the purpose of this policy, "consent" shall be defined as follows: the act of willingly and verbally agreeing to engage in specific sexual contact or conduct.

2. If sexual contact and/or conduct is not mutually and simultaneously initiated, then the person who initiates sexual contact/conduct is responsible for getting the verbal consent of the other individual(s) involved.

3. Obtaining consent is an ongoing process in any sexual interaction. Verbal consent should be obtained with each new level of physical and/or sexual contact/conduct in any given interaction, regardless of who initiates it. Asking "Do you want to have sex with me?" is not enough. The request for consent must be specific to each act.

4. The person with whom sexual contact/conduct is initiated is responsible to express verbally and/or physically her/his willingness or lack of willingness when reasonably possible.

5. If someone has initially consented but then stops consenting during a sexual interaction, she/he should communicate withdrawal verbally and/or through physical resistance. The other individual(s) must stop immediately.

6. To knowingly take advantage of someone who is under the influence of alcohol, drugs, and/or prescribed medication is not acceptable behavior in the Antioch community.

CONSENSUAL SEX CONTRACT

This document, published in 1992 by the National Center for Men (a group supporting men's rights), provides a written record of "consent."

AGREEMENT BEFORE LOVEMAKING entered into by _____ and _____ , this _____ day of _____ , 199__.

WHEREAS, the parties to this agreement want to be sexually intimate, but also want to avoid the misunderstandings that sometimes occur after sex,

Now, THEREFORE, the parties enter into the following agreements (check one declaration from each pair):

_____ We want to have a relationship that may lead to sexual intercourse.
_____ We want to have sex but without intercourse.

_____ We want to have sex as a way of expressing an emotional commitment that may eventually lead to marriage.
_____ We want to have a sexual relationship but we're not ready for marriage.

_____ We want our relationship to be monogamous.
_____ We both want the freedom to see other people.

_____ We want to have sex in order to conceive a child.
_____ We're not ready to be parents now. If an unplanned pregnancy occurs, neither one of us will try to force the other into parenthood.

_____ We want our sexual encounter to be discreet.
_____ We want the whole world to know about our love for each other.

Neither of us may claim to be the victim of sexual harassment or assault or rape as a result of the acts which are the subject of this agreement. By signing this contract, we acknowledge that the anticipated sexual experience will be of mutual consent.

We understand that this contract may be terminated at any time by either one of us *except* during the sexual activity contemplated by this agreement.

We understand that no provision of this agreement relieves us of the obligation to treat each other with caring and mutual respect.

IN WITNESS THEREOF, the parties execute the aforementioned agreement.

_____   _____
(Man's signature)   *(Woman's signature)*

—*Mel Feit,*
the National Center for Men

After reading these documents, refer to the questions on page 23 as well as these:

- Is each of these definitions primarily denotative or connotative? Explain.
- Is one more realistic than the other, in your view? Explain.
- Is either document adequate in defining "consent"? Explain.

Working in small groups, compare your reactions to these two documents, and decide on a group response. Appoint one group member to take detailed notes of the proceedings, one to draft the group's response, one to revise it, one to edit all versions, and one to present the final draft to the class.

· ·

OPTION FOR ESSAY WRITING

Along with changing times come changes in our way of seeing. Some terms that held meanings for us two or three years ago may have acquired radically different meanings by now. If we once defined *success* narrowly as social status and income bracket, we might now define it in broader words: leading the kind of life that puts us in close touch with ourselves and the world around us. Similarly, the meanings of many other terms (education, friendship, freedom, maturity, self-fulfillment, pain, love, home, family, career, patriotism) may have changed. Although some terms take on more positive meanings, others acquire more negative ones. Your connotations of *marriage* may depend on whether you have witnessed (or experienced) marriages that have been happy and constructive or bitter and destructive. And quite often an entire society's definition of something changes, *marriage* being a good example.

Identify something that has changed in meaning, either for you individually or for our society as a whole—such as the term "The American Dream." Discuss both the traditional and the new meanings (choosing a serious, ironic, or humorous point of view) in such a way that your definition makes a specific point or commentary, either stated or implied, about society's values or your own.

SPECIAL ISSUES IN PERSUASION

*A*s we have seen, the strategies in Chapters 10 to 16 can be used to draw readers into the writer's special viewpoint. This purpose can be called "persuasive" because it asks readers to agree with particular viewpoints such as these:

- media reports on African Americans often are biased (page 179)
- the "wifely" stereotype persists in today's generation (page 26)
- children are developing sexual awareness much too early (page 214)
- today's young people have little interest in public affairs (page 229)

Writing for the *primary* goal of persuasion often takes a stand on even more controversial topics—issues on which people always disagree. Examples: Do the risks of nuclear power outweigh its advantages? Should your school require athletes to maintain good grades? Should your dorm be coed? We write about these issues in hopes of winning readers over to our side—or at least inducing them to appreciate our position.

In a free society, you can expect some readers to disagree with your stand on a controversy no matter how long and how brilliantly you argue. But even though you won't change *everyone's* mind, a strong persuasive argument can make a difference to *some people.*

ANTICIPATING AUDIENCE RESISTANCE

Argument focuses on its audience; it addresses issues in which people are directly involved. But people rarely change their minds about such issues without good reason. Expect resistance from your readers, and defensive questions such as these:

What readers of argument want to know

- *Why should I even read this?*
- *Why should I change my mind?*
- *Can you prove it?*
- *How do you know?*
- *Says who?*

Getting readers to admit you might be right means getting them to admit they might be wrong. The more strongly their "minds are made up"—the more strongly they identify with their position—the more resistance you can expect. To overcome this resistance, you have to put yourself in your audience's position and see things their way before you argue for your way. The persuasiveness of any argument ultimately depends on how convincing it is to its *audience.*

Making a good argument requires that you bring together all the strategies you've learned so far, along with features specific to argumentative writing:

1. a main point or claim that the audience finds debatable
2. convincing support for the claim
3. appeals to the audience's reason
4. appeals to the audience's emotions (as appropriate)
5. a clear and unmistakable line of thought
6. attention to the ethics of argument

HAVING A DEBATABLE POINT

The main point in an argument must be debatable (something open to dispute, something that can be viewed from more than one angle). Statements of fact are not debatable:

A fact is something whose certainty is established

> Several near-disastrous accidents have occurred recently in nuclear power plants.
>
> Women outlive men.
>
> Economic policies of this presidential administration have led to increases in student loan programs.
>
> More than 50 percent of traffic deaths are alcohol related.

Because these statements can be verified (shown to be true or accurate—at least with enough certainty so that reasonable people would agree), they cannot be debated. Questions of taste or personal opinion never can be debated, because they rest on no objective reasons:

Personal taste or opinion is based on preference, belief, or feeling—instead of fact

> I love oatmeal.
>
> Catholics are holier than Baptists.
>
> Professor Dreary's lectures put me to sleep.
>
> I hate the taste of garlic.

Even many assertions that call for expository support are not debatable for most audiences. Consider these assertions:

Once reasonable people know the facts, they would have to agree with these claims

> During the last decade, the Religious Right has gained political influence.
>
> Competition for good jobs is now fiercer than ever.
>
> Police roadblocks help deter drunk driving.
>
> Lowering the drinking age increases alcohol-related traffic fatalities.

Writing that demonstrates the truth of these assertions is primarily referential. Once the facts are established, the audience almost certainly will say, "Yes, it's true."

What, then, is *a debatable point?* It *is one that cannot be proved true, but only more or less probable.* For example, few readers would debate the notion that electronic games have altered the play habits of millions of American children. But some would disagree that electronic games are dominating children's lives.

No amount of evidence can prove or disprove these claims

> The political activities of the Religious Right violate the constitutional separation of church and state.
>
> Schools should place more emphasis on competition.
>
> Police roadblocks are a justifiable deterrent against drunk driving.
>
> All states should maintain the drinking age at twenty-one.

Even though the rightness or wrongness of these controversial issues never can be proved, writers can argue (more or less persuasively) for one side or the other. And—unlike an assertion of personal opinion or taste—an arguable assertion can be judged by the quality of support the writer presents. How does the assertion hold up against *opposing* assertions?

Always state your arguable point directly and clearly as a thesis. While other development strategies (especially description and narration) may allow the thesis merely to be implied, argumentative writing almost never does. Let readers know exactly where you stand.

SUPPORTING YOUR CLAIM

Chapter 6 shows how any credible assertion rests on opinions derived from facts. But facts out of context can be interpreted in various ways. Legitimate argument offers convincing reasons, reliable sources, careful interpretation, and valid conclusions.

OFFERING CONVINCING REASONS

Any argument is only as convincing as the reasons that support it. Before readers will change their minds, they need to know why. They expect you to complete a version of this statement, in which your reasons follow the "because":

My position is _____ because _____.

Arguing effectively means using *only* those reasons likely to move your specific audience. Assume, for instance, that all students living on your campus have a meal plan with a 15-meal requirement (for weekdays), costing $1800 yearly. You belong to a group trying to reduce the required meals to 10 weekly. Before seeking students' support and lobbying the administration, your group constructs a list of reasons for its position. A quick brainstorming session produces this list:

> Required weekday meals should be reduced to ten per week because:
>
> *Subjective reasons matter to the writer— but not always to the reader* (margin)
>
> 1. Many students dislike the food.
> 2. Some students with only afternoon classes like to sleep late and should not have to rush to beat the 9:00 A.M. breakfast deadline.
> 3. The cafeteria atmosphere is too noisy, impersonal, and dreary.
> 4. The food selection is too limited.
> 5. The price of a yearly meal ticket has risen unfairly and is now more than 5 percent higher than last year's price.

You quickly spot a flaw in this list: all these reasons rest almost entirely on *subjective* grounds, on personal taste or opinion. For every reader who dislikes the food or sleeps late, another may like the food or rise early—and so on. Your intended audience (students, administrators) probably won't think these reasons very convincing. Your reasons should be based on *objective* evidence and on goals and values you and your readers share.

Offer Objective Evidence. Evidence—any information that supports your claim—is objective when it can be verified (shown to be factual) by everyone involved. Common types of objective evidence include statistics, examples, and expert testimony.

Numbers can be highly convincing. Many readers are interested in the "bottom line" (percentages, costs, savings, profits):

Cite the numbers (margin)

> Roughly 30 percent of the 500 students we surveyed in the cafeteria eat only 2 meals per day.

Always use statistics that your audience can identify with and that fit the point they are designed to illustrate. They should be accurate, trustworthy, and easy for readers to understand and verify. (See pages 341–344 for advice on avoiding statistical fallacies.) Always cite your sources.

Examples can help audiences visualize the idea or concept. For instance, the best way to explain what you mean by "wasteful" is to show "waste" occurring:

Show what you mean (margin)

> From 20 to 25 percent of the food prepared never is eaten.

Expert testimony—if it is unbiased and considered reliable by the audience—lends authority and credibility to any claim:

Cite the experts

Food service directors from three local colleges point out that their schools' optional meal plans have been highly successful.

Appeal to Shared Goals and Values. Evidence alone isn't always enough to change a reader's mind. Identify at least one goal you and your audience have in common. In the meal plan issue, for example, we can assume that everyone wants to eliminate wasteful practices. A persuasive argument therefore will take this goal into account:

Appeal to shared goals

These changes in the meal plan would eliminate waste of food, labor, and money.

Audiences in various situations have various goals shaped by certain values (qualities they believe in, ideals they stand for): friendship, loyalty, honesty, equality, fairness, and so on (Rokeach 57–58). They may value job security, being appreciated, a sense of belonging, safety, prosperity, or excitement. Look for a common, central goal. In the meal plan case, *fairness* might be an important value:

Appeal to shared values

No one should have to pay for meals she or he doesn't eat.

Here is how your group's final list of reasons might read:

Persuasive claims are backed up by reasons that matter to the reader

The number of required weekday meals should be reduced to ten per week because:

1. No one should have to pay for meals she or he doesn't eat.
2. Roughy 30 percent of the 500 students we surveyed in the cafeteria eat only two meals per day.
3. From 20 to 25 percent of the food prepared never is eaten—a waste of food, labor, and money.
4. Each dorm suite has its own kitchen, but these are seldom used.
5. Between kitchen suites and local restaurants, students on only the Monday-through-Friday plan do survive on weekends. Why couldn't they survive just as well during the week?
6. Food service directors from three local colleges point out that their schools' optional meal plans have been highly successful.

Reasonable audiences should find the above argument compelling because each reason is based on a verifiable fact or (as in item 1) good sense. Even audience members not moved to support your cause will understand why you've taken your stand.

Give your audience reasons that have meaning for *them* personally. For instance, in a recent study of teenage attitudes about smoking, respondents listed these reasons for not smoking: bad breath, difficulty concentrating, loss of friends, and trouble with adults. No respondents listed dying of cancer—presumably because this last reason carries little meaning for young people personally (Bauman et al. 510–30).

Finding objective evidence to support a claim often requires that we go beyond our own experience by doing some type of research (see Section Four).

APPEALING TO REASON

Although argument relies on some combination of description, narration, and exposition, many persuasive arguments are built around one or both of these reasoning patterns: *induction* (reasoning from specific evidence to a general conclusion) and *deduction* (applying a proven generalization to a specific case).

Just about any daily decision (including the ones you're asked to make in this book) is the product of inductive or deductive reasoning, or both. Suppose that on registration day you learn you've been assigned to Math 101 with Professor Digit. You immediately decide to transfer to some other section. Let's trace the reasoning that led to your decision.

First, you reasoned inductively, from this specific evidence to a generalization:

Inductive evidence

- *Fact:* Your older brother, a good mathematician and a serious student, received a D from Professor Digit two years ago, even though your brother slaved over his math assignments every night.
- *Fact:* 60 percent of Professor Digit's students receive a D or F.
- *Fact:* Professor Digit often remarks, in class, that he despises teaching "dull-witted, first-year students."
- *Fact:* Two friends, both good students, failed Professor Digit's course. Each repeated the course with a different instructor: one received a B+, one a B.
- *Fact:* About one-third of Professor Digit's students drop his course after receiving their first grade.

Based on the above evidence, you reached this generalization:

A generalization based
on inductive evidence | Professor Digit seems to grade his students unfairly.

The evidence led you to an informed opinion (a probability, not a fact). You reached this opinion through inductive reasoning. You used deductive reasoning to move from this generalization to a conclusion:

Generalization | Professor Digit seems to grade his students unfairly.

Specific instance | I am one of Professor Digit's students.

Conclusion | I am likely to be graded unfairly.

This conclusion led you to transfer to another section.

We use induction and deduction repeatedly, often unconsciously. Specific facts, statistics, observations, and experiences lead us inductively to generalizations such as these:

Other inductively based
generalizations | Pre-med majors must compete for the highest grades.

Politicians can't always be trusted.

Big cities can be dangerous.

A college degree alone does not ensure success.

On the other hand, deductive reasoning leads us from generalizations to specific instances to conclusions:

Generalization | Big cities can be dangerous.
Specific instance | New York is a big city.
Conclusion | New York can be dangerous.

Generalization | Pre-med majors must compete for the highest grades.
Specific instance | Brigitte will be a pre-med major next year.
Conclusion | Brigitte will have to compete for the highest grades.

When we write to persuade others, we need to use these processes deliberately and consciously.

USING INDUCTION

We use induction in two situations: (1) to move from specific evidence to a related generalization, or (2) to establish the cause or causes of something.

Assume you've been dating a Significant Other for a while, but recently you've made these observations:

Reviewing the evidence

My Significant Other (SO) hasn't returned my phone calls in a week.

My SO always wants to go home early.

My SO yawns a lot when we're together.

My SO talks to everyone but me at parties.

This evidence leads to an inductive generalization:

Generalizing from the evidence

My SO is losing interest in me.

The same kind of reasoning establishes the possible or probable causes of your SO's aloofness. As you reflect on the relationship, you recall a number of inconsiderate things you've done recently:

Establishing the cause

I've been awfully short-tempered lately.

I forgot all about my SO's birthday last week.

I'm usually late for our dates.

A few times, I've made wisecracks about my SO's creepy friends.

And so you conclude that your own inconsiderate behavior probably damaged the relationship.

Although generalizations aren't proof of anything, the better your evidence, the more likely it is that your generalizations are accurate. Avoid generalizing from too little evidence. That your Significant Other yawns a lot would not be a sufficient basis to conclude that she or he is losing interest. (Maybe he or she's ill or tired!) Or if your SO had yawned during only one evening, that fact alone would not support the hasty generalization that your relationship is on the rocks. Provide enough facts, examples, statistics, and informed opinions to make your assertions believable.

Consider the inductive reasoning in this passage from a 1963 letter by Martin Luther King, Jr. to white clergy after he had been jailed for organizing a civil-rights demonstration in Birmingham, Alabama.

An Inductive Argument

A key statistic (1)
Informed opinion (2)

Acknowledgment of opposing views (3)

[1]We have waited for more than 340 years for our constitutional and God-given rights. [2]The nations of Asia and Africa are moving with jetlike speed toward gaining political independence, but we still creep at horse-and-buggy pace toward gaining a cup of coffee at a lunch counter. [3]Perhaps it is easy for those who have never felt the stinging darts of segregation to

Examples (4)

say, "Wait." [4]But when you have seen vicious mobs lynch your mothers and fathers at will and drown your sisters and brothers at whim; when you have seen hate-filled policemen curse, kick, and even kill your black brothers and sisters; when you have seen the vast majority of your twenty million Negro brothers smothering in an airtight cage of poverty in the midst of an affluent society; when you suddenly find your tongue twisted and your speech stammering as you seek to explain to your six-year-old daughter why she can't go to the public amusement park that has just been advertised on television, and see tears welling up in her eyes when she is told that Funtown is closed to colored children, and see ominous clouds of inferiority beginning to form in her little mental sky, and see her beginning to distort her personality by developing an unconscious bitterness toward white people; when you have to concoct an answer for a five-year-old son who is asking, "Daddy, why do white people treat colored people so mean?"; when you take a cross-country drive and find it necessary to sleep night after night in the uncomfortable corners of your automobile because no motel will accept you; when you are humiliated day in and day out by nagging signs reading "white" and "colored"; when your first name becomes "nigger," your middle name becomes "boy" (however old you are) and your last name becomes "john," and your wife and mother are never given the respected title "Mrs."; when you are harried by day and haunted by night by the fact that you are a Negro, living constantly at tiptoe stance, never quite knowing what to expect next, and are plagued with inner fears and outer resentments; when you are forever fighting a degenerating sense of "nobodiness"—then you will understand why we find it difficult to wait. [5]There comes a time when the cup of endurance runs over, and [people] are no longer willing to be plunged into the abyss of despair. [6]I hope, sirs, you can understand our legitimate and unavoidable impatience.

A generalization from specifics (5)

Main point as a direct appeal (6)

—*Martin Luther King, Jr.*

Notice how the inductive argument is organized: sentence 4 carries the burden of support for Dr. King's stand. And the support itself is organized for greatest effect, with examples that progress from the injustice he has witnessed to the injustice he and his family have suffered to the humiliation he feels. Not only does he provide ample evidence to support his closing generalization (African Americans have reason to be impatient), but his evidence also adds up logically—and leads dramatically—to his conclusion.

USING DEDUCTION

You reason deductively when you use generalizations to arrive at specific conclusions. Once the generalization "African Americans have legitimate cause for impatience" is established *inductively* (and accepted), one can argue deductively by applying the generalization to a specific instance:

Generalization	African Americans have legitimate cause for impatience.
Specific instance	Ms. Gomes is African American.
Conclusion	Ms. Gomes has legitimate cause for impatience.

The conclusion is valid because (a) the generalization is accepted and (b) the specific instance is a fact. Both these conditions must exist in order for the conclusion to be sound.

Here is how you might use deductive reasoning daily:

Examples of deductive reasoning

- If you know that Professor Jones gives no make-up exams, and you sleep through her final, then you can expect to flunk her course.
- If you know that Batmobiles need frequent repairs, and you buy a Batmobile, then you can expect many repairs.

The soundness of deductive reasoning can be measured by sketching an argument in the form of a *syllogism*, the basic pattern of deductive arguments. Any syllogism has three parts: a major premise, a minor premise, and a conclusion:

A valid syllogism

All humans are mortal. [*Major premise*]

Feliciana is human. [*Minor premise*]

Feliciana is mortal. [*Conclusion*]

If readers accept both premises, they also must accept your conclusion. For the conclusion to be valid, the major premise must state an accepted generalization and the minor premise must state a factual instance of that generalization. Moreover, the conclusion must express the same degree of certainty as the premises (that is, if a "usually" appears in a premise, it must appear in the conclusion as well). Finally, the syllogism must be stated correctly, the minor premise linking its subject with the subject of the major premise; otherwise, the syllogism is faulty:

A faulty syllogism

All humans are mortal.

John is mortal. [*Minor premise is stated incorrectly; all creatures are mortal, but not all are human.*]

John is human.

Each premise in a syllogism actually is derived from inductive reasoning. Because every human being we've known so far has been mortal, we can reasonably conclude that all human beings are mortal. And once we have examined John thoroughly and classified him as human, we can connect the two premises to arrive at the conclusion that John is mortal.

Illogical deductive arguments may result from a faulty major premise (or generalization). We usually can verify a minor premise (as in the previous example, merely by observing John, to determine if he is human). But the major premise is a generalization; unless we have enough inductive evidence, the generalization can be faulty. How much evidence is enough? Let your good judgment tell you. Base your premise on *reasonable* evidence, so that your generalization reflects reality as discerning people would recognize it. Avoid unreasonable premises such as these:

Faulty generalizations

> All men are male chauvinists.
>
> School is boring.
>
> Long-haired men are drug addicts.
>
> People can't be trusted.
>
> Frailty, thy name is woman.

Notice the problem when one such generalization serves as the major premise in an argument:

What happens when the major premise is faulty

> People can't be trusted. [*Major premise*]
>
> My grandparents are people. [*Minor premise*]
>
> My grandparents can't be trusted. [*Conclusion*]

In ordinary conversation deductive arguments often are expressed as *enthymemes,* implicit syllogisms in which the generalizations are not stated explicitly; instead they are implied, or understood:

Enthymemes are implicit syllogisms

> Joe is ruining his health with cigarettes. [*Implied generalization: Cigarette smoking ruins health.*]
>
> Sally's low verbal scores on her college entrance exam suggest that she will need remedial help in composition. [*Implied generalization: Students with low verbal scores need extra help in composition.*]

Here's what happens to the conclusion when the unstated generalization is faulty:

Faulty enthymemes

> Martha is a feminist, and so she obviously hates men. [*All feminists hate men.*]

He's a member of the clergy, and so what he says must be true. [*Clergy members never are mistaken or dishonest.*]

Another danger in deductive arguments is the overstated generalization; that is, making a limited generalization apply to all cases. Be sure to modify your assertions with qualifying words such as **usually, often, sometimes,** and **some,** instead of absolute words such as **always, all, never,** and **nobody:**

Overstated generalizations

All Dobermans are vicious. [*Revised: "Some can be . . ."*]

Politicians never keep their promises. [*Revised: "Some politicians seldom . . ."*]

In such cases, remember that the conclusion that follows must also be qualified.

A Deductive Argument

[1]These ought to be the best of times for the human mind, but it is not so. [2]All sorts of things seem to be turning out wrong, and the century seems to be slipping through our fingers here at the end, with almost all promises unfulfilled. [3]I cannot begin to guess at all the causes of our cultural sadness, not even the most important ones, but I can think of one thing that is wrong with us and eats away at us: we do not know enough about ourselves. [4]We are ignorant about how we work, about where we fit in, and most of all about the enormous, imponderable system of life in which we are embedded as working parts. [5]We do not really understand nature, at all. [6]We have come a long way indeed, but just enough to become conscious of our ignorance. [7]It is not so bad a thing to be totally ignorant; the hard thing is to be partway along toward real knowledge, far enough to be aware of being ignorant. [8]It is embarrassing and depressing, and it is one of our troubles today.

—Lewis Thomas

The deductive argument in this paragraph proceeds like this:

Implied generalization | People who don't know enough about themselves are in a sad state of mind.

Specific instance | We don't know enough about ourselves.

Conclusion | Therefore, we are in a sad state of mind.

Decide whether the above argument is valid by answering these questions:

- Is the major premise acceptable?
- Is the minor premise verifiable?
- Does the argument avoid overstatement? If so how?
- Is the argument sufficiently focused?

RECOGNIZING ILLOGICAL REASONING

In induction or deduction, beware of the kinds of illogical reasoning called *fallacies* (assertions and statements derived from faulty logic) because they weaken your case.

MAKING FAULTY GENERALIZATIONS

When we accept research findings uncritically and we jump to conclusions about their meaning, we commit the error of *hasty generalization.* When we overestimate the extent to which the findings reveal some larger truth, we commit the error of *overstated generalization.*

A study in Greece on the role of fruits, vegetables, and olive oil in lowering breast cancer risk was widely publicized in 1995 because of the alleged benefits of olive oil for women who consume olive oil twice or more daily. Subsequent analysis of this study revealed that data about the women's food consumption covered only one year and were based on a single questionnaire asking women to estimate their previous year's diet. (Estimates of this type tend to be highly inaccurate.) Also, the study did not identify the quantities of olive oil individual users consumed. In this instance, then, the study's generalization about olive oil was shown to be *hasty* (based on insufficient evidence).

Further analysis revealed that only 99 respondents (of the nearly 2500 surveyed) claimed to have consumed olive oil twice or more daily ("Olive oil" 1). In this instance, the study's generalization was shown to be *overstated* (a limited generalization applied to all cases). Something true in one instance need not be true in other instances.

Although this particular study was flawed, many other studies support the generalization that fruits and vegetables do help lower the risk of cancer. Generalizing is vital and perfectly legitimate—when it is warranted.

How true are these generalizations?

Faulty generalizations

> Blondes have more fun.
>
> Television is worthless.
>
> Humanities majors rarely get good jobs.

A common version of faulty generalization is *stereotyping*, the simplistic and trite assignment of characteristics to groups.

Stereotypes

> All politicians are crooks.
>
> Southern cops are brutal.
>
> The Irish are big drinkers.

BEGGING THE QUESTION

You beg the question when you assume that a debatable premise (or premises) underlying your assertion already has been supported convincingly. In other words, you are "begging" readers to accept your premise before you have shown it to be reasonable:

Assertions that beg the question

> Useless subjects like composition should not be required.
>
> Voters should reject Candidate X's unfair accusation.
>
> Books like X and Y, which destroy the morals of our children, should be banned from school libraries.

If a subject is useless, obviously it should not be required. But a subject's uselessness is precisely what has to be established. Likewise, Candidate X's accusations have to be proved unfair, and books such as X and Y have to be proved corrupting. In each of these cases, the arguer is "begging the question" by asking for the desired conclusion without supporting it by reasoning.

AVOIDING THE QUESTION

As we will see in the next section, some appeals to emotions (pity, fear, and the like) are perfectly legitimate. But you avoid the question when you distract readers from the real issue with material that is irrelevant or that obscures the issue by making an irrational appeal to emotions.

An appeal to pity

> He should not be punished for his assault conviction because as a child he was beaten severely by his parents. [*Has no legal bearing on the real issue: his crime.*]

An appeal to fear

> If we outlaw guns, only outlaws will have guns. [*Ignores the deaths and injuries caused by "legally owned" guns.*]

An appeal to normalcy

> She is the best person for the teaching job because she is happily married and has two lovely children. [*Has nothing to do with the real issue: her qualifications as a teacher.*]

An appeal to flattery

> A person with your sophistication surely will agree that marriage is outmoded. [*Has nothing to do with the conclusion that remains to be verified.*]

An appeal to authority or patriotism

> Uncle Sam stands behind savings bonds. [*Ignores the question of whether savings bonds are a good investment: Although they are safe, they pay lower interest than many other investments.*]

The snob appeal to emotion persuades readers to accept your assertion because they want to be identified with respected or notable people.

Snob appeal

> "I want to be like Mike." [*Has nothing to do with the quality of the sneakers or hamburgers or other items being marketed.*]
>
> No All-American sports hero could be guilty of such a horrible crime. [*Ignores the evidence.*]

USING THE BANDWAGON APPEAL

The bandwagon approach urges readers to climb aboard by claiming that everyone else is doing it.

Bandwagon appeals

> This book is a best-seller. How could you ignore it?
>
> More Cadillac owners are switching to Continentals than ever before. [*Of course, if the numbers provided real evidence, the assertion would be legitimate.*]

ATTACKING YOUR OPPONENT

Another way to ignore the real question is by attacking your opponent through name-calling or derogatory statements about this person on the basis of age, gender, political or sexual orientation, or the like (ad hominem argument):

Ad hominem attacks

> The effete intellectual snobs in academia have no right to criticize our increase in military spending. [*Calling people names does not discredit their argument.*]
>
> How could a man be expected to understand a woman's emotional needs?
>
> College students are too immature to know what they want, so why should they have a say in the college curriculum?

USING FAULTY CAUSAL REASONING

Causal reasoning tries to explain *why* something happened or *what* will happen, often very complex questions. Anything but the simplest effect is likely to have multiple causes. Faulty causal reasoning oversimplifies or distorts the cause-effect relationship through errors like these:

Ignoring other causes

> Investment builds wealth. [*Ignores the role of knowledge, wisdom, timing, and luck in successful investing.*]

Ignoring other effects

> Running improves health. [*Ignores the fact that many runners get injured, and that some even drop dead while running.*]

Inventing a causal sequence	Right after buying a rabbit's foot, Felix won the state lottery. [*Posits an unwarranted causal relationship merely because one event follows another—the post hoc fallacy.*]
Confusing correlation with causation	Poverty causes disease. [*Ignores the fact that disease, while highly associated with poverty, has many causes unrelated to poverty.*]
Rationalizing	My grades were poor because my exams were unfair. [*Denies the real causes of one's failures.*]

ASSERTING A SLIPPERY-SLOPE FALLACY

We ski the slippery slope when we make some overstated prediction that one action will initiate other actions or events that lead to dire consequences.

Slippery slope assertions	Distributing condoms to high school students will lead to promiscuity.
	Unless we stop Communist aggression in Viet Nam, all of Southeast Asia will fall to Communism.

ARGUING FROM IGNORANCE

We argue from ignorance when we contend that an assertion is true because it has not been proven false—or that the assertion is false because it has not been proven true.

Arguments from ignorance	Drunk-driving laws are absurd: I know loads of people who drink and drive and who have never had an accident.
	Since the defendant can't offer evidence to prove her innocence, she must be guilty.

USING FAULTY ANALOGIES

Our analogies are faulty when they overstate the similarities between the two items being compared.

Faulty analogies	All my friends' parents are allowing them to hitchhike across country. Why can't I?
	In many instances, cancer cells can be eliminated by the appropriate treatment. Since violent criminals are a societal cancer, they should be eliminated by capital punishment.

IMPOSING THE EITHER-OR FALLACY

We commit the either-or fallacy when we reduce an array of choices to a dilemma: only two extreme positions or sides—black or white—even though other choices exist.

False dilemmas

> Students deserve the opportunity to do their best work. But deadlines force students to hand in something not carefully done, just to make sure it's on time. [*Ignores the possibility of doing it on time **and** doing it well.*]
>
> We have the choice between polluting our atmosphere or living without energy. [*Leaves out the possibility of generating clean energy.*]
>
> Marry me or I'll enter a monastery.

APPEALING TO EMOTION

Emotion is no substitute for reason, but some audiences are not persuaded by reason alone. In fact, the audience's attitude toward the writer is often the biggest factor in persuasion—no matter how solid the argument. Audiences are more receptive to people they like, trust, and respect.

Appeals to honesty, fairness, humor, and common sense are legitimate ways of enhancing a supportable argument. On the other hand, appeals to closed-mindedness, prejudice, paranoia, and ignorance (as in the logical fallacies covered earlier) merely hide the fact that an argument offers no authentic support.

Emotional transactions between writer and reader are complex, but the following strategies offer some guidance:

GUIDELINES FOR MAKING EMOTIONAL APPEALS

1. *Try to identify—empathize—with the reader's feelings.*
2. *Show respect for the reader's views.*
3. *Try to appear reasonable.*
4. *Know when and how to be forceful or satirical.*
5. *Know when to be humorous*

SHOWING EMPATHY

To show empathy is to identify with the reader's feelings and to express genuine concern for the reader's welfare. Consider the lack of empathy in this next paragraph.

A Message that Lacks Empathy

> Dear Buck,
>
> After a good deal of thought I've decided to write to you about your weight problem. Let's face it: you're much too fat. Last week's shopping trip convinced me of that. Remember the bathing suit you liked, the one that came only in smaller sizes? If you lost weight, you might be able to fit into those

kinds of suits. In addition to helping you look attractive, the loss of 30 or 40 pounds of ugly fat would improve your health. All you have to do is exercise more and eat less. I know it will work. Give me a call if you need any more help or suggestions.

This writer's superior tone can't help but alienate the reader. In this next version, he makes a distinct effort to empathize.

A More Empathetic Version

Dear Buck,

Remember that great bathing suit we saw in Stuart's the other day, the one you thought would be perfect for the beach party but that didn't come in your size? Because the party is still 3 weeks away, why not begin dieting and exercising so you can buy the suit? I know that losing weight is awfully hard, because I've had to struggle with that problem myself. Buck, you're one of my best friends, and you can count on me for support. A little effort on your part could make a big difference in your life.

Empathy is especially important in arguments that try getting the reader to *do* something.

ACKNOWLEDGING OPPOSING VIEWS

Before making your case, acknowledge the opposing case. This next writer takes a controversial position on a turning point in the high school experience. But by showing respect for the traditional view, she decreases readers' resistance to her own position.

An Acknowledgment of Opposing Views

Orienting statement (1)

Acknowledgment of opposing view (2–3)

Writer's argument (4)

[1]From our first steps into high school we learn to anticipate an essential rite of passage: the senior prom—one of those memories that last a lifetime. [2]Traditionally, prom night suggests a magical time when it's fun to get dressed up, have pictures taken with your date, enjoy a fancy dinner, and party with your friends; then, after a perfect evening, you kiss your date goodnight and go home. [3]This fairy tale chain of events is how our parents recount their long-ago experiences and it persists as part of the prom image. [4]But this benign image too often masks the reality of a night polluted by drugs and sex, a night based on competition and looks, a night hyped to unbelievable proportions, only to become a total letdown.

—Julia Conforti

MAINTAINING A MODERATE TONE

People are more inclined to accept the viewpoint of someone they *like*—someone who seems reasonable. Never overstate your case to make your point. Stay away from emotionally loaded words that boil up in the heat of argument. This next writer is unlikely to win converts:

Voice of the Hothead

Scientists are the culprits responsible for the rape of our environment. Although we never see these beady-eyed, amoral eggheads actually destroying our world, they are busy in their laboratories scheming new ways for industrialists and developers to ravage the landscape, pollute the air, and turn all our rivers, lakes, and oceans into stinking sewers. How anybody with a conscience or a sense of decency would become a scientist is beyond me.

Granted, this piece is forceful and sincere and does suggest the legitimate point that scientists share responsibility—but the writer doesn't seem very likable. The paragraph is more an attack than an argument. Besides generalizing recklessly and providing no evidence for the assertions, the writer uses emotionally loaded words (**eggheads, stinking sewers**) that overstate the position and surely will make readers skeptical.

Here is another version of this paragraph. Understating the controversial point makes the argument more convincing:

A More Reasonable Tone

[1]It might seem unfair to lay the blame for impending environmental disaster at the doorstep of the scientists. [2]Granted, the rape of the environment has been carried out, not by scientists, but by profiteering industrialists and myopic developers, with the eager support of a burgeoning population greedy to consume more than nature can provide and to waste more than nature can clear away. [3]But to absolve the scientific community from complicity in the matter is quite simply to ignore that science has been the only natural philosophy the western world has known since the age of Newton. [4]It is to ignore the key question: who provided us with the image of nature that invited the rape, and with the sensibility that licensed it? [5]It is not, after all, the normal thing for people to ruin their environment. [6]It is extraordinary and requires extraordinary incitement.

—*Theodore Roszak*

Notice how the above argument begins by acknowledging the opposing view (sentences 1–2). The tone is firm yet reasonable. When the writer points the blame at scientists, in sentences 3–4, he offers evidence.

Roszak softens his tone while making his point by using a rhetorical question in sentence 4. *Rhetorical questions* are really statements in the form of questions; because the answer is obvious, readers are invited (or challenged) to provide it for themselves. A rhetorical question can be a good way of impelling readers to confront the issue (as does the question in sentence 2 of the letter to Buck, page 268) without offending them.

But use rhetorical questions with caution. They can easily alienate readers, especially if the issue is personal.

Rhetorical Questions Used Offensively

> Your constant tardiness is an inconvenience to everyone. It's impossible to rely on a person who is never on time. Do you know how many times I've waited in crummy weather for you to pick me up? What about all the appointments I've been late for? Or how about all the other social functions we haven't "quite" made it to on time? It's annoying to everyone when you're always late.

The tone above seems far too aggressive for the situation.

Some strong issues may deserve the emotional emphasis created by rhetorical questions. This is another kind of decision you need to make continually about your audience and purpose.

USING SATIRE IN APPROPRIATE CIRCUMSTANCES

Satire can be one vehicle for expressing forceful anger, frustration, or outrage without alienating readers. No one enjoys being "told off" or ridiculed, but sometimes a jolt of lucid observation—"telling it like it is"—might help readers overcome denial in order to face an issue realistically.

Satire usually relies on irony and sarcasm. *Irony* is a form of expression that states one thing while clearly meaning another. For instance, Edward Abbey (page 177) lays out the horrifying scenario behind a "utopian" vision for transforming our national parks. *Sarcasm* employs a more blatant form of irony to mock or to ridicule. For instance, in the essay that follows, an undergraduate takes a hard look at the policy of eliminating "offensive" books from high school curricula.

As you read, think about how the satirical perspective forces a reexamination of attitudes.

Satire as a Persuasive Strategy
BONFIRE

> I've uncovered the root of all evil today. It lurks in our schools and in our communities. It hides in children's rooms and sits on our coffee tables. Books cause all of society's problems, from drugs to homosexuality to irreverence.
>
> Books like *Of Mice and Men* and *The Adventures of Huckleberry Finn* teach children violence, hatred, and blasphemy. After children read words like "damn," "hell," and "nigger," they will begin to use them. If they witness violence in literature, they will hit one another. After reading about George shooting Lenny in *Of Mice and Men,* they will regard killing their friends and carrying guns as acceptable. If they view a story like *Children of the Rainbow,* which contains homosexual characters, they will look at homosexuality in a positive light. Kids wouldn't think to become gay if they didn't read about it.

Brave New World and books of that type teach our children to have sex. Teen pregnancy and overpopulation originate from romance novels about fornication. *Go Ask Alice* introduces readers to drugs and therefore contributes to our society's drug problems. Kids won't participate in such evils if they don't know they exist.

If we shield our children from the world's harsh realities, they will grow up respectable citizens. We do this by burning books. Nothing makes me smile more than the flaming corpse of a smutty novel. While other families make hamburgers and hot dogs on their grills, I barbecue Twain. The smoke of *War and Peace* refreshes my nostrils after a long day. I bought 27 copies of *Catcher in the Rye* for a bonfire last August and this Christmas my living room will glow with the flames of that ancient pornography, the *Bible.*

No writing conveys a positive message, for even Dr. Seuss distorts reality for children. We should shut down all libraries, all bookstores, and all schools and end the use of the written word. After burning all books, we should eliminate magazines, newspapers and credits at the end of movies.

Libraries house Satan worshippers. Their message reaches our children through the schools. If you see your children with a library card, a membership card to Lucifer's kingdom, I urge you to destroy it and punish them. The future depends on eliminating texts which show the horrors of society. Keep the fires of hell away from your doorstep by setting aflame the contents of our libraries and the volumes in your bathrooms.

—*Adam Szymkowicz*

Some readers might feel offended or defensive about Adam's harsh assessment; however, satire deliberately seeks confrontation. So be sure that you understand its potential effect on your audience before deciding on a satirical perspective in your own writing.

ADDING HUMOR WHERE APPROPRIATE

Sometimes a bit of humor can rescue an argument that might cause hard feelings. In this next paragraph, the writer wanted to call attention to the delicate issue of his roommate's sloppiness.

Humor as a Persuasive Strategy

Jack,

If you never see me alive again, my body will be at the bottom of your dirty clothes pile that rises like a great mountain in the center of our room. How did I end up there? Well, while doing my math I ran out of paper and set out for my desk to get a few pieces—despite the risk I knew I was taking. I was met by a 6-foot wall of dirty laundry. You know how small our room is; I could not circumnavigate the pile. I thought I'd better write this note before going to the janitor's room for a shovel to dig my way through to my desk.

> The going will be tough and I doubt I'll survive. If the hard work doesn't kill me, the toxic fumes will. Three years from now, when you finally decide to do your wash, just hang my body up as a reminder to stash your dirty clothes in your closet where they will be out of sight and out of smell.
>
> —*Your dead roommate*

Again, anticipate how your audience will react; otherwise, humor can backfire.

Whichever strategies you employ, don't allow your tone to be voiceless. Readers need to sense a real person behind the words.

APPLICATION 17-1

Which of these statements are debatable, and why? (Review pages 252–253.)

1. Grades are an aid to education.
2. Forty percent of incoming first-year students at our school never graduate.
3. Physically and psychically, women are superior to men.
4. Pets should not be allowed on our campus.
5. Computer courses are boring.
6. Every student should be required to become computer literate.
7. The computer revolution is transforming American business.
8. French wines are better than domestic wines.
9. French wines generally are more subtle and complex than domestic wines.
10. The price of French wines has risen 20% in the past two years.

APPLICATION 17-2

Using your own subjects or those below, develop five arguable assertions. (Review pages 252–253.)

EXAMPLES

[*sex*] The sexual revolution has created more problems than it has solved.

[*education*] The heavy remedial emphasis at our school causes many introductory courses to be substandard.

education	law	pollution
sex	music	jobs
drugs	war	dorm life

APPLICATION 17-3

The statements below are followed by false or improbable conclusions. What specific supporting evidence would be needed to justify each conclusion so that it is not a specious generalization? (First, you need to infer the missing generalization or premise; then you have to decide what evidence would be needed for the premise to be acceptable.) (Review pages 253–256.)

EXAMPLE

Only 60 percent of incoming first-year students eventually graduate from this college. Therefore, the college is not doing its job.

To consider this conclusion valid, we would have to be shown that:

1. All first-year students want to attend college in the first place.
2. They are all capable of college-level work.
3. They did all assigned work promptly and responsibly.

1. Abner always speeds but never has an accident. Therefore, he must be an excellent driver.
2. Fifty percent of last year's college graduates did not find the jobs they wanted. Therefore, college is a waste of time and money.
3. Olga never sees a doctor. Therefore, she must be healthy.
4. This house is expensive. Therefore, it must be well built.
5. Felix is flunking first-year composition. Therefore, he must be stupid.

APPLICATION 17-4

Paragraph Warm-Up: Inductive Reasoning

Using Dr. King's paragraph (page 258) as a model, write a paragraph in which you use inductive reasoning to support a general conclusion about one of these subjects (after you have narrowed it) or about one of your own choice.

highway safety	minorities
a college core requirement	the legal drinking age
the changing role of women	credit cards

Identify your audience and purpose. Provide enough evidence so that readers can follow your line of reasoning to its conclusion.

APPLICATION 17-5

Paragraph Warm-Up: Deductive Reasoning

Select an accepted generalization from this list or choose one of your own as the topic statement in a paragraph using deductive reasoning. (Review pages 259–262.)

- "Beauty is in the eye of the beholder."
- "That person is richest whose pleasures are the cheapest."
- Some teachers can have a great influence on a student's attitude toward a subject.
- A college degree doesn't guarantee career success.

APPLICATION 17-6

Identify the fallacy in each of these sentences and revise the assertion to eliminate the error. (Review pages 263–267.)

EXAMPLE

Faulty   Television is worthless. [*sweeping generalization*]

Revised   Commercial television offers too few programs of educational value.

1. Big Goof received this chain letter, sent out twenty copies, and three days later won the lottery. Little Goof received this chain letter, threw it away, and fell off a cliff the next day.
2. Because our product is the best, it is worth the high price.
3. America—love it or leave it.
4. Three of my friends praise their Jettas, proving that Volkswagen makes the best car.
5. My grades last semester were poor because my exams were unfair.

6. Anyone who was expelled from Harvard for cheating could not be trusted as a president.

7. Until college students contribute to our society, they have no right to criticize our government.

8. Because Angela is a devout Christian, she will make a good doctor.

9. Anyone with common sense will vote for this candidate.

10. You should take up tennis; everyone else around here plays.

11. Hubert, a typical male, seems threatened by feminists.

12. Convex running shoes caused Karl Crane to win the Boston Marathon.

13. My doctor said "Mylanta."

14. How could voters expect any tax-and-spend liberal to know or understand the concerns of working people like us?

15. Sky diving is perfectly safe. After thirty dives it hasn't killed me yet!

16. If non-smokers think their lungs are being violated by smokers, it's a fact of life. Fumes from vehicles, woodstoves, and incinerators all damage everyone's lungs. Should we ban these things, too?

17. Vote for me, or our nation is doomed.

APPLICATION 17-7

Revise this next paragraph so that its tone is more moderate and reasonable, more like an intelligent argument than an attack. Feel free to add personal insights that might help the argument.

> People who argue that marijuana should remain outlawed are crazy. Beyond that, many of them are mere hypocrites—the boozers of our world who squander their salary in bars and come home to beat the wife and kids. Any intelligent person knows that alcohol bums out the brain, ruins the body, and destroys the personality. Marijuana is definitely safer; it leaves no hangover; it causes no physical damage or violent mood changes, as alcohol does; and it is not psychologically or physically addictive. Maybe if those redneck jerks who oppose marijuana would put down the beer cans and light a joint, the world would be a more peaceful place.

APPLICATION 17-8

After reading this paragraph, answer the questions that follow.

> [1]Responsible agronomists report that before the end of the year millions of people, if unaided, might starve to death. [2]Half a billion deaths by

starvation is not an uncommon estimate. [3]Even though the United States has done more than any other nation to feed the hungry, our relative affluence makes us morally vulnerable in the eyes of other nations and in our own eyes. [4]Garret Hardin, who has argued for a "lifeboat" ethic of survival (if you take all the passengers aboard, everybody drowns), admits that the decision not to feed all the hungry requires of us "a very hard psychological adjustment." [5]Indeed it would. [6]It has been estimated that the 3.5 million tons of fertilizer spread on American golf courses and lawns could provide up to 30 million tons of food in overseas agricultural production. [7]The nightmarish thought intrudes itself. [8]If we as a nation allow people to starve while we could, through some sacrifice, make more food available to them, what hope can any person have for the future of international relations? [9]If we cannot agree on this most basic of values—feed the hungry—what hopes for the future can we entertain? [10]Technology is imitable and nuclear weaponry certain to proliferate. [11]What appeals to trust and respect can be made if the most rudimentary of moral impulses—feed the hungry—is not strenuously incorporated into national policy?

—*James R. Kelly*

1. Is this argument inductive or deductive? Explain.

2. Does the author appeal to our emotions? If so, where and how?

3. In which sentences does he support his position with hard evidence?

4. Restate the main point as a declarative sentence. Is the point arguable? Explain.

5. Are the rhetorical questions effective here? Explain.

WORKS CITED

Bauman, K. E., et al. "Three Mass Media Campaigns to Prevent Adolescent Cigarette Smoking." *Preventive Medicine* 17 (1988): 510–30.

"Olive Oil and Breast Cancer: How Strong a Connection?" *University of California at Berkeley Wellness Letter* 11.7 (1995): 1–2.

Rokeach, Milton. *The Nature of Human Values.* New York: Free Press, 1973.

COMPOSING VARIOUS ARGUMENTS

*P*ersuasion, at best, is risky business, not least because no single approach is guaranteed to work. Your own approach will depend on the people involved, the relationships, and the topic. And your odds of succeeding improve immensely when your argument is clear, reasonable, and fair.

SHAPING A CLEAR LINE OF THOUGHT

Like all writing, persuasive writing has an introduction, body, and conclusion. But within this familiar shape, your argument should do some special things as well. Readers need to follow your reasoning; they expect to see how you've arrived at your conclusions. The facing model offers a standard shape for arguments. Each sample argument in this chapter is shaped around some version of that model. But remember that virtually no argument rigidly follows the order of elements shown in the outline. Select whatever shape you find most useful—as long as it reveals a clear line of thought.

AUDIENCE CONSIDERATIONS

In any persuasive writing, the audience is the main focus. Whenever you set out to influence someone's thinking, remember this principle:

No matter how brilliant, any argument rejected by its audience is a failed argument.

If readers find reason to dislike you or conclude that your argument has no meaning for them personally, they usually reject *anything* you say. Connecting with an audience means being able to see things from their perspective. The guidelines on page 280 can help you make that connection.

ETHICAL CONSIDERATIONS

Arguments can "win" without being ethical if they "win" at any cost. For instance, advertisers effectively win customers with an implied argument that "our product is just what you need!" Some of their more specific claims: "Our artificial sweetener is made of proteins that occur naturally in the human body [amino acids]" or "Our potato chips contain no cholesterol." Such claims are technically accurate, but misleading: amino acids in artificial sweeteners can alter body chemistry to cause headaches, seizures, and possibly brain tumors; potato chips often contain saturated fat—from which the liver produces cholesterol.

INTRODUCTION

Attract and Invite Your Readers and Provide a Forecast

- Identify the issue clearly and immediately. Show the audience that your essay deserves their attention.
- Acknowledge the opposing viewpoint accurately and concede its merit.
- Offer at least one point of your own that your audience can share.
- Offer significant background material so that your readers are fully prepared to understand your position.
- State a clear, concrete, and definite thesis. Never delay your thesis without good reason. For example, if your thesis is highly controversial, you might want to delay it until you've offered some convincing evidence.
- Keep the introduction short—no more than a few paragraphs.

BODY

Offer the Support and Refutation

- Use reasons that rest on impersonal grounds of support.
- In one or more paragraphs each, organize your supporting points for best emphasis. If you think your audience has little interest, begin with the more powerful material. Sometimes you can sandwich weaker points between stronger points. But if all your points are equally strong, begin with the most familiar and acceptable to your audience—to elicit some early agreement. In general, try to save the strongest points for last.
- Develop each supporting point with concrete, specific details (facts, examples, narratives, quotations, or other evidence that can be verified empirically or logically).
- Using transitions and other connectors, string your supporting points and their evidence together to show a definite line of reasoning.
- In at least one separate paragraph, refute opposing arguments (including any anticipated readers' objections to your points).

CONCLUSION

Sum Up Your Case and Make a Direct Appeal

- Summarize your main points and refutation, emphasizing your strongest material. Offer a short-and-sweet view of the Big Picture.
- End by appealing directly to readers for a definite action (where appropriate).
- Let readers know what they should do, think, or feel.

GUIDELINES FOR PERSUASION

1. *Be clear about what you want.* Diplomacy is important, but people won't like having to guess about your purpose.

2. *Never make a claim or ask for something you know readers will reject outright.* Be sure readers can live with whatever you're requesting or proposing. Develop a clear sense of what is *achievable* in this particular situation.

2. *Anticipate your audience's reaction.* Will they be defensive, surprised, annoyed, angry, or what? Try to address their biggest objections beforehand. Express your judgments ("We could do better") without making people defensive (It's all your fault").

4. *Avoid extreme personas.* **Persona** is the image or impression of the writer's personality suggested by the tone of a document. Resist the urge to "sound off," no matter how strongly you feel. Audiences tune out aggressive people—no matter how sensible the argument. Try to be likeable and reasonable. Admit the imperfections in your case. A little humility never hurts.

5. *Find points of agreement with your audience.* Focusing early on a shared value or goal or concern can reduce conflict and help win agreement on later points.

6. *Never distort the opponent's position.* A sure way to alienate people is to cast the opponent as more of a villain or simpleton than the facts warrant.

7. *Try to concede SOMETHING to the opponent.* Surely the opposing case is based on at least one good reason. Acknowledge the merits of that case before arguing for your own. Instead of seeming like a know-it-all, show some empathy and willingness to compromise.

8. *Use only your best material.* Not all your reasons or appeals will have equal strength or significance. Decide which material—from your *audience's* view—best advances your case.

9. *Make no claim or assertion unless you can support it with good reasons.* "Just because" does not constitute adequate support!

10. *Use your skills responsibly.* The obvious power of persuasive skills creates tremendous potential for abuse. People who feel they have been bullied or manipulated or deceived most likely will become your enemies.

We often are tempted to emphasize anything that advances our case and to ignore anything that impedes it. But a message is unethical if it prevents readers from making their best decision. Don't let readers down by doing "whatever it takes" to persuade. To ensure that your writing is ethical, ask yourself the questions on page 281.*

---

*Adapted from Brownell and Fitzgerald 18; Bryan 87; Johannesen 21–22; Larson 39; Unger 39–46; Yoos 50–55.

REVISION CHECKLIST

Ethics Checklist for Persuasive Writing

- ❑ Do I avoid exaggeration, understatement, sugarcoating, or any distortion or omission that leaves readers at a disadvantage?

- ❑ Do I make a clear distinction between "certainty" and "probability"?

- ❑ Have I explored all sides of the issue and all possible alternatives?

- ❑ Are my information sources valid, reliable, and unbiased?

- ❑ Am I being honest and fair with everyone involved?

- ❑ Am I reasonably sure that what I'm saying will harm no innocent persons or damage their reputation?

- ❑ Am I respecting all legitimate rights to privacy and confidentiality?

- ❑ Do I provide enough information and interpretation for readers to understand the facts as I know them?

- ❑ Do I state the case clearly, instead of hiding behind fallacies or generalities?

- ❑ Do I inform readers of the consequences or risks (as I am able to predict) of what I am advocating?

- ❑ Do I credit all contributors and sources of ideas and information?

- ❑ Do I give candid feedback or criticism, if it is warranted?

SPECIFIC GOALS OF ARGUMENT

Arguments can differ considerably in what they ask readers to do. The goal of an argument might be to influence readers' opinions, seek readers' support, propose some action, or change readers' behavior. Let's look at arguments that seek different levels of involvement from readers.

ARGUING TO INFLUENCE READERS' OPINIONS

An argument intended to change an opinion asks for minimal involvement from its readers. Maybe you want readers to agree that specific books and films should be censored, that women should be subject to military draft, that grades are a detriment to education. The specific goal behind any such argument is merely to get readers to change their thinking, to say "I agree."

ARGUING TO ENLIST READERS' SUPPORT

In seeking readers' support for our argument, we ask readers not only to agree with a position but to take a stand as well. Maybe you want readers to vote for a candidate, lobby for additional computer equipment at your school, or help enforce dorm or library "quiet" rules. The goal in this kind of argument is to get readers actively involved, to get them to ask "How can I help?"

MAKING A PROPOSAL

The world is full of problems to solve. And proposals are designed precisely to solve problems. The type of proposal we examine here typically asks readers to take some form of direct action (to improve dorm security, fund a new campus organization, or improve working conditions). But before you can induce readers to act, you must fulfill these preliminary persuasive tasks:

1. Spell out the problem (and its causes) in enough detail to convince readers of its importance
2. Point out the benefits of solving the problem
3. Offer a realistic solution
4. Address objections to your solution
5. Give reasons why your readers should be the ones to act

ARGUING TO CHANGE READERS' BEHAVIOR

Persuading readers to change their behavior is perhaps the biggest challenge in argument. Maybe you want your boss to treat employees more fairly, or a friend to be less competitive, or a teacher to be more supportive in the classroom. Whatever your goal, readers are bound to take your argument personally. And the more personal the issue, the greater resistance you can expect. You're trying to get readers to say, "I was wrong. From now on, I'll do it differently."

The four writing samples shown in Applications 18-1 through 18-4 are addressed to readers who have an increasing stake or involvement in the issue. Comparing these essays will show you how writers in various situations can convey their way of seeing.

....

APPLICATION 18-1

Essay Practice: Arguing to Influence Readers' Opinions

The following essay from *Newsweek* argues against the student-as-consumer attitude toward college grades. Read the essay, and answer the questions that follow. Then (as your instructor requests) select one of the essay assignments.

ESSAY FOR ANALYSIS AND RESPONSE

MAKING THE GRADE: MANY STUDENTS WHEEDLE FOR A DEGREE AS IF IT WERE A FREEBIE T SHIRT

[1]It was a rookie error. After 10 years I should have known better, but I went to my office the day after final grades were posted. There was a tentative knock on the door. "Professor Wiesenfeld? I took your Physics 2121 class? I flunked it? I wonder if there's anything I can do to improve my grade?" I thought: "Why are you asking me? Isn't it too late to worry about it? Do you dislike making declarative statements?"

[2]After the student gave his tale of woe and left, the phone rang. "I got a D in your class. Is there any way you can change it to 'Incomplete'?" Then the e-mail assault began: "I'm shy about coming in to talk to you, but I'm not shy about asking for a better grade. Anyway, it's worth a try." The next day I had three phone messages from students asking *me* to call *them.* I didn't.

[3]Time was, when you received a grade, that was it. You might groan and moan, but you accepted it as the outcome of your efforts or lack thereof (and, yes, sometimes a tough grader). In the last few years, however, some students have developed a disgruntled-consumer approach. If they don't like their grade, they go to the "return" counter to trade it in for something better.

[4]What alarms me is their indifference toward grades as an indication of personal effort and performance. Many, when pressed about why they think they deserve a better grade, admit they don't deserve one but would like one anyway. Having been raised on gold stars for effort and smiley faces for self-esteem, they've learned that they can get by without hard work and real talent if they can talk the professor into giving them a break. This attitude is beyond cynicism. There's a weird innocence to the assumption that one expects (even deserves) a better grade simply by begging for it. With that outlook, I guess I shouldn't be as flabbergasted as I was that 12 students asked me to change their grades *after* final grades were posted.

[5]That's 10 percent of my class who let three months of midterms, quizzes and lab reports slide until long past remedy. My graduate student calls it hyperrational thinking: if effort and intelligence don't matter, why should deadlines? What matters is getting a better grade through an unearned bonus, the academic equivalent of a freebie T shirt or toaster giveaway. Rewards are disconnected from the quality of one's work. An act and its consequences are unrelated, random events.

[6]Their arguments for wheedling better grades often ignore academic performance. Perhaps they feel it's not relevant. "If my grade isn't raised to a D I'll lose my scholarship." "If you don't give me a C, I'll flunk out." One sincerely overwrought student pleaded, "If I don't pass, my life is over." This is tough stuff to deal with. Apparently, I'm responsible for someone's losing a

scholarship, flunking out or deciding whether life has meaning. Perhaps these students see me as a commodities broker with something they want—a grade. Though intrinsically worthless, grades, if properly manipulated, can be traded for what has value: a degree, which means a job, which means money. The one thing college actually offers—a chance to learn—is considered irrelevant, even less than worthless, because of the long hours and hard work required.

[7]In a society saturated with surface values, love of knowledge for its own sake does sound eccentric. The benefits of fame and wealth are more obvious. So is it right to blame students for reflecting the superficial values saturating our society?

[8]Yes, of course it's right. These guys had better take themselves seriously now, because our country will be forced to take them seriously later, when the stakes are much higher. They must recognize that their attitude is not only self-destructive, but socially destructive. The erosion of quality control—giving appropriate grades for actual accomplishments—is a major concern in my department. One colleague noted that a physics major could obtain a degree without ever answering a written exam question completely. How? By pulling in enough partial credit and extra credit. And by getting breaks on grades.

[9]But what happens once she or he graduates and gets a job? That's when the misfortunes of eroding academic standards multiply. We lament that schoolchildren get "kicked upstairs" until they graduate from high school despite being illiterate and mathematically inept, but we seem unconcerned with college graduates whose less blatant deficiencies are far more harmful if their accreditation exceeds their qualifications.

[10]Most of my students are science and engineering majors. If they're good at getting partial credit but not at getting the answer right, then the new bridge breaks or the new drug doesn't work. One finds examples here in Atlanta. Last year a light tower in the Olympic Stadium collapsed, killing a worker. It collapsed because an engineer miscalculated how much weight it could hold. A new 12-story dormitory could develop dangerous cracks due to a foundation that's uneven by more than six inches. The error resulted from incorrect data being fed into a computer. I drive past that dorm daily on my way to work, wondering if a foundation crushed under kilotons of weight is repairable or if this structure will have to be demolished. Two 10,000-pound steel beams at the new natatorium collapsed in March, crashing into the student athletic complex. (Should we give partial credit since no one was hurt?) Those are real-world consequences of errors and lack of expertise.

[11]But the lesson is lost on the grade-grousing 10 percent. Say that you won't (not can't, but won't) change the grade they deserve to what they want, and they're frequently bewildered or angry. They don't think it's fair that they're judged according to their performance, not their desires or "potential." They don't think it's fair that they should jeopardize their scholar-

ships or be in danger of flunking out simply because they could not or did not do their work. But it's more than fair; it's necessary to help preserve a minimum standard of quality that our society needs to maintain safety and integrity. I don't know if the 13th-hour students will learn that lesson, but I've learned mine. From now on, after final grades are posted, I'll lie low until the next quarter starts.

—*Kurt Weisenfeld*

QUESTIONS ABOUT THE READING

CONTENT

- What assumptions does Weisenfeld make about the audience's knowledge and attitudes? Are these assumptions accurate? Why or why not?

- What is this writer's attitude toward his subject? Toward his audience? How do we know? What are the signals?

- What are the main issues for him? How has this essay affected your thinking about these issues?

- What point is the author making about educational expectations? Restate his point in your own words.

- Does the writer acknowledge the opposing viewpoint? If so, where?

- Does the writer concede anything to his opponents (give them credit for anything)? Explain.

- Does the thesis grow out of sufficient background details? Explain.

- Does the writer offer convincing reasons for his case? Explain.

- Does the writer make too much of an emotional appeal? Explain.

ORGANIZATION

- Which strategies of expository development are used here? Trace the line of thought by summarizing the topic of each paragraph. Is the material arranged in the best order?

STYLE

- How would you characterize the tone? Is it appropriate for the audience and purpose? Does the writer appear likable? Is he ever too extreme? Explain.

- Are the rhetorical questions effective? Explain.

RESPONDING TO YOUR READING

Explore your reactions to "Making the Grade" by using the questions on page 23. You might wish to challenge the author's view by arguing your own ideas about what students really want or the true purpose of education. (See, for example, essay option no. 2, page 286.) You might support his view by citing evidence from your own experience. Decide carefully on your audience and on what you want them to do, think, or feel after reading your essay. Be sure your essay supports a clear and definite point.

Be sure your essay has a clear thesis, and addresses a specific audience affected by the issue in some way. Although this essay will make an emotional appeal, your argument should not rest solely on subjective grounds (how you feel about it), but also on factual details.

OPTIONS FOR ESSAY WRITING

1. Argue for or against this assertion: Parents have the right to make major decisions in the lives of their teenagers.

2. Are grades an aid to education?

3. Sally and Sam have two children, ages 2 and 5. Sally, an attorney, is currently not working but has been offered an attractive full-time job. Sam believes Sally should not work until both children are in school. Should Sally take the job?

4. Recently, voters in several communities defeated or repealed ordinances protecting homosexuals from discrimination in housing and employment. Defend or attack these public decisions.

5. Should college scholarships be awarded for academic achievement or promise rather than for financial need?

6. During your more than 12 years in school, you've undoubtedly developed legitimate gripes about the quality of American education. Based on your experiences and perceptions and research, think about one specific problem in American education, and argue for its solution.

   Remember, you are writing an argument, not an attack; your goal is not to offend but to persuade readers—to move them to your way of seeing. After making sure that you have enough inductive evidence to support your main generalization, write an editorial essay for your campus newspaper: identify the problem; analyze its cause(s); and propose a solution. Possible topics:

   - too little (or too much) attention given to remedial students
   - too little (or too much) emphasis on practical education (career training)
   - too little (or too much) emphasis on competition
   - teachers' attitudes
   - parents' attitudes
   - students' attitudes

....

APPLICATION 18-2

Essay Practice: Arguing to Enlist Readers' Support

Read the next essay, and answer the questions that follow. Then (as your instructor requests) select one of the essay assignments.

ESSAY FOR ANALYSIS AND RESPONSE

STANDARDS YOU MEET AND DON'T DUCK

[1]I'm telling you about my son Mark, not because I want to embarrass him, but because I find it useful in discussing public-policy questions to ask what I would advocate if the people affected by my policy proposals were members of my own family.

[2]Mark, who is not quite 12, is a good kid: friendly, bright, a good athlete and (potentially) a very good student. But he has a tendency to be lazy about his studies.

[3]So at the beginning of the year, I issued an edict: He would perform acceptably well in school or he wouldn't be allowed to play organized sports outside school.

[4]He talked me into a modification: Rather than penalize him for last year's grades, earned before the new rule was announced, let him sign up for the Boys Club league now, and take him off the team if his mid-terms weren't up to par.

[5]Well, the mid-terms came out, and the basketball team is struggling along without the assistance of my son the shooting guard.

[6]All of which is a roundabout and perhaps too personal a way of saying my sentiments are with the Prince George's County (Md.) school officials. My suburban Washington neighbors, confronted with angry parents, disappointed students and decimated athletic teams, are under pressure to modify their new at-least-C-average-or-no-extracurriculars policy.

[7]I hope they will resist it. The new policy may not be perfect, but it reflects a proper sense of priorities, which is one of the things our children ought to be learning. It may turn out to be a very good thing for all concerned—including the 39 percent of the county's students who are temporarily ineligible for such outside activities as athletics, cheerleading, dramatics and band.

[8]I've heard the arguments on the other side, and while I don't dismiss them out of hand, they fall short of persuading me that the new standards are too tough or their application too rigid. I know that for some students, the extracurriculars are the only thing that keep school from being a complete downer. I know that some youngsters will be tempted to pass up Algebra II, chemistry and other tough courses in order to keep their extracurricular eligibility (weighted grade points could solve that problem). And I know

that for students whose strengths are other than academic, success in music or drama or sports can be an important source of self-esteem.

[9]Still I support the C-average rule—partly because of my assumption that it isn't all that tough a standard. We're not talking here about bell-shaped curves that automatically place some students above the median and some below it. I suspect that we're talking less about acceptable academic achievement than about acceptable levels of exertion. I find it hard to believe that Prince George's teachers will flunk kids who really do try: who pay attention in class, turn in all their work, seek special assistance when they need it and also bring athletic glory to their schools. (If it turns out that some youngsters are being penalized for inadequate gifts rather than insufficient effort, I'd support some modification of the rule.)

[10]The principal value of the new standard is that it helps the students, including those in the lower grades, to get their own priorities right: to understand that while outside activities can be an ego-boosting adjunct to classroom work, they cannot be a substitute for it. Even the truly gifted, whose nonacademic talents might earn them college scholarships or even professional careers, need as solid an academic footing as they can get.

[11]Pity, which is what we often feel for other people's children, says give the poor kids a break. Love, which is what we feel for our own, says let's help them get ready for real life—not by lowering the standards but by providing the resources to help them meet the standards. One principal who saw 38 percent of his students fall below the eligibility cutoff agrees. Said Thomas Kirby: "I don't see any point in having a kid who can bounce a basketball graduate from high school and not be able to read."

—*William Raspberry*

QUESTIONS ABOUT THE READING

CONTENT

- Does the writer acknowledge the opposing viewpoint, and does he address his opponents' biggest objection to his position?

- Where is the thesis? Is it easily found?

- Does the writer offer sound reasons for his case? Explain.

- Does the writer offer impersonal (as well as personal) support? Explain.

ORGANIZATION

- Is the introduction effective? Which of the tasks on page 279 does it perform? Explain.

- Does the writer place his strongest material near the beginning or the end of the essay? Is this placement effective?

- How does the writer achieve coherence and smooth transitions between paragraphs?

STYLE

- Does the writer avoid an extreme persona here (say, sounding like a righteous parent)? Explain.

RESPONDING TO YOUR READING

Explore your reactions to "Standards You Meet and Don't Duck" by using the questions on page 23. Then respond with your own essay supporting or opposing the author's view. Your goal is to get readers involved.

Perhaps you will want to argue from the viewpoint of athletes who are affected by grade standards. Or you might argue for some other school requirement, as in urging your old high school (or your college) to require an exit essay of its graduating seniors to ensure an acceptable level of literacy. Or maybe you feel that some school requirements are unfair.

Whatever your position, be sure that your essay has a clear thesis and that you address a specific audience whose support you seek. To be persuasive, base your support not only on personal grounds (how you feel about it), but on impersonal grounds (verifiable evidence), as well.

··

OPTIONS FOR ESSAY WRITING

1. Respond to the assertion that the liberal arts have become an unaffordable luxury. Be sure to consider the arguments for and against specialized vocational education versus a broadly humanistic—but less "practical"—education.

2. Your college is thinking of abolishing core requirements. Write a letter to the dean in which you argue for or against this change.

3. Should first-year composition be required at your school? Argue your position to the faculty senate.

4. Should your school (or institute) drop students' evaluations of teachers? Write to the student and faculty senates.

5. Perhaps you belong to a fraternity, a sorority, or some other organized group. Identify an important decision your group faces. In a letter, present your position on the issue to the group.

6. The Cultural Affairs Committee at your school has decided to sponsor a concert next fall, featuring some popular singer or musical group. Although the committee (mostly faculty) is aware that today's music reflects great diversity in personal taste and musical style, the committee members are uncertain about which performer or group would be a good choice for the event. In fact, most committee members admit to being ignorant of the characteristics that distinguish one performance or recording from another. To help in the decision, the committee has

invited the student body to submit essays (not letters) arguing for a performer or group. Free tickets will be awarded to the writer of the best essay. Compose your response.

7. Should your school have an attendance policy?

8. In a letter to the college newspaper, challenge an attitude or viewpoint that is widely held on your campus. Maybe you want to persuade your classmates that the time required to earn a bachelor's degree should be extended to five years. Or maybe you want to claim that the campus police should (or should not) wear guns. Or maybe you want to ask students to support a 10-percent tuition increase in order to make more computers and software available.

   What kind of resistance can you anticipate? How can you avoid outright rejection of your claim? What reasons will have meaning for your audience? What tone should you adopt?

· ·

APPLICATION 18-3

Essay Practice: Making a Proposal

The following proposal addresses a fairly common problem: a large television set in the campus center is causing congestion and wasting students' time. One student confronts the problem by writing a proposal to the director of the campus center.

Read the proposal carefully, and answer the questions that follow. If your instructor requests, select one of the essay assignments.

ESSAY FOR ANALYSIS

A PROPOSAL FOR BETTER USE OF THE TELEVISION SET IN THE CAMPUS CENTER

[1]Leaving the campus center yesterday for class, I found myself stuck in the daily pedestrian jam on the second-floor landing. People by the dozens had gathered on the stairway for their daily dose of "General Hospital." Fighting my way through the mesmerized bodies, I wondered about the appropriateness of the television set's location, and of the value of the shows aired on this set.

[2]Along with the recent upsurge of improvements at our school (in curriculum and standards), we should be considering ways to better use the campus center television. The tube plays relentlessly, offering soap operas and game shows to the addicts who block the stairway and main landing. Granted, television for students to enjoy between classes is a fine idea, but

no student needs to attend college to watch soap operas. By moving the set and improving the programs, we could eliminate the congestion and enrich the learning experience.

[3]The television needs a better location: out of the way of people who don't care to watch it, and into a larger, more comfortable setting for those who do. Background noise in the present location makes the set barely audible; and the raised seating in front of the set places the viewers on exhibit to all who walk by. A far better location would be the back wall of the North Lounge, outside the Sunset Room—a large, quiet, and comfortable space. Various meetings sometimes held in this room could be moved instead to the browsing area of the library.

[4]More important than the set's location is the quality of its programs. Videotaped movies might be a good alternative to the shows now aired. Our audiovisual department has a rich collection of excellent movies and educational programs on tape. People could request the shows they would like to see, and a student committee could be responsible for printing showtime information.

[5]The set might also serve as a primary learning tool by allowing communications students to create their own shows. Our school has the videotaping and sound equipment and would need only a faculty adviser to supervise the project. Students from scriptwriting, drama, political science, and journalism classes (to name a few) could combine their talents, providing shows of interest to their peers. We now have a student news program that is aired evenings on a local channel, but many who live some distance off campus cannot receive this channel on their sets at home. Why not make the program accessible to students during the day, here on campus?

[6]With resources already in our possession, we can make a few changes that will benefit almost everyone. Beyond providing more efficient use of campus center space, these changes could really stimulate people's minds. I urge you to allow students and faculty to vote on the questions of moving the television set and improving its programs.

—*Patricia Haith*

QUESTIONS ABOUT THE READING

CONTENT

- Does the proposal fulfill the tasks outlined on page 282? Explain.
- Does the writer offer the best reasons for her primary audience? Explain.
- For a different audience (say, students who avidly follow the soap operas), would the writer have to change her material? Explain.
- Is this argument primarily inductive or deductive?
- Does the writer establish agreement with the reader? If so, where?

ORGANIZATION

- Which expository strategy is used most in this essay?
- Is the narrative introduction effective? Explain.
- Does the conclusion perform all the tasks noted on page 279?

STYLE

- How do the outstanding style features of this essay contribute to its tone?
- Should the tone of this essay be more or less formal for this audience and purpose? Or is it appropriate? Explain.
- Is the writer's voice likable? Explain.

OPTION FOR ESSAY WRITING

Identify a problem in your school, community, family, or job. Develop a proposal for solving the problem. Stipulate a definite audience for your proposal. Here are some possible subjects:

- improving living conditions in your dorm
- improving security in your dorm
- creating a day-care center on campus
- saving labor, materials, or money at your job
- improving working conditions
- improving the services of your college library
- improving the food service on campus
- establishing more equitable use of computer terminals on campus

Be sure to spell out the problem, explain the benefits of change, offer a realistic plan, and urge your readers to definite action. Decide exactly what you want your readers to do.

APPLICATION 18-4

Essay Practice: Changing Readers' Behavior

This essay, a complaint letter from an employee to her boss, illustrates the challenge of trying to influence another person's behavior. Read it carefully, and answer the questions that follow. Then select one of the essay assignments.

ESSAY FOR ANALYSIS

LETTER TO THE BOSS

¹For several months I have been hesitant to approach you about a problem that has caused me great uneasiness at work. More recently, however, I've found that several other employees are equally upset, and I feel, as one of your close friends, that I should explain what's wrong. With you as our boss, we all have an exceptional employer-employee relationship, and I'd hate to see one small problem upset it.

²John, when you have criticism about any one of us at work, you never seem to deal directly with that specific person. When the chefs were coming in late, you didn't confront them directly to express your displeasure; instead, you discussed it with the other employees. When you suspected Alan's honesty and integrity as a bartender, you came to me rather than to Alan. I learned yesterday from the coat-checker that you are unhappy with the waitpersons for laughing and joking too much. And these are just a few of many such incidents.

³I understand how difficult it is to approach a person with constructive criticism—in fact, it's taken me several months to mention this problem to you! Having been on the receiving end of grapevine gossip, though, I would accept the complaint much more gracefully if it came directly from you. Many of the employees are needlessly upset, and our increasing dissatisfaction harms the quality of our work.

⁴Because I've never been a supervisor, I can only imagine your difficulty. I'm sure your task is magnified because when you bought this restaurant last spring, we employees all knew one another, but you knew none of us. You've told me many times how important it is for you to be a friend to all of us, but sometimes friendship can stand in the way of communication.

⁵Our old boss used to deal with the problem of making constructive suggestions in this way: Every other Saturday evening we would have a meeting at which he would voice his suggestions and we would voice ours. This arrangement worked out well, because none of us felt singled out for criticism, and we all had the chance to discuss any problems openly.

⁶I value your friendship, and I hope you will accept this letter in the sincere spirit in which it's offered. I'm sure that with a couple of good conversations we can work things out.

—Marcia White

QUESTIONS ABOUT THE READING

CONTENT

- Bracket all facts in this letter, and underline all statements of opinion (see Chapter 6). Are all opinions supported by facts? Explain.

- Does the writer acknowledge the opposing viewpoint? Explain.
- Does the writer admit the imperfections in her case? Explain.

ORGANIZATION

- In the introductory paragraph, is the writer guilty of "beating around the bush"? Explain.
- Which body paragraphs are deductive? Which inductive?
- Is the final body paragraph too indirect? Explain.
- Which is the most concrete paragraph? Explain its function.

STYLE

- In the second and third body paragraphs, identify one example of coordination. How does this structure reinforce the writer's meaning?
- Is the tone appropriate for the situation, audience, and purpose? Identify three sentences that contribute to the tone.
- Identify three sentences in which the writer expresses empathy with her reader.

OPTIONS FOR ESSAY WRITING

1. Everyone has habits that annoy others or are harmful in some way. Identify a bad habit of a friend, relative, coworker, or someone you spend a lot of time with, and write a letter trying to persuade the person to break the habit. Suggest specific actions that your reader might take to overcome the habit. (Stay away from the classic—cigarette smoking.) You're writing to someone close to you; you want to sound like an honest friend, not a judge. Your reader will be defensive; how can you defuse that defensiveness while getting your message across?

2. Think of a situation in which you recently encountered problems—in a job, in school, or as a consumer. Choose something about which you have a major complaint. Write a letter to the person in charge or otherwise responsible, laying out the issues and suggesting appropriate changes.

APPLICATION 18-5

Computer Application: The standard shape for an argument on page 279 suggests an effective arrangement for your thesis, your response to opposing views, your support paragraphs, and your conclusion. But throughout this book, we have seen that the standard shape can be varied in many productive ways. Using the word processing commands that allow you to move text, try out different placements for the various elements of one of your argumentative essays. What happens if you position the thesis after the response to opposing arguments instead of before it? What if you place the response to your opposition after the support? Get feedback from classmates about the various options. In particular, notice how different arrangements call for different transitions (see pages 101–103) between paragraphs and sections. Be sure to refine these transitions in the final version of the essay you select.

APPLICATION 18-6

Computer Application and Collaborative Project: Select one of the types of essays presented in this chapter. Using your *listserv* or E-mail, collaborate with a group of classmates on a joint paper addressed to an appropriate audience. Use the guidelines for collaborative work on page 47 (Section One) to brainstorm electronically for a topic, thesis, and support. Then distribute writing tasks, exchange and peer review your work, and construct a draft, using transitions to knit the sections together. Submit edited versions to the list and confer electronically about final decisions. As you work, take notes for a future paper about how the electronic process makes working together easier, more complex, or both.

WORKS CITED

Brownell, Judi, and Michael Fitzgerald. "Teaching Ethics in Business Communication: The Effective/Ethical Balancing Scale." *Bulletin of the Association for Business Communication* 55.3 (1992): 15–18.

Bryan, John. "Down the Slippery Slope: Ethics and the Technical Writer as Marketer." *Technical Communications Quarterly* 1.1 (1992): 73–88.

Johannesen, Richard L. *Ethics in Human Communication.* 2nd ed. Prospect Heights, IL: Waveland, 1983.

Larson, Charles U. *Persuasion: Perception and Responsibility.* 7th ed. Belmont, CA: Wadsworth: 1995.

Unger, Stephen H. *Controlling Technology: Ethics and Responsible Engineer.* New York: Holt, 1982.

Yoos, George. "A Revision of the Concept of Ethical Appeal." *Philosophy and Rhetoric* 12.4 (1979): 41–58.

THE RESEARCH REPORT PROCESS: A RESEARCH GUIDE FOR THE INFORMATION AGE

INTRODUCTION*

*My thanks to University of Massachusetts Dartmouth librarian Shaleen Barnes for inspiring this introduction.

*W*e do research to obtain facts or expert opinions or to understand issues. For example, we might want to inquire about the prices of building lots on Boca Grande Island, the latest findings in AIDS research, or what experts are saying about global warming. Or, suppose you learn that your well water is contaminated with benzene. Should you merely ask your neighbor's opinion about the dangers, or should you track down the answers for yourself?

In the workplace, professionals need to locate all kinds of information daily (*How do we market this product? How do we avoid accidents like this one? Are we headed for a recession?*). We all have to know where and how to look for answers, and how to communicate them *in writing*. Research is the way to find your own answers; a research report records and discusses your findings.

A *research report* involves a lot more than cooking up an old thesis, settling for the first material you happen to find, and then blending in a few juicy quotations and paraphrases to "prove" you've done the assigned work. Research is a deliberate form of inquiry, a process of *problem solving*. And we cannot begin to solve the problem until we have clearly defined it.

Parts of the research process follow a recognizable sequence. The following steps shown in Figure I4.1 are treated in these chapters:

FIGURE I4.1
Procedural stages in the research process

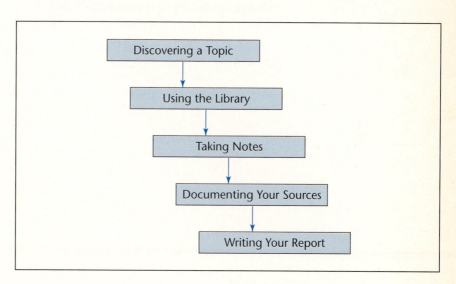

But research writing is never merely a "by-the-number" set of procedures ("First, do this; then do that"). The procedural stages depend on the many careful decisions that accompany any legitimate inquiry, depicted in Figure I4.2.

Let's consider how these inquiry stages of the research process lead to the kind of inquiry that makes a real difference.

FIGURE 14.2
Inquiry stages in the research process

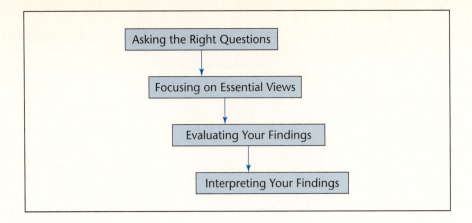

ASKING THE RIGHT QUESTIONS

The answers you uncover will depend on the questions you ask. Suppose, for instance, you've decided to research the following topic.

Defining and Refining a Research Question

The problem of violent crime on college campuses has received a good deal of recent publicity. So far your own school has been spared but, as a precautionary measure, campus decision makers are considering doubling the police force and allowing police to carry guns. Some groups are protesting, claiming that guns pose a needless hazard to students or that funding for additional police should be devoted to educational programs instead. On the student senate you and your colleagues have discussed the controversy, and you have been appointed to prepare a report that examines the trends regarding violent crime on campuses nationwide. Your report will form part of a document to be presented to the student and faculty senates in six weeks.

Your first task is to identify the exact question or questions you want answered. Before settling on a definite question, you need to navigate a long list of possible questions, like those in the Figure 14.3 tree chart. Any *one* of the questions could serve as the topic of a worthwhile research report on such a complex topic.

FOCUSING ON ESSENTIAL VIEWS

Note that we don't settle for the first or most comforting or convenient answer. We do research to discover the answer that stands the best chance of being right. To answer fairly and accurately, we have an ethical obligation to consider all perspectives from up-to-date and reputable sources, as depicted

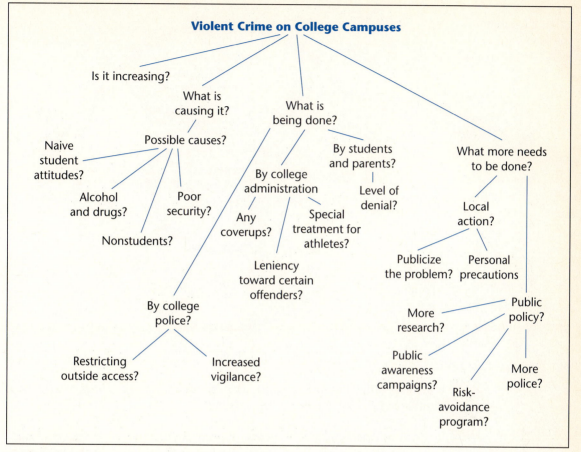

FIGURE 14.3
How the right questions help define a research problem

in Figure 14.4. Even "expert" testimony may not be enough, because experts can disagree or be mistaken.

Let's say you've chosen this question: *Violent crimes on college campuses: How common is it?* Now you can start considering information sources to consult (journals, reports, news articles, database searches, and so on). Figure 14.5 lists some likely sources of information.

ACHIEVING ADEQUATE DEPTH IN YOUR SEARCH*

Balanced research examines a *broad range* of evidence; thorough research, however, examines that evidence at an appropriate *depth*. As depicted in Fig-

---

*My thanks to University of Massachusetts Dartmouth librarian Ross LaBaugh for inspiring this section.

FIGURE 14.4
Effective research
considers multiple
perspectives

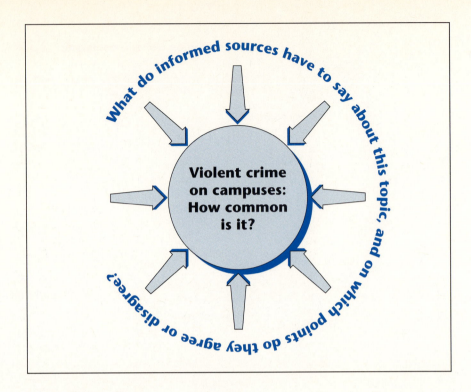

ure 14.6, different types of information about any topic can be seen to occupy different levels of detail and dependability.

1. At the surface layer are items from the popular press (newspapers, radio, TV, general magazines). Designed for general consumption, this layer of information often offers more journalistic interpretation than factual detail.

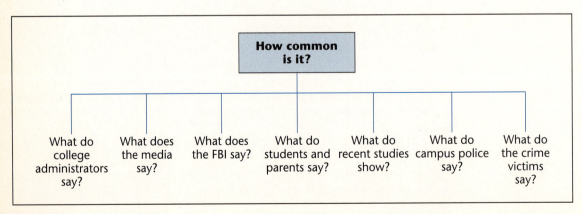

FIGURE 14.5
A range of essential viewpoints

2. At the next level are trade and business publications (*Law Enforcement Digest, The Chronicle of Higher Education,* and so on). Designed for readers who range from moderately informed to highly specialized, this layer of information focuses more on practice than on theory, on items considered newsworthy to group members, on issues affecting the field, on public relations, and on viewpoints that tend to reflect the particular biases of that field.

3. At a deeper level is the specialized literature (journals from professional associations: medical, legal, engineering, and so on). Designed for practicing professionals, this layer of information focuses on theory as well as practice; on descriptions of the latest studies—written by the researchers themselves and scrutinized by others for accuracy and objectivity; on debates among scholars and researchers; and on reviews, critiques, and refutations of prior studies and publications.

Also at this deeper level are government sources (studies and reports by NASA, EPA, FAA, FBI, the Congress; corporate documents available through the Freedom of Information Act [page 316]). Designed for anyone willing to investigate its complex resources, this layer of information offers hard facts and highly detailed and (in many instances) *relatively* impartial views of virtually any issue or topic in any field.

How "deep" is deep enough? This depends on your topic. But the real story and the hard facts more likely reside at the deeper levels of information.

FIGURE 14.6
Effective research achieves adequate depth

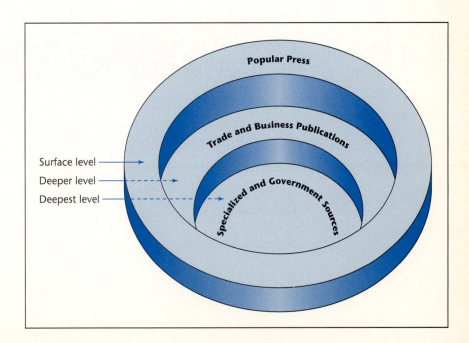

EVALUATING YOUR FINDINGS

Not all findings have equal value. Some information might be distorted, incomplete, or misleading. Information might be tainted by *source bias,* in which a source might understate or overstate certain facts, depending on whose interests that source represents—say, college administrators, or students, or a reporter seeking headlines.

QUESTIONS FOR EVALUATING A PARTICULAR FINDING

- *Is this information accurate, reliable, and relatively unbiased?*

- *Can the claim be verified by the facts?*

- *How much of it (if any) is useful?*

- *Is this the whole or the real story?*

- *Do I need more information?*

Remember, ethical researchers don't try to prove the "rightness" of some initial assumptions; instead, they research to find the *right* answers. And only near the end of your inquiry can you settle on a *definite* thesis based on what the facts suggest.

INTERPRETING YOUR FINDINGS

Once you've decided which of your findings seem legitimate, you need to decide what they all mean. The interpretation should fit the evidence and lead to an overall judgment about what the findings mean.

QUESTIONS FOR INTERPRETING YOUR FINDINGS

- *What are my conclusions?*
- *Do any findings conflict?*
- *Are other interpretations possible?*

- *Should I reconsider the evidence?*

- *What, if anything, should be done?*

Even the best research can produce contradictory or indefinite conclusions. For example (Lederman 5): What does a reported increase in violent

FIGURE 14.7
Critical thinking in the
research process

No single stage is
complete until all stages
are complete

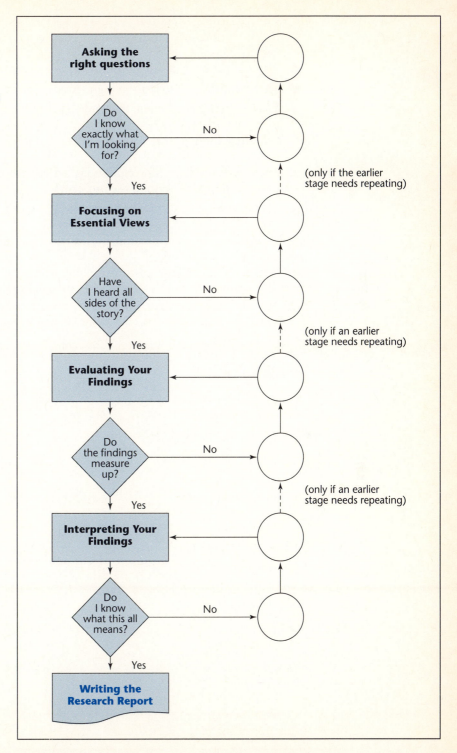

crime on U.S. college campuses mean—especially in light of national statistics that show violent crime decreasing?

- That college students are becoming more violent?
- That some drugs and guns in high schools end up on campuses?
- That off-campus criminals see students as easy targets?

Or could these findings mean something else entirely?

- That increased law enforcement has led to more campus arrests—and thus greater recognition of the problem?
- That crimes actually have not increased but more are being reported?

Depending on our interpretation, we might conclude that the problem is worsening—or improving!

Figure I4.7 shows the critical-thinking decisions crucial to worthwhile research: asking the right questions about your topic, your sources, your findings, and your conclusions. Like the writing process (Figure 1.2), the research process is *recursive:* stages are revisited and repeated as often as necessary.

WORK CITED

Lederman, Douglas. "Colleges Report Rise in Violent Crime," *Chronicle of Higher Education 3* Feb. 1995, sec. A: 31–42.

CHAPTER 19

ASKING QUESTIONS AND FINDING ANSWERS

DECIDING ON A RESEARCH TOPIC

A crucial step in developing a research report is deciding on a worthwhile topic. Begin with a subject with real meaning for you, and then decide on the specific question you want to ask about it. Pages 300–301 show how the subject of campus crime might be narrowed. Now let's try another subject.

Let's say you're disturbed about all the chemicals used to preserve or enhance flavor and color in foods—*food additives and preservatives.* What specific part of this subject would you like to focus on? This will be your *topic,* and it should be phrased as a question. To identify the possible questions you might ask, develop a tree chart (as on page 301). Your interests might lead you to this question: *What effects, if any, do food additives and preservatives have on children's behavior?*

GUIDELINES FOR CHOOSING A RESEARCH TOPIC

1. *Avoid topics that are too broad for a six- to twelve-page research report.* The topic "Do food additives and preservatives affect children?" would have to include children's growth and development, their intelligence, their susceptibility to diseases, and so on.

2. *Avoid topics that limit you to a fixed viewpoint before you've done your research:* "Which behavior disorders in children are caused by food additives and preservatives?" Presumably, you haven't yet established that such chemicals have any harmful effects. Your initial research is meant to find the facts, not to prove some point. Allow your thesis to grow from your collected facts, instead of manipulating the facts to fit your thesis.

3. *Avoid topics that have been exhausted:* abortion, capital punishment, gun control—unless, of course, you can approach such topics in a fresh way: "Could recent technological developments to help a fetus survive outside the womb cause the Supreme Court to reverse its 1973 ruling on abortion?"

4. *Avoid topics that can be summed up in an encyclopedia entry or in any one source:* "The Life of Thoreau," "How to Cross-Country Ski," or "The History of Microwave Technology." From a different angle, of course, any of these areas might allow you to draw your own, more interesting conclusions: "Was Thoreau Ever in Love?"; "How Do Injury Rates Compare Between Cross-Country and Downhill Skiing?"; "How Safe are Microwave Ovens?"

5. *Avoid religious, moral, or emotional topics that offer no objective basis for informed conclusions:* "Is Euthanasia Moral?"; "Will Jesus Save the World?"; "Should Prayer Be Allowed in Public Schools?" Questions debated throughout the ages by philosophers, judges, and social thinkers are unlikely to be answered definitely in your research paper.

But again, far more important than the subject you choose is the *question* you decide to ask about it. Plan to spend many hours in search of the right question.

USING THE LIBRARY

Figure 19.1 lists various options for beginning a library search:

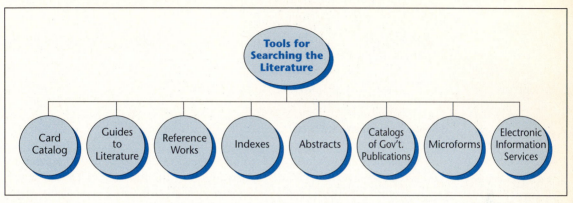

FIGURE 19.1
Ways you can search the literature

Where you begin your research will depend on whether you are searching for background and basic facts or seek the very latest information. If you have only limited knowledge or if you need to focus on your topic, you probably will want to begin with general reference sources.

REFERENCE WORKS

Reference works include encyclopedias, almanacs, handbooks, dictionaries, histories, and biographies. These provide background and bibliographies that can lead to more specific information. Make sure the work is current by checking the last copyright date.

Bibliographies   These comprehensive lists of publications about a subject are issued yearly, or even weekly. However, others can quickly become dated.

Annotated bibliographies (like the ones below, which include an abstract for each entry) are most helpful because they can point you to the most useful sources:

Bibliographies

> *MLA International Bibliography of Books and Articles on the Modern Languages and Literatures.* A comprehensive listing, published annually by the Modern Language Association.

> *Bibliographic Index.* Updated three times yearly, a listing (by subject) of bibliographies that contain at least 50 citations; to see which bibliographies are published in your field, begin here.

> *A Guide to U.S. Government Scientific and Technical Resources.* A list of everything published in these broad fields by the government.

Bibliographic Guide to Business and Economics. A list of all major business and economic publications.

Health Hazards of Video Display Terminals: An Annotated Bibliography. One of many bibliographies focused on a highly specific subject.

Encyclopedias   Encyclopedias provide basic information (which might be outdated). Sample listings:

Encyclopedias

> *Cassell's Encyclopedia of World Literature*
> *Encyclopedia of Social Sciences*
> *Encyclopedia of Food Technology*

Journals, newsletters, and other publications from professional organizations (such as the American Medical Association or the Institute of Electrical and Electronics Engineers) offer specialized information. The *Encyclopedia of Associations* offers a yearly listing of over 30,000 professional societies and organizations worldwide.

A growing number of organizations can be accessed via their Internet home page.

Dictionaries   Dictionaries can be generalized, or they can focus on specific disciplines or give biographical information. Sample listings:

Dictionaries

> *Webster's Third New International Dictionary of the English Language.* Considered the best general dictionary.
> *Dictionary of Engineering and Technology*
> *Dictionary of Telecommunications*
> *Dictionary of American Biography*

Handbooks   These research aids amass key facts (like formulas, tables, advice, and examples) about a field in condensed form. Sample listings:

Handbooks

> *Business Writer's Handbook*
> *Fire Protection Handbook*
> *The McGraw-Hill Computer Handbook*

Almanacs   Almanacs contain factual and statistical data. Sample listings:

Almanacs

> *World Almanac and Book of Facts*
> *Almanac for Computers*
> *Almanac of Business and Industrial Financial Ratios*

Directories In directories you will find updated information about organizations, companies, people, products, services, statistics, or careers, often including addresses and phone numbers:

Directories

> *The Career Guide: Dun's Employment Opportunities Directory*
> *Directory of Computer Software*
> *Standard & Poor's Register of Corporations, Directors, and Executives*
> *Directory of American Firms Operating in Foreign Countries*
> *Directory of Financial Aids for Women*
> *The Radical Right: A World Directory*

A growing number of directories and other reference works are accessible by computer.

THE CARD CATALOG

Printed Catalog Entries All materials held by a library usually are listed in its card catalog under three headings: *author, title,* and *subject.* Your library may place author, title, and subject cards in one alphabetical file or may provide individual catalogs labeled "Author," "Title," and "Subject." Say you are looking for a book on campus crime by Curtis Ostrander. Locate the "O" cards in the "Author" section of the catalog. Figure 19.2 shows a typical author catalog card:

Call number.................................	HV 6250. 4. S78
Author..	**Ostrander, Curtis**
Title...	Crime at college: the student guide to personal safety
Co-author....................................	/by Curtis Ostrander and Joseph Schwartz.
Publisher, Date.............................	Ithaca, NY: New Strategist Publications, 1994.
Physical features	191p.; 23 cm.
Other headings............................. under which this work is cataloged	1.College students--crimes against--United States. 2.School violence--United States. 3.Women college students--crimes against--United States. 4.Crime prevention--United States. 5.Alcoholism and crime. 6.Drugs and crime.

FIGURE 19.2
Catalog card classified by author

Library of Congress Guide to Subject Headings   If you know neither authors nor titles of works on your subject, use the *subject listing*. The *Library of Congress Subject Headings* (large books in the card catalog area) list related subject headings. Among the listings under *Campus* or *Crimes* you would see these:

Listings by subject headings

Campus	**Crimes**
Campus police	Crimes against students
Campus security	Student criminal offenses
Campus violence	Student victims of crime

You now have an array of subjects under which to search for useful material in the card catalog.

Electronic Catalog Entries   Most libraries are automating their card catalogs. Fast and easy to use, electronic card catalogs offer access points beyond *author, title,* and *subject,* including:

Access points for electronic catalog entries

- *Descriptor:* for retrieving works on the basis of a key word or phrase (say, "food additives" or "diet and behavior") in the subject heading, in the work's title, or the full text of its bibliographic record (its catalog entry or abstract).

- *Document type:* for retrieving works in a specific format (videotape, audiotape, compact disk, motion picture).

- *Organizations and conferences:* for retrieving works produced under the name of an institution or professional association (Smithsonian Institution, American Cancer Society).

- *Publisher:* for retrieving works produced by a particular publisher (Little, Brown and Co.).

- *Combination:* for retrieving works by combining any available access points (a book about a particular subject by a particular author or institution).

If the computer responds to your descriptors with a "no record" screen, consult the *Library of Congress Subject Headings* (above) for other possible key terms.

Through a computer network such as the *Internet,* an electronic catalog can be searched from home or office or anywhere in the world. Also through the Internet, electronic catalogs from major libraries worldwide (including the British Library, Harvard, and the Library of Congress) can be searched via computer. Note, however, that any misspelling or typographical error in key terms can result in a false indication of "no record."

GUIDES TO LITERATURE

If you simply don't know which books, journals, indexes, and reference works are available for your topic, consult a guide to literature. For a general listing of books in various disciplines, see Walford's *Guide to Reference Material* or Sheehy's *Guide to Reference Books*.

Ask your reference librarian about specialized guides such as *The Encyclopedia of Business Information Sources* or *Sources of Information in the Social Sciences* for works on your topic.

INDEXES

Indexes are good sources for current information

Indexes are lists of books, newspaper articles, journal articles, or other works on particular subjects. Because different indexes list sources in different ways, always read the introductory pages for instructions. Or ask a librarian for help.

Book Indexes A book index lists works by author, title, or subject. Sample listings (shown with annotations):

Book indexes

> *Books in Print.* An annual listing of all books published in the United States.
>
> *Cumulative Book Index.* A monthly worldwide listing of books in English.
>
> *Scientific and Technical Books and Serials in Print.* An annual listing of literature in science and technology.
>
> *Medical Books and Serials in Print.* An annual listing of works from medicine and psychology.

Remember that no book is likely to offer the very latest information because of time required to publish a book manuscript (from several months to over one year).

Newspaper Indexes These indexes list articles by subject. *The New York Times Index* is best known, but other major newspapers have their own indexes. Sample Listings:

Newspaper indexes

> *Boston Globe Index*
>
> *Christian Science Monitor Index*
>
> *Wall Street Journal Index*

Periodical Indexes A periodical index will provide you with recent information in magazines and journals. First decide whether you seek general or specialized information. Two general indexes are the *Magazine Index,* a subject index on microfilm, and the *Readers' Guide to Periodical Literature,* which is updated every few weeks. Codes for abbreviated journal titles are at the front of each volume.

Consult the *periodicals holding list* to determine which periodicals are held by your library. Copies of the list are available where indexes are shelved. Sometimes a periodical not held by your library is available in nearby libraries or through interlibrary loan.

If the article is in a very recent issue, look on the current periodical shelves. In some libraries, older issues are bound together in hardcover bindings instead of being microfilmed.

One recent and highly useful general index searchable by CD-ROM is the *Expanded Academic Index,* which provides complete bibliographic information on items from roughly 1200 journals, including the full text and images (charts, graphs, and so on) of roughly 60 percent of these works.

For specialized information, consult indexes that list journal articles in specific disciplines, such as *Ulrich's International Periodicals Directory,* the *Applied Science and Technology Index,* or the *Humanities Index.* For business articles, consult the *Business Periodicals Index.*

Chapters in books or current essays about an artist, author, issue, region, figure, or other topic in humanities and social sciences may be part of larger collections. To locate such material, consult the yearly *Essay and General Literature Index.*

Specific disciplines have their own indexes. Sample listings:

Periodical indexes

Agricultural Index

Education Index

Energy Index

Environment Index

International Nursing Index

Ask your librarian about the best indexes for your topic and about the many indexes that can be searched by computer.

INDEXES TO CONFERENCE PROCEEDINGS

Many of the papers presented at the more than 10,000 professional conferences are collected and then indexed in printed or computerized listings such as these:

Indexes to conference proceedings

Proceedings in Print

Index to Scientific and Technical Proceedings

Engineering Meetings (an *Engineering Index* database)

The very latest ideas, explorations, or advances in a field often are presented during such proceedings, before appearing as journal publications.

ABSTRACTS

Beyond indexing various works, abstracts summarize each article and can save you from going all the way to the journal in order to decide whether to read the article or to skip it. Abstracts usually are titled by discipline and increasingly are searchable by computer. A sample list:

Collections of abstracts

Biological Abstracts

Computer Abstracts

Environment Abstracts

Excerpta Medica

Forestry Abstracts

International Aerospace Abstracts

You might also consider abstracts of doctoral dissertations in *Dissertation Abstracts International.*

Abstracts increasingly are searchable by computer. Check with your librarian.

ACCESS TOOLS FOR FEDERAL GOVERNMENT PUBLICATIONS

The federal government publishes maps, periodicals, books, pamphlets, manuals, monographs, annual reports, research reports, and a remarkable array of other information, often searchable by computer.

Here are the basic access tools for government documents as well as for many privately sponsored documents:

Access tools for government publications

- *The Monthly Catalog of the United States Government* is the major access to government publications and reports.

- *Government Reports Announcements & Index* is a listing published every two weeks by the National Technical Information Service (NTIS), a branch of the U.S. Department of Commerce that serves as a clearinghouse for scientific and technical information—all stored in a computer database. The collection stores summaries of more than 1 million federally sponsored research reports and patents since 1964.

- The *Statistical Abstract of the United States,* updated yearly, offers an array of statistics on population, health, employment, crime, and the like. It can be accessed via the World Wide Web. CD-Rom versions are available beginning with the 1997 edition.

The government also issues *Selected Government Publications,* a monthly list of roughly 150 titles (with descriptive abstracts), ranging from highly general (*Questions About the Ocean*) to highly technical (*An Emission-Line*

Survey of the Milky Way). Finally, the government publishes bibliographies on hundreds of subjects, ranging from "Accidents and Accident Prevention" to "Home Gardening of Fruits and Vegetables."

Many unpublished documents are available under the Freedom of Information Act. The FOIA grants public access to all federal agency records except for classified documents, trade secrets, certain law enforcement files, records protected by personal privacy law, and similar categories of exempted information.

Publicly accessible government records

> Suppose you have heard that a certain toy has been recalled as a safety hazard and you want to know the details. In this case, the Consumer Product Safety Commission could help you. Perhaps you want to read the latest inspection report on conditions at a nursing home certified for Medicare. Your local Social Security office keeps such records on file. Or you might want to know if the Federal Bureau of Investigation has a file that includes you. In all these examples, you may use the FOIA to request information from the appropriate federal agency. (U.S. General Services Administration 1)

Contact the specific agency that would hold the records you seek: for workplace accident records, the Department of Labor; for industrial pollution records, the Environmental Protection Agency, and so on.

A growing body of government information is posted to the Internet or the World Wide Web. For example the Food and Drug Administration's electronic bulletin board lists information on experimental drugs to fight AIDS, drug and device approvals, recalls and litigations involving drugs or devices, health fraud, and a host of related items. The Department of Energy offers a Web homepage for information on human radiation experiments. Ask your librarian for electronic addresses of selected government agencies.

MICROFORMS

Microform technology enables vast quantities of printed information—government documents, technical reports, newspapers, business directories, and translated documents worldwide—to be reproduced and stored on rolls of microfilm or packets of microfiche (Lavin 12). This material is read on machines that magnify the reduced image. Ask your librarian for assistance.

USING ELECTRONIC INFORMATION SERVICES

Compared with manual searches of printed resources, electronic searches offer greater speed. Most importantly, they offer greater access (Gibaldi 6–7, 14–15):

Advantages of
electronic literature
searches

- *Sources can be located on the basis of limited information.* If you know only part of a full title or only an author's last name, the computer searches the database for all titles containing those words or authors sharing that last name.

- *Searches can be broadened.* A keyword search (using, say, "campus crime") scans not only subject headings or titles, but also a work's complete bibliographic record, including its abstract. Keyword searches therefore uncover a broad range of material that might have been overlooked in a traditional search by subject or title.

- *Searches can be customized.* The amount of information now available on most topics is overwhelming. But you can limit an electronic search to specific dates or to specific media (books, journals, newspapers, films, and so on).

- *A source's full text often can be accessed directly.* With a database that offers the full text of its listings, you no longer need to search the library for a printed equivalent of the work you seek. After scanning abstracts of selected titles, you can access the full texts to be read on-screen or downloaded and printed.

Major libraries across the globe are accessible by personal computer via the Internet and the World Wide Web.

Following is a sampling of the electronic search tools commonly available to researchers in virtually any discipline, working from virtually any location.

COMPACT DISKS AND DISKETTES

A single CD-ROM disk stores the equivalent of an entire encyclopedia and serves as a portable database.

One useful CD-ROM disk for business information is ProQuest, whose *ABI/INFORM* database indexes over 800 journals in management, marketing, and business since 1989, and whose *UMI* database indexes major U.S. newspapers. A keyword search of ProQuest's subject headings, titles, and abstracts yields a listing of relevant titles. You then can obtain the full bibliographic record, including the abstract, for each title of interest.

Another useful CD-ROM disk for information about psychology, nursing, education, and social policy is SilverPlatter, whose databases are easily accessed via keyword searches. Both ProQuest and SilverPlatter databases are updated frequently and subscribers (libraries and other organizations) receive revised disks on a regular basis.

ON-LINE DATABASES

Most college libraries subscribe to retrieval services that can access thousands of databases stored on centralized computers. From a library terminal (or in some cases, a microcomputer), you can access indexes, journals, books, monographs, dissertations, and reports. Compared with CDs, mainframe databases tend to be more specialized and more current, often updated daily (as opposed to weekly, monthly, or quarterly updating of CD databases).

Types of on-line databases

On-line retrieval systems offer three types of databases: *bibliographic, full-text,* and *factual* (Lavin 14). Bibliographic databases list publications in a field and sometimes include abstracts of each entry.

Full-text databases display the entire article or document (usually excluding graphics) directly on the computer screen and then will print the article on command.

Factual databases provide facts of all kinds: global and up-to-the-minute stock quotations, weather data, lists of new patents filed, and credit ratings of major companies, to name a few.

The following sections discuss four popular database services.

OCLC and RLIN You can easily compile a comprehensive list of works on your subject at any library that belongs to the Online Computer Library Center (OCLC) or the Research Libraries Information Network (RLIN). OCLC and RLIN databases store millions of records that have the same information found in a printed card catalog. Using a networked terminal, you type in author or title. You then get a listing of the publication you seek and information about where to find it. If your library doesn't have the publication, your librarian can activate the Interlibrary Loan System (ILS). Your order will arrive by mail in a week or two.

DIALOG Many libraries subscribe to DIALOG, a comprehensive network of more than 150 independent databases covering a broad range of subjects. You retrieve information by typing in key terms; the computer scans bibliography lists for titles containing those terms. Say you need information on *campus crime*. You instruct the computer to search ERIC, an education database, for titles including these words or synonymous words, such as *assault, violence, rape*. The system provides full bibliographies and abstracts of the most recent articles on your topic.

DIALOG also provides financial and product information about companies, names and addresses of company officers, statistical data, and patent information. Here are a few of DIALOG's databases:

DIALOG databases

AIDS Weekly

American Journal of Diseases of Children

Career Placement Registry

Conference Papers Index

Electronic Yellow Pages (for retailers, services, manufacturers)

Enviroline

Philosopher's Index

BRS Bibliographic Retrieval Services (BRS) is another popular database providing bibliographies and abstracts from life sciences, physical sciences, business, or social sciences. These are a few from the more than 50 BRS databases:

BRS databases

American Chemical Society Journals
Dissertation Abstracts International
Government Reports Announcements & Index
Harvard Business Review
International Pharmaceutical Abstracts
Pollution Abstracts
Robotics Information Database

THE INTERNET

Brief history of the INTERNET

A worldwide computer and supercomputer network, the INTERNET has evolved from ARAPANET, a network created in 1969 for university computer researchers to exchange files and share data. As the NET's potential for the open exchange of information became recognized, network sites increased and commercial on-line services began offering access to general subscribers. By 1989 the INTERNET had become a global vehicle for ideas and information of all kinds (Levy 179–80). Today's INTERNET connects more than 20 million computer users.

Commercial on-line services such as *Prodigy, Compuserve, America On-line,* and *Microsoft Network* provide Internet access via "gateways," along with aids for navigating its many resources, including the following:

INTERNET resources and navigation tools

- *Usenet,* a global bulletin board for sharing information and getting answers to questions on topics of common interest, categorized according to particular *newsgroups.* Newsgroups offer public access to more than 10,000 topics ranging from rain-forest preservation to intellectual property laws to witchcraft.

- *Listservs,* discussion groups on more specialized topics, usually among experts (say, cancer researchers), before their findings or opinions appear in published form. *Listserv* access is limited to subscribers.

- *Gopher,* a broad-based tool for retrieving information, searches database sites, library catalogs, and electronic publications worldwide for information under specific subject headings (say, "Crime on College Campuses"). To help users keep track of items searched and retrieve them if needed, *Gopher* provides a "bookmark" for each item searched.

- *Archie,* for locating and downloading free computer files or software from file-transfer sites worldwide.

- *Veronica, Jughead* and *WAIS* (*Wide Area Information Service*), for specialized searches of various types.

- *World Wide Web,* a global network of databases, documents, images, and sounds. All types of information from anywhere in the Web network can be accessed and explored through navigation programs such as *Yahoo, Mosaic,* or *Netscape,* known as *browsers.* Hypertext links among Web resources enable users to explore information along different paths by clicking on key words or icons that reveal additional paths for browsing and discovery.

  Each Web site has its own *homepage,* a type of electronic billboard that serves as introduction to the site and is linked to additional "pages" that individual users can explore according to their information needs.

Using a modem, a phone line, and an access provider such as *America Online* you can search INTERNET databases from a home, office, or laptop computer. You can join various INTERNET newsgroups, subscribe to discussion lists, send E-mail inquiries to NASA or the White House, or gain access to publications that exist only in electronic form (page 358). Using navigational and retrieval tools such as *Netscape* and *Mosaic,* you can explore sites on the World Wide Web, locate experts in all types of specialties, read the latest articles in journals such as *Nature* or *Science* or the latest newspaper listings of jobs in your field. For on-line databases in your field, ask your librarian.

Caution: Assume that any material obtained from the Internet is protected by copyright. Before using this material anyplace other than a college paper, obtain written permission from its owner.

ELECTRONIC MAIL

Perhaps the most widely used application on the Internet is electronic mail, or E-mail, which provides a connection to discussion forums on *Listserv* and *Usenet* and carries day-to-day communication as well.

How E-mail works

E-mail transmits an electronic document via networked computer terminals to recipients in the same building or across the globe. Specific codes direct the message to any electronic "mailbox" designated by the sender—or to all the mailboxes on a "mailing list." Alerted by an audio signal, the recipient "opens" the on-screen mailbox, reads the message, and then either responds, files the message, prints it out, forwards it, or deletes it. E-mail messages can be exchanged instantaneously or at the convenience of the communicating parties.

In addition to being a fast, convenient, and effective way to communicate, E-mail offers the following benefits to writers and researchers:

E-mail benefits for writers and researchers

- *E-mail can foster creative thinking.* E-mail dialogues involve a give-and-take, much like a conversation. Writers feel encouraged to express their thoughts spontaneously as they write and respond—without worrying about page design, paragraph structure, or perfect phrasing. This relatively free exchange of views can lead to new insights or ideas (Bruhn 43).

- *E-mail is an excellent tool for collaborative work and research.* Collaborative teams keep in touch via E-mail, and researchers contact people who have the answers they need.

E-Mail Guidelines*

Recipients who consider an E-mail message poorly written, irrelevant, offensive, or inappropriate will only end up resenting the sender. These guidelines offer suggestions for effective E-mail use:

- *Use E-mail to reach a lot of people quickly with a relatively brief, informal message.*

- *Don't use E-mail to send confidential information.* Avoid complaining, criticizing, or evaluating people or saying anything that warrants privacy.

- *Don't use E-mail to send formal correspondence.* For instance, don't apply for a job or a scholarship application via E-mail, unless recipients request or approve this method beforehand.

- *Check your distribution list before each mailing.* Be sure the message reaches all intended readers—but no unintended ones.

- *Assume your E-mail correspondence is permanent and could be read by anyone anytime.* Ask yourself whether you've written anything you couldn't say to another person's face. Avoid flaming (making rude remarks).

- *Before you forward an incoming message to other recipients, obtain permission from the sender.* Assume that any material you receive is the private property of the sender.

- *Limit your message to a single topic.* Keep the whole thing focused and concise. (Yours may be one of many messages confronting the recipient.) Avoid the temptation to ramble.

- *Use a clear subject line to identify your topic:* ("Subject: Request for Make-up Exam in Enl 278"). This helps recipients decide whether to read the message immediately, and makes it easier to file and retrieve for later reference.

- *Refer clearly to the message to which you are responding:* ("Here are the available meeting dates you requested on Oct. 10.")

- *Keep sentences and paragraphs short, for easy reading.*

- *Don't write in FULL CAPS—unless you want to SCREAM at the recipient!*

*These guidelines largely are adapted from the following sources: Bruhn (43); Goodman (33–35, 167); Kawasaki (286); Nantz and Drexel (45–51); Peyser and Rhodes (82). Full citations appear at end of chapter.

Despite their speed, currency, and efficiency automated searches also have limitations.

Limitations of automated searches

- Most computerized bibliographies include no entries before the mid-1960s.

- A manual search provides the whole "database" (the bound index or abstracts). As you browse, you often *randomly* discover something useful.*

- Automated searches can be expensive, depending on how many databases you search and how long you spend on-line.

For any automated search, a manual (random) search is usually needed as well. And a thorough search calls for a preliminary conference with a trained librarian.

As soon as you are familiar with your library, do a quick search of the card catalog, reference books, and indexes. Compile a working bibliography of at least a dozen works. Maybe you won't use all this material, or maybe you will need more—your bibliography will grow as you read. And many books you examine will have their own bibliographies leading to additional sources.

EXPLORING PRIMARY SOURCES

For many topics, you will want *primary* as well as *secondary* sources. Primary research is a firsthand study of the topic from observation, questionnaires, interviews, inquiry letters, works of literature, or personal documents (letters, diaries, journals). If your topic is the love life of Thoreau, a good primary source will be his journals, poems, and letters—or an interview with a specialist in the English Department. Secondary research is based on information and conclusions that other researchers—by their primary research—have compiled in books and articles. Secondary sources are *about* primary sources. Whenever possible, combine these approaches.

THE INFORMATIVE INTERVIEW

An excellent primary source for data that cannot be found in any publication is the *personal interview.* Much of what an expert knows may never be submitted for publication (Pugliano 6). Also, a respondent might refer you to other respondents or sources of information.

---

*University of Massachusetts Dartmouth librarian Charles McNeil cautions against assuming that computers yield the best material: "The material in the computer is what is cheapest to put there." Librarian Ross LaBaugh warns of a built-in bias in databases: "The company that assembles the bibliographic or full-text database often includes a disproportionate number of its own publications." Like any collection of information, a database can reflect the biases of its assemblers.

GUIDELINES FOR INFORMATIVE INTERVIEWS

PREPARING FOR THE INTERVIEW

1. *Know exactly what you are seeking.* Learn all you can about the topic beforehand. Be sure the information this person might provide is unavailable in print.

2. *Request the interview at your respondent's convenience.* Give the respondent ample notice and time to prepare, and ask whether she or he objects to being quoted or taped.

3. *Make questions unambiguous and specific.* Avoid questions that can be answered with a simple "yes" or "no."

4. *Write out each question on a separate notecard.* Use the notecard to summarize the response during the interview.

5. *Stick to your interview plan.* If the respondent wanders, politely bring the conversation back on track (unless the additional information is useful).

6. *Be a good listener.* Don't stare out the window or doodle.

7. *Ask for clarification or explanation whenever necessary.*

8. *Be ready to ask follow-up questions.* Some answers may reveal new directions for the interview.

9. *Keep note-taking to a minimum.* Record statistics, dates, names, and other precise data, but don't record every word. Jot significant terms that later can refresh your memory.

CONDUCTING THE INTERVIEW

1. *Make a good start.* Thank your respondent; restate your purpose; explain why you feel he or she can be helpful; explain exactly how the information will be used.

2. *Ask questions clearly, in the order you prepared them.*

3. *Be assertive but courteous.* Ask pointed questions, but remember that the respondent is doing you a favor.

4. *Let the respondent do most of the talking.* Keep opinions to yourself.

CONCLUDING THE INTERVIEW

1. *Ask for closing comments.* Perhaps the respondent can lead you to additional information.

2. *Invite the respondent to review your version.* If the interview is to be published, ask the respondent to approve your final draft before you quote him or her in print. Offer to provide copies of any document in which this information appears.

3. *As soon as you leave the interview, write a complete summary.* Do this while responses are fresh in your memory.

GUIDELINES FOR DEVELOPING A QUESTIONNAIRE

1. *Decide on the types of questions* (Adams and Schvaneveldt 202–12; Velotta 390). Questions can be *open-ended* or *closed-ended.* Open-ended questions allow respondents to express exactly what they're thinking or feeling in a word, phrase, sentence, or short essay:

Open-ended questions

How much do you know about crime at our school?

What do you think should be done about crime at our school?

Since one never knows what people will say, open-ended questions are a good way to uncover attitudes and obtain unexpected information. Essay-type questions though are hard to answer and tabulate.

When you want to measure where people stand on an issue, choose closed-ended questions:

Closed-ended questions

Are you interested in joining a group of concerned students? Yes _____ No _____

Characterize your degree of concern about crime problems at our school.

High _____ Moderate _____
Low _____ No concern _____

Circle the number that indicates your view about the administration's proposal to allow campus police to carry handguns.

1   2   3   4   5   6   7
STRONGLY   NO   STRONGLY
APPROVE   OPINION   DISAPPROVE

Respondents may be asked to *rate* one item on a scale (from high to low, best to worse), to *rank* two or more items (in order of importance, desirability), or to select items from a list. Other questions measure percentages or frequency

How often do you . . . ?

Always _____ Often _____
Sometimes _____ Rarely _____
Never _____ .

Although they are easy to answer, tabulate, measure, and analyze, closed-ended questions create the potential for biased responses. Some people, for instance, automatically prefer items near the top of a list or the left side of a rating scale (Plumb and Spyridakis 633). Also, people generally are prone to agree rather than disagree with assertions in a questionnaire (Sherblom, Sullivan, and Sherblom 61).

2. *Design an engaging introduction and opening questions.* Persuade respondents that the survey relates to their concerns, that their answers matter, and that their anonymity is assured. Explain how respondents will benefit from your findings, or offer an incentive (say, a copy of your final report).

A survey introduction

Your answers will enable our Senate representative to convey your views about handguns for the campus police. Results of this survey will appear in our campus newspaper. Thank you.

Begin with the easiest questions. Once respondents commit to these, they are likely to complete later, more difficult questions.

3. *Make each question unambiguous and unbiased.* All respondents should be able to interpret identical questions identically.

An ambiguous question

Do you favor weapons for campus police? Yes _____ No _____

"Weapons" might mean tear gas, clubs, handguns, all three, or two out of three. Consequently, responses to the above question would produce a misleading statistic, such as "Over 95 percent of students favor handguns for campus police" when the accurate conclusion might be "Over 95 percent of students favor some form of weapon." Moreover, the limited choice ("Yes/No") reduces an array of possible opinions to an either/or choice.

A clear and incisive question

Do you favor (check all that apply):

_____ The current policy, in which campus police carry mace and a club?

_____ Having campus police carry non-lethal "stun guns"?

_____ Having campus police store handguns in their cruisers?

_____ Having campus police carry only small-caliber handguns?

_____ Having campus police carry handguns of large caliber?

_____ Having campus police carry no weapons whatsoever?

_____ Don't know.

To ensure a full range of possible responses, include options such as "Other _____," "Don't know," "Not applicable," or an "Additional comments" section.

Avoid *loaded questions* that invite or advocate a particular viewpoint or bias:

A loaded question

Should our campus tolerate the needless endangerment of innocent students by lethal weapons? Yes _____ No _____

Emotionally loaded and judgmental words ("endangerment," "innocent," "tolerate," "needless," "lethal") in a survey are unethical because their built-in judgments manipulate people's responses (Hayakawa 40).

4. *Keep the questionnaire as short as possible.* Try to limit questions and response space to two sides of a single page.

SURVEYS AND QUESTIONNAIRES

Surveys enable us to develop profiles and estimates about the concerns, preferences, attitudes, beliefs, or perceptions of a large, identifiable group (*a target population*) by studying representatives of that group (*a sample group*).

Surveys help us make assessments like these

- *What percentage of students feel safe on our campus?*
- *Is public confidence in technology increasing or decreasing?*
- *Do consumers prefer brand A or brand B?*

The tool for conducting surveys is the *questionnaire*. While interviews allow for greater clarity and depth, questionnaires offer an inexpensive way to survey a large group. Respondents can answer privately and anonymously—and often more candidly than in an interview.

INQUIRY LETTERS OR CALLS

Letters, phone calls, or E-mail inquiries are handy for obtaining specific information from government agencies, legislators, private companies, university research centers, trade associations, and research foundations such as the Brookings Institution and the Rand Corporation (Lavin 9). Keep in mind, however, that unsolicited inquiries, especially by phone or E-mail, can be intrusive and offensive.

ORGANIZATIONAL PUBLICATIONS

Most organizations also publish pamphlets, brochures, annual reports, or prospectuses for consumers, employees, investors, or voters. But be alert for bias in company literature. If you were evaluating the safety measures at a local nuclear power plant, you would want the complete picture. Along with the company's literature, you would want studies and reports from government agencies and publications from environmental groups.

PERSONAL OBSERVATION

If possible, amplify and verify your findings with a firsthand look. Observation should be your final step, because you now know what to look for. Have a plan. Know how, where, and when to look, and jot down observations immediately. You might even take photos or make drawings.

Keep in mind that even direct observation is not foolproof: for instance, you might be biased about what you see (say, focusing on the wrong events or ignoring something important) or, instead of behaving normally, people who know they are being observed might exhibit behavior they think you expect (Adams and Schvaneveldt 244).

APPLICATION 19-1

Prepare a research report by completing these steps. (Your instructor might establish a timetable for your process.)

PHASE ONE: PRELIMINARY STEPS

1. Choose a topic of *immediate practical importance,* something that affects you or your community directly. Develop a tree chart to help you ask the right questions.
2. Identify a specific audience and its intended use of your information.
3. Narrow your topic, checking with your instructor for approval and advice.
4. Identify the various viewpoints that will lead to your own balanced viewpoint.
5. Make a working bibliography to ensure sufficient primary and secondary resources. Don't delay this step!
6. List the information you already have about your topic.
7. Submit a clear statement of purpose to your instructor.
8. Make a working outline.

PHASE TWO: COLLECTING, EVALUATING, AND INTERPRETING DATA

Read Chapter 20 in preparation for this phase.

1. In your research, move from the general to the specific; begin with general reference works for an overview.
2. Skim the sources, looking for high points.
3. Evaluate each finding for accuracy, reliability, fairness, and completeness.
4. Take notes *selectively.* Use notecards or electronic file software.
5. Decide what your findings mean.
6. Settle on your thesis.
7. Use the checklist on page 344 to assess your methods, interpretations, and reasoning.

PHASE THREE: ORGANIZING YOUR DATA AND WRITING THE REPORT

1. Revise your working outline, as needed.
2. Follow the introduction-body-conclusion format.
3. Fully document all sources of information.
4. Write your final draft according to the checklist on page 377.
5. Proofread carefully.

DUE DATES

- List of possible topics due: _____
- Final topic due: _____
- Working bibliography and working outline due: _____
- Notecards due: _____
- Revised outline due: _____
- First draft of report due: _____
- Final draft of report with full documentation due: _____

APPLICATION 19-2

Computer Project: In addition to Web searches through a Web Browser, many universities offer *Telnet* or *Gopher* search options. If your institution provides workshops on *Gopher* searches through *Veronica* or *Archie* (search tools named after cartoon characters), sign up for one, then augment your Web search with one of these other options. As you gather information, note the differences in the quantity and type of material you find.

WORKS CITED

Adams, Gerald R., and Jay D. Schvaneveldt, *Understanding Research Methods.* New York: Longman, 1985.

Bruhn, Mark J. "E-Mail's Conversational Value." *Business Communication Quarterly* 58.3 (1995): 43–44.

Gibaldi, Joseph. *MLA Handbook for Writers of Research Papers.* 4th ed. New York: Modern Language Assn., 1995.

Goodman, Danny. *Living at Light Speed.* New York: Random, 1994.

Hayakawa, S. I. *Language in Thought and Action.* 3rd ed. New York: Harcourt, 1972.

Kawasaki, Guy. "The Rules of E-Mail." *MACWORLD* Oct. 1995: 286.

Lavin, Michael R. *Business Information: How to Find It. How to Use It.* 2nd ed. Phoenix: Oryx, 1992.

Levi, Stephen. "Optimism about the Net." *MACWORLD* July 1994: 179–80.

Nantz, Karen S., and Cynthia L. Drexel. "Incorporating Electronic Mail with the Business Communication Course." *Business Communication Quarterly* 58.3 (1995) 45–51.

"Online." *Chronicle of Higher Education* 14 Oct. 1992: sec. A:1.

Peyser, Marc, and Steve Rhodes. "When E-Mail Is Oops-Mail." *Newsweek* 16 Oct. 1995: 82.

Plumb, Carolyn, and Jan H. Spyridakis, "Survey Research in Technical Communication: Designing and Administering Questionnaires." *Technical Communication* 39.4 (1992): 625–38.

Pugliano, Fiore. Unpublished review, 1991.

Sherblom, John C., Claire F. Sullivan, and Elizabeth C. Sherblom, "The What, the Whom, and the Hows of Survey Research," *Bulletin of the Association for Business Communication* 56:12 (1993): 58–64.

U.S. General Services Administration. *Your Rights to Federal Records.* Washington: GPO, 1995.

Velotta, Christopher. "How to Design and Implement a Questionnaire." *Technical Communications* 38.3 (1991): 387–92.

Watkins, Beverly T. "Many Campuses Start Building Tomorrow's Electronic Library." *Chronicle of Higher Education* 2 Sep. 1992: sec A: 1+.

Weinstein, Edith. Unpublished review, 1991.

CHAPTER 20

RECORDING, EVALUATING, AND INTERPRETING YOUR FINDINGS

Whether you work with your own findings or those of other researchers, you confront questions like these: *How much is worth keeping? How should I record it? Can I trust this information? What, exactly, does it mean? Has my inquiry been adequate?* These latter stages of the research process call for the same quality of critical thinking required by the earlier stages.

RECORDING THE FINDINGS

Findings should be recorded in ways that enable you to easily locate, organize, shuffle, and control the material.

TAKING NOTES

Notecards are easy to organize and reorganize.

GUIDELINES FOR RECORDING RESEARCH FINDINGS

1. *Make a separate bibliography card for each work you consult.* Record that work's complete entry (Figure 20.1), using the citation format that will appear in your report. (See pages 350–360 for sample entries.) Record the information accurately so that you won't have to relocate a source at the last minute.

    When searching an on-line catalog, you often can print out the full bibliographic record for each work, thereby ensuring an accurate citation.

2. *Skim the entire work to locate relevant material.* Look over the table of contents and the index. Check the introduction for an overview or thesis. Look for informative headings.

3. *Go back and decide what to record.* Use a separate card for each item.

4. *Be selective.* Don't copy or paraphrase every word. (See the page 336 guidelines for summarizing.)

5. *Record the item as a quotation or a paraphrase.* When quoting others directly, record words and punctuation accurately. When restating or adapting material in your own words, preserve the original meaning and emphasis.

    In place of notecards, many researchers take notes on a laptop computer, using electronic file software that allows notes to be filed, shuffled, and retrieved by author, title, topic, date, or keywords.

QUOTING THE WORK OF OTHERS

You must place quotation marks around all exact wording you borrow, whether the words were written or spoken (as in an interview or presenta-

FIGURE 20.1
Bibliography card

Record each
bibliographic citation
exactly as it will appear
in your final report

HV 6250. 4. W65v53

National Research Council.

Understanding Violence against Women.

Washington, DC: National Academy Press, 1996.

Plagiarism often is
unintentional

tion) or whether they appeared in electronic form. Even a single borrowed sentence or phrase, or a single word used in a special way, needs quotation marks, with the exact source properly cited.

If your notes don't identify quoted material accurately, you might forget to credit the source. Even when this omission is unintentional, writers face the charge of *plagiarism* (misrepresenting as one's own the words or ideas of someone else). Possible consequences of plagiarism include expulsion from school, the loss of a job, and a lawsuit.

For a direct quotation, copy the selection word for word (Figure 20.2) and include the page number(s). If your quotation omits parts of a sentence, use an *ellipsis* (three periods equally spaced: . . .) to indicate each part that you have omitted from the original. If your quotation omits the end of a sentence, the beginning of the subsequent sentence, or whole sentences or paragraphs, show the ellipsis with four periods (. . . .).

Ellipsis within and
between sentences

> If your quotation omits parts . . . use an ellipsis. . . . If your quotation omits the end. . . .

Your elliptical expression must be grammatical and must not distort the original meaning. Any clarifying comments of your own within the quotation should be *placed inside brackets* to distinguish your words from those of your source, as shown on page 333.

FIGURE 20.2
Notecard for a
quotation

> National Research Council. <u>Understanding</u>
> <u>Violence.</u> p. 137.
>
> "School-based programs to prevent date rape and
> intimate partner violence, as well as programs on
> conflict resolution and general violence prevention,
> have become popular in recent years. However, these
> programs have seldom been evaluated, and the
> evaluations that have been done usually look only
> at short-term attitudinal change."

Place quotation marks
around all directly
quoted material

Brackets setting off
personal comments
within quoted material

This occupation [campus police officer] requires excellent judgment.

(For more on brackets and ellipses, see pages 448, 449.)

Generally, audience needs require that integrated quotations be introduced by phrases such as "Jones argues that," "Smith suggests that," so that readers will know who said what. More importantly, readers need a transitional phrase to see the relationship between the quoted idea and the sentence that precedes it:

An introduction that
unifies a quotation with
the discussion

One investigation of sexual assault on college campuses found that "college athletes and fraternity men are a protected species" (Johnson 1991, p. 34).

Your integrated sentences should be grammatical:

Quoted material
integrated
grammatically with the
writer's words

"Alcohol has become the social drug of choice at American colleges," reports Matthews, "and a fuel for campus crime" (1993, p. 41).

(For quoting long passages and for punctuating at the end of a quotation, see pages 447–448.)

Use direct quotations only when precision, clarity, or emphasis requires the original words. Avoid excessively long quoted passages; paraphrase, instead of quoting, most borrowed material.

PARAPHRASING THE WORK OF OTHERS

Paraphrasing means more than changing or shuffling a few words; it means restating the original idea in your own words, sometimes in a clearer, more direct, and emphatic way, and giving full credit to the source.

Faulty paraphrasing is a form of plagiarism

To borrow or adapt someone else's ideas or reasoning without properly documenting the source is plagiarism. To offer as a paraphrase an original passage only slightly altered—even when you document the source—also is plagiarism. Equally unethical is offering a paraphrase, although documented, that distorts the original meaning.

An effective paraphrase generally displays all or most of the following elements (Weinstein 3):

GUIDELINES FOR PARAPHRASING

1. *Refer to the author early in the paraphrase, to indicate the beginning of the borrowed passage.*

2. *Retain keywords from the original, to preserve its meaning.*

3. *Restructure and combine original sentences, for emphasis and fluency.*

4. *Delete needless words from the original for conciseness.*

5. *Use your own words and phrases to explain the author's ideas, for clarity.*

6. *Cite (in parentheses) the exact source, to mark the end of the borrowed passage and to give full credit.*

7. *Be sure to preserve the author's original intent.*

Figure 20.3 shows an entry paraphrased from the passage on page 333. Paraphrased material is not enclosed within quotation marks, but it is documented to acknowledge your debt to the source.

PREPARING SUMMARIES AND ABSTRACTS

As we record our research findings, we summarize and paraphrase to capture the main ideas in compressed form. Also, researchers and readers who must act on information need to identify quickly what is most important in a long document. An abstract is a type of summary that does three things: (1) shows what the document is all about; (2) helps readers decide whether to read all of it, parts of it, or none of it; and (3) gives readers a framework for understanding what follows.

Whether you summarize your own writing (like the sample on page 380) or someone else's, readers expect the qualities listed on page 335.

FIGURE 20.3
Notecard for a
paraphrase

National Research Council. Understanding Violence.

According to the National Research Council, school programs for date-rape and violence prevention have grown, but their effectiveness has not been measured adequately (137).

Signal the beginning of the paraphrase by citing the author, and the end by citing the source.

What readers expect from an abstract

- *Accuracy:* Readers expect an abstract to sketch precisely the content, emphasis, and line of reasoning of the original.
- *Completeness:* Readers expect to consult the original document only for more detail—not to make sense of the main ideas and their relationships.
- *Readability:* Readers expect an abstract to be clear and straightforward—easy to follow and understand.
- *Conciseness:* Readers expect an abstract to be informative yet brief, and they may stipulate a word limit (say, 200 words).

For college papers, the abstract normally appears on a separate page right before the text of the paper or report.

EVALUATING THE SOURCES

Not all sources are equally dependable. A source might offer information that is out-of-date, inaccurate, incomplete, mistaken, or biased.

"Is the source up-to-date?"

- *Determine the currency of the source.* Certain types of information become outdated more quickly than others. For topics that focus on *technology* (Internet censorship, alternative cancer treatments), information more than a few months old may be outdated. But for topics that focus

GUIDELINES FOR SUMMARIZING INFORMATION AND PREPARING AN ABSTRACT

1. *Be considerate of later users.* Unless you own the book, journal, or magazine, work from a photocopy.

2. *Read the entire original.* When summarizing the work of another writer, grasp the total picture before picking up your pencil.

3. *Reread and underline.* Identify the issue or need that led to the article or report. Focus on the main ideas: thesis, topic sentences, findings, conclusions, and recommendations.

4. *Pare down your underlined material.* Omit lengthy background, examples, technical details, explanations or anything unessential to the overall meaning. In abstracting the writing of others, avoid direct quotations; if you must quote some crucial word or phrase directly, be sure to use quotation marks.

5. *Rewrite in your own words.* Even if this first draft is too long, include everything that seems essential; you can trim later.

6. *Edit for conciseness.* Once your draft contains everything readers need, find ways to trim. (Review pages 118–124.)

    a. Cross out needless words—but keep sentences clear and grammatical:

    Needless words omitted

    > As far as artificial intelligence is concerned, the technology is only in its infancy.

    b. Cross out needless prefaces:

    Needless prefaces omitted

    > The writer argues that . . .
    > Also discussed is. . . .

    c. Combine related ideas in order to emphasize important connections:

    Disconnected

    > The nuclear core approached critical temperature. The loss-of-coolant alarm was triggered. The operations manager immediately ordered the reactor shutdown.

    Connected

    > As the nuclear core approached critical temperature, triggering the loss-of-coolant alarm, the operations manager immediately ordered the reactor shutdown.

    d. Use numerals for numbers, except to begin a sentence.

7. *Check your edited version against the original.* Verify this version's accuracy and completeness. Add no new information.

8. *Rewrite your edited version.* In this final draft, strive for readability and conciseness. Respect any stipulated word limit.

9. *Document your source.* Cite the full source (Chapter 21) below any abstract not accompanied by its original.

on *people,* (student motivation, gender equality), historical perspectives often are helpful.

"Is the source dependable?"

■ *Assess the dependability of a printed source.* Some sources are more reputable, unbiased, and authoritative than others. For research on alternative cancer treatments, you could depend more on reports in the *New England Journal of Medicine* or *Scientific American* than on those in scandal sheets or movie magazines. Even researchers with expert credentials, however, can disagree or be mistaken.

One way to assess a publication's reputation is to check its copyright page. Is the work published by a university, professional society, museum, or respected news organization? Do members of the editorial and advisory board have distinguished titles and degrees? Is the publication *refereed* (submissions reviewed by experts prior to acceptance)? Publications often provide brief biographies or descriptions of authors' earlier publications and achievements.

"Can the source be trusted?"

■ *Assess the dependability of an Internet or database source.* The Internet offers information that never appears in other sources, for example from *listservs* and *newsgroups.* But much of this information may reflect the bias of the special-interest groups that provide it. Moreover, anyone can publish almost anything on the Internet—including a great deal of misinformation—without having it verified, edited, or reviewed for accuracy. Don't expect to find everything you need on the Internet.

Even in a commercial database (say, DIALOG or BRS), decisions about what to include and what to leave out depend on the biases, priorities, or interests of those who assemble that database.

"Who sponsored the study, and why?"

■ *Consider the sponsorship and the motives for the study.* Much of today's research is paid for by private companies or special-interest groups, who have their own agendas (Crossen 14, 19). Medical research may be sponsored by drug or tobacco companies; nutritional research, by food manufacturers; environmental research, by oil or chemical companies. Instead of a neutral and balanced inquiry, this kind of "strategic research" is designed to support one special interest or another (132–34). Furthermore, those who pay for strategic research are not likely to publicize findings that contradict their original claims or opinions or beliefs. Research consumers need to know exactly what the sponsors of a particular study stand to gain or lose from the results (234).*

---

*Some issues (the need for defense spending or causes of inflation) always are controversial, and will never be resolved. Although we can get verifiable data and can reason persuasively on some subjects, no close reasoning by any expert and no supporting statistical analysis will "prove" anything about a controversial subject. For instance, one could only *argue* (more or less effectively) that federal funds will or will not alleviate poverty or unemployment. Some problems simply are more resistant to solution than others, no matter how dependable the sources.

"What do similar sources say about this?"

- *Cross-check the source against other, similar sources.* Try not to rely on any single information source. Verify against other, equivalent sources.

EVALUATING THE EVIDENCE

Evidence is any finding used to support or refute a particular conclusion. While evidence can serve the truth, it also can create distortion, misinformation, and deception. For example, how much does recycling really save? How well are public schools educating children? Which automobiles are safest? Conclusions about such matters are based on evidence that often can be manipulated in support of one view or another. As consumers of research we have to assess for ourselves the quality of evidence presented.

"Is there enough evidence?"

- *Determine the sufficiency of the evidence.* Evidence is sufficient when it enables us to reach an accurate judgment or a conclusion. Say you are researching the alleged benefits of low-impact aerobics for reducing stress among employees at a fireworks factory. You would need to interview or survey a broad sample: people who have practiced aerobics for a long time; people of both genders, different ages, different occupations, different lifestyles before they began aerobics, and so on. Even responses from hundreds of practitioners might constitute insufficient evidence unless those responses were supported by laboratory measurements of metabolic and heart rates, blood pressure, and so on.

  Personal experience usually offers insufficient evidence from which to generalize. You cannot tell whether your experience is representative, regardless of how long you might have practiced aerobics. Although anecdotal evidence ("This worked great for me!") might offer a good starting point for an investigation, personal experience should be evaluated within the broader context of *all* available evidence.

"Can the evidence be verified?"

- *Differentiate hard from soft evidence.* Hard evidence consists of factual statements, expert opinion, or statistics that can be verified. Soft evidence consists of uninformed opinion or speculation, data that were obtained or analyzed unscientifically, and findings that have not been replicated or reviewed by experts.

INTERPRETING YOUR FINDINGS

Interpreting means trying to reach an overall judgment about what the findings mean and what conclusion or action they suggest.

Unfortunately, research does not always yield answers that are clear or conclusive. Instead of settling for the most *convenient* answer, we pursue the most *reasonable* answer by examining critically a full range of possible meanings.

IDENTIFY YOUR LEVEL OF CERTAINTY

Research can yield three distinct and very different levels of certainty:

1. The ultimate truth: the *conclusive answer:*

A practical definition of "truth"

> Truth is *what is so* about something, as distinguished from what people wish, believe, or assert to be so. In the words of Harvard philosopher Israel Scheffler, truth is the view "which is fated to be ultimately agreed to by all who investigate."* The word *ultimately* is important. Investigation may produce a wrong answer for years, even for centuries. For example, in the second century A.D., Ptolemy's view of the universe placed the earth at its center—and though untrue, this judgment was based on the best information available at that time. And Ptolemy's view survived for 13 centuries, even after new information had discredited this belief. When Galileo proposed a more truthful view in the fifteenth century, he was labeled a heretic.
>
> One way to spare yourself any further confusion about truth is to reserve the word *truth* for the final answer to an issue. Get in the habit of using the words *belief, theory,* and *present understanding* more often. (Ruggiero 21–22)

2. The *probable answer:* the answer that stands the best chance of being true or accurate—given the most we can know at this particular time. Probable answers are subject to revision in the light of new information.
3. The *inconclusive answer:* the realization that the truth of the matter is more elusive or ambiguous or complex than we expected.

Exactly how certain are we?

We need to decide what level of certainty our findings warrant. For example, we are *highly certain* about the perils of smoking, *reasonably certain* about the health benefits of fruits and vegetables, but *less* certain about the perils of coffee drinking or the benefits of vitamin supplements.

Can you think of additional examples of information about which we are *highly, reasonably,* or *barely* certain?

BE ALERT FOR PERSONAL BIAS

When the issue is controversial, our own bias might cause us to overestimate (or deny) the certainty of our findings.

Personal bias is a fact of life

> Expect yourself to be biased, and expect your bias to affect your efforts to construct arguments. Unless you are perfectly neutral about the issue, an unlikely circumstance, at the very outset . . . you will believe one side of the is-

---

*From *Reason and Teaching.* New York: Bobbs-Merrill, 1973.

> sue to be right, and that belief will incline you to . . . present more and better arguments for the side of the issue you prefer. (Ruggiero 134)

Because personal bias is hard to transcend, *rationalizing* often becomes a substitute for *reasoning*:

Reasoning versus
rationalizing

> You are reasoning if your belief follows the evidence—that is, if you examine the evidence first and then make up your mind. You are rationalizing if the evidence follows your belief—if you first decide what you'll believe and then select and interpret evidence to justify it. (Ruggiero 44)

Personal bias often is unconscious until we examine our own value systems, attitudes long held but never analyzed, notions we've inherited from our backgrounds, and so on. Recognizing our own biases is a crucial first step in managing them.

EXAMINE THE UNDERLYING ASSUMPTIONS

Assumptions are notions we take for granted, things we accept without proof. The research process rests on assumptions like these: that a sample group accurately represents a larger target group, that survey respondents remember certain facts accurately, that mice and humans share enough biological similarities for meaningful research. For a particular study to be valid, the underlying assumptions have to be accurate.

Assume, for instance, you are an education consultant evaluating the accuracy of IQ testing as a predictor of academic performance. Reviewing the evidence, you perceive an association between low IQ scores and low achievers. You then check your statistics by examining a cross-section of reliable sources. Should you feel justified in concluding that IQ tests do predict performance accurately? This conclusion might be invalid unless you could verify the following assumptions:

1. That neither parents nor teachers nor the children tested had seen individual test scores and had thus been able to develop biased expectations.
2. That, regardless of their IQ scores, all children had been exposed to an identical pace, instead of being "tracked" on the basis of individual scores.

The evidence could be evaluated and interpreted only within the framework of these underlying assumptions.

AVOIDING STATISTICAL FALLACIES

How numbers can
mislead

The purpose of statistical analysis is to determine the meaning of a collected set of numbers. Surveys and questionnaires often lead to some kind of numerical interpretation. ("What percentage of respondents prefer *X?*" "How often does *Y* happen?") In our own research, we often rely on numbers collected by survey researchers.

Numbers seem more precise, more objective, more scientific, and less ambiguous than words. They are easier to summarize, measure, compare, and analyze. But numbers can be totally misleading. For example, radio or television phone-in surveys produce grossly distorted data: although 90 percent of callers might express support for a particular viewpoint, people who call tend to be those with the greatest anger or extreme feelings about the issue—representing only a fraction of overall attitudes (Fineman 24). Mail-in surveys can produce similar distortion because only people with certain attitudes might choose to respond.

Before relying on any set of numbers, we need to know exactly where they come from, how they were collected, and how they were analyzed (Lavin 275–76). Are the numbers accurate and, if so, what do they mean?

COMMON STATISTICAL FALLACIES

Faulty statistical reasoning produces conclusions that are unwarranted, inaccurate, or deceptive. Here are some typical fallacies:

"Exactly *how well* are we doing?"

■ *The sanitized statistic:* Numbers are manipulated (or "cleaned up") to obscure the facts. For instance, the College Board's recent "recentering" of SAT scores has raised the "average" math score from 478 to 500 and the average verbal score from 424 to 500 (a boost of almost 5 and 18 percent, respectively), although actual student performance remains unchanged (Samuelson 44).

"How many rats was that?"

■ *The meaningless statistic:* Exact numbers are used to quantify something so inexact or vaguely defined that it should only be approximated (Huff 247; Lavin 278): "Boston has 3,247,561 rats." "Zappo detergent makes laundry 10 percent brighter." An exact number looks impressive, but it can hide the fact that certain subjects (child abuse, cheating in college, virginity, drug and alcohol abuse on the job, eating habits) cannot be quantified exactly because respondents don't always tell the truth (because of denial or embarrassment or merely guessing). Or they respond in ways they think the researcher expects.

"Why is *everybody* griping?"

■ *The undefined average:* The mean, median, and mode are confused in determining an average (Huff 244; Lavin 279). The *mean* is the result of adding up the value of each item in a set of numbers, and then dividing by the number of items. The *median* is the result of ranking all the values from high to low, then choosing the middle value (or the 50th percentile, as in calculating SAT scores). The *mode* is the value that occurs most often in a set of numbers.

Each of these three measurements represents some kind of average. But unless we know which "average" is being presented, we cannot interpret the figures accurately.

Assume, for instance, that we are computing the average salary among female vice presidents at XYZ Corporation (ranked from high to low):

Vice President	Salary
"A"	$90,000
"B"	$90,000
"C"	$80,000
"D"	$65,000
"E"	$60,000
"F"	$55,000
"G"	$50,000

In the above example, the mean salary (total salaries divided by people) equals $70,000; the median salary (middle value) equals $65,000; the mode (most frequent value) equals $90,000. Each is, legitimately, an "average," and each could be used to support or refute a particular assertion (for example, "Women receive too little" or "Women receive too much").

Research expert Michael Lavin sums up the potential for bias in reporting averages:

> Depending on the circumstances, any one of these measurements may describe a group of numbers better than the other two. . . . [But] people typically chose the value which best presents their case, whether or not it is the most appropriate to use. (279)

Although the mean is the most commonly computed average, this measurement is misleading when one or more values on either end of the scale deviate excessively from the normal distribution (or spread) of values. Suppose, for instance, that Vice President "A" (above) was paid $200,000: because this figure deviates so much from the normal range of salary figures for "B" through "G," it distorts the average for the whole group—increasing the "mean salary" by more than 20 percent (Plumb and Spyridakis 636).

"Is 51 percent really a majority?"

■ *The distorted percentage figure:* Percentages are reported without explanation of the original numbers used in the calculation (Adams and Schvaneveldt 359; Lavin 280); "Seventy-five percent of respondents prefer our brand over the competing brand"—without mention that only four people were surveyed.

Another fallacy in reporting percentages occurs when the *margin of error* is ignored. This is the margin within which the true figure lies, based on estimated sampling errors in a survey. For example, a claim that most people surveyed prefer Brand X might be based on the fact that 51 percent of respondents expressed this preference; but if the survey carried a 2 percent margin of error, the real figure could be as low as 49 percent or as high as 51 percent. In a survey with a high margin of error, the true figure may be so uncertain that no definite conclusion may be drawn.

"Which car should we buy?"

- *The bogus ranking:* This happens when items are compared on the basis of ill-defined criteria (Adams and Schvaneveldt 212; Lavin 284): "Last year, the Batmobile was the number-one selling car in America"—without mention that some competing car makers actually sold *more* cars to private individuals, and that the Batmobile figures were inflated by hefty sales to rental-car companies and corporate fleets. Unless we know how the ranked items were chosen and how they were compared (the criteria), a ranking can produce a scientific-seeming number based on a completely unscientific method.

"Does X actually cause Y?"

- *Confusion of correlation with causation: Correlation* is the measure of association between two variables (between smoking and increased lung cancer risk or between education and income). *Causation* is the demonstrable production of a specific effect (smoking causes lung cancer). Correlations between smoking and lung cancer or education and income signal a causal relationship that has been proven by many studies. But not every correlation implies causation. For instance, a recently discovered correlation between moderate alcohol consumption and decreased heart disease risk offers no sufficient proof that moderate drinking *causes* less heart disease.

    Many highly publicized correlations are the product of "data dredging": In this process, computers randomly compare one set of variables (say, eating habits) with another set (say, a range of diseases). From these countless comparisons, certain relationships reveal themselves (say, between coffee drinking and pancreatic cancer risk). As dramatic as such isolated correlations may be, they constitute no proof of causation and often lead to hasty conclusions (Ross 135).

"Is this good news or bad news?"

- *Misleading terminology:* The terms used to interpret statistics sometimes hide their real meaning. For instance, the widely publicized figure that people treated for cancer have a "50 percent survival rate" is misleading in two ways; (1) *Survival* to laypersons means "staying alive," but to medical experts, staying alive for only five years after diagnosis qualifies as survival; (2) the "50 percent" survival figure covers *all* cancers, including certain skin or thyroid cancers that have extremely high *cure rates,* as well as other cancers (such as lung or ovarian) that rarely are curable and have extremely low *survival rates* ("Are We" 6).

    Even the most valid and reliable statistics require us to interpret the reality behind the numbers. For instance, the overall cancer rate today is "higher" than it was in 1910. What this may mean is that people are living longer and thus are more likely to die of cancer and that cancer today rarely is misdiagnosed—or mislabeled because of stigma ("Are We" 4). The finding that rates for certain cancers "double" after prolonged exposure to electromagnetic waves may really mean that cancer risk actually increases from 1 in 10,000 to 2 in 10,000.

These are only a few examples of statistics and interpretations that seem highly persuasive but that in fact cannot always be trusted. Any interpretation of statistical data carries the possibility that other, more accurate interpretations have been overlooked or deliberately excluded (Barnett 45).

☑ CHECKLIST FOR THE RESEARCH PROCESS

(Numbers in parentheses refer to the first page of discussion.)

Methods

- ❑ Did I ask the right questions? (300)
- ❑ Are the sources appropriately up-to-date? (335)
- ❑ Is each source reputable, trustworthy, relatively unbiased, and borne out by other, similar sources? (337)
- ❑ Does the evidence clearly support the conclusions? (338)
- ❑ Can all the evidence be verified? (338)
- ❑ Is a fair balance of viewpoints presented? (300)
- ❑ Has my research achieved adequate depth? (301)

Reasoning

- ❑ Am I reasonably certain about the meaning of these findings? (339)

- ❑ Can I rule out other possible interpretations or conclusions? (304)
- ❑ Am I reasoning instead of rationalizing? (340)
- ❑ Am I confident that my causal reasoning is correct? (343)
- ❑ Can all the numbers and statistics be trusted? (340)
- ❑ Have I resolved (or at least acknowledged) any conflicts among my findings? (304)
- ❑ Have I decided whether my final answer is definitive, probable, or inconclusive? (339)
- ❑ Is this the most reasonable conclusion (or merely the most convenient)? (338)
- ❑ Have I accounted for all sources of bias, including my own? (340)
- ❑ Should the evidence be reconsidered? (345)

ASSESSING YOUR INQUIRY

The inquiry phases of the research process present a minefield of potential errors in where we search, how we interpret, and how we reason. So before preparing the actual report, examine critically your methods, interpretations, and reasoning with the page 344 checklist.

WORKS CITED

Adams, Gerald R., and Jay D. Schvaneveldt. *Understanding Research Methods.* New York: Longman, 1985.

"Are We in the Middle of a Cancer Epidemic?" *University of California at Berkeley Wellness Letter* 10.9 (1994): 4–5.

Barnett, Arnold. "How Numbers Can Trick You." *Technology Review* Oct. 1994: 38–45.

Crossen, Cynthia. *Tainted Truth: The Manipulation of Fact in America.* New York: Simon, 1994.

Fineman, Howard, "The Power of Talk." *Newsweek* 8 Feb. 1993: 24–28.

Huff, Darrell. *How to Lie with Statistics.* New York: Norton, 1954.

Lavin, Michael R. *Business Information: How to Find It, How to Use It.* 2nd ed. Phoenix, AZ: Oryx, 1992.

Plumb, Carolyn, and Jan H. Spyridakis. "Survey Research in Technical Communication: Designing and Administering Questionnaires." *Technical Communication* 39.4 (1992): 625–38.

Ross, Philip E. "Lies, Damned Lies, and Medical Statistics." *Forbes* 14 Aug. 1995: 130–35.

Ruggiero, Vincent R. *The Art of Thinking.* 3rd ed. New York: Harper, 1991.

Samuelson, Robert. "Merchants of Mediocrity." *Newsweek* 1 Aug. 1994: 44.

Weinstein, Edith K. Unpublished review, 1991.

DOCUMENTING YOUR SOURCES

*D*ocumenting research means acknowledging one's debt to each information source. Proper documentation satisfies professional requirements for ethics, efficiency, and authority.

WHY YOU SHOULD DOCUMENT

Documentation is a matter of *ethics*, for the originator of borrowed material deserves full credit and recognition. Moreover, all published material is protected by copyright law. Failure to credit a source could make you liable to legal action, even if your omission was unintentional.

Documentation also is a matter of *efficiency*. It provides a network for organizing and locating the world's recorded knowledge. If you cite a particular source correctly, your reference will enable interested readers to locate that source themselves.

Finally, documentation is a matter of *authority*. In making any claim (say, "A Mercedes-Benz is more reliable than a Ford Taurus") you invite challenge: "Says who?" Data on road tests, frequency of repairs, resale value, workmanship, and owner comments can help validate your claim by showing its basis in *fact*. A claim's credibility increases in relation to the expert references supporting it. For a controversial topic, you may need to cite several authorities who hold various views, as in this next example, instead of forcing a simplistic conclusion on your material:

Citing a balance of views

> Opinion is mixed as to whether a marketable quantity of oil rests beneath Georges Bank. Cape Cod Geologist John Blocke feels that extensive reserves are improbable ("Geologist Dampens Hopes" 3). Oil geologist Donald Marshall is uncertain about the existence of any oil in quantity at this location ("Offshore Oil Drilling" 2). But the U.S. Interior Department reports that the Atlantic continental shelf may contain 5.5 billion barrels of oil (Kemprecos 8).

Readers of your research report expect the *complete picture*.

WHAT YOU SHOULD DOCUMENT

Document any insight, assertion, fact, finding, interpretation, judgment or other "appropriated material that readers might otherwise mistake for your own" (Gibaldi and Achtert 155)—whether the material appears in published form or not. Specifically you must document those sources listed on page 348.

Sources that require documentation

- any source from which you use exact wording, or
- any source from which you adapt material in your own words, or
- any visual illustration: charts, graphs, drawings, or the like

How to document a confidential source

In some instances, you might have reason to preserve the anonymity of unpublished sources: say, to allow people to respond candidly without fear of reprisal (as with employee criticism of the company), or to protect their privacy (as with certain material from E-mail inquiries or electronic newsgroups). You still must document the fact that you are not the originator of this material by providing a general acknowledgment in the text ("A number of faculty expressed frustration with . . . ") along with a general citation in your list of References or Works Cited ("Interviews with campus faculty, May 1996").

Common knowledge need not be documented

You don't need to document anything considered *common knowledge:* material that appears repeatedly in general sources. In medicine, for instance, it has become common knowledge that foods containing animal fat (meat, butter, cheese, whole milk) contribute to blood cholesterol levels. And so in a research report on fatty diets and heart disease, you probably would not need to document that well-known fact. But you would document information about how the fat-cholesterol connection was discovered, subsequent studies (say, of the role of saturated versus unsaturated fats), and any information for which some other person could claim specific credit. If the borrowed material can be found in only one specific source, and not in multiple sources, document it. When in doubt, document the source.

HOW YOU SHOULD DOCUMENT

Cite borrowed material twice: at the exact place you use that material, and at the end of your paper. Documentation practices vary widely, but all systems work almost identically: a brief reference in the text names the source and refers readers to the complete citation, which enables the source to be retrieved.

This chapter illustrates citations and entries for two styles widely used for documenting sources in college writing:

- Modern Language Association (MLA) style, for the humanities
- American Psychological Association (APA) style, for social sciences

Unless your audience has a particular preference, either of these styles can be adapted to most research writing. Use one style consistently throughout your paper.

MLA DOCUMENTATION STYLE

Use this alternative to footnotes and bibliographies

Traditional MLA documentation used superscripted numbers (like this:[1]) in the text, followed by complete citations at page bottom (footnotes) or at document's end (endnotes) and, finally, by a bibliography. But a more current form of documentation appears in the *MLA Handbook for Writers of Research Papers,* 4th ed., New York: Modern Language Association, 1995. Footnotes or endnotes are now used only to comment on material in the text or on sources or to suggest additional sources. (Place these notes at page bottom or in a "Notes" section at document's end.)

Cite a source briefly in your text and fully at the end

In current MLA style, in-text parenthetical references briefly identify the source(s). The complete citation then appears in a "Works Cited" section at paper's end.

A parenthetical reference usually includes the author's surname and the exact page number(s) of the borrowed material:

Parenthetical reference in the text

> Recent data provided by 796 colleges indicate that violent crime on campus is increasing (Lederman 31).

Readers seeking the complete citation for Lederman can refer easily to Works Cited, listed alphabetically by author:

Full citation at paper's end

> Lederman, Douglas. "Colleges Report Rise in Violent Crime." Chronicle of Higher Education 3 Feb. 1995, sec. A: 31–42.

This complete citation includes page numbers for the entire article.

MLA Parenthetical References

How to cite briefly in your text

For clear and informative parenthetical references, observe these guidelines:

- If your discussion names the author, do not repeat the name in your parenthetical reference; simply give the page number(s):

Citing page numbers only

> Lederman points out that data provided by 796 colleges indicate that violent crime on campus is increasing (31).

- If you cite two or more works in a single parenthetical reference, separate the citations with semicolons:

Three works in a single reference

> (Jones 32; Leduc 41; Gomez 293–94)

■ If you cite two or more authors with the same surname, include the first initial in your parenthetical reference to each author:

Two authors with identical surnames

| (R. Jones   32)   (S. Jones   14–15)

■ If you cite two or more works by the same author, include the first significant word from each work's title, or a shortened version:

Two works by one author

| (Lamont, Biophysics 100–01)   (Lamont, Diagnostic Tests 81)

■ If the work is by an institutional or corporate author or if it is unsigned (that is, author unknown), use only the first few words of the institutional name or the work's title in your parenthetical reference:

Institutional, corporate, or anonymous author

| (American Medical Assn. 2)   ("Distribution Systems" 18)

To avoid distracting the reader, keep each parenthetical reference as brief as possible. (One method is to name the source in your discussion, and to place only the page number[s] in parentheses.)

Where to place a parenthetical reference

For a paraphrase, place the parenthetical reference *before* the closing punctuation mark. For a quotation that runs into the text, place the reference *between* the final quotation mark and the closing punctuation mark. For a quotation set off (indented) from the text, place the reference two spaces *after* the closing punctuation mark.

MLA WORKS-CITED ENTRIES

How to space and indent entries

The Works Cited list includes each source that you have paraphrased or quoted. In preparing the list, type the first line of each entry flush with the left margin. Indent the second and subsequent lines five spaces. Double-space within and between each entry. Use one character space after any period, comma, or colon.

How to cite fully at the end

Following are examples of complete citations as they would appear in the Works Cited section of your report. Shown italicized below each citation is its corresponding parenthetical reference as it would appear in the text. Note capitalization, abbreviations, spacing, and punctuation in the sample entries.

What to include in an MLA citation for a book

MLA Works-Cited Entries for Books.   Any citation for a book should contain the following information (found on the book's title and copyright pages): author, title, editor or translator, edition, volume number, and facts about publication (city, publisher, date).

INDEX TO SAMPLE ENTRIES FOR MLA WORKS-CITED LIST

1. Book, Single Author—MLA

Reardon, Kathleen Kelley. <u>They Don't Get It, Do They?: Communication in the Workplace—Closing the Gap Between Women and Men</u>. Boston: Little, 1995.

Parenthetical reference: (Reardon 3–4)

Identify the state of publication by U.S. Postal Service abbreviations. If the city of publication is well known (Boston, Chicago, and so on), omit the state abbreviation. If several cities are listed on the title page, give only the first. For Canada, include the province abbreviation after the city. For all other countries, include an abbreviation of the country name.

2. Book, Two or Three Authors—MLA

Aronson, Linda, Roger Katz, and Candide Moustafa. Toxic Waste Disposal

Methods. New Haven: Yale UP, 1997.

Parenthetical Reference: (Aronson, Katz, and Moustafa 121–23)

Shorten publishers' names, as in "Simon" for Simon & Schuster, "GPO" for Government Printing Office, or "Yale UP" for Yale University Press. For page numbers having more than two digits, give only the final two digits for the second number.

3. Book, Four or More Authors—MLA

Santos, Ruth J., et al. Environmental Crises in Developing Countries. New

York: Harper, 1995.

Parenthetical reference: (Santos et al. 9)

"Et al." is the abbreviated form of the Latin "et alia," meaning "and others."

4. Book, Anonymous Author(s)—MLA

Structured Programming. Boston: Meredith, 1995.

Parenthetical reference: (Structured 67)

5. Multiple Books, Same Author(s)—MLA

Chang, John W. Biophysics. Boston: Little, 1997.

---. Diagnostic Techniques. New York: Radon, 1994.

Parenthetical references: (Chang, Biophysics 123–26) (Chang, Diagnostic 87)

When citing more than one work by the same author, do not repeat the author's name; simply type three hyphens followed by a period. List the works alphabetically by title.

6. Book, One or More Editors—MLA

Morris, A. J., and Louise B. Pardin-Walker, eds. Handbook of New

Information Technology. New York: Harper, 1996.

Parenthetical reference: (Morris and Pardin-Walker 34)

For more than three editors, name only the first, followed by "et al."

7. Book, Indirect Source—MLA

Kline, Thomas. Automated Systems. Boston: Rhodes, 1992.

Stubbs, John. White-Collar Productivity. Miami: Harris, 1996.

Parenthetical reference: (qtd. in Stubbs 116)

When your source (as in Stubbs, above) has quoted or cited another source, list each source in its appropriate alphabetical place in the Works Cited list. Use the name of the original source (here, Kline) in your text and begin the parenthetical reference with "qtd. in," or "cited in" for a paraphrase.

8. Anthology Selection or Book Chapter—MLA

Bowman, Joel P. "Electronic Conferencing." Communication and

Technology: Today and Tomorrow. Ed. Al Williams. Denton, TX: Assn.

for Business Communication, 1994. 123–42.

Parenthetical reference: (Bowman 129)

The page numbers in the complete citation are for the selection cited from the anthology.

What to include in an MLA citation for a periodical

MLA Works-Cited Entries for Periodicals. Give all available information in this order: author, article title, periodical title, volume and issue, date (day, month, year), and page numbers for the entire article—not just pages cited.

9. Article, Magazine—MLA

DesMarteau, Kathleen. "Study Links Sewing Machine Use to Alzheimer's

Disease." Bobbin Oct. 1994: 36–38.

Parenthetical reference: (DesMarteau 36)

No punctuation separates the magazine title and date. Nor is the abbreviation "p." or "pp." used to designate page numbers. If no author is given, list all other information:

"Video Games for the Next Decade." Power Technology Magazine 18 Oct.

1996: 18+.

Parenthetical reference: ("Video Games" 18)

This article began on page 18 and then continued on page 21. When an article does not appear on consecutive pages, give only the number of the first page, followed immediately by a plus sign. A three-letter abbreviation denotes any month spelled with five or more letters.

10. Article, Journal with New Pagination Each Issue—MLA

Thackman-White, Joan R. "Computer-Assisted Research." American Library

Journal 51.1 (1997): 3–9.

Parenthetical reference: (Thackman-White 4–5)

Because each issue for that year will have page numbers beginning with "1," readers need the number of this issue. The "51" denotes the volume number; the "1" denotes the issue number. Omit "The" or "A" or any other introductory article from a journal or magazine title.

11. Article, Journal with Continuous Pagination—MLA

Barnstead, Marion H. "The Writing Crisis." Journal of Writing Theory 12

(1994): 415–33.

Parenthetical reference: (Barnstead 418)

When page numbers continue from issue to issue for the full year, readers won't need the issue number, because no other issue in that year repeats these same page numbers. (Include the issue number if you think it will help readers retrieve the article more easily.) The "12" denotes the volume number.

12. Article, Newspaper—MLA

Baranski, Vida H. "Errors in Medical Diagnosis." Boston Times 15 Jan. 1997,

evening ed., sec. B: 3.

Parenthetical reference: (Baranski 3)

When a daily newspaper has more than one edition, cite the specific edition after the date. Omit any introductory article in the newspaper's name (not The Boston Times). If no author is given, list all other information. If the newspaper's name does not contain the city of publication, insert it, using brackets: "Sippican Sentinel [Marion MA]."

What to include in an
MLA citation for a
miscellaneous source

MLA Works-Cited Entries for Other Sources Miscellaneous sources range from unsigned encyclopedia entries to conference presentations to government publications. A full citation should give this information (as available): author, title, city, publisher, date, and page numbers.

13. Encyclopedia, Dictionary, Other Alphabetical Reference—MLA

''Communication.'' The Business Reference Book. 1993 ed.

Parenthetical reference: (''Communication'')

Begin a signed entry with the author's name. For any work arranged alphabetically, omit page numbers in the complete citation and the parenthetical reference. For a well-known reference book, include only an edition (if stated) and a date. For other reference books, give the full publication information.

14. Report—MLA

Electrical Power Research Institute (EPRI). Epidemiologic Studies of Electric

Utility Employees. (Report No. RP2964.5). Palo Alto, CA: EPRI, Nov.

1994.

Parenthetical reference: (Electrical Power Research Institute [EPRI] 27)

If no author is given, begin with the organization that sponsored the report.

For any report or other document with group authorship, as above, include the group's abbreviated name in your first parenthetical reference, and then use only that abbreviation in any subsequent reference.

15. Conference Presentation—MLA

Smith, Abelard A. ''Multicultural Stereotypes in Elizabethan Prose Fiction.''

First British Symposium in Multicultural Studies. London, 11–13 Oct.

1995. Ed. Anne Hodkins. London: Harrison, 1996. 106–21.

Parenthetical reference: (Smith 109)

The above example shows a presentation that has been included in the published proceedings of a conference. For an unpublished presentation, include the presenter's name, the title of the presentation, and the conference title, location, and date, but do not underline or italicize the conference information.

16. Interview, Personally Conducted—MLA

Nasson, Gamela. Chief of Campus Police. Rangeley, ME. 2 Apr. 1997.

Parenthetical reference: (Nasson)

17. Interview, Published—MLA

Lescault, James. "The Future of Graphics," Executive Views of Automation.

Ed. Karen Prell. Miami: Haber, 1997. 216–31.

Parenthetical reference: (Lescault 218)

The interviewee's name is placed in the entry's author slot.

18. Letter, Unpublished—MLA

Rogers, Leonard. Letter to the author. 15 May 1993.

Parenthetical reference: (Rogers)

19. Questionnaire—MLA

Taynes, Lorraine. Questionnaire sent to 61 college administrators. 14 Feb.

1997.

Parenthetical reference: (Taylor)

20. Brochure or Pamphlet—MLA

Career Strategies for the 21st Century. San Francisco: Blount Economics

Assn., 1997.

Parenthetical reference: (Career)

If the work is signed, begin with its author.

21. Lecture—MLA

Dumont, R. A. "Androgyny and the Rhetorical Tradition." Lecture,

University of Massachusetts at Dartmouth, 15 Jan. 1996.

Parenthetical reference: (Dumont)

If the lecture title is not known, write Address, Lecture, or Reading but do not use quotation marks. Include the sponsor and the location if they are available.

22. Government Document—MLA

If the author is unknown, begin with the information in this order: name of the government, name of the issuing agency, document title, place, publisher, and date:

Virginia. Highway Dept. Standards for Bridge Maintenance. Richmond:

Virginia Highway Dept., 1991.

Parenthetical reference: (Virginia Highway Dept. 49)

For any Congressional document, identify the house of Congress (Senate or House of Representatives) before the title, and the number and session of Congress after the title:

United States Cong. House. Armed Services Committee. Funding for the

Military Academies. 103rd Congress, 2nd, sess. Washington: GPO,

1995.

Parenthetical reference: (Armed Services Committee 41)

("GPO" is the abbreviation for the United States Government Printing Office.)

For an entry from the Congressional Record, give only date and pages:

Cong. Rec. 10 Mar. 1994: 2178–92.

Parenthetical reference: (Cong. Rec. 2184)

23. Document with Corporate Authorship—MLA

Hermitage Foundation. Global Warming Scenarios for the Year 2030.

Washington: Natl. Res. Council, 1996.

Parenthetical reference: (Hermitage Foun. 123)

24. Map or Other Visual Aid—MLA

Deaths Caused by Breast Cancer, by County. Map. Scientific American Oct.

1995: 32D.

Parenthetical reference: (Deaths Caused)

If the creator of the visual is listed, list that name first. Identify the type of visual (Map, Graph, Table, Diagram) immediately following its title.

25. Miscellaneous Items (Unpublished Report, Dissertation, and so on)—MLA

Author (if known), title (in quotes), sponsoring organization or publisher,

date, page number(s).

For any work that has group authorship (corporation, committee, task force), cite the name of the group or agency in place of the author's name.

What to include in an MLA citation for an electronic source

MLA Works-Cited Entries for Electronic Sources. In general, citation for an electronic source with a printed equivalent should begin with that publication information (see relevant sections above). But whether or not a printed equivalent exists, any citation should enable readers to retrieve the material electronically.

26. On-line Database Source—MLA

Sahl, J. D. "Power Lines, Viruses, and Childhood Leukemia." Cancer Causes

Control 6.1 (Jan. 1995): 83. MEDLINE. On-line. Dialog. 7 Nov. 1995.

Parenthetical reference: (Sahl 83)

For entries with a printed equivalent, begin with the publication information for the printed source, then the database title (underlined), the "On-line" designation to indicate the medium, the service provider, and date of access. The access date is important because frequent updatings of databases can produce different versions of the material.

For entries with no printed equivalent, give the title and date of the work in quotation marks, followed by the electronic source information:

Argent, Roger R. "An Analysis of International Exchange Rates for 1995."

Accu-Data. On-line. Dow Jones News Retrieval. 10 Jan. 1996.

Parenthetical reference: ("An Analysis" 4)

If the author is not known, begin with the work's title.

27. Computer Software—MLA

Virtual Collaboration. Diskette. New York: Harper, 1994.

Parenthetical reference: (Virtual)

Begin with the author's name, if known.

28. CD-ROM Source—MLA

Canalte, Henry A. "Violent-Crime Statistics: Good News and Bad News."

Law Enforcement Feb. 1995: 8. ABI/INFORM. CD-ROM. Proquest. Sept.

1995.

Parenthetical reference: (Canalte 8)

If the material also is available in print, begin with the information about the printed source, followed by the electronic source information: name of database (underlined), "CD-ROM" designation, vendor name, and electronic publication date. If the material has no printed equivalent, list its author (if known) and its title (in quotation marks), followed by the electronic source information. If you are citing merely an abstract (page 422) of the complete work, insert "Abstract," followed by a period, immediately after the work's page number(s)—as in "8" in the previous entry.

For CD-ROM reference works and other material that is not routinely updated, give the work title followed by the "CD-ROM" designation, place, electronic publisher, and date:

Time Almanac. CD-ROM. Washington: Compact, 1994.

Parenthetical reference: (Time Almanac 74)

Begin with the author's name, if known.

29. Internet Posting (Bulletin Board, Discussion List)—MLA

Templeton, Brad. "10 Big Myths about Copyright Explained." Intellectual

Property Caucus Discussion List (29 Nov. 1994): 6pp. On-line posting.

BITNET. 6 May 1995.

Parenthetical reference: (Templeton)

Begin with the author's name (if known), followed by the title of the work (in quotation marks), title of the list or group (underlined), publication date, number of pages, the "On-line posting" designation, name of network, and date of access. If appropriate, include the on-line address at the end of your entry, after the word "Available." The parenthetical reference includes no page number because none is given in the on-line posting.

30. E-Mail—MLA

Wallin, John Luther. "Frog Reveries." E-mail to author. 12 Oct. 1997.

Cite personal E-mail as you would printed correspondence. If the document has a subject line or title, enclose it in quotation marks.

For publicly posted E-mail (say, for a newsgroup or discussion list) include the address and the date of access.

31. Web Source—MLA

Dumont, R. A. "An On-line Course in Composition." 10 Dec. 1995. On-line

    posting. http://www.umassd.edu/englishdepartment (6 Jan. 1996).

Parenthetical reference: (Dumont 7–9)

Begin with the author's name (if known), followed by title of the work (in quotation marks), the posting date, the "On-line" designation, the Web address, and the date of access. In place of (or in addition to) the Web address, include the name of the Web site (underlined), if available:

Rogers, S. E. "Chemical Risk Assessment Guidelines." 12 Feb. 1996.

    OTA Online. http://www.ota.gov (10 Mar. 1996).

"OTA" stands for Office of Technology Assessment.

MLA Sample List of Works Cited

Place your "Works Cited" section on a separate page at document's end. (See pages 420–424.) Arrange entries alphabetically by author's surname. When the author is unknown, list the title alphabetically according to its first word (excluding introductory articles). For a title that begins with a digit ("5," "6," etc.), alphabetize the entry as if the digit were spelled out.

ACW Documentation for Unconventional Electronic Sources*

Examples of unconventional electronic sources

Unconventional electronic sources include MUDs (multi-user dungeons), MOOs (MUD object-oriented software), IRC (internet relay chat); FTPs (file transfer protocols), and others listed below. Conventions for documenting these sources continue to evolve. One useful system has been developed by Professor Janice R. Walker, University of South Florida, and endorsed by The Alliance for Computers and Writing (ACW).

The ACW system observes MLA conventions wherever possible, but also provides formats for unique documentation often required by unconven-

---

*Discussion adapted and examples reproduced from the style sheet prepared by Janice R. Walker and its version published in Hairston, Maxine and John J. Ruskiewicz. *The Scott Foresman Handbook for Writers.* 4th ed. New York: Harper, 1996: 671–75.

tional sources. For example, if the author is not named, your parenthetical reference might include instead the Internet or Web site and date:

Parenthetical citation
in the text

| (MediaMOO 10 Mar. 1996)

If page numbers are not given, a reference might include the author and date:

| (Walker April 1995)

The full citation for each parenthetical reference appears alphabetically on a Works Cited page at paper's end. A typical entry contains the following information (as available or appropriate):

What to include in an
ACW citation for an
unconventional
electronic source

| Author's Last Name, First Name. "Title of Work." Title of Complete Work.

[protocol (e.g., ftp, telnet, gopher) and address] [search path] (date of

message or visit)].

Following are examples of specific entries as they would appear in the Works Cited section of your document—along with MLA entries for conventional print and electronic sources.

FTP Site—ACW. A file transfer protocol site enables files to be transferred between computers via phone lines.

Bruckman, Amy. "Approaches to Managing Deviant Behavior in Virtual

Communities." ftp.media.mit.edu/pub/asb/papers/deviance-chi94 (4

Dec. 1996).

WWW Site—ACW. A World Wide Web site is accessed via a web browser such as *Yahoo, Netscape, InfoSeek, WebCrawler,* or *Lynx.*

Burka, Lauren P. "A Hypertext History of Multi-User Dimensions." MUD

History. http://www.ccs.neu.edu/home/lpb/mud-history.html

(5 Dec. 1996).

Telnet Site—ACW. Telnet provides users direct access to files in other computers on the Internet.

Gomes, Lee. "Xerox's On-Line neighborhood: A Great Place to Visit."

Mercury News 3 May 1992. telnet   lambda.parc.xerox.com 8888,

@go#50827, press 13   (5 Dec. 1996).

Synchronous Communication (MOOs, MUDs, IRC)—ACW. Synchronous communication occurs in "real time": the message typed in by the sender appears instantly on the screen of the recipient, as in a personal interview. Begin the citation with the name of the communicator(s) and indicate the type of communication (e.g., personal interview).

> Pine-Guest. Personal Interview. telnet world/sensemedia.net 1234
>
> (12 Dec. 1996).

Gopher Site—ACW. Gopher is a software tool for locating and searching internet databases and retrieving and downloading files.

> Quittner, Joshua. "Far Out: Welcome to Their World Built of MUD."
>
> Published in Newsday, 7 Nov. 1993.   gopher/University of
>
> Koeln/About Muds, MCOs and MUSEs in Education/Selected
>
> Papers/newsday (5 Dec. 1995).

Listserv and Newslist—ACW. In these sites messages are posted about a single topic. Indicate the subject line of the posting in quotes.

> Seabrook, Richard H. C. "Community and Progress."
>
> cybermind@jefferson.village.virginia.edu   (22 Jan. 1994).

E-mail—ACW. Indicate the author and the subject line of the posting. For personal E-mail entries, the address usually is omitted.

> Walker, Janice. "Electronic Documentation." Personal e-mail (1 May 1996).

APA DOCUMENTATION STYLE

One popular alternative to MLA style appears in the *Publication Manual of the American Psychological Association*, 4th ed. Washington, DC: American Psychological Association, 1994. APA style is useful when writers wish to emphasize the publication dates of their references. A parenthetical reference in the text briefly identifies the source, date, and page number(s):

Reference cited in the text

> Recent data provided by 796 colleges indicate that violent crime on campus is increasing (Lederman, 1995, p. 31).

The full citation then appears in the alphabetical listing of "References" at paper's end:

Full citation at paper's end	Lederman, D. (1995). Colleges report rise in violent crime. <u>Chronicle of</u> <u>Higher Education</u>, pp. 31–42.

Because it emphasizes the date, APA style (or any similar author-date style) is preferred in the sciences and social sciences, where information quickly becomes outdated.

APA PARENTHETICAL REFERENCES

How APA and MLA parenthetical references differ

APA's parenthetical references differ from MLA's (pages 349–350) as follows: the citation includes the publication date; a comma separates each item in the reference; and "p." or "pp." precedes the page number (which is optional in the APA system). When a subsequent reference to a work follows closely after the initial reference, the date need not be included. Here are specific guidelines:

- If your discussion names the author, do not repeat the name in your parenthetical reference; simply give the date and page number(s):

Author named in the text

Lederman points out that recent data provided by 796 colleges indicate that violent crime on campus is increasing (1995, p. 31).

When two authors of a work are named in your text, their names are connected by "and," but in a parenthetical reference their names are connected by an ampersand, "&."

- If you cite two or more works in a single reference, list the authors in alphabetical order and separate the citations with semicolons:

Two or more works in a single reference

(Jones, 1994; Gomez, 1992; Leduc, 1997)

- If you cite a work with three to five authors, try to name them in your text, to avoid an excessively long parenthetical reference:

A work with three to five authors

Franks, Oblesky, Ryan, Jablar, and Perkins (1993) studied the role of electro-magnetic fields in tumor formation.

In any subsequent references to this work, name only the first author, followed by "et al." (Latin abbreviation for "and others").

- If you cite two or more works by the same author published in the same year, assign a different letter to each work:

Two or more works by the same author in the same year

(Lamont 1994a, p. 135) (Lamont 1994b, pp. 67–68)

Other examples of parenthetical references appear with their corresponding entries in the following discussion of the reference-list entries.

APA REFERENCE-LIST ENTRIES

How to space and indent entries

The APA reference list includes each source you have cited in your paper. In preparing the list of references for a student paper, type the first line of each entry flush with the left margin. Indent the second and subsequent lines five spaces. Double-space within and between each entry. Skip one character space after any period, comma, or colon.

Following are examples of complete citations as they would appear in the "References" section of your paper. Shown immediately below each entry is its corresponding parenthetical reference as it would appear in the text. Note the capitalization, abbreviation, spacing, and punctuation in the sample entries.

What to include in an APA citation for a book

APA Entries for Books.   Any citation for a book should contain all applicable information in the following order: author, date, title, editor or translator, edition, volume number, and facts about publication (city and publisher).

1. Book, Single Author—APA

Reardon, K. K. (1995). They don't get it, do they?: Communication in the

workplace—closing the gap between women and men. Boston: Little,

Brown.

Parenthetical reference: (Reardon, 1995, pp. 3–4)

Use only initials for an author's first and middle name. Capitalize only the first words of a book's title and subtitle and any proper names. Identify a later edition in parentheses between the title and the period.

2. Book, Two to Five Authors—APA

Aronson, L., Katz, R., & Moustafa, C. (1996). Toxic waste disposal methods.

New Haven: Yale University Press.

Parenthetical reference: (Aronson, Katz, & Moustafa, 1996)

Use an ampersand (&) before the name of the final author listed in an entry. As an alternative parenthetical reference, name the authors in your text and include date (and page numbers, if appropriate) in parentheses.

INDEX TO SAMPLE ENTRIES FOR APA REFERENCES

3. Book, Six or More Authors—APA

Fogle, S. T., et al. (1995). <u>Hyperspace technology</u>. Boston: Little, Brown.

Parenthetical reference: (Fogle, et al., 1995, p. 34)

"Et al." is the Latin abbreviation for "et alia," meaning "and others."

4. Book, Anonymous Author—APA

<u>Structured programming</u>. (1995). Boston: Merideth Press.

Parenthetical reference: (Structured Programming, 1995, p. 67)

In your list of references, place an anonymous work alphabetically by the first key word (not "The," "A," or "An") in its title. In your parenthetical reference, capitalize all key words in a book, article, or journal title.

5. Multiple Books, Same Author(s)—APA

Chang, J. W. (1997a). Biophysics. Boston: Little, Brown.

Chang, J. W. (1997b). MindQuest. Chicago: John Pressler.

Parenthetical reference: (Chang, 1997a)   (Chang, 1997b)

Two or more works by the same author not published in the same year are distinguished by their respective dates alone, without the added letter.

6. Book, One to Five Editors—APA

Morris, A. J., & Pardin-Walker, L. B. (Eds.). (1996). Handbook of new

information technology. New York: HarperCollins.

Parenthetical reference: (Morris & Pardin-Walker, 1996, p. 79)

For more than five editors, name only the first, followed by "et al."

7. Book, Indirect Source

Stubbs, J. (1996). White-collar productivity. Miami: Harris.

Parenthetical reference: (cited in Stubbs, 1996, p. 47)

When your source (as in Stubbs, above) has cited another source, list only this second source, but name the original source in your text: "Kline's study (cited in Stubbs, 1996, p. 47) supports this conclusion."

8. Anthology Selection or Book Chapter—APA

Bowman, J. (1994). Electronic conferencing. In A. Williams (Ed.),

Communication and technology: Today and tomorrow. (pp. 123–142).

Denton, TX: Association for Business Communication.

Parenthetical reference: (Bowman, 1994, p. 126)

The page numbers in the complete reference are for the selection cited from the anthology.

What to include in an APA citation for a periodical

APA Entries for Periodicals A citation for an article should give this information (as available), in order: author, publication, date, article title (without quotation marks), volume or number (or both), and page numbers for the entire article—not just the page(s) cited.

9. Article, Magazine—APA

DesMarteau K. (1994, October). Study links sewing machine use to

Alzheimer's disease. Bobbin, 36, 36–38.

Parenthetical reference: (DesMarteau, 1994, p. 36)

If no author is given, provide all other information. Capitalize only the first words in an article's title and subtitle. Capitalize all key words in a periodical title. Show a continuous underline for the periodical title, volume number, and comma.

10. Article, Journal with New Pagination for Each Issue—APA

Thackman-White, J. R. (1997). Computer-assisted research. American

Library Journal, 51 (1), 3–9.

Parenthetical reference: (Thackman-White, 1997, pp. 4-5)

Because each issue for a given year has page numbers that begin at "1," readers need the issue number (in this instance, "1"). The "51" denotes the volume number, which is underlined.

11. Article, Journal with Continuous Pagination—APA

Barnstead, M. H. (1994). "The Writing Crisis." Journal of Writing Theory,

12, 415–433.

Parenthetical reference: (Barnstead, 1994, pp. 415–416)

The "12" denotes the volume number. When page numbers continue from issue to issue for the full year, readers won't need the issue number, because no other issue in that year repeats these same page numbers. (You can include the issue number if you think it will help readers retrieve the article more easily.)

12. Article, Newspaper—APA

Baranski, V. H. (1997, January 15). Errors in medical diagnosis. The Boston

Times, p. B3.

In addition to the year of publication, include the month and date. If the newspaper's name begins with 'The," include it in your citation. Include "p." or "pp." before page numbers. For an article on nonconsecutive pages, list each page, separated by a comma.

What to include in an APA citation for a miscellanous source

APA Entries for Other Sources. Miscellaneous sources range from unsigned encyclopedia entries to conference presentations to government documents. A full citation should give this information (as available); author, publication date, work title, city, publisher (or volume and issue number), and page numbers (if applicable).

13. Encyclopedia, Dictionary, Alphabetical Reference—APA

Communication. (1993). In The business reference book.

Parenthetical reference: ("Communication," 1993)

For an entry that is signed, begin with the author's name and publication date.

14. Report—APA

Electrical Power Research Institute. (1994). Epidemiologic studies of electric

utility employees. (Report No. RP2964.5). Palo Alto, CA: Author.

Parenthetical reference: (Electrical Power Research Institute [EPRI], 1994, p. 12)

If authors are named, list them first, followed by the publication date. When citing a group author, as above, include the group's abbreviated name in your first parenthetical reference, and use only that abbreviation in any subsequent reference. When the agency (or organization) and publisher are the same, list "Author" in the publisher's slot.

15. Conference Presentation—APA

Smith, A. A. (1996). Multicultural stereotypes in Elizabethan prose fiction. In

A. Hodkins (Ed.), First British Symposium on Multicultural Studies (pp.

106–121). London: Harrison Press, 1996.

Parenthetical reference: (Smith, 1996, p. 109)

In parentheses is the date of the presentation. The name of the symposium is a proper name, and so is capitalized. Following the publisher's name is the date of publication.

For an unpublished presentation, include the presenter's name, year and month, title of the presentation (underlined), and all available information about the conference or meeting: "Symposium held at. . . ." Do not underline or italicize this last information.

16. Interview, Personally Conducted—APA

This material is considered a "nonrecoverable" source, and so is cited in the text only, as a parenthetical reference:

Parenthetical reference: (G. Nasson, personal interview, April 2, 1997)

If you name the interviewee in your text, do not repeat the name in your citation.

17. Interview, Published—APA

Jable, C. K. (1996, June 7). The future of graphics. [Interview with James

Lescault]. In K. Prell (Ed.), Executive views of automation (pp.

216–231). Miami: Haber Press, 1997.

Parenthetical reference: (Jable, 1996, pp. 218–223)

Begin with the name of the interviewer, followed by the interview date and title (if available), the designation (in brackets), and the publication information, including the date.

18. Personal Correspondence—APA

This material is considered nonrecoverable data and so is cited in the text

only, as a parenthetical reference:

Parenthetical reference: (L. Rogers, personal correspondence, May 15, 1993)

If you name the correspondent in your text, do not repeat the name in your citation.

19. Brochure or Pamphlet—APA

This material follows the citation format for a book entry (pages 364–366).

20. Unpublished Lecture—APA

Dumont, R. A. (1999, January 15). Androgyny and the rhetorical tradition.

Lecture presented at the University of Massachusetts at Dartmouth.

Parenthetical reference: (R. A. Dumont, 1996).

If you name the lecturer in your text, do not repeat the name in your citation.

21. Government Document—APA

If the author is unknown, present the information in this order: name of the issuing agency, publication date, document title, place, and publisher.

> Virginia Highway Department. (1991). <u>Standards for bridge maintenance</u>.
>
> Richmond: Author.

Parenthetical reference: (Virginia Highway Department, 1991, p. 49)

When the issuing agency is both author and publisher, list "Author" in the publisher's slot.

For any Congressional document, identify the house of Congress (Senate or House of Representatives) before the date.

> United States Congress. House. Armed Services Committee. (1995).
>
> <u>Funding for the military academies</u>. Washington, DC: U.S. Government
>
> Printing Office.

Parenthetical reference: (Armed Services Committee, 1995, p. 41)

22. Miscellaneous Items (Unpublished manuscript, Dissertation, and so on)—APA

> Author (if known), date of publication, title of work, sponsoring
>
> organization or publisher, page numbers.

For any work that has group authorship (corporation, committee, and so on), cite the name of the group or agency in place of the author's name.

What to include in an APA citation for an electronic source

APA Entries for Electronic Sources.   APA documentation standards for electronic sources continue to be refined and defined. A sampling of currently preferred formats is presented below. Any citation for electronic media should enable readers to identify the original source (printed or electronic) and provide an electronic path for retrieving the material.

Begin with the publication information for the printed equivalent. Then name the electronic source ([On-line], [CD-ROM], [Computer software]), the protocol* (Bitnet, Dialog, FTP, Telnet) and any other items that define a clear path (service provider, database title, and access code, retrieval number, or site address).

---

*A protocol is a body of standards that ensure compatibility among the different products designed to work together on a particular network.

23. On-line Database Abstract—APA

Sahl, J. D. (1995). Power lines, viruses, and childhood leukemia [On-line].

    Cancer Causes Control, 6 (1), 83. Abstract from DIALOG File: MEDLINE

    Item: 93-04881

Parenthetical reference: (Sahl, 1995)

Note the absence of closing punctuation. Any punctuation added to the availability statement could interfere with retrieval.

24. On-line Database Article—APA

Alley, R. A. (1995, January). Social influences on worker satisfaction

    [29 paragraphs]. Industrial Psychology [On-line serial], 5(11). Available

    FTP: Hostname:publisher.com Directory:pub/journals/industrial.

    psychology/1995

Parenthetical reference: (Alley, 1995)

Give the length of the article [in paragraphs], after its title. Add no terminal punctuation to the availability statement.

25. Computer Software or Software Manual—APA

Virtual collaboration [Computer software]. (1994). New York: HarperCollins

    Publishers.

Parenthetical reference: (Virtual, 1994)

For citing a manual, replace the "Computer software" designation in brackets with "Software manual."

26. CD-ROM Abstract—APA

Canalte, H. A. (1995, February). Violent-crime statistics: Good news and

    bad news [CD-ROM]. Law Enforcement, 8. Abstract from: Proquest File:

    ABI/Inform Item: 978032

Parenthetical reference: (Canalte, 1995)

The "8" in the above entry denotes the page number of this one-page article.

27. CD-ROM Reference Work—APA

Time almanac. (1994). Washington Compact, 1994.

Parenthetical reference: (Time Almanac, 1994)

If the work on CD-ROM has a printed equivalent, APA currently prefers that it be cited in its printed form. As more works appear in electronic form, this convention may be revised.

28. Electronic Bulletin Boards, Discussion Lists, E-Mail—APA

Parenthetical reference: Fred Flynn (personal communication, May 10, 1996)

provided these statistics.

This material is considered personal communication in APA style. Instead of being included in the list of references, it is cited directly in the text. According to APA's current standards, material from discussion lists and electronic bulletin boards has limited research value because it does not undergo the kind of review and verification process used in scholarly publications.

APA SAMPLE LIST OF REFERENCES

APA's "References" section is an alphabetical listing (by author) equivalent to MLA's "Works Cited" section (page 360). Like Works Cited, the References section includes only those works actually cited. (A bibliography usually would include background works or works consulted as well.) In one notable difference from MLA style, APA style calls for only "recoverable" sources to appear in the reference list. Therefore, personal interviews, E-mail messages, and other unpublished materials are cited in the text only, as shown on page 391.

. . . .

APPLICATION 21-1

Computer Project: Both MLA and APA have issued new guidelines (pages 358, 370) for documenting sources from the Internet or Web. In addition, the Alliance for Computers and Writing (ACW) has issued a suggested format (page 360).

But electronic documentation presents special problems. First, authors or sponsoring organizations for material posted directly to the Internet can be hard to find. Material on the Internet may have appeared somewhere else first, and this original source is sometimes not indicated clearly. Internet addresses won't take you back to the same site if you fail to copy them exactly—even though they may be several lines long. Pages often aren't numbered. Finally, it's sometimes hard to verify the quality of Internet sources, since on the Internet, *anyone* can claim to be an expert.

As you conduct your own electronic searches, use the list of problems above as a starting point and compile your own list of documentation issues in electronic research. For your classmates, compose a set of guidelines that will help them deal with these difficulties. Then examine the MLA, APA, and ACW formats for electronic documentation. Which seems most useful? Why? Can you suggest changes that will make the formats more effective for students like you as they try to document their work?

....

WORK CITED

Gibaldi, Joseph, and Walter S. Achtert. *MLA Handbook for Writers of Research Papers.* 3rd ed. New York: Modern Language Assn., 1988.

CHAPTER 22

COMPOSING THE RESEARCH REPORT

DEVELOPING A WORKING THESIS AND OUTLINE

Don't expect to arrive at your thesis until you have evaluated and interpreted your findings (as discussed on pages 338–344). Your thesis should emerge from the most accurate and reliable information you have been able to find. On page 301 you phrased your topic as this question:

Research topic

Violent Crime on College Campuses: How Common Is It?

Near the completion of your research, you should have at least a tentative answer to that question:

Tentative thesis

Violent crime on college campuses is more common than many people like to believe.

As your research proceeds, you might revise this tentative thesis any number of times.

Now you need a road map—a working outline. Perhaps your topic itself or your reading suggested a rough, working outline:

A working outline

    I. The extent of the problem
       A. Recent examples of highly publicized campus crimes
       B. National crime statistics
       C. The 1992 Campus Awareness and Security Act
   II. Direct causes of campus crime
       A. Alcohol and drug use by students
       B. Offenders from off-campus
  III. Indirect causes of campus crime
       A. Naive assumptions by parents
       B. Carefree student attitudes
       C. Deceptive publicity by some colleges
       D. Special treatment for athletes and fraternities
       E. Denial and cover-up by administrators
  IV. Actions required
       A. Greater candor and publicity
       B. Change in student habits
       C. Prevention programs

Of course, by the time you compose your final outline the shape of your report may have changed radically (see pages 382–389).

DRAFTING YOUR REPORT

When you have collected and reviewed your material, organized your note-cards, and settled on a workable thesis, you are ready to write the first draft of your report.

Begin by revising your working outline. At this stage, try to develop a detailed formal outline, using at each level either topic phrases (page 375) or full sentences (page 400).

A formal outline needs logical notation and consistent format. *Notation* is the system of numbers and letters marking the logical divisions; *format* is the arrangement of your material on the page (indention, spacing, and so on). Proper notation and format show the subordination of some parts of your topic to others. The general pattern of outline notation goes like this:

The logical divisions of
a formal outline

        I.
            A.
                1.
                2.*
            B.
                1.
                2.
                        a.
                        b. (1)†
                            (2)
            C.
        II. etc.

(For a discussion of a sample formal outline, see page 401.) When your outline is complete, check your tentative thesis to make sure it promises *exactly* what your report will deliver.

Now you can begin to write. Students often find this the most intimidating part of research: pulling together a large body of information. Don't frantically throw everything on the page simply to get done. Concentrate on only one section at a time.

Begin by classifying your notecards in groups according to the section of your outline to which each card is keyed. Next, arrange the notecards for your introduction in order. Now, lay them out in rows, as you would lay out playing cards. You are ready to write your first section. As you move from subsection to subsection, provide commentary and transitions, and document each source.

---

*Note each level of division yields at least two items. If you cannot divide a major item into at least two subordinate items, retain only your major heading.
†Carry further subdivisions as far as needed, but keep notation for each level individualized and consistent.

REVISING YOUR REPORT

After completing and documenting a first draft, use the Revision Checklist for essays in Chapter 5, along with the following Research Report checklist, to revise the report.

....

 RESEARCH REPORT CHECKLIST

(Numbers in parentheses refer to the first page of discussion.)

Contents

❑ Does the report grow from a clear thesis? (375)

❑ Does the title offer an accurate forecast? (52)

❑ Does the evidence support the conclusion? (339)

❑ Is the report based on reliable sources and evidence? (335, 338)

❑ Is the information complete? (304)

❑ Does the report avoid reliance on a single source? (300)

❑ Is the evidence free of weak spots? (338)

❑ Are all data clearly and fully interpreted? (338)

❑ Can anything be cut? (331)

❑ Is anything missing? (304)

Organization

❑ Does the introduction state clearly the purpose and thesis? (383)

❑ Does the report follow the outline? (401)

❑ Is each paragraph focused on one main thought? (88)

❑ Is the line of reasoning clear and easy to follow? (39)

Documentation

❑ Is all quoted material marked clearly throughout the text? (331)

❑ Are all sources other than common knowledge documented? (347)

❑ Are direct quotations used sparingly and appropriately? (333)

❑ Are all quotations accurate and integrated grammatically? (332)

❑ Is the report free of excessively long quotations? (333)

❑ Are all paraphrases accurate and clear? (334)

❑ Is the documentation consistent, complete, and correct? (348)

Figure 22.1 shows the completed report, documented according to the APA style guidelines discussed in Chapter 21.

A SAMPLE REPORT IN APA STYLE

The following report was written in response to scenario on page 300. As you read the report, evaluate its content, organization, and documentation by referring to the Checklist on page 377.

Campus Crime   1

Campus Crime: A Hidden Issue

Julia Conforti

University of Massachusetts, Dartmouth
Professor J. M. Lannon

Intermediate Composition

Section 1

May 5, 1997

FIGURE 22.1
A research report in APA Style

Campus Crime   2

2

ABSTRACT

Violent crime on college campuses, usually student-on-student and triggered by
alcohol and drugs, is far more common than many people like to believe.
Campus crime remains a largely hidden issue because of naive assumptions by
parents, carefree student attitudes, deceptive publicity by some colleges, special
treatment for athletes and other privileged groups, and frequent denial and
cover-up by college administrators. Recent government legislation, improved
security measures, and prevention and support programs offer partial solutions.
Most needed, however, is more responsible behavior from students and greater
candor and publicity from college officials.

FIGURE 22.1
A research report in APA Style   (*Continued*)

DISCUSSION OF RESEARCH REPORT IN APA STYLE
APA FRONT MATTER (ITEMS THAT PRECEDE THE REPORT): 1–2

1. *Title page:* Center the title and all other lines. Do not underline the title or use all capital letters. Double space between lines. Number the title page and all subsequent pages in the upper-right corner and include a shortened title as a running head for each page.

2. *Abstract:* Papers in APA style usually contain a one-paragraph abstract (roughly 100 words) that previews the main points and shows how they are related. Place the abstract on a separate page, following the title page. Center the heading; double-space the abstract; use no paragraph indent. (To prepare an abstract, see page 334.)

3
4
5
6
7
8
9
10
11

Campus Crime: A Hidden Issue

Parents, students, and school administrators view college campuses through rose-colored glasses. We tend to think a college campus is a fairy land in which good prevails and, on rare occasions, evil briefly invades and then quickly retreats. According to journalist Anne Matthews (1993), "when aware of campus crime at all, [we] frequently attribute it to faceless hit-and-retreat raiders from the world beyond the ivy curtain" (p. 38). Like characters in a make-believe world, we enjoy feeling content and secure. The real world, however, tells a different story.

How Secure Is the Typical College Campus?

Benign images of campus life often conceal a pattern of violence. In 1986, at Lehigh University a female student was "robbed, sodomized, and murdered in her dorm bed by a fellow student she had never met" (Pfister, 1994, p. 26). In 1990, "one male and three female students at the University of Florida and another woman at Santa Fe Community College were found stabbed or bludgeoned to death. . . . Three of the victims were mutilated; one, an 18-year-old female honor student, was decapitated" ("Campus Ripper," 1990, p. 43). In 1991, "five University of Iowa employees—three professors, one staff member, and an associate vice president—were shot to death by a former physics graduate student irate at losing a research prize" (Matthews, 1993, p. 38). In 1992, "student Wayne Lo, 18, roamed Simon's Rock College, shooting four people and killing a professor and a fellow student" (Matthews, 1993, p. 38).

FIGURE 22.1
A research report in APA Style　(*Continued*)

APA Body Elements: 3–12

3. Include the shortened title as a running head on each page and continue the page numbering.

4. Repeat the title exactly as it appears on the title page and center it.

5. Use one-inch margins all around. Begin the first paragraph two lines below the title and use double spacing throughout. Use a five-space indent for the first line of each paragraph. Do not hyphenate words at the right margin or justify the right margin (i.e., make it even).

6. Use the introduction to invite readers in and present your main idea. Show readers that your topic has meaning to them *personally* (as our writer here does by using "We"). For immediate credibility, try to include brief quotations from one or more authorities.

7. Introduce brief quotes by naming the author or speaker so that readers will know who said what. Combine the quoted material with your own words to make complete sentences. Use brackets to signal any alteration of the original quotation.

8. Use section headings to orient readers and show them what to expect. When you use questions as headings, phrase the questions the way readers might ask them. Phrase all section headings consistently.

9. Use vivid examples to make the problem real for readers.

10. Cite each source in parentheses, inside the period, but outside any quotation marks.

11. Use a shortened title to identify a source with no author named.

12

Countless additional crimes occur on college campuses and their number is increasing. For example, Lederman (1995) points out that campus robberies and assaults increased by nearly 3 percent from 1992 to 1993, following a similar increase from 1991 to 1992 (p. 31). For this same period, the FBI National Press Office (1996) reports consecutive annual declines in violent crime nationwide of roughly 1.5 percent. Campus officials reportedly offer "no clear explanation why violent crime would be on the upswing on campuses if it is dropping elsewhere" (Lederman, 1995, p. 31).

Why Does Campus Crime Receive Scant Attention?

To find the right college for their child, parents look for many qualities in a school: a strong academic program, an accomplished faculty, an attractive campus, clean and roomy dormitories, and so on. But parents rarely consider campus crime because they assume that college campuses are safe. School officials attribute such naivete to parents' belief in the notion of in loco parentis— the assumption that a university stands in for the student's parents. According to a University of South Carolina law enforcement official, parents have unrealistic expectations when they send children off to college: "They expect the university to be able to control students' behavior. We can't always do that" (Dodge, 1991, p. 30). One safety official at Rutgers University agrees that too many parents "feel like they are turning their child over to the university for the university to care for in the same way that the child was cared for at home; that is just not possible" (McClarin, 1994, p. 11).

FIGURE 22.1
A research report in APA Style   *(Continued)*

12. When you name the author in your text, include the date of the work immediately afterward, and the page numbers at citation's end. In the APA system, page numbers are optional in citing paraphrased material, but required in citing direct quotations.

Most students also feel safe in the serene and attractive setting of the typical college, failing to realize that roughly 80 percent of campus crime is student-on-student (McClarin, 1994, p. 11). In his review of recent research, Kier (1986) observes that as many as one of ten women on college campuses is sexually assaulted by an acquaintance. Pfister (1994), notes that overall estimates of campus sexual assault range from one in twenty-five to one in four (p. 26). Despite these alarming figures, student respondents to a survey at St. Augustine's College attributed the crime problem mostly to nonstudents (Ayres, 1994, p. 14).

In addition, like their parents, students assume they will be safeguarded from any danger by administrators or security personnel. They often consider themselves invincible and have the attitude "I get to do whatever I want but you have to protect me" (Matthews, 1993, p. 47). But students make themselves vulnerable to crime by drinking and partying until all hours and then just plopping down, wherever they may be, and sleeping until they sober up. Prior to the 1986 rape and murder at Lehigh University, for example, students routinely left room and dorm doors unlocked for the convenience of friends and roommates (Pfister, 1994, p. 26).

College crime statistics show that carefree attitudes about alcohol contribute to campus crime. Matthews (1993) asserts that "alcohol has become the drug of use at American Colleges, and a fuel for campus crime" (p. 41). In 1989, Towson State's Center for the Study and Prevention of Campus Violence surveyed 1,100 colleges and universities and found that "student crime victims drink and use drugs significantly more than nonvictims" (Matthews, 1993, p. 40). A 1992 survey of 17,000 students on 140 campuses found that 42 percent of college students are "binge drinkers" (five or more drinks in a row within any

FIGURE 22.1
A research report in APA Style   (*Continued*)

two weeks), and that female students on high-binge campuses reported a higher number of unwanted sexual advances (Cage, 1992, p. 30). A 1994 survey by Columbia University's Center on Addiction and Abuse found that 95 percent of campus crimes as well as 90 percent of campus rapes involve alcohol ("Outlook," 1994, p. 21).

Administrators know the exact dangers that exist on any college campus, but too often they choose to ignore the unpleasant facts—to avoid scaring off prospective students. Bright, glossy brochures promote every aspect of a particular school but rarely mention campus safety—let alone crime statistics. Transcripts of Congressional hearings (1990) reveal that, when campus crime does hit home, administrators often deny that any of their students are involved (p. 61).

Administrators sometimes cover up campus crime because the offenders are prominent student athletes or drunken fraternity members. While investigating sexual assault on college campuses, Johnson (1991) found that "college athletes and fraternity men are a protected species" (p. 34). Beyond avoiding bad publicity, campus officials protect these assailants for fear of antagonizing their parents or school athletic fans and contributors (Matthews, 1993, p. 42). One prominent university recently awarded a grant to a basketball player who had pleaded guilty to sexual assault. This same school then offered his victim an academic scholarship (Blum, 1995, p. 29).

Any violent crime on a college campus causes temporary wariness among parents, students, and faculty. For a few weeks following a rape, assault, or other crime, everyone behaves more cautiously. Parents warn students to be careful. Administrators post fliers with police phone numbers in large, bold print. Students walk in groups and avoid usual shortcuts through woods or poorly lit areas. Extra police are on patrol; emergency phones are repaired;

Campus Crime   7

dorm security is increased. But as the immediate shock wears off, students again take their safety for granted. They begin walking alone again at night; they resume their usual shortcuts.

At our school, only four weeks after a female nearly was raped while awaiting a bus outside the library and a male student was assaulted by a knife-wielding attacker, most students seem to have resumed their carefree ways. On any late evening, males and females alike can be seen walking or jogging alone.

Is Enough Being Done?

The rise in campus crime led to passage of the Crime Awareness and Security Act in 1990, requiring all schools to disclose information about security measures and crime statistics to current or prospective students and employees ("Rates," 1994, p. 2). This legislation was followed in 1992 by the Campus Sexual Assault Victim's Bill of Rights, requiring all colleges to establish set policies for assisting victims. Also passed in 1992 was the Buckley Amendment Clarification Act, designating campus police records as no longer confidential (Security, 1996). Perhaps most significant, Fossley and Smith (1995) note that courts are increasingly holding schools responsible for crimes on their campuses.

Although schools routinely offer sessions on campus safety and sexual assault for incoming students, these programs tend to be "one-shot deals." Also, safety measures such as increased lighting and police patrols, emergency phones, and escort services help prevent assault by strangers—but not by acquaintances. Clearly, more needs to be done: for example, prevention programs, periodic safety-awareness sessions, self-defense classes, and mandatory crime-awareness seminars in which student victims share their experiences with other students. These seminars might even be offered as one-credit classes. Current crime

FIGURE 22.1
A research report in APA Style   (*Continued*)

statistics could be published weekly in the campus newspaper. Measures like these would heighten safety awareness and possibly reduce campus crime.

Resources for students are increasingly available on the INTERNET. For example, Security on Campus, Inc., a non-profit organization for preventing campus violence, has helped victims and families take legal action against various schools for negligence and "failure to protect" (Security, 1997). Survivors of Stalking, an independently funded advocacy and resource center, offers help for victims (Survivors, 1997). Campus Outreach Service circulates an on-line petition to ensure that all colleges comply with the Federal laws discussed earlier (Campus, 1997).

College students have every right to feel safe on campus, but they must recognize that campus crime is real. Student and dorm director Lisa Fiorini (1996) observes that students at our school "have not listened to the warnings around them. . . . They don't believe [campus crime] really happens because it never happens to anyone they know" (p. 2). While the specter of campus crime should not taint the freedoms and joys of college life, parents must become more realistic; students, more responsible for their actions; and colleges, more candid.

Crime is a fact of life on college campuses—just as in the real world. The sooner parents, students, and administrators accept this fact, the safer college campuses might become.

13

14

References

15   Ayres, B. D., Jr. (1993, September 10). College requires applicants to come clean about crime. New York Times, p. A14.   *[newspaper article]*

16   Blum, D. E. (1995, June 30). A controversial scholarship [On-line]. The Chronicle of Higher Education, pp. A29–A30. Abstract from: SilverPlatter File: ERIC Item:EJ508567   *[CD-ROM abstract]*

Cage, M. C. (1992, September 30). 42% of college students engage in "binge drinking," survey shows. The Chronicle of Higher Education, p. A30.

17   Campus Outreach Services. (1997). A college petition for restoration of effect to federal sexual assault laws [On-line web site]. Available WWW: http:www.cs.utk.edu/~bartley/cos/petition.html   *[web site]*

18   Campus ripper. (1990, September 14). Time, 43.   *[magazine article]*

Dodge, S. (1991, February 18). With campus crime capturing public attention, colleges re-evaluate security measures and stiffen some penalties. The

19   Chronicle of Higher Education, pp. A29, A31.

FBI National Press Office (1996, October 13). Uniform crime reporting program press release [On-line web site]. Available WWW:http://www.fbi.gov/ucr/ucr95prs.htm

Fiorini, Lisa, K. (1996, December 2). Letter to the editor. UMass Dartmouth Torch, P. 2.   *[college newspaper]*

FIGURE 22.1
A research report in APA Style   *(Continued)*

APA List of References: 13–21

13. Continue the running heads and page numbers. Use one-inch margins.

14. Center the "References" title at the top of a new page. Include only recoverable data (material that readers could retrieve for themselves); cite personal interviews, unpublished lectures, electronic discussion lists, and E-mail and other personal correspondence parenthetically in the text only. (See also items 17 and 21 in this list.)

15. Double space entries and order them alphabetically by author's last name (excluding A, An, or The). List initials only for authors' first and middle names. Write out names of all months. Capitalize only the first word in article or book titles and subtitles, and any proper nouns. Capitalize all key words in magazine, journal, or newspaper titles. Do not enclose article titles in quotation marks. Underline or italicize periodical titles.

16. In student papers, indent the second and subsequent lines of an entry five spaces. In papers submitted for publication in an APA journal the first line instead is indented.

17. List all web sites that directly contributed to your paper, and provide the electronic address, especially for resources that readers might wish to consult. If no author is named, list the organization sponsoring the web site (e.g., Campus Outreach Services) in the author slot. Omit your punctuation from the end of an electronic address.

18. Use the first key word in the title to alphabetize works whose author is not named.

19. For a magazine or newspaper article on nonconsecutive pages, list each page, separated by a comma.

Campus Crime   10

20

Fosley R., & Smith, M. (1995, Summer) Institutional liability for campus rapes: The emerging law. [On-line] Journal of Law and Education, 24(3), 377–401. Abstract from: WWW: http://www.educlaw.edu/jle/cc.htm   *[on-line abstract]*

Johnson, C. (1991, October 7). When sex is the issue. U.S. News and World Report, 34–35.

21

Kier, F. (1996, January). Acquaintance rape on college campuses: A review of the literature. Paper presented at the annual meeting of the Southwest Educational Research Association, New Orleans.   *[unpublished conference paper]*

Lederman, D. (1995, February 3). Colleges report rise in violent crime. The Chronicle of Higher Education, pp. A31–A42.

Matthews, A. (1993, March 4). The campus crime wave. The New York Times Magazine, 30–42.

McClarin, K. (1994, September 7). Fear prompts self-defense as crime comes to college. New York Times, pp. 1A, 4A.

Outlook: Campus drinking: Who, why and how much. (1994, June 13). U.S. News and World Report, 21.

Pfister, B. (1994, Spring). Swept awake! On the Issues, 20–26.

Rates of campus crime. (1994, March/April). Society, 2–3.

Security on Campus, Inc. (1997). History, Accomplishments, and Programs [On-line web site]. Available WWW: http://www.socoline.org.htm   *[web site]*

Survivors of Stalking. (1997). Ending the silence that kills [On-line web site]. Available WWW: http://www.gate.net/~soshelp/one.htm

U.S. House of Representatives. (1990). Hearing on H.R. 3344: The crime awareness and security act. Washington, DC: U.S. Government Printing Office.   *[gov't publication—no author named]*

FIGURE 22.1
A research report in APA Style   (*Continued*)

APA LIST OF REFERENCES (CONTINUED)

20. For more than one author or editor, use ampersands instead of spelling out "and." Use italics or a continuous underline for a journal article's title, volume number, and the comma. Give the issue number in parentheses only if each issue begins on page 1. Do not include "p." or "pp." before journal page numbers (only before page numbers from a newspaper). For page numbers of three or more digits, provide all digits in the second number.

21. Treat an unpublished conference presentation as a "recoverable" source, including it in your list of references instead of merely citing it parenthetically in your text.

CASE STUDY: A SAMPLE RESEARCH PROJECT

*T*his chapter will follow one student writer's problem-solving, from the day her report was assigned until she submitted her final draft.

DISCOVERING A WORTHWHILE TOPIC

As soon as Shirley Haley learned that a research report was due in six weeks, she began to search for a worthwhile topic. Although many of Haley's college friends had adjusted to the hectic pace of the first-year student, others were not doing so well: some had developed insomnia; others had gained or lost a good deal of weight; one friend was sleeping more than 12 hours a day. Other disorders ranged from compulsive eating and indigestion to chronic headaches and skin problems—all seemingly since the beginning of the semester. Haley wondered why, beyond the obvious pressures of college life, so many of her friends had become so unhealthy.

A psychology major, Haley recently had read about *stress* in an introductory textbook. She wondered about a connection between stress and her friends' problems.

FOCUSING THE INQUIRY

But Haley knew that, to come up with the right answers, she would have to ask the right questions. Here is her tree chart:

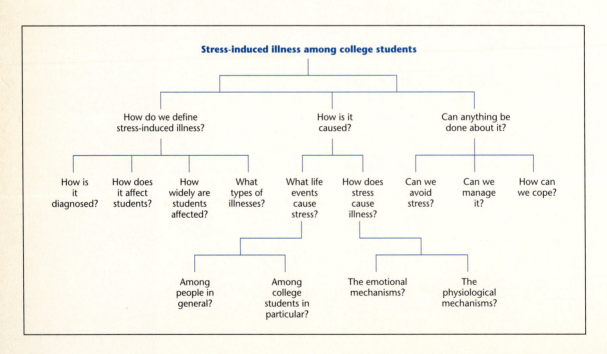

Once she knew what information she was looking for, Haley focused on the various viewpoints that would give her a balanced picture:

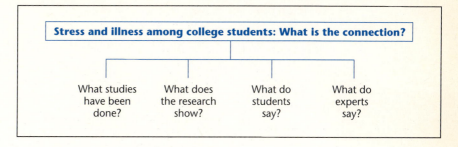

Now that she knew what questions to ask and where to get the answers, Haley was ready to research.

SEARCHING THE LITERATURE

Because Haley already had read a description of *stress* in her psychology textbook, she did not need general reference works such as encyclopedias and specialized dictionaries. She went straight to the *Readers' Guide to Periodical Literature,* the most recent volume of which listed numerous articles under "Stress." Haley also checked under "College students"; there, under the subheading "Psychology," she found other relevant titles. Also checking earlier volumes of the *Readers' Guide,* she recorded full citations of interesting articles on bibliography cards.

Next Haley searched through recent volumes of *Psychological Abstracts* for studies on stress and college students. Besides finding yet more titles, she could look up and read abstracts of promising articles. Under "College Students" she found some key articles addressing her friends' health problems.

Now Haley checked her library's periodicals holdings list (page 314) to see which of these key articles the library held. Some she found collected in bound volumes; others were on microfilm. The librarian helped her use a microfilm reader and also ordered two articles from other libraries.

At the card catalog, Haley jotted down a few book titles and call numbers. In the stacks, she browsed through the books on the shelves. She also checked the "Selected Bibliography" section of her psychology textbook, continuing to record citations on bibliography cards.

Finally, Haley browsed World Wide Web sites and on-line databases for the most recent electronic sources on her topic.

RECORDING AND REVIEWING FINDINGS

Armed with a good stock of sources, Haley skimmed the most promising works, evaluating each finding for accuracy, reliability, fairness, and completeness. She recorded useful material on notecards, indicating source and page numbers and recording quotations word for word. Because she found a good body of information on stress management, she decided to structure her report in this way:

Problem ⟶ Causes and Effects ⟶ Solutions

SETTLING ON A THESIS

The evidence pointed toward a definite conclusion: Stress was indeed a real factor in students' poor health. Now she could formulate a tentative thesis:

| Stress is a definite cause of illness among college students.

Haley would later refine and expand her thesis, but, for now, she had a good focal point for developing her report.

WRITING AND DOCUMENTING THE REPORT IN MLA STYLE

Haley continued to read, record information, outline, and organize her note-cards. Finally, she decided she knew enough to write her first draft. Using the revision checklists, she reworked her first and second drafts into the final draft that appears on the following pages. (Marginal numbers refer to the writer's decisions discussed on the facing pages.)

1

Students Under Stress: College Can Make You Sick

by
Shirley Haley

English 101, Section 1432
Professor Lannon
December 8, 19xx

FIGURE 23.1
A research report in MLA style

Haley   i

OUTLINE

Thesis: Because of disruptive changes and pressures in their personal, social, and academic lives, college students are highly vulnerable to the physical effects of stress.

I. The Problem: Stress increasingly is recognized as a definite cause of physical disorders.

A. The mechanisms have been studied for years, but stress still is making us sick.

B. Stress has a technical and a personal definition, and both are accurate.

C. More and more of us suffer the physical effects of stress.

D. College students are among the groups most affected.

II. Specific Causes: Stress-induced illness is caused by emotional responses that have physical consequences.

A. Stress originates when the body works too hard to maintain equilibrium.

1. If the alarm reaction persists, the body is forever ready for action.

2. Psychosomatic illness is not imaginary.

B. A major study showed a connection between the stress of common life events and illness.

C. Even a series of ordinary events in the lives of college students can cause dangerous levels of stress.

D. Various studies of college students confirm the stress-illness link.

III. Possible Solutions: Now that the problem is recognized, solutions are being found.

A. The effect stress has on us depends on how well we cope.

1. We need both coping strategies and help from others.

2. Without coping mechanisms, we are almost certain to be overwhelmed.

B. Students need to develop more realistic expectations of college life.

1. College orientation should be more realistic.

2. Stress-management courses should be offered by more colleges.

C. Some type of stress-management training should be available to every college student.

FIGURE 23.1
A research report in MLA style   (*Continued*)

1. *Title page:* Many reports for government, business, and industry are prefaced by a title page with these standard items: report title, author's name, course or department, intended reader's name, and date. Haley centers and spaces these items for visual appeal. The title page is not numbered.

2. *Outline* (on next page): The running head for all pages is the author's last name, followed by one space and page number (small roman numerals for outline, Arabic for paper). Haley prefaces her sentence outline with her thesis, so that readers can understand her plan at a glance. Her three major sections (*The Problem, Specific Causes,* and *Possible Solutions*) reveal a clear and sensible effect-to-cause development (see pages 211–212).

Notice that each level of division in the outline yields at least *two* parts.

3

Haley   1

The Problem: Stress-Induced Illness

Stress can cause physical illness. The mechanisms have been studied for years, but stress still is making us sick.

4

Over 60 years ago, the search began for a link between stress and illness. Walter Cannon identified the "fight or flight" response in 1929. Showing that emotional arousal causes physical reactions such as increased respiration and pulse rate and elevated blood pressure, Cannon laid the groundwork for stress research. In the 1930s Dr. Adolf Mayer, who began charting patients' life events to aid his medical diagnoses, recorded "the changes of habit, of school entrances, graduations or changes, or failures; the various jobs . . . and other important events" (Dohrenwend and Dohrenwend 3). And Hans Selye in 1936 described the body's reaction to stress as "the syndrome of just being sick" ("Stress Concept" 72).

5

6

Stress has a technical and a personal definition. Technically, stress is a response to life events that disrupt the physical being. In personal terms, stress is part of what happens when a person falls in or out of love, receives good or bad news, drives a car, receives a traffic ticket, takes final exams, or graduates. All life experiences, good and bad, entail stress. In fact, some degree of anxiety is a good motivator—we work better under stress. According to Dr. Kenneth Greenspan, director of the stress lab at New York Presbyterian Hospital, "as with a violin string, there is an optimal note: not all slack—not all taut" (Adler and Gosnell 107). But when stress becomes excessive, it endangers our physical health.

7

8

More and more of us suffer physical effects of stress: ulcers and colitis, fatigue and exhaustion, high blood pressure and headache. Stress probably makes us susceptible to infectious disease and cancer by inhibiting our "natural killer (NK) cells." These killer cells help the body fight colds, flu, pneumonia, and other infections, and they destroy malignant cells. In one study, young adults who

FIGURE 23.1
A research report in MLA style   (*Continued*)

3. *Headings and page numbering:* Because she uses a title page, Haley does not repeat her title on page 1. Instead she uses section headings to keep readers on track. Each page of the paper itself (including Works Cited) has an Arabic number after the author's last name as running head.

4. *Background information:* Haley's opening grabs our attention by showing immediately that stress makes us sick. She summarizes a half-century of stress research, to show that the stress issue is no mere fad. Brief quotations from authorities lend credibility.

5. *Using quoted material:* Haley introduces brief quotes by naming the author and by combining the quotations with her own words to make complete sentences.

6. *In-text citations:* Haley cites each source in parentheses, inside the period, but outside any quotation marks. Because one of the authors cited in the first paragraph has more than one work listed in Haley's "Works Cited" section, Haley lists a shortened version of this work's title when she refers to that author.

7. *Defining the problem:* Haley *defines* her subject before discussing it, clarifying her definition with concrete examples. She quotes an authority to point out that *some* stress can be beneficial, but that too much is destructive.

8. *Relating the material to the audience:* Readers want to know what something means to *them* personally; Haley therefore includes a paragraph on the common effects and signs of stress.

Haley   2

reported highly stressful lives showed decreased NK cell activity and a high rate of
infectious illness (Bower 141). Recent work by John Cacioppo and colleagues at
Ohio State University shows that stress definitely weakens the immune system.

Stress has warning signs, cues to seek help before our bodies actually break
down. Among the commonest signs are an overpowering urge to cry or run away,
persistent anxiety for no reason, insomnia, and a feeling of being "keyed up." (See
Appendix A for other signs.) Overeating and alcohol or drug use are often the result
of stress beyond endurance, an attempt to escape (Selye, Stress of Life 175).

Among the groups most exposed to life changes, and thus most affected by
stress, are college students. In a 1992 Irish study, Tyrell found that students' main
sources of stress were "fear of falling behind, finding the motivation to study, time
pressures, financial worries, and concern about academic ability" (185–88). Stanford
psychologist Alejandro Martinez regards stress as one of the three major problems
(along with family and relationships) faced by college students (Nikravesh).

Students' battles with stress can begin early. Even before graduating from high
school they worry about admission to the college of their choice. Or they feel
pressure to measure up to parents' achievements and expectations, or keep up with
successful older siblings. "Second-rate doesn't rate at all in a majority of the
households from which these [students] come—and they know it" (Brooks 613).
Transition to college creates more stress as students leave a friendly and familiar
environment for one that seems impersonal and demanding, academically and
socially (Compas et al. 243). Moreover, today's students struggle with tuition
increases, reductions in financial aid, and feelings of hopelessness about finding
decent jobs after graduation (Cage 26). Others worry about coping with sexual
experiences or being the victims of sexual assault (White and Humphrey).

Such disruptive changes and pressures in their personal, social, and academic
lives make students vulnerable to the physical effects of stress.

FIGURE 23.1
A research report in MLA style   (*Continued*)

9. *Citing an electronic source with no printed equivalent:* The page numbers for this electronic text are not available, so Haley names the author in her discussion, to avoid the in-text parenthetical citation.

10. *Referring to appendices:* Haley refers us to an appendix at report's end for details that we might find useful but that would interrupt the flow of the report itself.

11. *Thesis paragraphs:* Now Haley can focus specifically on stress in the lives of college students. This paragraph and the next lead into her thesis (bottom of page "2").

12. *Citing a source whose author is named in the text:* Because Haley has named the author (Tyrell) in her paragraph, she merely lists the page numbers in her parenthetical citation.

13. *Citing an online source:* The "Nikravesh" citation includes no page numbers because none are available from the online source.

14. *Citing an abstract:* The "White and Humphrey" citation includes no page numbers because merely the abstract is being cited.

Haley   3

15

Specific Causes of Stress-Induced Illness

Stress originates when the body works too hard to maintain the equilibrium necessary for a healthy life. Any disruption or demand, good or bad, sets off an adjustment that allows the body to regain its equilibrium. When a stimulus sets off this adjustment, when an "alarm reaction" puts the body "on alert," adrenaline prepares the body for action: blood pressure rises to increase blood flow to muscles; digestion temporarily shuts down; blood sugar rises to increase energy; perspiration increases; and other physical changes occur, to prepare the body for "fight or flight" (Selye, "Stress Concept" 76).

16

If the alarm reaction persists, the body is forever ready for action. That is when stress becomes destructive. We can run away from a speeding car as we cross the street, and when the danger passes, so does the stress. But we can't run away from some inner threat, such as the pressure for good grades. And as the stress endures, our bodies become less able to maintain the equilibrium needed for health.

Far from being imaginary, psychosomatic illness is real disease that can be diagnosed and treated. But the cause of psychosomatic illness is unmanaged stress. Until the stress is controlled, the disease can't be cured. Because of previous illness or heredity, one organ or system (heart, digestive system, skin) in a person's body tends to be most vulnerable. This part of the body is like the weak link in a chain; no matter what pulls the chain, good or bad, the chain breaks (Selye, "Stress Concept" 77).

17

A connection between the stress of common life events and illness was first demonstrated in a 1967 study. First, researchers assigned point values to 43 specific life events (divorce, illness, marriage, job loss). After collecting health histories, the researchers asked their subjects to total the points for recent events in their lives. (The scale ranged from 100 points for the death of a spouse to 11

FIGURE 23.1
A research report in MLA style   *(Continued)*

15. *Tracing the causes:* Before Haley covers the disruptive situations that cause stress, she explains how the body reacts to such situations. We need this background to understand the later connection between life events and illness.

16. *Interpreting research findings:* This paragraph shows us that Haley is interpreting her material, not merely giving us a collection of findings to sort out for ourselves.

17. *Establishing the link:* Haley describes the major study that demonstrated the stress-illness connection. Again, she refers us to an appendix for details.

Haley   4

for a traffic violation—see Appendix B for a full listing.) Comparing the health histories to point totals, the researchers discovered that any group of life events totaling 150 or more points in one year was connected to a major illness (requiring a physician's care) for 93 percent of the subjects. And the harmful effects of a high point total lasted as long as two years (Holmes and Masuda 50–56).

Studies of college students confirm the stress-illness link. Even a collection of ordinary events in students' lives can place them in a danger category, as shown in Table 1:

TABLE 1: A Life-Events Scale for College Students

Event	Points	Event	Points
Beginning or ending of school	26	Change in church activities	19
Change in living conditions	25	Change in social activities	18
Revision of personal habits	24	Loan of less than $10,000	17
Change in work hours or conditions	20	Change in sleeping habits	16
Change in residence	20	Change in eating habits	15

Source: Adapted from Holmes and Rahe, Table 3:216.

The life events in Table 1 alone total 200 points—disregarding any other points students collect from out-of-school experiences. One recent study shows that even "computer technology hassles" are a major source of stress—even among experienced computer users (Ballance and Ballance 682).

More than half the medical students in one study "experienced major health changes" within two years after entering school. A college life-events scale was given to 54 incoming first-year medical students; those with the highest scores reported most illness before the end of the second year (Holmes and Masuda 64). The stress of starting school can strongly affect one's health.

FIGURE 23.1
A research report in MLA style   (*Continued*)

18. *Focusing on college students:* Haley now interprets her general findings in specific relation to college students, leading into a detailed discussion of studies on college students.

19. *Using visuals:* Haley chooses a table for her numerical data. She numbers the table, introduces it, cites her source, and interprets the data for her readers. Tables longer than one text page would go in an appendix (see pages 8–10). Other visuals (charts, graphs, diagrams, maps, photos) can provide concrete and vivid illustrations.

20. *Citing sources selectively:* Rather than listing all studies confirming the stress-illness link, Haley is *selective*, giving us only what we need.

In a related study, Holmes and Masuda found a connection between life changes and the number of injuries sustained by 100 college football players. High scores on the life-change survey equaled more injuries on the field. Of the ten players who had multiple injuries, seven were from the group with highest scores in the life-events survey (66).

21

Recent findings suggest that outside pressure to succeed in college causes far more stress than self-imposed pressure. In a 1995 study of Japanese college students, Ohtani and Sakurai found that "socially-prescribed perfectionism" was a potent stress producer while self-oriented perfectionism was not. Self-motivated students apparently are better off than those who merely try to please others.

22

One major study suggests that stress-induced illness can be self-perpetuating, that symptoms initiated by stressful events can help create further stressful events: "For example, divorce of one's parents may lead to symptoms of depression [anxiety, insomnia, loss of appetite, hopelessness, etc.], which in turn may lead to disruption of interpersonal relationships and poor performance in school" (Compas 242). Merely treating the symptoms—without confronting the causes—traps many students in this cycle of stress and illness.

23

Possible Solutions

24

Because stress is unlikely to disappear, our only solution is to learn to cope. "It is our ability to cope with the demands made by the events in our lives, not the quality or intensity of the events, that counts. What matters is not so much what happens to us, but the way we take it" (Selye, "Stress Concept" 83). And "the way we take it" has a lot to do with heredity, with the coping strategies we've learned, and with the helping resources available to us now.

Without coping mechanisms, we are likely to be overwhelmed. Richard Lazarus of the University of California at Berkeley suggests: "coping is the core

FIGURE 23.1
A research report in MLA style   (*Continued*)

21.   *Citing an abstract:* No page numbers are given because the source is merely an abstract.

22.   *Transition:* Haley's transitional sentence sums up the causes and leads into her final discussion of solutions.

23.   *Arriving at solutions:* Haley's reasoning in this part proceeds from the importance of coping, to specific coping strategies, to students' coping needs, to programs designed to help students cope. She has *shaped* her material to clarify her thought.

24.   *Punctuating quotations.* Commas and periods following a quotation belong inside the quotation marks. Any other punctuation belongs outside the quotation marks—unless it belongs to the quoted material itself *(What did he mean when he said "I'm through"? or His response was "I'm through!")*.

Haley   6

25
26

problem [of stress]," and George Vaillant of Harvard speculates that "stress does not kill us so much as ingenious adaptation to stress . . . facilitates our survival" (Adler and Gosnell 108).

For students, coping depends on realistic expectations of college life. A 1984 counseling study at Kansas State University found that students tend to be unrealistic about their chances of succeeding in college. They suffer from what Levine calls the Titanic Ethic: "They see doom in the world around them but still feel they [personally] will somehow survive" (qtd. in Newton 541). Students are so certain of survival, they make few plans for coping with anticipated problems; instead they rely on the hope that problems will take care of themselves (Newton 540–42).

27

28

To help students avoid shattered expectations, college orientation should be more realistic. Newton suggests that, besides playing games, registering, testing, and waving goodbye until fall, orientation should include stress-management counseling and a no-nonsense look at all sides of college life (541).

Realistic approaches to college life also must include the effective use of leisure time. Stanford's Dr. Martinez emphasizes the importance, during stressful periods, of persisting with activities that do us good, such as exercise (Nikravesh). A recent study shows that students who know how to relax through recreational activities (hobbies, sports, exercise groups) report reduced feelings of stress (Mounir and McKinney 7–9). Meditation training seems particularly effective in stress reduction (Janowiak and Hackman 108–09).

Some schools now offer credit courses in stress management. For example, University of Minnesota counselor John Romano offers "Psychology and the Management of Stress." The course's goal is to "teach students how to implement personal change strategies before emotional and physical crises develop." Focus is on three areas: diet, exercise, and life-style (Romano 533–34). In all three areas, students learn to accept responsibility for changing their lives.

FIGURE 23.1
A research report in MLA style   (*Continued*)

25. *Using brackets in quotations:* To clarify some quotations, Haley inserts a word or phrase in brackets. The brackets signal that the writer has altered the original quotation; the bracketed comments are Haley's, not the author's.

26. *Using ellipses in quotations:* Haley uses ellipses (. . .) to shorten otherwise long quotations. In fact, no quotation in the report is more than a few lines long. A research report does not merely catalog other people's ideas and words. Instead, writers give this material their own concise shape—without distorting the original information.

A quotation of more than four typewritten lines would have been indented ten spaces and double-spaced, without quotation marks.

27. *Quoting an indirect source:* In her research, Haley came across a key phrase—"the Titanic Ethic"—to characterize college students. But Haley's source quoted this phrase from another source, and her source gave no page number from the original. Unable to trace the original, Haley includes the abbreviation "qtd."—for "quoted in"—in the parenthetical citation of her indirect source. As we will see, she includes the indirect source (Newton) in her Works Cited list.

28. *Paraphrased and summarized material:* To save space and improve coherence, Haley paraphrases and summarizes throughout her report. (See pages 334 and 336 for guidelines.) Here is the original passage for this paraphrase:

> Selective blindness may be a more difficult illness to prevent when the fantasy vision may seem more pleasant than reality. As a recommendation, to shock students into an awareness of reality now may be more beneficial than the rude awakening of tomorrow. So far, the best suggestion is to conduct "future shock" and "future cope" workshops that confront students with situations and problems that will need to be resolved. Perhaps, orientation programs should strive to show more of the realities of college life rather than the present-day programs of welcoming, testing, registering, and saying "I'll see you in the fall."

Haley   7

To teach students how to cope with stress and learn to relax, the University of California at Irvine offers a "stress lab." Here, students find warm surroundings, homelike furniture, literature, videotapes, interactive stress-reduction programs, and even a biofeedback machine (Murray).

These are a mere sample of the resources now available to students under stress. A quick Internet search reveals that many colleges now offer web sites with all sorts of information on stress reduction.

29

In conclusion, although stress in college is unavoidable, it can be managed. Stress-management training should be offered to all students, to make them aware of the realities of college life and of their responsibility for their own well-being. All students should make it a point to explore the resources offered by their schools. As the research clearly shows, students who do learn to manage stress will be less likely to find that college makes them sick.

FIGURE 23.1
A research report in MLA style   (*Continued*)

29. *Conclusion:* Haley's closing suggestions are keyed specifically to her thesis, summarizing and rounding out the discussion and reemphasizing the major points.

Haley   8

30

Appendix A: Warning Signals of Stress

Stress has definite warning signals, emotional and physical. Here are the commonest:

Emotional Signs of Stress

- being emotionally very "up" or very "down"
- impulsive behavior and emotional instability
- uncontrollable urge to cry or run away
- inability to concentrate
- feelings of unreality
- loss of "joy of life"
- feeling "keyed up"
- being easily startled
- nightmares; insomnia
- a general sense of anxiety or dread

Physical Signs of Stress

- pounding heart (may indicate high blood pressure)
- constantly dry throat and mouth
- weakness; dizziness
- feelings of tiredness
- trembling; nervous tics
- high-pitched, nervous laughter
- grinding of teeth
- constant aimless motion
- excessive perspiring
- diarrhea; indigestion; queasy stomach
- headaches
- pain in the neck or lower back (because of muscle tension)
- excessive or lost appetite
- proneness to accidents

Source: Adapted from Selye, The Stress of Life: 175.

FIGURE 23.1
A research report in MLA style   (*Continued*)

30. *Appendices* (this and the next two pages): An appendix is a catchall for material that is important but difficult to integrate into the body of a report. Appendices might include:

- details of an experiment
- specific measurements
- maps
- quotations longer than one page of text
- photographs
- long lists or visuals using more than one full page
- texts of laws, regulations, literary passages, and so on

But readers should not have to turn to appendices to understand the report. Haley distills the essentials from her appendices and includes them in the main text.

Each appendix is labeled clearly, with a separate one for each major item. Appendices appear at the end of the text but before the Works Cited pages.

Appendix B: Stress Values of Common Life Events

In their 1967 study, Holmes and Rahe ranked life events in descending order according to their stress value. This table shows the rating scale.

Social Readjustment Rating Scale

Rank	Life Event	Mean Value
1	Death of spouse	100
2	Divorce	73
3	Marital separation from mate	65
4	Detention in jail or other institution	63
5	Death of a close family member	63
6	Major personal injury or illness	53
7	Marriage	50
8	Being fired at work	47
9	Marital reconciliation with mate	45
10	Retirement from work	45
11	Major change in the health or behavior of a family member	44
12	Pregnancy	40
13	Sexual difficulties	39
14	Getting a new family member (e.g., through birth, adoption, oldster moving in, etc.)	39
15	Major business readjustment (e.g., merger, reorganization, bankruptcy, etc.)	39
16	Major change in financial state (e.g., a lot worse off or a lot better off than usual)	38
17	Death of a close friend	37
18	Changing to a different line of work	36
19	Major change in the number of arguments with spouse (e.g., either a lot more or a lot less than usual regarding child rearing, personal habits, etc.)	35
20	Taking out a mortgage or loan for a major purchase (e.g., for a home, business, etc.)	31
21	Foreclosure on a mortgage or loan	30
22	Major change in responsibilities at work (e.g., promotion, demotion, lateral transfer)	29
23	Son or daughter leaving home (e.g., marriage, attending college, etc.)	29
24	Trouble with in-laws	29

FIGURE 23.1
A research report in MLA style   (*Continued*)

Haley   10

Appendix B: (Continued)

Social Readjustment Rating Scale

Rank	Life Event	Mean Value
25	Outstanding personal achievement	28
26	Wife beginning or ceasing work outside the home	26
27	Beginning or ceasing formal schooling	26
28	Major change in living conditions (e.g., building a new home, remodeling, deterioration of home or neighborhood)	25
29	Revision of personal habits (dress, manners, associations, etc.)	24
30	Trouble with the boss	23
31	Major change in working hours or conditions	20
32	Change in residence	20
33	Changing to a new school	20
34	Major change in usual type and/or amount of recreation	19
35	Major change in church activities (e.g., a lot more or a lot less than usual)	19
36	Major change in social activities (e.g., clubs, dancing, movies, visiting, etc.)	18
37	Taking out a mortgage or loan for a lesser purchase (e.g., for a car, TV, freezer, etc.)	17
38	Major change in sleeping habits (a lot more or a lot less sleep, or change in part of day when asleep)	16
39	Major change in number of family get-togethers (e.g., a lot more or a lot less than usual)	15
40	Major change in eating habits (a lot more or a lot less food intake, or very different meal hours or surroundings)	15
41	Vacation	13
42	Christmas	12
43	Minor violations of the law (e.g., traffic tickets, jaywalking, disturbing the peace, etc.)	11

Source: "The Social Readjustment Scale": 216.

FIGURE 23.1
A research report in MLA style   (*Continued*)

Haley   11

31

Works Cited

32 Adler, Jerry, and Mariana Gosnell. "Stress: How It Can Hurt." Newsweek 21 Apr.

1980: 106–08.   *[magazine article]*

33 Ballance, C. T., and V. V. Ballance. "Relating Self-Rated Computer Experience to

Computer Stress." Psychological Reports 72.2 (1993): 680–82. MEDLINE.

Online. DIALOG. 8 Nov. 1996.   *[journal article from online database]*

Bower, Bruce. "Setting the Stage for Infection." Science News 26 Aug. 1989: 141.

Brooks, Andre A. "Educating the Children of Fast-Track Parents." Phi Delta Kappan

April 1990: 612–15.

34 Cacioppo, John T. "Stress: Interplay between Social and Biological Processes." 18

Dec. 1995. Online posting. 8 Nov. 1996. Available WWW:

http://www.acs.ohio-state,edu/units/psych/s-psych/jtc.html   *[web site]*

35 Cage, Mary C. "Students Face Pressures as Never Before, But Counseling Help Has

Withered." Chronicle of Higher Education 18 Nov. 1992, Sec A: 2.

[newspaper article]

Compas, Bruce E., et al. "A Prospective Study of Life Events, Social Support, and

Psychological Symptomatology During the Transition from High School to

College." American Journal of Community Psychology 14 (1986): 241–56.

[journal article from print source]

36 Dohrenwend, Barbara Snell, and Bruce Dohrenwend, eds. Stressful Life Events:

Their Nature and Effects. New York: Wiley, 1974.

37 Holmes, Thomas H., and Minoru Masuda. "Life Change and Illness Susceptibility."

Dohrenwend and Dohrenwend. 45–72.

FIGURE 23.1
A research report in MLA style   (*Continued*)

31. *Works Cited* (including the continuation on the next page): One inch from the top of the page is the centered heading "Works Cited." Two spaces below the heading is the first entry. Each entry is double spaced, with second and subsequent lines indented five spaces from the left margin. Entries are in alphabetical order, with double spacing between them. The Works Cited section follows the numbering of the text pages.

32. Article titles appear in quotation marks; book or periodical titles are underlined or italicized. All key words in the title are capitalized. Articles, prepositions, or conjunctions are capitalized only if they come first or last. Three-letter abbreviations denote months having five or more letters. Volume numbers for magazines are not cited. No punctuation separates magazine title and date.

33. An entry for an online database or any electronic source that is updated periodically should include your date of access (as in "8 Nov.").

34. A citation for a web source begins with the author's name (if known), followed by the work's title (in quotations marks), the posting date, the "online" designation, and the user's access data. No closing punctuation appears after the web address.

35. Omit the introductory article ("The") in the newspaper's name.

36. In this collection of essays by various authors, the editors also are the authors of the introduction to the anthology.

37. Since this essay appears in an anthology cited elsewhere in this list (i.e., Dohrenwend and Dohrenwend) the only information needed is the editor's name and the page numbers.

Holmes, Thomas H., and R. H. Rahe. "The Social Readjustment Scale." Journal of
    Psychosomatic Research 11 (1967): 213–18.

Janowiak, J. J., and R. Hackman. "Meditation and College Students' Self-
    Actualization and Rated Stress." Psychological Reports 75.2 (1994):
    1007–10.

Levine, A. When Dreams and Heroes Died: A Portrait of Today's College Student.
    San Francisco: Jossey, 1980.   *[book—one author]*

Mounir, Raghet, and Jennifer McKinney. "Campus Recreation and Perceived
    Academic Stress." Journal of College Student Development 34.1 (1993):
    5–10.

38 Murray, Bridget. "University 'Stress Lab' Helps Students Unwind." APA Monitor
    March 1996: n. pag. Online. 11 Nov. 1996. Available WWW:
    http://www.apa.org/monitor/mar96/stress.html

39 Newton, Fred B., et al. "The Assessment of College Student Needs: First Step in a
    Prevention Response." Personnel and Guidance Journal 62 (1984): 537–43.

40 Nikravesh, Bita, "Stress in College." National Student News Service 16 Feb. 1996:
    n. pag. Online. 10 Nov. 1996. Available WWW:
    http://acs5.gac.peachnet.edu/~colonade/1996/021396/college-stress.html

                                                        [electronic publication]

41 Ohtani, Y., and S. Sakurai. "Relationship of Perfectionism to Depression and
    Hopelessness in College Students." Shiriqaku Kenkyu 66.1 (1995): 41–47.
    Abstract. Trans. MEDLINE. Online. DIALOG. 9 Nov. 1996.   *[online abstract]*

Romano, John L. "Stress Management and Wellness: Reaching Beyond the
    Counselor's Office." Personnel and Guidance Journal 62 (1984): 533–36.

FIGURE 23.1
A research report in MLA style   (*Continued*)

38. Although this online article has a printed equivalent, "n. pag." denotes that this web source provided no page numbers.

39. An entry for a work with four or more authors or editors cites only the first person's name, followed by "et al."

40. An electronic publication has no printed equivalent.

41. Here Haley cites merely the abstract, translated from an article in Japanese. Note the "Abstract" designation, followed by "Trans." Since there are no page numbers Haley avoids a parenthetical citation by naming the authors in her discussion (page "5").

42 Selye, Hans. "The Stress Concept: Past, Present, and Future." <u>Stress Research:</u>

<u>Issues for the 80's</u>. Ed. Cary L. Cooper. Chichester, England: Wiley, 1983:

69–87.   *[article, anthology]*

43 ---. <u>The Stress of Life</u>. Rev. ed. New York: McGraw, 1976.

44 Tyrell, Jeanne. "Sources of Stress among Psychology Undergraduates." <u>Irish</u>

<u>Journal of Psychology</u> 13.2 (1992): 184–92.

45 White, Jaquelyn W., and John A. Humphrey. "Sexual Revictimization: A

Longitudinal Perspective." Paper Presented at the 101st Annual Meeting of

the American Psychological Association, 20–24 Aug. 1993. Toronto, Ontario.

Abstract. <u>ERIC</u>. CD-ROM. SilverPlatter. 3 Sept. 1996. ERIC Item: ED 374 363.

[conference paper—CD-ROM abstract]

FIGURE 23.1
A research report in MLA style   (*Continued*)

42. An entry for an article in a collection of works compiled by an editor.

43. An entry for a revised edition of a book. Books with no edition number on the title page are cited as first editions. Otherwise, the edition is identified by number, name, or year, as given on the title page. Shorten publishers' names ("McGraw" for "McGraw-Hill" or "Harper" for "HarperCollins"). Also, multiple works by the same author are listed alphabetically according to title. Three hyphens followed by a period denote a second work by the same author.

44. For page numbers with more than two digits, type only the final two digits of the second number.

45. A citation for a CD-ROM database that is updated often should include the date of electronic publication for that particular disk (as in "3 Sept. 1996"). The "Abstract" designation shows that Haley is citing merely the abstract of this conference presentation.

EDITING FOR GRAMMAR, PUNCTUATION, AND MECHANICS

*T*he rear endsheets display editing and revision symbols and their page references. When your instructor marks a symbol on your paper, turn to the appropriate section for explanations and examples.

COMMON SENTENCE ERRORS

The following common sentence errors are easy to repair.

frag

SENTENCE FRAGMENT

A sentence expresses a logically complete idea. Any complete idea must contain a subject and a verb and must not depend on another complete idea to make sense. Your sentence might contain several complete ideas, but it must contain at least one!

> *[incomplete idea]*   *[complete idea]*   *[complete idea]*
> Although Mary was injured, she grabbed the line, and she saved the boat.

Omitting some essential element (the subject, the verb, or another complete idea), leaves only a piece of a sentence—a *fragment*.

> Grabbed the line. [*a fragment because it lacks a subject*]
>
> Although Mary was injured. [*a fragment because—although it contains a subject and a verb—it needs to be joined with a complete idea to make sense*]
>
> Sam an electronics technician.

This last statement leaves the reader asking, "What about Sam the electronics technician?" The verb—the word that makes things happen—is missing. Adding a verb changes this fragment to a complete sentence.

Simple verb	Sam **is** an electronics technician.
Verb plus adverb	Sam, an electronics technician, **works hard.**
Dependent clause, verb, and subjective complement	**Although he is well paid,** Sam, an electronics technician, **is not happy.**

Do not, however, mistake the following statement—which seems to contain a verb—for a complete sentence:

> Sam being an electronics technician.

Such "-ing" forms do not function as verbs unless accompanied by such other verbs as **is, was,** and **will be.**

> **Sam,** being an electronics technician, **was responsible for checking the circuitry.**

Likewise, the "to + verb" form (infinitive) is not a verb.

Fragment   To become an electronics technician.

Complete   To become an electronics technician, **Sam had to complete a two-year apprenticeship.**

Sometimes we inadvertently create fragments by adding certain words (**because, since, it, although, while, unless, until, when, where,** and others) to an already complete sentence.

> **Although** Sam is an electronics technician.

Such words subordinate the words that follow them; that is, they make the statement dependent on an additional idea, which must itself have a subject and a verb and be a complete sentence. (See also "Subordination"—pages 114–115.) We can complete the subordinate statement by adding an independent clause.

> Although Sam is an electronics technician, **he hopes to become an electrical engineer.**

Note: Because the incomplete idea (dependent clause) depends on the complete idea (independent clause) for its meaning, you need only a *pause* (symbolized by a comma), not a *break* (symbolized by a semicolon). Here are some fragments from students' writing. Each is repaired in two ways. Can you think of other ways of making these statements complete?

Fragment   She spent her first week on the job as a researcher. **Selecting and compiling technical information from digests and journals.**

Revised   She spent her first week on the job as a researcher, selecting and compiling technical information from digests and journals.

In her first week on the job as a researcher, she selected and compiled technical information from digests and journals.

Fragment	**Because the operator was careless.** The new computer was damaged.
Revised	Because the operator was careless, the new computer was damaged.
	The operator was careless; as a result, the new computer was damaged.
Fragment	**When each spool is in place.** Advance your film.
Revised	When each spool is in place, advance your film.
	Be sure that each spool is in place before advancing your film.

ACCEPTABLE FRAGMENTS

A fragmented sentence is acceptable in commands or exclamations because the subject ("you") is understood.

Acceptable fragments	Slow down.
	Give me a hand.
	Look out!

Also, questions and answers sometimes are expressed as incomplete sentences.

Acceptable fragments	How? By investing wisely.
	When? At three o'clock.
	Who? Bill.

In general, however, avoid fragments unless you have good reason to use one for special tone or emphasis.

APPLICATION A-1

Correct these sentence fragments by rewriting each in two ways.

1. Fred is a terrible math student. But an excellent writer.
2. As they entered the haunted house. The floors began to groan.
3. Hoping for a A in biology. Sally studied every night.
4. Although many students flunk out of this college. Its graduates find excellent jobs.
5. Three teenagers out of every ten have some sort of addiction. Whether it is to alcohol or drugs.

cs

COMMA SPLICE

In a comma splice, two complete ideas (independent clauses), which should be *separated* by a period or a semicolon, are incorrectly *joined* by a comma:

| Sarah did a great job, she was promoted.

You can choose among several possibilities for repair:

1. Substitute a period followed by a capital letter:

| Sarah did a great job. She was promoted.

2. Substitute a semicolon to signal a relationship between the two items:

| Sarah did a great job; she was promoted.

3. Use a semicolon with a connecting adverb (a transitional word):

| Sarah did a great job; **consequently,** she was promoted.

4. Use a subordinating word to make the less important clause incomplete, thereby dependent on the other:

| **Because** Sarah did a great job, she was promoted.

5. Add a connecting word after the comma:

| Sarah did a great job, **and** she was promoted.

The following revisions show that your choice of construction will depend on the exact meaning or tone you wish to convey:

Comma splice	This is a fairly new product, therefore, some people don't trust it.
Revised	This is a fairly new product. Some people don't trust it.
	This is a fairly new product; therefore, some people don't trust it.
	Because this is a fairly new product, some people don't trust it.
Comma splice	Ms. Gomez was a strick supervisor, she was well liked by her employees.

Revised	Ms. Gomez was a strict supervisor. She was well liked by her employees.
	Ms. Gomez was a strict supervisor; **however,** she was well liked by her employees.
	Although Ms. Gomez was a strict supervisor, she was well liked by her employees.
	Ms. Gomez was a strict supervisor, **but** she was well liked by her employees.

APPLICATION A-2

Correct these comma splices by rewriting each in two ways.

1. Efforts are being made to halt water pollution, however, there is no simple solution to the problem.
2. Bill slept through his final, he had forgotten to set his alarm.
3. Ellen must be a genius, she never studies yet always gets A's.
4. We arrived at the picnic late, there were no hamburgers left.
5. My part-time job is excellent, it pays well, provides good experience, and offers a real challenge.

RUN-ON SENTENCE

ro

The run-on sentence, a cousin to the comma splice, crams too many ideas without needed breaks or pauses.

Run-on	The hourglass is more accurate than the waterclock for the water in a waterclock must always be at the same temperature in order to flow with the same speed since water evaporates it must be replenished at regular intervals thus not being as effective in measuring time as the hourglass.
Revised	The hourglass is more accurate than the waterclock because water in a waterclock must always be at the same temperature to flow at the same speed. Also, water evaporates and must be replenished at regular intervals. These temperature and volume problems make the waterclock less effective than the hourglass in measuring time.

APPLICATION A-3

Revise these run-on sentences.

1. The gale blew all day by evening the sloop was taking on water.
2. Jennifer felt hopeless about passing English however the writing center helped her complete the course.
3. The professor glared at John he had been dozing in the back row.
4. Our drama club produces three plays a year I love the opening nights.
5. Pets should not be allowed on our campus they are messy and sometimes dangerous.

FAULTY AGREEMENT—SUBJECT AND VERB

The subject should agree in number with the verb. Faulty agreement seldom occurs in short sentences, where subject and verb are not far apart: "Jack eat too much" instead of "Jack eats too much." But when the subject is separated from its verb by other words, we sometimes lose track of the subject-verb relationship.

> **Faulty**   The lion's **share** of diesels **are** sold in Europe.

Although **diesels** is closest to the verb, the subject is **share,** a singular subject that needs a singular verb.

> **Revised**   The lion's **share** of diesels **is** sold in Europe.

Agreement errors are easy to correct once subject and verb are identified.

> **Faulty**   There **is** an estimated 29,000 **women** living in our city.
> **Revised**   There **are** an estimated 29,000 **women** living in our city.
> **Faulty**   A **system** of lines **extend** horizontally to form a grid.
> **Revised**   A **system** of lines **extends** horizontally to form a grid.

A second problem with subject-verb agreement occurs with indefinite subject pronouns such as **each, everyone, anybody,** and **somebody.** They usually take a singular verb.

> **Faulty**   **Each** of the crew members **were** injured during the storm.
> **Revised**   **Each** of the crew members **was** injured during the storm.
> **Faulty**   **Everyone** in the group **have** practiced long hours.
> **Revised**   **Everyone** in the group **has** practiced long hours.

Collective nouns such as **herd, family, union, group, army, team, committee,** and **board** can call for a singular or plural verb, depending on your intended meaning. When denoting the group as a whole, use a singular verb.

> **Correct**   The **committee meets** weekly to discuss new business.
>
> The editorial **board** of this magazine **has** high standards.

To denote individual members of the group, use a plural verb.

> **Correct**   The **committee disagree** on whether to hire Jim.
>
> The editorial **board are** all published authors.

When two subjects are joined by **either . . . or** or **neither . . . nor,** the verb is singular if both subjects are singular and plural if both subjects are plural. If one subject is plural and one is singular, the verb agrees with the one closer to the verb.

> **Correct**   Neither **John** nor **Bill works** regularly.
>
> Either **apples** or **oranges are** good vitamin sources.
>
> Either Felix or his **friends are** crazy.
>
> Neither the boys nor their **father likes** the home team.

If, on the other hand, two subjects (singular, plural, or mixed) are joined by **both . . . and,** the verb will be plural.

> **Correct**   **Both** Joe and Bill **are** resigning.

A single **and** between subjects makes for a plural subject.

Faulty Agreement—Pronoun and Referent

agr p

A pronoun must refer to a specific noun (its referent or antecedent), with which it must agree in gender and number.

> **Correct**   **Jane** lost **her** book.
>
> The **students** complained that **they** had been treated unfairly.

When an indefinite pronoun such as **each, everyone, anybody, someone,** or **none** serves as the pronoun referent, the pronoun is singular.

> **Correct**   **Anyone** can get **his** degree from that college.
>
> **Anyone** can get **his** or **her** degree from that college.
>
> **Each** candidate described **her** plans in detail.

APPLICATION A-4

Revise these sentences to make their subjects and verbs agree in number or their pronouns and referents agree in gender and number.

1. Ten years ago the mineral rights to this land was sold to a mining company.
2. Each of the students in our dorm have a serious complaint about living conditions.
3. Neither the students nor the instructor like this classroom.
4. Neither Fred nor Mary expect to pass this course.
6. Anyone wanting to enhance their career should take a computer course.

FAULTY PRONOUN CASE

ca

A pronoun's case (nominative, objective, or possessive) is determined by its role in the sentence: as subject, object, or indicator of possession.

If the pronoun serves as the subject of a sentence (**I, we, you, she, he, it, they, who**), its case is *nominative*.

> **She** completed her graduate program in record time.
>
> **Who** broke the chair?

When a pronoun follows a version of the verb **to be** (a linking verb), it explains (complements) the subject, and so its case is nominative.

> The killer was **she.**
>
> The professor who perfected our new distillation process is **he.**

If the pronoun serves as the object of a verb or a preposition (**me, us, you, her, him, it, them, whom**), its case is *objective*.

Object of the verb   The employees gave **her** a parting gift.

Object of the preposition   To **whom** do you wish to complain?

If a pronoun indicates possession (**my, mine, our, ours, yours, yours, his, her, hers, its, their, whose**), its case is *possessive*.

The brown briefcase is **mine.**

Her offer was accepted.

Whose opinion do you value most?

Here are some frequent errors in pronoun case:

Faulty	**Whom** is responsible to **who?** [*The subject should be nominative and the object should be objective.*]
Revised	**Who** is responsible to **whom?**
Faulty	The debate was between Marsha and **I.** [*As object of the preposition, the pronoun should be objective.*]
Revised	The debate was between Marsha and **me.**
Faulty	**Us** students are accountable for our decisions. [*The pronoun accompanies the subject, "students," and thus should be nominative.*]
Revised	**We** students are accountable for our decisions.
Faulty	A group of **we** students will fly to California. [*The pronoun accompanies the object of the preposition, "students," and thus should be objective.*]
Revised	A group of **us** students will fly to California.

Deleting the accompanying noun from the two latter examples reveals the correct pronoun case ("We . . . are accountable . . ."; "A group of us . . . will fly . . .").

....

APPLICATION A-5

Select the appropriate pronoun case from each of these pairs (in parentheses).

1. By (who, whom) was the job offer made?
2. The argument was among Bill, Terry, and (I, me).
3. A committee of (we, us) concerned citizens is working to make our neighborhood safer.
4. (Us, we) students are being hurt by federal cuts in loan programs.
5. The liar is (he, him).

shift

SENTENCE SHIFTS

Shifts in point of view damage coherence. If you begin a sentence or paragraph with one subject or person, do not shift to another.

Shift in person	When **one** finishes such a great book, **you** will have a sense of achievement.
Revised	When **you** finish such a great book, **you** will have a sense of achievement.
Shift in number	**One** should sift the flour before **they** make the pie.
Revised	**One** should sift the flour before **one** makes the pie. *(Or better: Sift the flour before making the pie.)*

Do not begin a sentence in the active voice and then shift to the passive voice.

| Shift in voice | **He** delivered the plans for the apartment complex, and the building site **was also inspected by him.** |
| Revised | He **delivered** the plans for the apartment complex and also **inspected** the building site. |

Do not shift tenses without good reason.

| Shift in tense | She **delivered** the blueprints, **inspected** the foundation, **wrote** her report, and **takes** the afternoon off. |
| Revised | She **delivered** the blueprints, **inspected** the foundation, **wrote** her report, and **took** the afternoon off. |

Do not shift from one verb mood to another (as from imperative to indicative mood in a set of instructions).

| Shift in mood | **Unscrew** the valve and then steel wool **should be used** to clean the fittings. |
| Revised | **Unscrew** the valve and then **use** steel wool to clean the fitting. |

APPLICATION A-6

Revise these sentences to eliminate shifts in person, mood, voice, tense, or number.

1. People should keep themselves politically informed; otherwise, you will not be living up to your democratic responsibilities.
2. Barbara made the Dean's List and the Junior Achievement award was also won by her.

3. As soon as he walked into his dorm room, George sees the mess left by his roommate.

4. When one is being stalked by a bear, you should not snack on sardines.

5. First loosen the lug nuts; then you should jack up the car.

EFFECTIVE PUNCTUATION

pct

Punctuation marks are like road signs and traffic signals. They govern reading speed and provide clues for navigation through a network of ideas; they mark intersections, detours, and road repairs; they draw attention to points of interest along the route; and they mark geographic boundaries.

Let's review the four used most often. These marks can be ranked in order of their relative strengths.

1. *Period.* A period signals a complete stop at the end of an independent idea (independent clause). The first word in the idea following the period begins with a capital letter.

   Jack is a fat cat. His friends urge him to diet.

2. *Semicolon.* A semicolon signals a brief stop after an independent idea but does not end the sentence; instead, it announces that the forthcoming independent idea is **closely related** to the preceding idea.

   Jack is a fat cat; he eats too much.

3. *Colon.* A colon usually follows an independent idea and, like the semicolon, signals a brief stop but does not end the sentence. The colon and semicolon, however, are never interchangeable. A colon symbolizes "explanation to follow." Information after the colon (which need not be an independent idea) explains or clarifies the idea expressed before the colon.

   Jack is a fat cat: he weighs forty pounds. [*The information after the colon answers "How fat?"*]

   or

   Jack is a fat cat: forty pounds worth! [*The second clause is not independent.*]

4. *Comma.* The weakest of these four marks, a comma signals only a pause within or between ideas in the sentence. A comma often indicates that the word, phrase, or clause set off from the independent idea cannot stand alone but must rely on the independent idea for its meaning.

Jack, a fat cat, is a jolly fellow.

Although he diets often, Jack is a fat cat.

A comma is used between two independent clauses only if accompanied by a coordinating conjunction (**and, but, or, nor, yet**).

Comma splice	Jack is a party animal, he is loved everywhere.
Correct	Jack is a party animal, **and** he is loved everywhere.

END PUNCTUATION

The three marks of end punctuation—period, question mark, and exclamation point—work like a red traffic light by signaling a complete stop.

Period A period ends a sentence and is the final mark in some abbreviations.

Ms.	Assn.	N.Y.
M.D.	Inc.	B.A.

Periods serve as decimal points for numbers.

$15.95

21.4%

Question Mark A question mark follows a direct question.

Where is the essay that was due today?

Do not use a question mark to end an indirect question.

Faulty	Professor Grim asked if all students had completed the essay?
Revised	Professor Grim asked if all students had completed the essay.
	or
	Professor Grim asked, "Did all students complete the essay?"

Exclamation Point Use an exclamation point only when expression of strong feeling is appropriate.

Appropriate	Oh, no!
	Pay up!

SEMICOLON

; /

Like a blinking red traffic light at an intersection, a semicolon signals a brief but definite stop.

Semicolons Separating Independent Clauses Semicolons separate independent clauses (logically complete ideas) whose contents are closely related and are not connected by a coordinating conjunction.

> The project was finally completed; we had done a good week's work.

The semicolon can replace the conjunction-comma combination that joins two independent ideas.

> The project was finally completed, and we were elated.
> The project was finally completed; we were elated.

The second version emphasizes the sense of elation.

Semicolons Used with Adverbs as Conjunctions and Other Transitional Expressions Semicolons must accompany conjunctive adverbs like **besides, otherwise, still, however, furthermore, moreover, consequently, therefore, on the other hand, in contrast,** or **in fact.**

> The job is filled; however, we will keep your résumé on file.
> Your background is impressive; in fact, it is the best among our applicants.

Semicolons Separating Items in a Series When items in a series contain internal commas, semicolons provide clear separation between items.

> I am applying for summer jobs in Santa Fe, New Mexico; Albany, New York; Montgomery, Alabama, and Moscow, Idaho.
> Members of the survey crew were Juan Jimenez, a geologist; Hector Lightfoot, a surveyor; and Mary Shelley, a graduate student.

COLON

: /

Like a flare in the road, a colon signals you to stop and then proceed, paying attention to the situation ahead. Usually a colon follows an introductory statement that requires a follow-up explanation.

> We need this equipment immediately: a voltmeter, a portable generator, and three pairs of insulated gloves.
> She is an ideal colleague: honest, reliable, and competent.

Except for salutations in formal correspondence (e.g., Dear Ms. Jones:) colons follow independent (logically and grammatically complete) statements.

> **Faulty**   My plans include: finishing college, traveling for two years, and settling down in Sante Fe.

No punctuation should follow "include."
Colons can introduce quotations.

> The supervisor's message was clear enough: "You're fired."

A colon can replace a semicolon between two related, complete statements when the second one explains or amplifies the first.

> Pam's reason for accepting the lowest-paying job offer was simple: she had always wanted to live in the Northwest.

APPLICATION A-7

Insert semicolons or colons as needed in these expressions.

1. June had finally arrived it was time to graduate.
2. I have two friends who are like brothers Sam and Daniel.
3. Joe did not get the job however, he was high on the list of finalists.
4. The wine was superb an 1898 Margaux.
5. Our student senators are Joan Blake, a geology major Helen Simms, a nursing major and Henry Drew, an English major.

Comma

The comma is the most frequently used—and abused—punctuation mark. It works like a blinking yellow traffic light, for which you slow down briefly without stopping. Never use a comma to signal a *break* between independent ideas.

Comma as a Pause Between Complete Ideas   In a compound sentence in which a coordinating conjunction (**and, or, nor, for, but**) connects equal (independent) statements, a comma usually precedes the conjunction.

> This is an excellent course, **but** the work is difficult.

Comma as a Pause Between an Incomplete and a Complete Idea A comma usually is placed between a complete and an incomplete statement in a complex sentence when the incomplete statement comes first.

> **Because he is a fat cat,** Jack diets often.
>
> **When he eats too much,** Jack gains weight.

When the order is reversed (complete idea followed by incomplete), the comma usually is omitted.

> Jack diets often **because he is a fat cat.**
>
> Jack gains weight **when he eats too much.**

Reading a sentence aloud should tell you whether or not to pause (and use a comma).

Commas Separating Items (Words, Phrases, or Clauses) in a Series Use commas after items in a series, including the next to last item.

> **Helen, Joe, Marsha,** and **John** are joining us on the term project.
>
> He works hard **at home, on the job,** and even **during his vacation.**
>
> The new employee complained **that the hours were long, that the pay was low, that the work was boring, and that the supervisor was paranoid.**

Use no commas if **or** or **and** appears between all items in a series.

> She is willing to study in San Francisco or Seattle or even in Anchorage.

Comma Setting Off Introductory Phrases Infinitive, prepositional, or verbal phrases introducing a sentence usually are set off by commas, as are interjections.

Infinitive phrase	**To be or not to be,** that is the question.
Prepositional phrase	**In Rome,** do as the Romans do.
Participial phrase	**Being fat,** Jack was slow at catching mice.
	Moving quickly, the army surrounded the enemy.
Interjection	**Oh, is** that the verdict?

Commas Setting Off Nonrestrictive Elements   A *restrictive* phrase or clause modifies or defines the subject in such a way that deleting the modifier would change the meaning of the sentence.

> All students **who have work experience** will receive preference.

Without **who have work experience,** which *restricts* the subject by limiting the category **students,** the meaning would be entirely different. All students will receive preference.

Because this phrase is essential to the sentence's meaning, it is *not* set off by commas.

A *nonrestrictive* phrase or clause could be deleted without changing the sentence's meaning and *is* set off by commas.

> Our new manager, **who has only six weeks' experience,** is highly competent.

> **Modifier deleted**   Our new manager is highly competent.

> This house, **riddled with carpenter ants,** is falling apart.

> **Modifier deleted**   This house is falling apart.

Commas Setting Off Parenthetical Elements   Items that interrupt the flow of a sentence (such as **of course, as a result, as I recall,** and **however**) are called parenthetical and are enclosed by commas. They may denote emphasis, afterthought, clarification, or transition.

> **Emphasis**   This deluxe model, **of course,** is more expensive.
>
> **Afterthought**   Your essay, **by the way,** was excellent.
>
> **Clarification**   The loss of my job was, **in a way,** a blessing.
>
> **Transition**   Our warranty, **however,** does not cover tire damage.

Direct address is parenthetical.

> Listen, **my children,** and you shall hear. . . .

A parenthetical expression at the beginning or the end of a sentence is set off by a comma.

> **Naturally,** we will expect a full guarantee.
>
> **My friends,** I think we have a problem.

You've done a good job, **Jim.**

Yes, you may use my name in your advertisement.

Commas Setting Off Quoted Material   Quoted items within a sentence are set off by commas.

The customer said, "I'll take it," as soon as he laid eyes on our new model.

Commas Setting Off Appositives   An appositive, a word or words explaining a noun and placed immediately after it, is set off by commas when the appositive is nonrestrictive. (See page 442.)

Martha Jones, **our new president,** is overhauling all personnel policies.

Alpha waves, **the most prominent of the brain waves,** typically are recorded in a waking subject whose eyes are closed.

Please make all checks payable to Sam Sawbuck, **school treasurer.**

Commas Used in Common Practice   Commas set off the day of the month from the year, in a date.

May 10, 1989

Commas set off numbers in three-digit intervals.

11,215

6,463,657

They also set off street, city, and state in an address.

Mail the bill to J. B. Smith, 18 Sea Street, Albany, Iowa 01642.

When the address is written vertically, however, the omitted commas are those which would otherwise occur at the end of each address line.

J. B. Smith

18 Sea Street

Albany, Iowa 01642

Commas set off an address or date in a sentence.

Room 3C, Margate Complex, is my summer address.

June 15, 1987, is my graduation date.

They set off degrees and titles from proper nouns.

> Roger P. Cayer, M.D.
>
> Gordon Browne, Jr.
>
> Sandra Mello, Ph.D.

Commas Used Erroneously Avoid needless or inappropriate commas. Read a sentence aloud to identify inappropriate pauses.

Faulty   The instructor told me, that I was late. [*separates the indirect from the direct object*]

The most universal symptom of the suicide impulse, is depression. [*separates the subject from its verb*]

This has been a long, difficult, semester. [*second comma separates the final adjective from its noun*]

John, Bill, and Sally, are joining us on the trip home. [*third comma separates the final subject from its verb*]

An employee, who expects rapid promotion, must quickly prove his or her worth. [*separates a modifier that should be restrictive*]

I spoke by phone with John, and Marsha. [*separates two nouns linked by a coordinating conjunction*]

The room was, 18 feet long. [*separates the linking verb from the subjective complement*]

We painted the room, red. [*separates the object from its complement*]

APPLICATION A-8

Insert commas where needed in these sentences.

1. In modern society highways seem as necessary as food water or air.
2. Everyone though frustrated by pollution can play a part in improving the environment.
3. Professor Jones who has written three books is considered an authority in her field.
4. Amanda Ford of course is the best candidate for governor.
5. Terrified by the noise Sally ran never looking back.
6. One book however will not solve all your writing problems.

APPLICATION A-9

Eliminate needless or inappropriate commas from these sentences.

1. Students, who smoke marijuana, tend to do poorly in school.
2. As I started the car, I saw him, dash into the woods.
3. This has been a semester of boring, dreadful, experiences.
4. Sarah mistakenly made dates on the same evening with Joe, and Bill, even though she had promised herself to be more careful.
5. In fact, a writer's reaction to criticism, is often defensiveness.

APOSTROPHE

ap /

Apostrophes indicate the possessive, a contraction, and the plural of numbers, letters, and figures.

Apostrophe Indicating the Possessive At the end of a singular word, or of a plural word that does not end in **s,** add an apostrophe plus **s** to indicate the possessive. Single-syllable nouns that end in **s** take the apostrophe before an added **s.**

> The **people's** candidate won.
>
> The chainsaw was **Emma's.**
>
> The **women's** locker room burned.
>
> I borrowed **Chris's** book.

Do not add **s** to words that already end in **s** and have more than one syllable; add an apostrophe only.

> **Aristophanes'** death

Do not use an apostrophe to indicate the possessive form of either singular or plural pronouns.

> The book was hers.
>
> Ours is the best school in the county.
>
> The fault was theirs.

At the end of a plural word that ends in **s,** add an apostrophe only.

> the **cows'** water supply
>
> the **Jacksons'** wine cellar

At the end of a compound noun, add an apostrophe plus **s.**

| my **father-in-law's** false teeth

At the end of the last word in nouns of joint possession, add an apostrophe plus **s** if both own one item.

| **Joe and Sam's** lakefront cottage

Add an apostrophe plus **s** to both nouns if each owns specific items.

| **Joe's** and **Sam's** passports

Apostrophe Indicating a Contraction An apostrophe shows that you have omitted one or more letters in a phrase that is usually a combination of a pronoun and a verb.

| I'm   they're
| he's   you'd
| you're   who's

Don't confuse **they're** with **their** or **there.**

Faulty	there books
	their now leaving
	living their
Correct	their books
	they're now leaving
	living there

Remember the distinction this way:

| Their friend knows they're there.

It's means "it is." **Its** is the possessive.

| It's watching its reflection in the pond.

Who's means "who is," whereas **whose** indicates the possessive.

| Who's interrupting whose work?

Other contractions are formed from the verb and the negative.

isn't	can't
don't	haven't
won't	wasn't

Apostrophe Indicating the Plural of Numbers, Letters, and Figures

The **6's** on this new printer look like smudged **G's**, **9's** are illegible, and the **%'s** are unclear.

QUOTATION MARKS

Quotation marks set off the exact words borrowed from another speaker or writer. The period or comma at the end is placed within the quotation marks.

Periods and commas belong within quotation marks

"Hurry up," Jack whispered.

Jack told Felicia, "I'm depressed."

The colon or semicolon always is placed outside quotation marks.

Colons and semicolons belong outside quotation marks

Our student handbook clearly defines "core requirements"; however, it does not list all the courses that fulfill the requirement.

When a question mark or exclamation point is part of a quotation, it belongs within the quotation marks, replacing the comma or period.

Some punctuation belongs within quotation marks

"Help!" he screamed.

Marsha asked John, "Can't we agree about anything?"

But if the question mark or exclamation point pertains to the attitude of the person quoting instead of the person being quoted, it is placed outside the quotation mark.

Some punctuation belongs outside quotation marks

Why did Boris wink and whisper, "It's a big secret"?

Use quotation marks around titles of articles, paintings, book chapters, and poems.

Certain titles belong within quotation marks   The enclosed article, "The Job Market for College Graduates," should provide some helpful insights.

But titles of books, journals, or newsapers should be underlined or italicized.

Finally, use quotation marks (with restraint) to indicate your ironic use of a word.

Quotation marks to indicate irony   She is some "friend"!

APPLICATION A-10

Insert apostrophes and quotation marks as needed in these sentences.

1. Our countrys future, as well as the worlds, depends on everyone working for a cleaner environment.
2. Once you understand the problem, Professor Jones explained, you find its worse than you possibly could have expected.
3. Can we help? asked the captain.
4. Its a shame that my dog had its leg injured in the accident.
5. All the players bats were eaten by the cranky beaver.

ELLIPSES

... /

Three dots in a row (. . .) indicate you have omitted material from a quotation. If the omitted words come at the end of the original sentence, a fourth dot indicates the period. (Also see pages 332, 333.)

> "Three dots . . . indicate . . . omitted . . . material. . . . A fourth dot indicates the period. . . ."

ITALICS

In typing or longhand writing, indicate italics by underlining. On a word processor, use italic print for titles of books, periodicals, films, newspapers, and plays; for the names of ships; for foreign words or scientific names; sparingly, for emphasizing a word; and for indicating the special use of a word.

The *Oxford English Dictionary* is a handy reference tool.

The *Lusitania* sank rapidly.

She reads *The Boston Globe* often.

My only advice is *caveat emptor*.

Bacillus anthracis is a highly virulent organism.

Do not inhale these fumes under any circumstances!

Our contract defines a *work-study student* as one who works a minimum of 20 hours weekly.

PARENTHESES

( )/

Use commas normally to set off parenthetical elements, dashes to give some emphasis to the material that is set off, and parentheses to enclose material that defines or explains the statement that precedes it.

An anaerobic **(airless)** environment must be maintained for the cultivation of this organism.

The cost of running our college has increased by 15 percent in one year **(see Appendix A for full cost breakdown).**

This new calculator **(made by Ilco Corporation)** is perfect for science students.

Material between parentheses, like all other parenthetical material discussed earlier, can be deleted without harming the logical and grammatical structure of the sentence.

BRACKETS

[ ]/

Brackets in a quotation set off material that was not in the original quotation but is needed for clarification, such as an antecedent (or referent) for a pronoun. (Also see pages 332, 333.)

"She **[Amy]** was the outstanding candidate for the scholarship."

Brackets can enclose information taken from some other location within the context of the quotation.

"It was in early spring **[April 2, to be exact]** that the tornado hit."

Use **sic** ("thus," or "so") when quoting an error in a quotation.

The assistant's comment was clear: "He don't **[sic]** want any."

DASHES

Dashes can be effective—if not overused. Parentheses deemphasize the enclosed material; dashes emphasize it.

> Have a good vacation—but watch out for sandfleas.
>
> Mary—a true friend—spent hours helping me rehearse.

....

APPLICATION A-11

Insert parentheses or dashes as appropriate in these sentences.

1. Writing is a deliberate process of deliberate decisions about a writer's purpose, audience, and message.
2. Have fun but be careful.
3. She worked hard summers at three jobs actually to earn money for agricultural school.
4. To achieve peace and contentment that is the meaning of success.
5. Fido a loyal pet saved my life during the fire.

EFFECTIVE MECHANICS

Correctness in abbreviation, hyphenation, capitalization, use of numbers, and spelling demonstrates your attention to detail.

ABBREVIATIONS

Avoid abbreviations in formal writing or in situations that might confuse your reader. When in doubt, write the word out.

Abbreviate some words and titles when they precede or immediately follow a proper name, but not military, religious, or political titles.

Correct	Mr. Jones
	Dr. Jekyll
	Raymond Dumont, Jr.
	Reverend Ormsby
	President Clinton

Abbreviate time designations only when they are used with actual times.

Correct	400 B.C.
	5:15 a.m.
Faulty	Plato lived sometime in the B.C. period.
	She arrived in the a.m.

Most dictionaries provide an alphabetical list of other abbreviations. For abbreviations in documentation of research sources, see pages 351–362.

HYPHEN

Hyphens divide words at the right-hand margin and join two or more words used as a single adjective if they precede the noun but not if they follow it:

> com-puter
> the rough-hewn wood
> the all-too-human error
> The wood was rough hewn.
> The error was all too human.

Some other commonly hyphenated words:

- Most words that begin with the prefix self-. (Check your dictionary.)

> self-reliance
> self-discipline

- Combinations that might be ambiguous.

> re-creation [*a new creation*]
> recreation [*leisure activity*]

- Words that begin with **ex** only if **ex** means "past."

> ex-faculty member
> excommunicate

- All fractions, along with ratios that are used as adjectives and that precede the noun (but not those that follow it), and compound numbers from twenty-one through ninety-nine.

a **two-thirds** majority

In a **four-to-one** vote, the student senate defeated the proposal.

The proposal was voted down **four to one.**

Thirty-eight windows were broken.

CAPITALIZATION

cap

Capitalize the first words of all sentences as well as titles of people, books, and chapters; languages; days of the week; the months; holidays; names of organizations or groups; races and nationalities; historical events; important documents; and names of structures or vehicles. In titles of books, films, and the like, capitalize the first word and all those following except articles or prepositions.

Items that are capitalized

Joe Schmoe	Russian
A Tale of Two Cities	Labor Day
Protestant	Dupont Chemical Company
Wednesday	Senator Barbara Boxer
the *Queen Mary*	France
the Statue of Liberty	The War of 1812

Do not capitalize the seasons (**spring, winter**) or general groups (the **younger generation, the leisure class**).

Capitalize adjectives that are derived from proper nouns.

Chaucerian English

Capitalize titles preceding a proper noun but not those following.

State Senator Marsha Smith

Marsha Smith, state senator

Capitalize words such as **street, road, corporation,** and **college** only when they accompany a proper noun.

Bob Jones University

High Street

The Rand Corporation

Capitalize **north, south, east,** and **west** when they denote specific locations, not when they are simply directions.

> the South
>
> the Northwest
>
> Turn east at the next set of lights.

Use of Numbers

Numbers expressed in one or two words can be written out or written as numerals. Use numerals to express larger numbers, decimals, fractions, precise technical figures, or any other exact measurements.

> | | |
> |---|---|
> | 543 | 2,800,357 |
> | $3\frac{1}{4}$ | 15 pounds of pressure |
> | 50 kilowatts | 4000 rpm |

Use numerals for dates, census figures, addresses, page numbers, exact units of measurement, percentages, times with a.m. or p.m. designations, and monetary and mileage figures.

> | | |
> |---|---|
> | page 14 | 1:15 p.m. |
> | 18.4 pounds | 9 feet |
> | 12 gallons | $15 |

Do not begin a sentence with a numeral. If your figure needs more than two words, revise your word order.

> Six hundred students applied for the 102 available jobs.
>
> The 102 available jobs brought 780 applicants.

Do not use numerals to express approximate figures, time not designated as a.m. or p.m., or streets named by numbers less than 100.

> about seven hundred fifty
>
> four fifteen
>
> 108 East Forty-second Street

Spelling

Take the time to use your dictionary for all writing assignments. When you read, note the spelling of words that give you trouble. Compile a list of troublesome words.

APPLICATION A-12

In these sentences, make any needed mechanical corrections in abbreviations, hyphens, numbers, or capitalization.

1. Dr. Jones, our english prof., drives a red maserati.
2. Eighty five students in the survey rated self-discipline as essential for success in college.
3. Since nineteen eighty seven, my goal has been to live in the northwest.
4. Senator tarbell has collected forty five hand made rugs from the middle east.
5. During my third year at Margate university, I wrote twenty three page papers on the Russian revolution.
6. 100 bottles of beer are on the wall.

FORMAT GUIDELINES FOR SUBMITTING YOUR MANUSCRIPT

*F*ormat is the look of a page, the visual arrangement of words and spacing. A well-formatted manuscript invites readers in, guides them through the material, and helps them understand it.

1. *Use the right paper and ink.* Type or print in black ink, on $8\frac{1}{2} \times 11$ inch, low-gloss, white paper. Use rag-bond paper (2 pounds or heavier) with a high fiber content (25 percent minimum). Onion skin and erasable paper smudge too easily and are difficult for instructors to write on.

2. *Use high-quality type or print.* On typewritten copy, keep erasures to a minimum, and redo all smudged pages. On a computer, print your hard copy on a letter-quality printer, a laser printer, or a dot-matrix printer (with a fresh ribbon) in the letter-quality mode.

3. *Use standard type sizes and typefaces.* Standard type sizes for manuscripts run from 10 to 12 points—depending on the particular typeface. (Certain typefaces, such as "pica," usually call for a 10-point type size whereas others, such as "elite," call for a 12-point typesize.) Use other sizes only for headings, titles, or special emphasis.

   Word-processing programs offer a variety of typefaces (or fonts). Except for special emphasis, use conservative typefaces; the more ornate ones are harder to read and inappropriate for most manuscripts.

4. *Number pages consistently.* Number your first and subsequent pages with arabic numerals (1, 2, 3), one-half inch from the top of the page and aligned with the right margin or centered in the top or bottom margin. For numbering pages in a research report, see pages 401, 403.

5. *Provide ample margins.* Small margins make a page look crowded and difficult, and allow no room for peer or instructor comments. Provide margins of at least $1\frac{1}{2}$ inches top and bottom, and $1\frac{1}{4}$ inches right and left. If the manuscript is to be bound in some kind of cover, widen your left margin to 2 inches.

6. *Keep line spacing and indentation consistent.* Double space within and between paragraphs. Indent the first line of each paragraph five spaces from the left margin. (Indent five spaces on a computer by striking the Tab key.)

7. *Design your first page.* If your instructor requires a title page, see pages 399–401. For the first page of a manuscript without a separate title page, follow the format your instructor recommends.

8. *Cite and document each source.* Consult Chapter 21. For designing "Works Cited" pages in a documented essay, see pages 420–425.

9. *Proofread your final manuscript.* On a computer, spell checkers and grammar checkers can reveal certain errors, but are no substitute for your own careful evaluation.

How to insert corrections on final copy

If you need to make a few handwritten corrections on your final copy, use a caret (^) to denote the insertion:

> *make*
> If you need to ^ a few handwritten. . . .

Any page requiring more than three or four such corrections should be retyped or reprinted.

10. *Bind your manuscript for readers' convenience.* Do not use a cover unless your instructor requests one. Use a staple or large paper clip in the upper left-hand corner.

11. *Make a backup copy.* Print out or photocopy a backup paper, which you should keep—just in case the original you submit gets lost or misplaced.

FORMAT CHECKLIST

Before submitting any manuscript, evaluate its format by using the following checklist.

- ❑ Do paper and ink meet quality standards?
- ❑ Is the type or print neat, crisp, and easy to read?
- ❑ Are type sizes and typefaces appropriate and easy to read?
- ❑ Are pages numbered consistently?
- ❑ Are all margins adequate?
- ❑ Are line spacing and indentation consistent?
- ❑ Are the first and subsequent pages appropriately designed?
- ❑ Is each source correctly cited and documented?
- ❑ Has the manuscript been proofread carefully?
- ❑ Is the manuscript bound for readers' convenience?
- ❑ Has a backup copy been made?

Abbey, Edward. From "Episodes and Visions" in *Desert Solitaire* by Edward Abbey. Copyright © 1968 by Edward Abbey, renewed 1996 by Clarke Abbey. Reprinted by permission of Don Congdon Associates, Inc.

Allison, Jay. "About Men: Back at the Ranch" by Jay Allison from *The New York Times Magazine*, May 27, 1990. Copyright © 1990 by The New York Times Co. Reprinted by permission.

"The Antioch College Sexual Offense Policy." Reprinted by permission of Antioch College.

Asimov, Isaac. "The Case Against Man" from *Science Past–Science Future* by Isaac Asimov. Published by permission of The Estate of Isaac Asimov, c/o Ralph M. Vicinanza, Ltd.

Baumeister, Roy F. Excerpt from "Should Schools Try to Boost Self-Esteem?" by Roy F. Baumeister as appeared in *American Educator*, Summer 1996. Reprinted by permission of American Federation of Teachers and the author.

Brooks, John. *Telephone: The First Hundred Years.* New York: Harper & Row, Publishers, Inc., 1975, 1976.

Carson, Rachel. From *The Edge of the Sea* by Rachel Carson. Copyright © 1955 by Rachel L. Carson, © renewed 1983 by Roger Christie. Reprinted by permission of Houghton Mifflin Co. All rights reserved.

Cousins, Norman. "How to Make People Smaller Than They Are." *Saturday Review*, December 1978.

Eighner, Lars. From *Travels with Lizbeth: Three Years On the Road and On the Streets* by Lars Eighner. Copyright © 1993 by Lars Eighner. Reprinted by permission of St. Martin's Press Incorporated.

Feit, Mel. "Consensual Sex Contract" by Mel Feit. Reprinted by permission of the author.

Goleman, Daniel. "Why the Brain Blocks Daytime Dreams" by Daniel Goleman. Reprinted with permission from *Psychology Today* Magazine, Copyright © 1976 (Sussex Publishers, Inc.).

Gorman, James. "Like, Uptalk?" by James Gorman from *The New York Times Magazine*, August 15, 1993. Copyright © 1993 by the New York Times Co. Reprinted by permission.

Hemingway, Ernest. Excerpt from "Bull Fighting: A Tragedy" from *By-Line: Ernest Hemingway*, edited by William White. Reprinted by permission of Scribner, a Division of Simon & Schuster, Copyright © 1967 by Mary Hemingway.

Hertzberg, Hendrick and David C. K. McClelland. "Paranoia" by Hendrick Hertzberg and David C. K. McClelland. Copyright © 1974 by *Harper's* Magazine. All rights reserved. Reproduced from the June issue by special permission.

Holmes, Thomas H. and R. H. Rahe. Table, "The Social Readjustment Rating Scale" by Thomas H. Holmes and R. H. Rahe from *Journal of Psychosomatic Research* 11(2), 1967: 213-218. Reprinted by permission of Elsevier Science Inc.

Huxley, Aldous. Excerpt from BRAVE NEW WORLD REVISITED by Aldous Huxley. Copyright © 1958 by Aldous Huxley. Reprinted by permission of HarperCollins Publishers, Inc. and Random House UK.

Kelley, James R. From "The Limits of Reason" by James R. Kelley as appeared in *Commonweal*, September 12, 1975. Reprinted by permission.

Kemelman, Harry. *Common Sense in Education*. New York: Crown Publishers, Inc., 1970, pp. 34–35.

King, Martin Luther, Jr. "Letter from Birmingham Jail" by Martin Luther King, Jr. Copyright 1963 by Martin Luther King, Jr., copyright renewed 1991 by Coretta Scott King. Reprinted by arrangement with The Heirs to the Estate of Martin Luther King, Jr., c/o Writers House, Inc. as agent for the proprietor.

Lifton, Robert Jay and Eric Olson. *Living and Dying*. New York: Praeger Publishers, 1974, p. 129.

Lindbergh, Anne Morrow. From *Gift from the Sea*. Copyright © 1955 by Anne Morrow Lindbergh. Reprinted by permission of Pantheon Books, a division of Random House, Inc.

Lutz, William. Excerpt from "Doubts about Double-Speak" by William Lutz as appeared in *State Government News,* July 1993, Vol. 36, No. 7, pp. 22-24. Copyright ©1993, Council of State Governments. Reprinted with permission from *State Governments News*.

Menninger, Karl. From *The Crime of Punishment* by Karl Menninger. Copyright © 1966, 1968 by Karl Menninger. Used by permission of Viking Penguin, a division of Penguin Books USA Inc.

Moody, Edward J. From "Urban Witches" by Edward J. Moody as appeared in *Conformity and Conflict: Readings in Cultural Anthropology,* Fifth edition by James P. Spradley and David W. McCurdy. Copyright ©1997 by Barbara A. Spradley and David W. McCurdy. Reprinted by permission of Addison-Wesley Educational Publishers Inc.

Morgan, Ted. From *On Becoming American* by Ted Morgan. Copyright ©1978 by Ted Morgan. Reprinted by permission of Houghton Mifflin Company. All rights reserved.

Morris, Willie. *North Toward Home*. Boston: Houghton Mifflin Co., 1967.

Murray, Donald. *A Writer Teaches Writing*, Second edition. Boston, MA: Houghton Mifflin Co.

The New York Times. Excerpt from *The New York Times*, April 4, 1973. Copyright © 1973 by The New York Times Co. Reprinted by permission.

Oreskes, Michael. "Profiles of Today's Youth: They Couldn't Care Less" by Michael Oreskes from *The New York Times*, July 28, 1990. Copyright © 1990 by The New York Times Co. Reprinted by permission.

Orwell, George. Excerpt from *Shooting an Elephant and Other Essays* by George Orwell. Copyright © 1950 by Sonia Brownell Orwell and renewed 1978 by Sonia Pitt-Rivers. Reprinted by permission of Harcourt Brace & Company and Martin Secker and Warburg Ltd.

Overbeck, Joy. "Sex, Kids, and the Slut Look" by Joy Overbeck from "My Turn" column in *Newsweek*, July 26, 1993. Copyright © 1993, Newsweek, Inc. All rights reserved. Reprinted by permission.

Raspberry, William. "Standards You Meet and Don't Duck" by William Raspberry from *The Washington Post*, February 18, 1985. Copyright © 1985, The Washington Post. Reprinted by permission.

Raybon, Patricia. "A Case of Severe Bias" by Patricia Raybon as appeared in *Newsweek*, October 2, 1989. Reprinted by permission of the author.

Roszak, Theodore. *Where the Wasteland Ends*. New York: Bantam Doubleday Dell.

Selye, Hans, M. D. *The Stress of Life*, Revised Edition. New York: McGraw-Hill Book Company, 1956, 1976.

Staples, Brent. "Black Men and Public Space" by Brent Staples as appeared in *MS Magazine*, September 1986. Brent Staples writes editorials for *The New York Times* and is the author of the memoir, *Parallel Time: Growing Up in Black and White*. Reprinted by permission of the author.

Syfers, Judy Brady. "Why I Want a Wife" by Judy Brady Syfers as appeared in *MS Magazine*, December 31, 1971. Reprinted by permission of the author.

Thomas, Lewis. "Biomedical Science and Human Health: The Long-Range Prospect" by Lewis Thomas reprinted by permission of *Daedalus*, Journal of the American Academy of Arts and Sciences, from the issue entitled, "Discoveries and Interpretations: Studies in Contemporary Scholarship, Volume I," Summer 1977, Vol. 106, No. 3.

Editing and Revision Symbols

Symbol	Problem	Page*	Symbol	Problem	Page*
ab	incorrect abbreviation	450	ital	italics needed for emphasis	448
agr p	error in pronoun agreement	433	mod	a modifying word or phrase misplaced	109
agr sv	error in subject-verb agreement	432	neg	negative construction needs rephrasing	122
apl	missing or misused possessive apostrophe	445	nom	nominalization (nouns made from verbs)	121
av	active voice needed	115	num	error in the use of numbers	453
bias	biased language needs rephrasing	143	np	a needless phrase, creates wordiness	120
ca	pronoun in the wrong case	434	over	overstatement or exaggeration	133
cap	capital letter needed	452	par	parallel phrasing needed	112
cl	word that merely adds clutter	123	pct	error in punctuation	437
comb	choppy sentences need to be combined	126	[ ]/	brackets	449
cont	faulty contraction	446	:/	colon	439
coord	coordination needed or faulty	114	,/	comma	440
cs	comma splice, links two sentences only by a comma	430	--/	dash	450
			.../	ellipses	448
			!/	exclamation point	438
			-/	hyphen	451
dgl	dangling modifier	110	( )/	parentheses	449
euph	euphemism that misleads	133	./	period	438
			?/	question mark	438
frag	a fragment used as a sentence	427	"/"	quotation mark	447
			;/	semicolon	439

*Numbers refer to the first page of major discussion in the text.